D0151940

# ALEXANDER BLOK

*Selected Poems*

Александръ Блокъ

# ALEXANDER BLOK

*Selected Poems*

INTRODUCED AND EDITED BY
AVRIL PYMAN, Ph. D.

ILLUSTRATED BY
KIRILL SOKOLOV

# PERGAMON PRESS

OXFORD · NEW YORK · TORONTO
SYDNEY · BRAUNSCHWEIG

Pergamon Press Ltd., Headington Hill Hall, Oxford

Pergamon Press Inc., Maxwell House, Fairview Park, Elmsford, New York 10523

Pergamon of Canada Ltd., 207 Queen's Quay West, Toronto 1

Pergamon Press (Aust.) Pty. Ltd., 19a Boundary Street, Rushcutters Bay,
N.S.W. 2011, Australia

Vieweg & Sohn GmbH, Burgplatz 1, Braunschweig

First edition 1972

Library of Congress Catalog Card No. 67–31506

*Printed in Germany*

08 012184 5 (flexicover)
08 012185 3 (hard cover)

# CONTENTS

## PART I.    JUVENILIA

## PART II.   POEMS FROM VOLUME I

### VERSES FROM THE COLLECTION "ANTE LUCEM"

### VERSES FROM THE COLLECTION "СТИХИ О ПРЕКРАСНОЙ ДАМЕ" (1901–1902)

### РАСПУТЬЯ

## PART III. POEMS FROM VOLUME II

### POEMS OF THE 1905 REVOLUTION
### FROM THE COLLECTIONS
### "РАЗНЫЕ СТИХОТВОРЕНИЯ" and "ГОРОД"

### VERSES FROM THE COLLECTION
### "ПУЗЫРИ ЗЕМЛИ" (1904–1905)

### VERSES FROM THE COLLECTIONS
### "РАЗНЫЕ СТИХОТВОРЕНИЯ" (1904–1908)
### and "ГОРОД" (1904–1908)

### VERSES FROM THE COLLECTIONS
### "СНЕЖНАЯ МАСКА" (1907), "ВОЛЬНЫЕ МЫСЛИ" (1907),
### and "ФАИНА" (1906–1908)

## PART IV.   POEMS FROM VOLUME III
### VERSES FROM THE COLLECTION
### "СТРАШНЫЙ МИР" (1909–1916)

### VERSES FROM THE COLLECTION
### "ВОЗМЕЗДИЕ" (1908–1913)

### VERSES FROM THE COLLECTION
### "ЯМБЫ" (1907–1914)

### VERSES FROM THE COLLECTION
### "ИТАЛЬЯНСКИЕ СТИХИ" (1909)

### VERSES FROM THE COLLECTION
### "РАЗНЫЕ СТИХОТВОРЕНИЯ" (1908–1916)

### VERSES FROM THE COLLECTION
#### "АРФЫ И СКРИПКИ" (1908–1916)

### VERSES FROM THE COLLECTION
#### "КАРМЕН" (1914)

### VERSES FROM THE COLLECTION
#### "РОДИНА" (1907–1916)

### AN EXTRACT FROM THE LONG POEM
#### "ВОЗМЕЗДИЕ"

### VERSES FROM THE COLLECTION
#### "О ЧЁМ ПОЁТ ВЕТЕР" (1913)

# LIST OF ILLUSTRATIONS

# EDITOR'S PREFACE

THE ONLY effective introduction to a poet is through his verse and this book has been conceived first and foremost as an *introduction* to the life and work of Alexander Blok. Readers who are sufficiently interested can go on to the nine-volume *Collected Works* recently published to which cross-references have been made throughout this work.

Blok's total poetic output includes more than 1700 published verses, counting parodies and translations. This book offers 103 poems, one extract from a long poem and one prose passage. Obviously, the editor has had to be rigorously selective and has had constantly to bear in mind the primary purpose of producing an annotated edition of Blok's poetry for the English-speaking reader: that is, to give that reader an immediate over-all impression of Blok's complex development as a poet—full, as he says himself, of "divagations, falls, doubts and regrets"—and, on a deeper level, some knowledge of what Blok called his "road"—"straight as an arrow in its ultimate direction and, like an arrow, purposeful".

In order to give this bird's-eye view, the selection of verses has been made on a strictly representational basis. Two or three poems have been chosen from each book or cycle in an endeavour to convey the dominant quality of each period of the poet's formative years and, subsequently, of each major theme which he wove into the symphony of his mature poetry. The task of editing Blok's poetry is made easier by the fact that he himself edited the first three editions of his poems (1912, 1916, 1918) and, before his death, worked out a detailed plan for the publication of his collected works, the first four volumes of which, comprising his lyric poetry and his plays, were actually ready for publication when he died.* Blok divided his poetry into three volumes, each markedly different in theme and texture, yet differing only as wayside scenery differs seen through the eyes of one purposeful traveller.

The First Volume is a book of the Dawn, of Revelation and of Awakening. Already, Blok writes not only of himself but, albeit quite unknowingly, of his time and of his country. Later, he often pictured Russia as a Sleeping Beauty and this early poetry describes the casting off of an evil enchantment of sloth and pessimism, a prayerful reawakening to a golden morning in which, as Blok's contemporary and spiritual "brother" Andrey Bely was to recall after Blok's death, "... we experienced the violent change in our temporal world as the onslaught of Eternity". "This poor child of my Youth", Blok called his First Volume in 1916, but he added: "The Verses about the Most Beautiful Lady remain the *best*. Time should not touch them, however weak I may have been as an artist." It has been possible to print the extracts from the First Volume in the order in which Blok last arranged them and in which they have appeared in all subsequent Soviet editions of his work because, as he says, there was in this early poetry "a single-stringed quality of soul which made it possible to arrange all the verses... in strictly chronological order; here, the chapters are divided up into years, in the following books— according to subject".

However, in so brief an anthology, in which only a few poems must represent a whole range of ideas and experiences, it seemed to make for greater clarity to rearrange chronologically the poems written between the years 1904 and 1908 which go to make up Blok's transitional Second Volume. This rearrangement of the material gives a clearer picture of the way in which the themes of Blok's mature poetry gradually crystallized in the

---

* For the history of this edition see Vl. Orlov, "Литературное Наследство Александра Блока", *Литературное Наследство*, 27–28 М., 1937, стр. 505–74.

melting-pot of spiritual turmoil, rebellion, revolution and reaction which is the poetry of the Second Volume. Blok considered the poetry which he wrote during the year 1901 to be "of primary significance both for the first volume and for the whole trilogy... the 'magic crystal' through which I first beheld, albeit indistinctly, all the 'distance of a free romance'". If, in the "Verses about the Most Beautiful Lady", Blok stands, as it were, on a high mountain, surveying the country through which he is about to travel through a golden morning haze, in the Second Volume he is like a man who has plunged impatiently down into the mists, forgetting both guide and compass in his eagerness to test his own strength. Dimly, he is conscious of other people, who, like him, seem to have waded in heedlessly and prematurely and to be making towards the same distant goal; there are many of them and they seem to know better than he where they are going and what they want. Momentarily, the poet is acutely aware that it is these half-glimpsed, grey figures who carry in themselves the vitality and patience to reach that Promised Land which he had glimpsed from the mountain-top and taken for a private paradise. But ancient and powerful forces are working against them. Because they have set forth unprepared, they are scattered and defeated and the poet is left alone in a great, hushed expanse of treacherous marshland and wreathing mists. Because this is the actual order of the experience mirrored in Blok's poetry, the verses written about and during the 1904–1905 Revolution are placed *before* those from the cycle "Bubbles of the Earth" with which Blok himself elected to begin his Second Volume, even though most of them were written in the summer and autumn of 1905 when he was already beginning to lose interest in the revolutionary situation in Petersburg. After "Bubbles of the Earth", a chronological arrangement has been attempted of Blok's sorrowful post-1905 poetry, in which the "mystic" theme of "The Stranger" is interwoven with the haunting humanity of "The Ring of Suffering"—verses originally grouped, together with the poetry of the Revolution, in two collections entitled simply "Various Verses" and "The Town". Immediately after the Revolution, the stillness which resettled over the country in a leaden, thundery hush seemed to eat its way into the very heart of the poet. Still sustained by the memory of the Perfection from which he had come and which, he believed, still awaited him with pardon and healing at the end of his road, he is, for the moment, lost—drifting and circling, living in the moment and not, as he believed one *should* live, for the future, transforming his life into art, dreaming dreams and chasing shadows. But, as the darkness deepens, the first snow-flakes of the soft winter of 1906 begin to fall—and the poet is engulfed suddenly in a blizzard of snow and stars. Turning his back on stillness and resignation, he surrenders himself to the elements—from which he emerges, shaken and sober, into the bright, prosaic light of day. "Free Thoughts", the blank-verse cycle written during the summer of 1907, is the firstfruit of this new clarity of vision and has been restored to its chronological place between "The Snow-Mask" (January 1907) and the poetry written in the autumn and winter of the same year. For the Second Volume ends naturally, in poetry and in time, with the setting in of winter.

> For at the end of the road, full of falls, contradictions, bitter ecstasies and useless melancholy, there stretches one eternal and boundless plain, our home from the beginning, perhaps Russia herself. And the snows which have dimmed the shining of the One Star will die away. And the snows which have covered the earth—are there only until the Spring. But in the meantime, the snow blinds the eyes and the cold freezes the soul and blocks the roads.... (From Blok's own introduction to "The Earth in Snow".)

The Third Volume does not recount a process. The poet is mature and, in the settled winter of his heart, is free to write of things other than himself, to fulfil his function as "a witness", to put the "excellent grand-piano" of his talent at the service of the Spirit of his Age. Russia, particularly, he has come to feel "as his own soul". But her course and his are already predetermined by what has gone before, the situation has already crystallized, the road ahead is seen with painful clarity, and it remains only to "bear witness", to await events and, when they come, not to waste time opposing the Music of History but to welcome the new harmonies and to preserve what is worth preserving of the old in faith and dignity. For, Blok wrote, "it is my destiny to become a catacomb". There is no development in Blok's mature poetry—only various moods of varying intensity. For this reason, the editor has felt free to adhere to Blok's own grouping—this time "according to subject".

In the introduction, an attempt has been made to write briefly about Blok's poetry in the context of his life and time. The notes are more detailed. Their purpose is not only to make available in English much material contained in the notes to the first three volumes of the nine-volume Soviet *Collected Works*, but also to supplement these notes by providing references to English translations, by making available relevant material from unpublished sources, and by cross-references to published works about specific aspects of Blok's poetry and also to the poet's own letters, diaries, prose, plays and other poems. Cross-references to Blok's published works have been given, wherever possible, to the nine-volume *Collected Works*. The last three volumes, however, which contain Blok's letters, diaries, and notebooks, had not come out at the time of writing, so that all references to these materials give only the dates and, in the case of letters, the names of the recipients. Exceptions have been made for letters only so far available in separate publications (monographs, newspapers, journals, etc.), and for those contained in the two-volume *Letters to Relatives*, where the page reference has been given. Other material is not difficult to locate under the date of writing. Letters and extracts from Blok's diaries and notebooks have been published in a number of editions of his works. P. Medvedev edited and published one volume of Blok's notebooks (1930) and two of his diaries (1928). These, however, are not always easy to come by, which is why it has not been thought necessary to give page references to these particular editions, although the editor has been careful to distinguish between the notebooks and the two diaries which is not done, for instance, in the two-volume edition of Blok's *Selected Works* published in Moscow 1955. Volumes 7 and 9 of the new *Collected Works* give the fullest publications from the diaries and notebooks available to date.

Much bibliographical material is contained in the notes. The Bibliography at the end of this book aims to acquaint the reader in some detail with the literature about Blok published outside the Soviet Union in English, French, German, Italian and Russian, with other bibliographies which provide an excellent coverage of works on Blok in the U.S.S.R. until the end of 1957, and with the *main* works on Blok's life and poetry published in Russian and other European languages which have been listed in chronological order for the convenience of the student. I am particularly grateful to Tartu University for permission to republish the sections on Blok in English, French, German and Italian and would like to mention the great debt I owe to librarians and bibliographers all over Europe and in the U.S.A. and the U.S.S.R. who helped me in this work and whom I have thanked more fittingly by name in the Tartu publication. I am also most grateful to the Academy of Sciences of the U.S.S.R. for permission to reprint (after the section on Blok in English) a revised and extended list of Blok's verses in English translation originally published in the collection *Международные Связи Русской Литературы*, ed M. P. Alekseyev, Moscow–Leningrad, 1963.

The chronology was an afterthought but, it is hoped, one that will be found useful.

Finally, as editor, I would like to express my profound gratitude to the personnel of the Manuscript Department of the Pushkin House, Leningrad; of the Manuscript Room of the Lenin Library, Moscow; and of the Central State Archives of Literature and Art, Moscow. They not only gave me access to almost all the material I wished to see, but also co-operated tirelessly and enthusiastically in deciphering difficult handwriting and in locating and suggesting material. I should like also to thank the British Council, whose Graduate Exchange Scheme enabled me to spend two years in the Soviet Union preparing this book, a great privilege which would have been quite unthinkable without their patience in negotiation and organization. There are, of course, always individuals also "without whom this book could not have been written"—in this case, my parents, who kept me in peace and plenty for two years on my return from Russia, and Dr. Nikolay Andreyev, who, ever since he set my feet on the path of learning, has helped me in every conceivable way and whose letters of introduction opened many doors to me—in Paris, Germany, Russia and at home in England—which might otherwise have never creaked ajar. Warmest thanks are also due to the following individuals who bore patiently with my insatiable curiosity: the late O. V. Kirschbaum, Blok's cousin and my dear grandmother-in-law, who remembered the poet as a youth reciting Shakespeare at family parties; V. P. Verigina, who still smiles at the memory of an Alexander Blok of hypnotic charm, wild imagination and irresistible humour; N. N. Volokhova, who "took Blok down from the bookshelf" for me and showed me an artist of explosive, youthful talent, not without affectation in life but, as an artist, dedicated beyond the measure of his fellows; N. A. Pavlovich, who loves and remembers a stern teacher, a tragic figure of absolute spiritual integrity; Yuriy Shaporin, the musician, who talked of Blok's punctilious courtesy and of his "piercing, inhuman beauty"; N. A. Kogan-Nolle, who evokes in her reminiscences a sophisticated and experienced man of literature—but a man with his own deep and radiant dreams into which she modestly refrained from prying; E. F. Knipovich, almost the only person to "get on" with Blok, his wife and his mother during the poet's last years, who talked with affection of Lyubov' Dmitriyevna's elemental spontaneity, of Alexandra Andreyevna and her sister Mariya—"incredibly 'sweet-scented' old ladies—in a spiritual sense, that is—living for ideas and literature, pure and disinterested and quite cut off from life", and of Blok himself who "like all good men had much of the little boy in him", who loved, at the age of 39, to ride on the back of trams, dangling his legs in the sun, or to see a squirrel running across his path when out walking. Sincere thanks are also due to the late Professor Gudzy, who helped to cut a great deal of red tape for me in Moscow; to Vladimir Orlov, who spent a whole day showing me Blok's Petersburg; and to many younger and so far less distinguished friends who helped explore the town, find Blok's old school, photograph his last home, follow in his footsteps along the sandy dunes above the Stranger's Lake at Ozerki, or risked being caught by the bridges, which are drawn up between two and four in the morning to let the shipping pass through, in order to wander about Blok's "Islands" when the canals reflect the glowing green skies of the White Nights and the tall cranes and factory chimneys appear to hang weightless above the insomniac city. Above all, my thanks are due to my Director of Studies in Leningrad, D. E. Maksimov, who helped me with his advice, assisted me to gain access to archive materials and who, both through his weekly seminars at the University and through his own sensitive, exacting and profound appreciation of Blok's poetry, taught me how much Blok still means for us today, how the influence of one great poet of severe integrity can work on through a scholar, a class-room, a conference-chamber, a crowded lecture hall, exposing the false, searing the indifferent, generously and trustingly discovering worlds of beauty and faith to all true feeling and honest thought.

# INTRODUCTION

In Dostoyevsky, there are people who "reject" the world and there are people who "accept" the world. There are also such people in real life, but neither type is often to be met with on this earth.

An enormous effort of concentration of the whole being and a sensitive attunement of the soul are needed if man is to "accept" or to "reject" anything. For this reason, not all who are content to walk the earth "accept" the world.

Sincere and ardent "acceptance" is crucifixion, joyful and anguished.

Joy, ah joy that is suffering
Pain of wounds unprobed.

Both the joy of "acceptance" and the yearning sadness of "rejection" are equal in quality and intensity.

Roman Gul'

Blok, "raised up out of hell", burnt with fire, loved and hated the world in a new way.

P. M. Medvedev

1

Alexander Blok believed that life was only worth living on the basis of "all or nothing". The theme of his experience is the theme of "Joy-Suffering", of which he made a compound word in his play *The Rose and the Cross*. But his art deals with matters more humble and more human—with the exception of the First Book, which is an attempt to write about Salvation in the form of the Eternal Feminine, the Most Beautiful Lady. From this theme Blok fell away, partly because it was too great to be contained by the small, "drawing-room" world into which he had been born, partly because—perceiving the "End" but not the "Way"—he became lost in a world "beyond good and evil" and "betrayed" his vocation.

> No, in my present state (cruelty, awkwardness, maturity, sickness) I cannot, I have no right to speak of anything *more* than the human. My theme is certainly not "the Cross and the Rose"—that is outside my scope. Let it be the fate of a man, a failure and, perhaps, if I am able to "humble myself" before art, it may be that some-one will glimpse through my theme—something more.

To be, in life, an ordinary man—and to write simply of the human condition in such a way as to imply the existence of "something more"—in this is the whole pathos of Blok's mature work. On a lyrical plane, it is the poetry of a soul which remembers and seeks Salvation, but which has "only yearning, sparse, lyrical thoughts" about God and which flees Christ. On a less subjective level, it is the poetry of the decay of a civilization seen through the prism of the whole heritage of classical and Christian learning. Either way, it is a great poetry of Beginnings and Ends, a search for "the true link between the temporal and that which is outside time", a poetry in which, as Blok himself declared, the devil himself might break his leg trying to distinguish between the "lyrical" and the "objective".

The demands Blok made on life and people were absolute, and his poetry is correspondingly harsh. A contemporary wrote that, with Blok's death, Faith also died from Russian literature "but perhaps we writers became rather more kindly towards one another". All that Blok wrote is instinct with love, but it is a love "which burns and destroys", a bent and broken love destined to find no consummation in an imperfect world, yawing between the passions and the spirit, now shrouded and listless in the dark vapours of sensuality, now streaming rent and tattered in winds that blow between the spheres.

In the strength of this love, Blok "rejected the world" with a cold implacability scarcely equalled by the most uncompromising modern pessimism. He could conjure the "evil eternity" to which our generation has devoted so many volumes in eight lines of starkly simple verse, his only "props" "a street", "a lamp", "a chemist's shop". He added new dimensions of terror and emptiness to the old romantic images of Don Juan and Carmen. Hamlet and

Ophelia are at home in his poetry; Lear and Cordelia in his thought; the mysterious gaseous interplay of life and fate which boils and bubbles in the tragedy of Macbeth boils and bubbles also in Blok's fate—and in his poetry. The Pierrot weeps; the Harlequin leaps lightly into empty space; the Daemon broods over the world in beautiful isolation, hungry for fresh life; and somewhere, by a still woodland pool, a hermit raises deep eyes and allows them to follow the white, dusty highway... far, far away from the object of contemplation to where, on a darkened, granite street, a dark and broken man tries desperately to light a street-lamp, or searches vainly for the little end of string which only needs to be pulled for the world to change.

Blok's poetry is, perhaps, the supreme example of the ludicrous inadequacy of literary rubrics. He is classified as the greatest of the Russian symbolists but there is nothing easier than to prove that the formative influences of his youth were Russian nineteenth-century poetry and German romanticism, that much of his later poetry ("Ravenna", for instance, or the unfinished narrative poem "Retribution") bears the true classic stamp, or that he sought, and prized greatly, simplicity, psychological realism, real content. Trying to evoke the atmosphere of his poetry, critics often quote the lines:

> Средь видений, сновидений
> Голосов миров иных.

> (Voices between dreams and daydreams
> Sound from other worlds than this.)

Yet Blok also wrote: "I never loved 'dreams' and, at my best, when I really succeed in saying something truly 'mine', something worth-while—I even detest dreams, I would rather have the greyest reality." Nevertheless, any attempt to isolate Blok from his symbolist background is foredoomed to failure. His whole approach to words, as to life, is symbolist in the Russian sense: that is, he sees all outward form as the shell of reality.

Blok believed in the *objective reality* of other worlds. Yet, because this was a real belief, healthily rooted in a life-long love of Plato and in a sober and severe understanding of the nature of religion, he was free to fight the *poisons* of symbolism, the cloudy emanations of decadent mysticism; free to look for his other worlds in the distorting mirror of the everyday; free for just so long as he kept in mind that the everyday *was* a distorting-mirror. In a letter to his friend Andrey Bely, he attempted to explain why, although he would never accept the outward forms of life as the ultimate reality, he could no longer write only of the ideal:

I am thinking of a scepticism worthy of terror. It *must not* "be gone round", but at the same time it is early to overcome it. What if we build *on it*.... We have not the strength to go away and to forget (forget the higher calling of the service of the Ideal Reality A. P.). In that is the living foundation of that scepticism of which I am talking.

It would be good, ah, how good, say I, to stop, to look around, to rejoice in everything phenomenal, to stand lost in happiness before the "seeming" the "appearance",(Φαινὄ-μενον). ... Those who have approached once, even once, will not forget. And that cross is already enough to bear!

Entering reality, Blok, gloriously equipped by nature and society to "stand lost in happiness" before her fortuitous and temporal blessings, determined from the beginning to maintain a sceptical attitude, to remember always that the mirror distorts. He betrayed his first calling, or believed he had betrayed it; but to this second resolution he remained consistently faithful and this is the basis of his art.

Жизнь без начала и конца.
Нас всех подстерегает случай.
Над нами – сумрак неминучий,
Иль ясность божьего лица.
И ты, художник, твёрдо веруй
В начала и концы. Ты знай,
Где стерегут нас ад и рай.
Тебе дано бесстрастной мерой
Измерить всё, что видишь ты.
Твой взгляд – да будет твёрд и ясен.
Сотри случайные черты –
И ты увидишь: мир прекрасен.
Познай, где свет, – поймёшь, где тьма.
Пускай же всё пройдёт неспешно,
Что в мире свято, что в нём грешно,
Сквозь жар души, сквозь хлад ума.

(Life is without beginning, without end.
And each of us is subject to blind chance.
Above us lowers the everlasting dark,
Or else the radiance of the face of God.
But you, the artist, steadfastly believe
In ends and in beginnings. You must know,
Where Heaven watches over us—where Hell.
With a fair judgement is it given you
To measure all things that you here may see.
And let your eye be single, firm and clear.
Eliminate the aimless strokes of chance,
And you will see: the world is beautiful.
Learn where to look for light, and you will learn
Where darkness is. And let all holy things
And all things sinful filter slowly through
The fever of the heart, the cold of mind.)

Alexander Blok was born on 16th November 1880 in the house of the Rector of the University of St. Petersburg, a small eighteenth-century building on the Vasilievsky Island whose windows look across the wide sweep of the

Neva to the formal, lion-guarded steps of the Admiralty anchorage. His family background was immensely important to him; so much so that his brief autobiography is almost all about his parents, grandparents and other relatives. For the rest, apart from a paragraph about the University and another giving factual details about books, people and events which influenced his adult development, he refers "those who are interested" to his poetry and to the article "On the Present State of Russian Symbolism".*

Blok's father, Alexander L'vovich Blok, was Professor of Law at Warsaw University. The Baltic family von Blok of Mecklenburg had come to Russia in 1755. Johannes, the founder of the family fortunes, was appointed personal physician to Paul I, who, in 1796, conferred on him patents of heredity nobility. The Bloks soon became russified, although they retained their Lutheran faith until the time of Alexander L'vovich's father, who married a woman of Cossack extraction, the daughter of the Governor of Novgorod, who had her children christened in the Orthodox Church. Blok's aunt and biographer, Mariya Beketova, believes that the strain of cruelty which made Alexander L'vovich so impossible a husband was probably inherited from his Cossack ancestors. Be that as it may, there was a history of mental instability on the Blok side of the family. The poet's paternal grandfather died in a mental home and his father, though a brilliant scholar, was eccentric to the point of abnormality. He suffered from various manias, among the most pronounced of which seems to have been an exaggerated sense of economy in words, money, time and even physical movement. He spent twenty years of his life revising his magnum opus, *Politics in the Sphere of the Sciences*, striving always to find more and more laconic expression for his thought; two wives, both of whom seem to have loved him, were forced to leave him not only on account of his tyrannous temperament but also because he quite literally kept them short of food; towards the end of his life, when he lived alone, his whole household was arranged so as to economize movement, every object being so placed that he should have to make no unnecessary gestures in his daily routine. Nevertheless, he was a man of great culture, an excellent musician and, in his youth, a romantic, daemonic figure. A favourite family legend tells how Dostoyevsky once noticed him at a reception and remarked that he would like to write a novel about him. Undoubtedly, it was from his father that Blok inherited his "Dionysiac" approach to art, the capacity to abandon himself utterly to the elemental power of "music", although, being tone-deaf, he was denied the spontaneous relief of pouring out his feelings at the piano as his father did, but had instead to transform "sounds" into "words". Also like his father, Blok was paradoxically tidy and systematic

* A detailed summary of this article is given in English by Sir Cecil Kisch in his book *Alexander Blok, Prophet of Revolution*, London, 1960, pp. 62–66.

in everyday life, perhaps, as one contemporary memorist remarked, as a "kind of self-defence against inner chaos".

In the narrative poem "Retribution", Blok describes how his father descended like a hawk on the gentle and courteous Beketov family, impressed the old people with his brilliant, paradoxical conversation, and carried off the youthful, defenceless but far from unwilling third daughter. Two years later, when Alexandra Beketova was expecting her first child, her husband brought her back from Warsaw to Petersburg to visit her parents. They were shocked at the change in their formally vivacious and high-spirited daughter. One day, her father heard her cry out from her room and ran upstairs to discover her husband in the act of striking her. Professor Beketov, the most gentle and civilized of men, was at a loss for words when his son-in-law stalked past him out of the room with a muttered apology to the effect that he had "thought everyone was out". The upshot of all this was that Alexandra Andreyevna's parents persuaded her to remain with them for the birth of her child and, finally, to leave her husband although, in their happier moments, the couple appear to have enjoyed a rare lyrical and intellectual affinity and Blok's father at first made vigorous efforts to persuade his wife to return to him. Her sister Mariya records that it was principally fear of putting her child at the mercy of so unstable a being which decided Alexandra Andreyevna to leave and eventually to divorce her husband. The couple saw each other occasionally (a hazy memory of Blok's childhood was a feeling of violent jealousy for his father on the occasion of one of his visits, and of creeping up behind him to stick a pin into his arm as he sat talking to his mother) and Alexander L'vovich accepted full financial responsibility for his child and occasionally wrote him rather dry, minatory letters. Blok, in his turn, was brought up to write regularly to his father, but the somewhat stilted style of these epistolary exercises tell their own tale. It was not until summoned to his father's death-bed in 1909 that he was overcome by a sharp sense of nearness to and compassion for this extraordinary man, who died respected by his students but abandoned by friends and family, his second wife having also left him after the birth of a daughter, Blok's half-sister Angelina. Blok was conscious of having inherited something of his father's dark and violent temperament and of a certain fellow-feeling for his aristocratic and misanthropic rejection of the modern world. At the same time, he saw his father as a figure of guilt; the manuscript of the autobiographical poem "Retribution" contains an extraordinarily revealing "doodle", a caricature of Blok's father, the face bearing an uncanny resemblance to Blok's own face on his death-bed but the pose and the expression oddly degenerate, almost clownish, underneath which Blok has scribbled in his firm, black hand: "подсудимый", "The Prisoner at the Bar". Without wishing to stress the point unduly, it does seem possible that Blok's temperamental inability to reverence a masculine deity, his exclusive devotion to the cult of the "eternal Feminine", which, as many of his letters witness, he realized *logically* was not enough, had its roots in his relationship to his own father and in the fact that, from his birth, Providence had appeared to him only in the guise of a woman.

"I was brought up in my mother's family", Blok begins his autobiography. He goes on to describe his grandfather, the distinguished botanist, Andrey Nikolayevich Beketov, one-time Rector of Petersburg University, active and disinterested enthusiast for liberal reform, most gentlemanly and unworldly of radicals. Pasternak considered that Blok, for all his stormy premonitions and his vagabond's artist's life, in fact followed closely in his respectable grandfather's footsteps:

И жил ещё дед-якобинец,
Кристальной души радикал,
От коего не на мизинец
И ветренник внук не отстал.

(And there was also a Jacobin-grandfather
A radical of crystalline soul
And the man of the winds, the grandson,
Strayed from his steps not at all.)

As a little boy, Blok would walk all day with his grandfather through the woods watching for wild creatures, looking for rare botanical specimens and for the "magic fern" which flowers only on Midsummer's Eve. He retained the happiest memories of these expeditions and on them he could hardly fail to absorb something of the old scholar's philosophy.

Amongst Blok's books (his entire library is preserved in the Pushkin House in Leningrad) there is one entitled: *From the Life of Nature and of People, a Collection of Popular Articles, by A. Beketov* inscribed with the dedication "To my dear little Sasha from the Author" (Милому моему Сашуреньке от автора). This book contains an article entitled "Harmony in Nature" in which Beketov writes with touching conviction of the essential harmony between man and nature and between all natural phenomena. "The task of science", he claims, "is to understand the laws of world harmony and, in this sense, all sciences are a part of one indivisible whole."

This conception of the underlying harmony of scientifically observed reality and of the "wholeness" of culture is the mainspring of Blok's "mysticism" and of all his poetry. The Beketovs were modest and hard-working servants of enlightenment, and Blok was not brought up to expect the discovery of harmony to be easy. One of his favourite quotations, constantly on his pen during the Revolution, was Plato's Χαλεπὰ τὰ καλὰ (The Beautiful is difficult). In the same spirit of humble toil and high endeavour as his grandfather set out to discover the laws of plant-life, Blok set out to become, in his poetry, "a releaser of harmony". When his fiancée, the daughter of a still more distinguished scientist, the famous chemist Mendeleyev, showed herself impatient of the poet's "mysticism", he protested:

> ... but this very "mysticism" (which you think of as something not of this world, beyond our sphere, "theoretical"), this is the very best that I have ever had in me.... Mysticism is not a "theory", it is the *constant* sensation and constatation in oneself and in all around of mysterious, *living*, indestructible links, one thing with another and, through this, with the unknown. It is a religious awareness and not a misty clouding-up of thought.... Your father accomplished a *mystic* action when, in the great concentration of his creative work, he discovered a *biological* law (a law of life), and these *biological* laws themselves are *mystical*, for they tell us of *causality*, that is of "*determinism*" (of dependence from). When the living sap rises through the stem what is going forward is a *mystical process*.
>
> Mysticism comes from the Greek word *mysterion* which means *mystery*. In the final analysis not even the materialists (or variants of the same type, the positivists), who maintain that almost *everything* has been discovered and that it only remains to discover "a little bit", deny the existence of mysteries. The question is, whether we poor children of the Earth will succeed in discovering, dissecting and analysing God?
>
> That is what mysticism is. It accepts me whole, I am in it and it is in me. It is my nature. From it I write poetry.
>
> ... I know many things more than other people. God grant that I shall come to know still more and more.... When you say "Without mysticism, please" it is as though you were pronouncing the death-sentence not only over me but even over my verses. And they sing to You and of You.*

The influence of Blok's grandmother, Elizaveta Grigor'evna Karelina, a delightful matriarch in whom, as Blok remembered, "an exceptionally definite character was united to a mind as clear as the country summer mornings on which she would rise to work before first light", was as happy as that of the grandfather. The daughter of a well-known explorer, she translated novels, scientific books and children's stories from English, French and German so successfully that some of her translations are still on sale in the Soviet Union today. She enjoyed a sunny temperament and a rich sense of humour. Less lyrically-minded than her husband, she disliked Goethe's *Faust* which, she maintained, had been written solely in order "to keep all those deep-thinking Germans guessing", and had a Voltairian contempt for all forms of religious ritual. Indeed, though the Beketov's were nominally Orthodox Christians, they were at the same time fairly typical products of the free-thinking intelligentsia in an age when the gap between the Church and the intelligentsia in Russia was very much wider than in the twentieth century. The old people never went to their village church and their children only very occasionally. Mariya Beketova records that the village priest at

* Letter of 31/I/1903, ЦГАЛИ, Ф 55, Опись № 1, Ед. Хр. №. 97.

first tried to refuse her father Christian burial, and there was also some trouble over Blok's marriage. It is a mistake to picture Blok as a spiritual revolutionary breaking away from an Orthodox religious background. On the contrary, he and Andrey Bely, a young Muscovite poet of the same age, the son of a professor of mathematics and himself, by training, a natural scientist, were among the first of a new wave of educated men of the scientific tradition to show serious respect for the faith of their forefathers. The anticlerical notes which abound in Blok's later poetry reflect the Beketov contempt for an ignorant priesthood as well as Blok's deep private anger against the degradation of an idea which, if he did not accept, he at least profoundly respected.

The other member of Blok's family who was so close to him that it is virtually impossible to assess her influence was, of course, his mother. Alexandra Andreyevna did not share her father's serene belief that all that was needed to uncover the underlying harmonies of existence was hard work and moral rectitude. Like him and like her son she believed "that we can do everything, there is nothing impossible for man. What would be the point of all our ardent efforts if this were not so? Man should set no limit to his desires, or to his efforts to attain them."* But, unlike the older Beketovs, she was a hypersensitive being, nervous to the point of neuroticism. "*I can't bear it*", she writes to the same correspondent, "I get ill from the barbarity of people's interest, opinions, amusements, views: from their measureless, limitless indifference to Good and Evil."† This was quite true. She did "get ill" and several times attempted suicide; and her son was always conscious of these cyclic fits of acute depression, even from a distance, experiencing the same kind of thing himself in a less acute physical form. From his poetry, she considered strangely her own the lines "Сердцу влюбленному негде укрыться от боли" (For the heart in love there is no shelter from pain), "Пьяна, весела моя боль" (Drunk and joyful my pain), and again "Опаленным, смятенным, соженным до тла—Хвала!" (To the scorched, swept away, to the burnt to the ground—Glory!).

This destructive pathos was something quite new in the Beketov family; in this, doubtless, lay Alexandra Andreyevna's affinity with Blok's father, and thus the poet had to struggle all his life with a difficult double heredity of nervous instability. It is a curious fact that he sought in his wife that reassuring, rich and earthy tenderness which he had failed to find in his mother. "Try to understand", he once wrote to her, "that there is definitely no-one but you to whom I can turn for support, because Mama's love for me is full of anxiety...." Nevertheless, Blok's relationship with his mother, who was

* Letter to M.P. Ivanova, 24/III/1913, ЦГАЛИ, Ф №. 55, Опись №. 1, Ед. Хр. №. 539.
† Letter to M.P. Ivanova, 31/X/1908, ЦГАЛИ, Ф №. 55, Опись №. 1, Ед. Хр. №. 534.

only just twenty years his senior, was in many ways an extraordinarily happy one. The intrusion of a stepfather (Alexandra Andreyevna remarried when her son was 8 years old) seems to have made remarkably little difference. During the winter, Sasha and his mother now lived in the officer's quarters allotted to her second husband, F. F. Kublitsky-Piottukh, instead of with her parents. But Shakhmatovo, Blok's grandfather's modest country estate near Moscow, remained their "home". Petersburg had never offered them a home in this sense. Professor Beketov had lost his rectorship for defending insurgent students in 1883, and with it the charming and comparatively spacious Rector's house. Since then, the Beketov family had been rather short of funds, an unpleasant fact which they faced with the supreme indifference of the highly principled, quietly and unobtrusively cutting their coat to suit their cloth, and had moved several times from flat to flat. Blok's new Petersburg home in the Grenadiers' Barracks overlooked a major tributary of the Neva and was situated way at the back of the "Petrogradskaya Storona", the island which had originally been the heart and centre of Peter the Great's extraordinary capital but which had since become a strangely provincial and endlessly fascinating no-man's land between the ordered, eighteenth-century elegance of the city centre and the sprawling, chaotic human power-house of Petersburg's industrial suburbs. The new home was, if anything, an improvement, and imbued Blok with a lasting love for the sleepy outskirts of his city, for the busy canals and the shabby islands. Franz Feliksovich, a kindly man of part-Polish origin who adored his clever and generous-hearted wife, came and went, quietly deferring to the intellectual superiority of the family into which he had married. Why Alexandra Andreyevna ever accepted him is something of a mystery. He was a good man but his well-meaning serenity and conventional opinions irritated her and they seem to have had nothing in common. Blok retained without difficulty his unique place in his mother's heart. It was to her that he first showed his verses; in his first diary, he noted that she understood him "in everything"; to his fiancée he explained that it was possible to let his mother into the secret of their betrothal "because she understands everything that it's possible to understand, because she knows and loves *me* better than anyone else in the world (without exception)"*. As for Alexandra Andreyevna, she *lived* through her love for her son and through her participation in his vocation (cf. the poem *Son and Mother*, No. 44, and note)†. "Perhaps you are right in all that you wrote about my

---

* Letter of 28/XII/1902 to L. D. Mendeleyeva, ЦГАЛИ, Ф №. 55, Опись №. 1, Ед. Хр. №. 97.

† Numbers given after the title of poems by Blok refer to the numbers of these poems (and the notes) in this publication. Cross-references are also made between number and number in the notes themselves.

relationship with Sasha", she admitted to a woman who knew and loved them both. "My sin is that all my world is in him."*

Like all very close and intense relationships, Blok and his mother's love for one another was at times a painful burden to them both but, for the growing boy, his mother's understanding and undivided attention was merely one of the most pleasant aspects of an exceptionally pleasant life. To her credit, Alexandra Andreyevna was never possessive and appreciated her son's friends, and later his loves, with a generous objectivity and a complete disregard for whether or not they liked her. An unusual feature of their family was a complete and merciless frankness, a dispassionate predilection for home truths. In this respect, Alexandra Andreyevna failed her son only once. When, on his death-bed, he asked her whether he were dying, she tried to tell him that he would get better. He turned away from her as though his last support had gone. She never forgave herself.

Even when Blok was a small child, he was in no way dominated by his mother. Her *exalté* influence was diluted by the more common-sensical natures of her mother and sisters. Blok was thankful all his life for the circumstance that "family traditions" and his "sheltered existence" conditioned the fact that he "knew not one line of the so-called 'new poetry' until after entering the University". His early reading was confined to adventure stories, the classics of world literature (including, of course, his own) and, in poetry, first and foremost to the high romanticism of the early nineteenth century and the neo-Classic, neo-Romantic verse of Maykov, Fet, Polonsky and Apukhtin. Although his own element was *musique*, in the sense in which Verlaine applied the word to poetry, Blok always considered it a good thing that he was brought up among lovers of "dear, old-fashioned *éloquence*", and was profoundly grateful to "the sober and healthy people" whose influence forearmed him in his youth against "the infection of that mystic charlatanism which, a few years later, became fashionable in certain literary circles". Someone who knew Blok well towards the end of his life told me that "spiritual health" was one of his outstanding characteristics and that, had he been able to bring himself to accept Christ, he would undoubtedly have turned to the Orthodox Christian tradition rather than to any of the new "mystic" religions such as Spiritism or Steiner's Theosophy, which attracted so many of his contemporaries from Andrey Bely to W. B. Yeats. This "spiritual health" Blok owed largely to the Beketovs and to the country air of Shakhmatovo.

Life at Shakhmatovo where the Beketovs spent all their summers was, outwardly at least, an idyllic affair. Under the aegis of their easy-going, busy parents, who finally died within three months of one another in 1902, the

* Letter of 15/IV/1910 to M. P. Ivanova, ЦГАЛИ, Ф №. 55, Опись №. 1, Ед. Хр. №. 535.

Beketov sisters wrote, made jam, pickled mushrooms, translated, entertained
their admirers, talked long and passionately of life and literature under the
ancient lilacs and provided a loving and admiring chorus for the antics of
little Beeba, Alexandra's beautiful and mercurial baby son. Sometimes
Shakhmatovo was shared by two young cousins, the sons of an elder Beketov
sister, but always Sasha, as he came to be called when he got out of skirts and
stopped looking, as one admiring acquaintance remarked, "like a marquise
in a powder-robe", was the ringleader, losing himself and his companions in
games of the imagination, organizing terrible battles, inventing charades, or
editing a family magazine to which he and his cousins contributed transla-
tions from French and Latin, verses, jokes, puzzles and serial stories which
show the unmistakable influence of Conan Doyle, Jules Verne and Fenimore
Cooper. Even after the cataclysm of the 1917 revolution, Blok remembered
the deeper, personal shock of his first day at school, his sense of being
"irrevocably given away". When he came back home and his mother asked
him what he had seen at school, he replied in an awed voice: "People". This
sense of shock, however, soon gave way to bored tolerance. Blok was a
sturdy, intelligent lad, well able to hold his own in class and protected from
"people" by impeccable manners and a certain inborn consciousness of
"being out of the top drawer". At school, he absorbed enough conventional
learning to enable him to enter the Faculty of Law at Petersburg University
and, finally, to graduate from the Philological Faculty with a first-class
degree. But his real education, "a Russian Gentleman's *Education Sentimen-
tale*", as he later called it, went on at home.

At Shakhmatovo, Blok would lose himself for hours on foot or on horse-
back in the fragrant meadows, the clean-floored, fairy-tale woodlands and
the fields of clover and tall, white rye which surrounded his home and which
were to become the dream-illumined landscape of his early poetry. Dogs,
chickens, horses and a variety of other pets and domestic animals were an
integral part of this life. Blok learnt to work with his hands, to garden, to fell
trees, to construct. He became an excellent carpenter. From the example of
his industrious grandparents, he must also have absorbed the rudiments of
estate management, a sense of responsibility (and of property), and the ability
to keep accounts. Yet there was nothing of the yokel squire about the young
Blok. Like most educated Russians, the Beketovs knew instinctively how to
combine simplicity with refinement. Protected from infancy from any kind
of spiritual vulgarity, Blok never lost his sense of rather aloof astonishment
when confronted with the ignoble, the insincere or, for that matter, with
anything aesthetically or morally unpleasing.

Only when he came to understand the prevalence of these things in the
outside world and the way in which the majority of his fellow-beings accepted

them as inevitable, as "life", and, at the same time, to realize that his own responsibility as an artist was to wake people up to the necessity of non-acceptance, was it that they reduced him to helpless anger, despair, flaunting, self-destructive debauchery and to that state which was, perhaps, ultimately responsible for his early death, and which another poet, Khodasevich, diagnosed in the unforgettable phrase: "insomnia of the heart".

Of course, there were "people" at Shakhmatovo, too—quaint and lovable people called "peasants". True, they were regrettably ignorant, often drunk and not always quite honest. This, however, was the fault of the antiquated social system which, Blok's grandfather, at least, was convinced, would soon be replaced by some form of Utopian Socialism along the lines thought out in France by Saint Simon and Fourier. Meanwhile, one did what one could, tried to stop them being too servile and calling you their "father" and them-selves your "children", treated them with unfailing courtesy and, if at a loss, clapped them in a friendly way on the shoulder and muttered encouragingly, "Eh bien, mon petit!" When Blok, at the age of 18, fell in love with the daughter of his grandfather's friend and colleague, Dmitry Ivanovich Mendeleyev, who owned the neighbouring estate of Boblovo, and discovered in her a serious ambition to become an actress which matched his own romantic determination to tread the boards and even, when his time came, to die "on the stage of a heart-attack", the young people of the two families even invited the peasants to watch their performance of scenes from Shake-speare and the Russian classics.

There is a photograph of the fifteen-year-old Lyubov' Dmitriyevna as Ophe-lia, her heavy, red-gold hair entwined with real wild-flowers, her eyes childishly pathetic under heavy, puckered brows, her whole figure expressive of a kind of touching bewilderment in the face of an unkind world. Another photo-graph shows Blok himself, a youthfully ravaged Hamlet in a black velvet costume. The elders of the two houses were genuinely moved by the sincerity and talent of the young people and, perhaps most of all, by their beauty. But Mariya Andreyevna recalls that "the performances themselves sometimes entailed great disappointments. The public, apart from relatives and neigh-bours, was made up of peasants from the neighbouring villages .... In the middle of the most pathetic declarations of Hamlet, Chatsky or Romeo they would begin to laugh ... and the more intense the scene, the louder the laughter." For the time being, Blok remained deaf to this discordant laughter. The peasants were a picturesque part of his background and he had not yet realized that there was something absurdly anachronistic about a nineteenth-century university professor being treated by his tenants as though he were their medieval suzerain. For one thing, he witnessed no overt injustices for, as Chukovsky observes in his reminiscences of Blok, "The upper-class way

of life of the old gentry was ennobled in his family by the great culture of all
its members, who from generation to generation had rendered devoted
service to scholarship", and Blok was not yet aware, or at least not fully
aware, that "this very continuity of the cultivated mind was in itself the
privilege of well-born families". For another, love is traditionally blind and
Blok, no sooner did he emerge from the schoolroom and begin to think for
himself, fell in love with Lyubov' Dmitriyevna Mendeleyeva, with his own
childhood, with a legendary Russia which, in reality, had long since passed
into history, but which could be "conjured up" and "re-enacted" with
intoxicating realism in the setting of Shakhmatovo and Boblovo. In Blok's
early love poetry, the lyrical hero is often a wandering Prince, his Beloved a
Princess living in some secluded and pastoral retreat. In fact, so great was the
power of suggestion radiated by the stately young couple against their
natural background of flowering gardens and gentle countryside that even
the memoirs of Blok's friends and contemporaries invariably fall into the
language of legend when they try to describe them. Even their wedding was
like a scene from a fairy-tale, the peasants bringing the traditional gifts of
white geese, bread and salt to the door of the ancient private chapel in which
they were married and then foregathering in the courtyard of the Mendeleyev
home, dressed in holiday costume, to cheer the bride and groom—for which,
as at all landowners' weddings, they received gifts of money and sweets.

All this was too beautiful and, in a sense, too flattering to be lightly cast
aside. Blok found it easy to relegate an underlying sense of the incongruities
of his existence to the "depths of the archives of the Police Department of his
soul". To these "archives" he also relegated his discovery, at the age of 15 or
so, of a troublesome and "dark" sensuality. Yet he tells us that, from then on,
he was "subject to fits of despair and irony which found an outlet only many
years later in my first attempt at drama ('The Puppet-Show')". This, however,
is something less than the truth. Blok's earliest poetry, contained in the book
*Ante Lucem*, is heavily shadowed by the pessimism of the age. His heroine is
Ophelia, cast off because Hamlet believes life itself unfit for her; his hero, a
man indifferent, grey and old before his time; his theme, Paradise Lost and
the helpless, dumb resentment of man. Meanwhile, however, he was leading
the gayest of gay lives, "preparing, outwardly, to become an actor".

In August 1898 Blok went to stay with his mother's cousin, the artist, Olga
Solov'ev, wife of Mikhail, brother to the famous philosopher Vladimir
Solov'ev. These people were the first, outside his immediate family, to take an
interest in him as a poet, and Blok rates his acquaintance with them as among
the most important events in his young life. Their son, Sergey, however,
gives a description of his cousin's arrival which is far from suggestive of any
immediate profundity in their relationships:

> ... I went to meet Blok in the little wood bordering our estate. A governess-cart appeared. In it a young man, elegantly dressed, with an aureole of golden curls, a rose in his button-hole and a swagger-cane. At his side—a young lady. He had just finished school and was out for fun. The theatre, flirtations, verses...

In a letter to Blok's mother, Olga Solov'ev confirms her son's first impression:

> ... I expect you're wondering why I don't write more about Sasha. I haven't really got to know him from the inside, but from the outside I find him extremely handsome. I do so love that type, just like a Van Dyck portrait. ... I couldn't get to know him because he's always on the go and very much in demand, and it would be such a bore for him. Sergey is in ecstasies over him and in his eyes Sasha has become *the* authority on every conceivable question.*

However, the Solov'ev household, where it was no unusual thing to be woken up by some supremely self-centred young poet from the scandalous group known as the Moscow symbolists, unshakably determined to deliver his views on Anti-Christ over the family breakfast-table, as utterly oblivious of his hostess's negligé as of her husband's frail health, where art, religion, history and philosophy were the small change of conversation even more than at the Beketovs', where Blok first became familiar with the ideas of Vladimir Solov'ev, could not fail to make a deep impression on him. Olga Solov'ev was instrumental in interesting Valeriy Bryusov (the founder of the Symbolist School in Moscow and the editor of the almanac *The Northern Flowers* [Северные Цветы]) in Blok's verses. She also effected an introduction between Blok and another young poet, Boris Bugayev, who was later to become famous under the pen-name Andrey Bely. She showed Bely Blok's poems some time before he had succeeded in finding a publisher and Bely, steeped still more deeply than Blok in the philosophy of Vladimir Solov'ev and more especially in his cult of the Divine Sophia, at once recognized "a brother". Thanks to Olga Solov'ev, the two young men struck up a correspondence and later met and formed, together with the younger but extremely precocious Sergey, the nucleus of an esoteric and intimate group which, regrettably, but not inappropriately, they frequently referred to as the "Brotherhood of the Dawn". This "brotherhood" was in fact a perfectly natural friendship between three young men of similar tastes and backgrounds, which was given a curious lyrical profundity and intensity at its inception when, a whole year before they actually met, Bely and Blok found themselves called upon to rally round and support Sergey in the tragic loss of both his parents. His father, a gentle invalid, died naturally on 17th January 1903 and his mother, an enchantingly amusing, gay and sympathetic woman, deliberately, in full possession of her faculties, shot herself on the same day.

* Undated letter of between 9/II and 27/VIII/1898, ЦГАЛИ, Ф №. 55, Опись №.I, Ед. Хр. №. 551.

The friendship did not last, but it was of the first importance for Blok's later development. Meanwhile, it is enough that his acquaintanceship with the Solov'evs led him to think more deeply on religious subjects.

In the autumn of 1898 Blok entered the Faculty of Law at Petersburg University, following rather spinelessly in his father's footsteps. Here he remained for the next two years, falling deeper and deeper in love with Lyubov' Dmitriyevna, who was extremely shy of him and did not know what to make of his exalted tone, more especially as it was combined with sudden lapses into sophisticated irony far above her schoolgirl head. Blok took her shyness for indifference and severity and dared not tell her he loved her. Instead, he began to study religious writers, mystics, Plato and the neo-Platonists. Here he found a real religious force, not just a logical system or a stimulus to vague mystic "experiences"; a force which, he felt in his heart, could bring Regeneration and Salvation but which, in return, demanded total selfsurrender. "There began a period of submission to God and Plato", he wrote of the winter of 1900–1. The Divine Feminine Being, of whom he had already written, in November 1900, "In Thee—Salvation" (No. 5 and note), became the object of his worshipful contemplation. In the spring of 1901 he began to read Vladimir Solov'ev's poetry to the Divine Sophia. The poems written under the direct influence of Solov'ev during the "mystic summer" of 1901 Blok regarded as "of primary importance not only to the first volume but to the whole trilology" [i.e. the whole body of verse published during his lifetime, A.P.]; his first book, consisting of poems written between 1900 and 1905, was called *Verses About the Most Beautiful Lady*. It is still of the "Most Beautiful Lady" that Blok was writing when he declared, many years later:

> In our first youth we were given a true covenant. Of the soul of the people and of ours, together with theirs reduced to ashes, it is necessary to say in simple, courageous accents: "may they rise again". Perhaps we ourselves will die, but the dawn of that *first* love will remain.

For generations now critics have pondered what Blok meant by this "first love". Vladimir Orlov dismisses the whole question by stating categorically that the poetry of the first volume is a mere prologue to the work of the "real Blok" which, he says, begins "somewhere between 1906 and 1907". Sergey Solov'ev, on the other hand, and Blok's first editor, P.P. Pertsov, regarded the *Verses about the Most Beautiful Lady* as Blok's supreme achievement. Blok himself appeared, in later life, to value the content more than the form of those early verses (see Editor's preface). Sergey Makovsky, writing in 1956, voiced the general confusion: "To whom is addressed this Thou (with a capital letter)? To the woman of his choice? To an apparition of another world? Or—to Russia? For those who have read Blok carefully here is, in some sort, his essence."

Blok himself defined the Most Beautiful Lady as an "essence possessed of an independent existence" (see Note 9). Though himself beset by "demons and doubles", he admitted no dualism in Her. "She is *unique* in Her manifestations," he wrote to Bely, "has nothing in common with anything, the feeling of Her is *uncanny* and, in the highest moments, quite different from Astarte." "I feel Her", he wrote, still to Bely, "most often as a mood. I think it is possible to see Her, but not incarnate in a person, and this person cannot know whether She is present in them or not. Only momentarily (in a flash) can Her Shadow be perceived in another's face (and then only when that face is not animated)."

Such was Blok's subjective perception of the Lady. Objectively, although the concept of the Eternal Feminine was "in the air" and being talked about everywhere in literary circles, his ideas about her were deeply influenced by Vladimir Solov'ev (cf. Notes to the poem Ищу спасения) who, unlike Blok, claimed actually to have had visions of the "Divine Sophia" and who sung these visions in his poetry and rationalized them in his philosophy. The cult of Hagia Sophia which Solov'ev thus revived is of ancient origin. She is a Feminine Being born, like the created world, of chaos, and she embodies, *in Eternity, the redeemed creation which is at one with God and, in Time, the strivings of the fallen creation to re-establish this lost unity within the framework of the temporal process.* Blok's contemporaries, at least, connected Her with the Woman Clothed with the Sun of the Apocalypse. Vladimir Solov'ev says that she is "*no other than the true, pure and perfect humanity*";\* that she is not a shadow in the mind of God, but a distinct spiritual force who responds to the love of the Creator by a free act of her own love. This radiant image has been sung throughout world literature. For Dante she was Beatrice; Goethe called Her the Eternal Feminine. In the view of much idealist philosophy, it is the spark of the Eternal Feminine in every woman which attracts and holds her appointed lover, which frees him from the prison of abstract theory and introspection and leads him into communion with the rest of humanity, the rest of creation; a communion which it is essential that he should experience because the transformation or salvation of the individual is only possible as a part of the transformation or salvation of the whole cosmos.

How deeply this cult affected Blok's love story, and how inextricably his love story was interwoven with his belief in the Divine Sophia, is evident from his poetry and his letters. Even at 18, Blok was not without romantic experience, but his feeling for Lyubov' Dmitriyevna was the emotion of a boy for a dream figure miraculously embodied in "the girl next door", innocent as "first love" is supposed to be, so respectful that even marriage seemed,

\* Editor's italics.

although infinitely desirable, almost a desecration of the aerial quality of their relationship. For a short time, this Platonic passion seems to have heightened his sensitivity in a way which made him see the world once again in the magical, freshly awakened light of childhood. Every event of his daily life took on immense significance; even the changes in the weather were omens and portents; like a child, he lived in the present and like a child looked straight through the present into eternity. The first poem of the Beautiful Lady cycle (as printed according to Blok's own final arrangement) is about childhood and eternity and, throughout their married life, "Lyuba" and "Sasha" remained bound together by their childhood, preserving a Peter Pan ability to retreat from the difficulties and betrayals of the grown-up world into a land of their own which had its own language, full of allusions to "secret places" which they had both known, to animals and to people. Yet they were not children and, for some reason, probably because of unfortunate early experiences, Blok seemed to feel that the normal relationship between man and woman would degrade them. Lyubov' Dmitriyevna, too young to know much about such things, at first trusted herself to Blok absolutely and then asserted her right to live as a normal woman outside her marriage, a right which Blok could not but concede, with compassion, but not without bitterness, because he had been the first to "fall" from his impossibly confused standards, and was, in any case, rather doubtful of their validity. Even at the height of his dream-hushed "mystic summer" his perfectly normal feelings for his Lyubov', resolutely driven from his conscious mind, were beginning to "taint" his poetry. Although Blok's approach to love, which at this time resembled that of the medieval troubadours' cult of "chivalrous love", may sound very extraordinary to the modern ear, it is important to remember that it was not so extraordinary for his day and age. The two most powerful influences on his youth—Vladimir Solov'ev and the Merezhkovskys—held definite theories on this subject, which they expounded in weighty treatises. Blok was not a theoretician. He always sought the harmonious, intuitive solution; yet these theories undoubtedly influenced him. However, unlike their originators, he was not of the type to put them into practice. He was a strong, hot-blooded and healthy young man, burdened with a nervous temperament and gifted with a lucid, analytical mind and almost fanatical integrity. The combination of these factors made him suspicious of the purity of his deliberately disembodied dreams of love and led him to see himself now as "a dark slave of accursed blood", now as an old man "dried up by vigilance", now as a "smoky torch" predestined to burn for ever "on the threshold of the Ideal". The resolutely suppressed sensual impulses began to escape "the Police Department of his Soul", and encroached not only upon his feelings for Lyubov' Dmitriyevna but also

upon his subjective awareness of "The Most Beautiful Lady". In the
poem "I have forebodings of Thee" (Предчувствую Тебя. Года проходят
мимо, №. 9) written right in the middle of his "mystic Summer" in June 1901,
the poet already envisages the possibility of a "change of face" not so much
in the Beautiful Lady Herself as in his own awareness of Her. When, in No-
vember 1901, the sense of Her immanence began to fail him, he described
this as "the limit of the cognizance of God". In the same autumn, he no-
ted the waning power of Lyubov' Dmitriyevna. It is at this point that a
profane element entered the strange romance and Blok wrote: "In Novem-
ber began my open *sorcery* for I invoked doubles. ..." Yet he continued
to hope that, in some way, the human girl would save him, from the out-
side, as it were, and, in 1902, he wrote to her:

> I am not a decadent. People who think that are quite wrong. I am after the decadents.
> But, in order that I could emerge completely from the decadence which is contemporary
> to me and which attracts me by its formlessness and amorality... I had to meet that
> enchantment, sweetness and greatness which is in Thee.

But Lyubov' Dmitriyevna was so distressed and puzzled by Blok's apparent
inability to see her as herself, as "a living human being with a live heart"
rather than "as some kind of abstract idea" that, in the early spring of 1902,
she broke off relations with him, too shy to hand him the letter of explana-
tion from which these two phrases are taken. When they met again, in the
country in July, Blok confides to his diary that he does not know what he
wants, but adds with the Nietzschean *amor fati* which was to characterize him
all his life: "I want that which will happen. Because it is that which ought
to happen and what happens will be what I want." On 16th September he
roughed out an extraordinary, ironic-sincere letter to Lyubov' Dmitriyevna:
he is not just in love, but the world has no meaning for him except in so far as
it is connected with her. Half-ironically, he begs to be allowed to "approach
her more nearly": "Of course, that is both impertinent and, in essence, even im-
possible (we will discuss that later), but I am justified by my long and deep
faith in You (as the earthly embodiment of the famous Immaculate Virgin
or Eternal Feminine, if you want to know)." The tone of this letter is simply
not that in which Blok is wont to speak of the Most Beautiful Lady; it is the
tone of romantic irony, which he acknowledged to be one of the scourges of
his time. Already, he is more than doubtful of the validity of the mystic game
he has been playing and when, in November, he finally plucked up courage
to propose to Lyubov' Dmitriyevna and she accepted him, Blok, although
overjoyed, could not fully recover the enchantment of the "mystic summer"
of 1901. Now he was brought face to face with the dual nature of his love,
and his innocent fiancée could not help him. "The foundations are still the
same", he wrote to her, "but everything is upside down. I have recognized

every word in these legends which say that You are not and never will be
with me. And I have grown accustomed to them—and felt at home with
them. I am familiar with separation, tormenting and infinite. I am not yet
familiar with reunion". "I can only love, I understand nothing, I want noth-
ing, I love you", she answered him, "to understand, to reason, to want—is
your *duty*."

Although Blok a few years later had to renounce all attempt to write of
"The Most Beautiful Lady", although his marriage was in many ways un-
happy, yet his wife always fulfilled for him the function of Hagia Sophia
working through the Beloved: she lent substance to his higher self and, to his
spiritual existence, an earthly significance which it lacked without her, thus
remaining always "the holy place of his soul".

> If you should go, I shall completely "disappear" from the face of the earth, "shall
> dissolve" in the creation and in creating. When you are not there, I am so unthinkable
> that I suspect that, finally, some people are beginning to notice that I don't act of my
> own volition, that something inspires me from without.*

So he wrote to her when they were still engaged. And again: "You are
doing a great thing for me. You are bringing me down to Earth" (Ты меня
опрощаешь). A friend described how she would listen to his poetry after
they became man and wife:

> She would remain silent, but A.A., sitting sideways to her, facing us, would listen to
> her in silence. In silence they understood one another, Alexander and Lyubov'. After
> all, Al. Blok also kept silence about his poetry.
>     In Lyubov' the earth was silent, as it is silent at sunrise, and the earth in her was
> profound, like the sunrise...
>     ... and now he has returned from the aerial battle, weary, exhausted, even wounded,
> and unearthly mists blow about him; they are alien, incomprehensible, and they
> frighten the earthly princess: desolately she caresses her Bridegroom's wounds and
> whispers to him, as though to her sick child: "Dear one, why, why?"

The simple human fact was that Blok needed Lyubov', and that he needed
her and all his life continued to need her as she was: simple, spontaneous,
healthy, intelligent and of the earth, earthy, in the same way he was later to
need the solid, demanding reality of his motherland to remind him that his
vision was a vision of the earth redeemed, of "a *life* of beauty, freedom and
light", and not a disembodied spiritual fantasy. In May 1903 he wrote:

> Когда я в сумерки проходил по дороге,
> Заприметился в окошке красный огонёк.
> Розовая девушка встала на пороге
> И сказала мне, что я красив и высок.
>
> В этом вся моя сказка, добрые люди.
> Мне больше не надо от вас ничего:
> Я никогда не мечтал о чуде –
> И вы успокойтесь – и забудьте про него.

* Letter to L. D. Blok of 30/XI/1902, Цгали, Ф №. 55, Опись №. I, Ед. Хр. №. 97.

(When I was passing along the road in the twilight
I saw a red glow in the window
A rosy girl stood on the threshhold
And told me that I was tall and handsome.

That is all my tale, good people,
Nothing more do I ask of you.
I never dreamt of a miracle,
So you calm down and forget about it too.)

The last poem of the third and last book of the group of poems to which Blok always referred as the "First Volume" and which he entitled *The Parting of the Ways* (Распутья), leaves his wife sleeping (cf. No. 25); there are no capital letters, and the poet promises that he will disturb her no longer. The first poem of the next book, "Thou hast gone into the fields without return" seems, in conjunction with this, to establish the final separation of the wife from the Divine Being:

Thou who holdest land and sea
Immovably in Thy slender hand. (Cf. No. 26.)

Lyubov' Dmitriyevna's plea to be loved for herself, "without mysticism", was, however, merely a contributory factor to Blok's growing difficulty in writing about the "Most Beautiful Lady".

From the beginning, he had felt Her to be "flying away" to some more important task than that of revealing Herself to individual prophets, moving towards "the Manifestation of Herself in History" and, here, Blok felt rather vaguely that She "has something to do with the End of the World". At the same time, he did *not* at first feel that "the people or society had any part in Her Grace". The remote immutability of Her perfection seemed to exclude all possibility of "kindliness", of interference in lowly human lives. This, in Blok's scheme of things, was the sphere of Christ, whom he *did* feel to be "kind" and actively benevolent towards "the people". (The quotation which he most often associates with the figure of Christ is the verse written on the open book which He is depicted as holding on Russian icons: "Come unto Me, all ye that labour and are heavy-laden.") But, although the revelation of the Beautiful Lady in Blok's life might fairly be termed a religious experience, it was not an experience accompanied by religious vocation. Of this, Blok wrote to Bely that he was not a mystic and had, indeed, always been a rake; one thing, however, he knew for certain, but this was "what" and not "how". As his sense of communion with the "what", with the Most Beautiful Lady Herself, faded, he was left increasingly empty and desolate. From the beginning, daemonic notes of resentment and rebellion had provided a kind of growling undertone to his religious aspiration. "Never will I go to be healed of Christ", he wrote to his Christian friend Zhenya Ivanov in June 1904 and, to Andrey Bely almost a year earlier, "I like to 'wave my cap in the air' and

I do *not want* the torments of the cross." And yet, refusing the road of self-abnegation, putting aside the easy yoke, he was conscious always that this road did in reality exist and might have been the better one for him. In this spirit he wrote to Bely in August 1903:

> You love Christ more than Her. I cannot. I know that you are ahead, without doubt. But—I cannot. From this it follows that you are free from a part of that tormenting, ancient, intellectual temptation which often tortures me: "eternal masculinity". For this reason, I do not know Her so well. .. By rights my place is with the real decadents—without top or bottom. But often this does not appeal to me, and I return again ...
> There my fall is watched
> By flights of joyous angels.

Beside the personal and the religious, there was also a third reason why Blok gradually gave up the attempt to write poetry about the Most Beautiful Lady: this was that he found art and religion increasingly incompatible. Instinctively, he had always shrunk from the idea of mixing the two, and it was with evident self-distrust that he noted in his diary in April 1902: "Surely I too am not coming round to deny the autonomy of art, to accept its inevitable transmutation into religion?"

This entry was made under the direct influence of Zinaida and Dmitry Merezhkovsky, at that time the undisputed leaders of the intellectual and artistic *élite* of Petersburg. Blok had just met them, and their influence on him was second only to that of the Solov'ev family. Not only was Merezhkovsky an accomplished poet and famous critic, not only was his wife, Zinaida Hippius, one of the most brilliant talents amongst the elder generation of Russian symbolists, not only were they connected, through Serge Dyaghilev's journal *The World of Art*, to everything that was most vital and alive in contemporary Russian art and letters, but the two stood at the very centre of an intellectual movement which, at that time, was of great interest to the young Blok: the attempt to bridge the gap between the intelligentsia and the Church through the medium of the so-called "Religious-Philosophical Meetings" and of their journal *The New Road* (Новый Путь). It was *The New Road* which, in March 1903, first published twelve of Blok's verses to The Most Beautiful Lady, but the friendship which sprang up between the young poet and the Merezhkovskys was more than purely literary. The Merezhkovskys whom, as another member of their "circle", Georgy Chul'kov, later recalled, literary Petersburg tended to regard as a kind of compound personality, were acquisitive and energetic soul-hunters. Blok became a frequent visitor and listened fascinated to their talk of the necessity of "hallowing" all human achievement, of the "two abysses" which reflect one another, of "the way of self-assertion" which leads to union with God as surely as "the way of self-abnegation". Dimly, Blok distrusted this reconciling of opposites, even as he distrusted the idea of a theurgical art which proceeded naturally from the notion of a "sacred culture". Merezhkovsky thought in dialectical antitheses, and Blok found this "scientifically correct" but "mystically" unsatisfying. As early as June 1902 he was questioning Hippius' idea that man could approach a final, religious "synthesis" of "Aesthetics and ethics, eros and 'courtly love', paganism and the 'old' Christianity ... without deliberately shutting out the sounds of life, so that they should not drown the Great Rushing Sound". For him, the only "synthesis" worth having was that revealed to Plotinus and Solov'ev "not logical, a different and already finally apocalyptic synthesis, that very one of which it has been said; 'And there shall be no more curse!'"

If the Lady had "something to do with the end of the world" and if this was how Blok envisaged the end of the world, it is clear that he could not go on writing about Her without "deliberately shutting out the sounds of life". But the "sounds" of life, the "music" of history are the very stuff of Blok's poetry. In a lovely poem written in May 1902, he expressed this dilemma in relation to the Beautiful Lady:

> Ты не ушла. Но может быть,
> В своем непостижимом строе
> Могла исчерпать и избыть
> Всё мной любимое, земное ...
>
> И нет разлуки тяжелей
> Тебе, как розе, безответней
> Пою я, серый соловей,
> В моей темнице многоцветной!

> (Thou hast not gone away. But perhaps
> In Thine unattainable sphere
> Thou mays't use up and exhaust
> All that I love, of the earth ...
>
> And there is no separation so hard to bear:
> To Thee, unanswering as a rose,
> I sing, a grey nightingale,
> In my many-coloured prison!)

In 1903 he wrote to Andrey Bely: "All the time I am haunted by the ineradicable suspicion: does not pure (?) service, constant standing in 'the unfailing light of the New Goddess', exclude the necessity and even the very possibility of poetic work?" In 1906 Blok finally solved these questions in one of his working notebooks:

Mysticism is the Bohemian element of the soul, religion is standing watch ... *true art does not correspond in its impulses with religion.** It is positivist or mystic (both spring from the same source). Art has its own Rule, it is a monastery of historical for-

* Editor's italics.

mation, that is a monastery which leaves no room for religion. Religion is that (about that) which is to come, mysticism—that which has been and which is.

Mysticism asserts itself most evidently (is at its most characteristic) in ecstasy (which might be defined as an alliance with the world against people). Religion is foreign to ecstasy (we should sleep and eat and read and walk religiously), it is an alliance with people against the world as *distortion* (?) N.B. Everything in the world which is revealed *in its undistorted state* (possibly even *everything*) immediately becomes the object of religion. ... It remains only to fall asleep (to wait long and patiently for the return of the old) or to break the window and, thrusting our head out, to see that life is simple (joyful, difficult, complicated). This last (through poverty) is the road to religion.

All his life Blok was to feel his own failure to devote himself to the religious ideal as a fall and, occasionally, in moments of nostalgia, bitterly regretted having adventured himself into what he repeatedly described as "the Hell of art", but he did not "repent". Possibly, he felt that only by finding out about "that which has been and which is" could he acquire the right to hope for "that which is to come".

"Absolute emancipation from the earthly idol can come to pass only by way of complete πάθος in earthly form", he wrote to Bely. Even as he wrote of the Most Beautiful Lady, Blok was becoming increasingly aware of the world beyond "the window", and its "distortions" showed up with abominable clarity against the white radiance of his dreams for the future.

All those picturesque peasants, for instance. Years later, when those same peasants sacked and burnt his beloved Shakhmatovo at the end of 1918, Blok was to think back to the time of the "Verses about the Most Beautiful Lady"—and to understand:

Yes, when I bore the great flame of love in my heart, made up of the usual simple elements, yet receiving a new content and a new meaning because the bearers of that love were Lyubov' Dmitriyevna and I—"exceptional people"—when I was full of that love which people will read about in my books after I am dead, I used to take pleasure in setting my beautiful horse prancing through the poverty-stricken village. Just to show off, I enjoyed asking the way, which I knew perfectly well beforehand, of some poor peasant or of some comely peasant-woman just in order to exchange flashing smiles with her and to make my heart jump a little for no better reason than that I was young, the mist damp, her eyes dark and my belt tight. And all this had absolutely no effect on my great love (or had it? What if all my future falls and disintegration had their origin in this?) but, on the contrary, set the flames of my youth, just my youth, leaping and, together with my youth, that *other*, greater flame...

The poor people were aware of all this. More aware of it than I was, more consciously so. They knew that the master was young, his horse stately, his smile attractive, that his fiancée was lovely and that both were—gentlefolk. And wait and see now—we'll show the gentry something, pleasant or not.

And they showed us.

And they are showing us. ... And—*I have not the right to judge.*

This awareness of slowly ripening anger crept up on Blok very gradually. In the *Verses about the Most Beautiful Lady* it is not yet identified—just a sound as of distant thunder:

Не жди последнего ответа
Его в сей жизни не найти
Но ясно чует слух поэта.
Далёкий гул в своём пути.

Он приклонил с вниманием ухо,
Он жадно внемлет, чутко ждёт,
И донеслось уже до слуха;
Цветёт, блаженствует, растёт ...

Всё ближе — чаянье сильнее,
Но, ах! — волненья не снести ...
И вещий падает, немея,
Заслыша близкий гул в пути.

(Do not expect the final answer,
It is not given in this life.
But the ear of the poet clearly catches
The distant thunder on his road.
He has bent his head attentively,
Eagerly, he takes it in, fine-strung, he waits,
And already he can hear it:
It flowers, it basks in bliss, it grows. ...
And nearer yet, the premonition stronger,
But, Ah! The expectation is unbearable ...
And the seer falls, struck dumb,
Hearing the thunder close upon the road)

—this thunderous roaring sound rumbles through all Blok's work: "Близкий гул в пути" (1901), "Тот гул, который возрастает так быстро, что с каждым годом мы слышим его ясней и ясней" (1908), "Люди культуры, сторонники прогресса, отборные интеллигенты—с пеной у рта строят машины, двигают вперёд науку, в тайной злобе, стараясь забыть и не слышать гул стихий земных и подземных, пробуждающийся то там, то здесь" (1908), "Есть немота—то гул набата" (1914), "Мне начинает казаться, что за городским гулом я слышу ещё какой-то гул" (August 1917), "На днях, лежа в темноте с открытыми глазами, слушал гул, гул: думал, что началось землетрясение" (9th January 1918) and on the day he finished "The Twelve" and "The Scythians": "Страшный шум возрастающий во мне и вокруг. Этот шум слышал Гоголь" (29th January 1918). In 1920 Blok confided to a young woman poet: "Kipling wrote a story called *The Light that Failed*. There's a man goes blind in it. Only I have gone deaf—for ever."

At the time he was writing the *Verses about the Most Beautiful Lady*, the roaring sound still seemed to come from "other worlds". Blok did not as yet consciously associate it with Revolution. Indeed, to judge by his correspondence, he appears to have looked on peasant uprisings, which, in the early years of the twentieth century were a sporadic, almost a seasonal, feature of Russian country life, as distressing evils in the nature of droughts and outbreaks of cholera, with which, in fact, they were not infrequently associated. He also preserved an attitude of Olympian aloofness towards undergraduate politics, writing with icy disdain of the demonstrations, boycotts, strikes and meetings which kept student opinion in a state of ferment throughout his university career. In a society where moral indignation and perpetual readiness to sacrifice reputation and career for the sake of "protest" were the distinguishing marks of the decent fellow ("порядочный человек"), this youthful arrogance showed a certain moral courage. It was not in Blok to seek popularity. For this, some lesser souls envied him and sought to corrupt or besmirch him. For this, as he grew older, others, more generous, trusted and followed him. For this, after the 1917 Revolution, when he worked in an advisory capacity with the actors of the Great Dramatic Theatre in Petrograd, they called him their "conscience". For this, Gor'ky, in later years Blok's most generous adversary on boards and committees, advised: "Trust Blok. He is a man of fearless sincerity", and said of him in another context: "Blok was uniquely beautiful, both as a man and as a personality—enviably beautiful."

There was, however, one aspect of Russia's social troubles which did impinge upon Blok's conscious mind—even during his years of "extreme individualism" before the First Revolution. This was the problem of man and the machine (see the poem "The Factory", No. 22 and note). He *did* feel a common humanity with the factory workers of Petersburg and, whereas he felt a bookish admiration for rather than indignation on behalf of the peasant behind the plough, he shrank with every fibre of his being from the idea of day after day spent in the service of machines. "But what of man?" he asks in the first chapter of the autobiographical poem "Retribution", in which he seeks to characterize the nineteenth century, and answers: "Not man was master, but machines and towns." And, to the twentieth century, he puts the question once again:

Что-же человек? За рёвом стали,
В огне, в пороховом дыму,
Какие огненные дали
Открылись взору твоему?
О чем – машин немолчный скрежет?

(But what of man? Behind the shriek of steel
Amid the flames, in smoking powder veiled,
What fiery distances have opened up
Before your wondering gaze?
What means this ceaseless grinding of machines?)

"All Europe grinds and whirls", he wrote to his mother in 1911, "and at heart there is no longer any reason for such activity, because everything is over already", and, in the same year, with considerable exasperation, to his wife, who had sent him a gleeful description of a shopping spree in Paris: "Try to understand that all objects of modern production are sheer vulgarity and not worth a brass farthing." Blok had no objection to industrialization as such (see "The New America", No. 94 and note; also note to No. 91), but, from the beginning, he was horrified at the thought of the machines taking over and of man binding himself to the service of his own greed: inventing for the sake of invention, launching out into space simply because the machines were there to take him, producing more and more useless goods, grinding out more and more terrible weapons and sacrificing his own life to this Moloch of his own creation. Again, it was not the idea of service to which Blok objected any more than the idea of industrialization. He had been brought up with an almost feudal conception of duty of which he once wrote: "Remember duty. It is the only music. Without duty, there is neither life nor passion." He maintained that work was "sacred, life-giving, an education for the mind, the will and the heart", but, he added: "From whence then is the curse attached to it? For there is a curse." It was compassion for those who *had* to work, not creatively and purposively but simply for a living, "to eat bread in the sweat of their brows", which inculcated in Blok a feeling of solidarity with his fellow-men far more profound than the often superficial liberalism of the universities. Although far from rich, he and his ancestors had been spared this curse, and had therefore grown into different kinds of men. But they had also become isolated, cut off from their roots, and had lost the will to live, the very instinct of self-preservation.

The people's will to live, on the other hand, Blok felt suddenly and overwhelmingly, when the first Revolution of 1904–5 brought them streaming out from the obscurity of their workshops and their slums to walk in procession through the streets of Petersburg. Here were the people who would know how to master the machines, who would have a use for them, who *needed* them in order to obtain the leisure and security to become, each last one of them, "exceptional human beings"; the people "who desperately wanted to live a little like rich people". So, when Blok eventually "joined in" politics, it was not to demand the freedom of the Press or even Representative Government. It was to march rather vaguely with a red flag at the head of a worker's procession, to the ill-contained amusement of some of his more aesthetic colleagues such as Valeriy Bryusov. In the same way when, after 1917, he clearly felt himself to be an internationalist, his vision was the ultra-modern one of the older nations "walking arm in arm" with the new, under-developed countries destined to build a new culture on the ruins of the old. Blok was not interested in "abstractions", either political or philosophic.

Although the revolution of 1904–1905 caused an emotional upheaval that

liberated many thoughts and intuitions which Blok had formerly contrived
to ignore, these thoughts and intuitions had been present, albeit dormant, in
all the poetry of his First Volume. The Most Beautiful Lady Herself is outside
the chronology of Blok's development. While he felt Her as an imminent
presence all other themes faded in awe before Her Majesty:

И другие песни спою когда-нибудь

(And the other songs I shall sing some other time.)

Yet in his later work, particularly in the poems of the Third Volume, while
She is not always present as revelation, she *is* present as dogma. Occasionally,
in Blok's most tragic verses, the very desolation of Her absence seems to
underline his belief in Her objective existence. Had this not been so, surely
the poet would have laid aside his pen and made an end:

Над нами *сумрак неминучий**
Иль ясность божьего лица.

(Above us lowers *the eternal dark**
Or else the radiance of the face of God.)

Either, or: "Blok was a maximalist", wrote Andrey Bely, and again, "He
was interested only in direct experience". Finding that he *could* not write
about the Eternal, he decided to write about the temporal, but this does not
mean that the Eternal ceased to exist for him. The Lady, then, is a constant:
greater than Blok's poetry, greater than the historical process: the goal and
inspiration of both. But Blok's "mysticism", his sorcery, his daemonism and
conjuring of "Astarte" and of "doubles" are not constants. They do have a
place in the chronology of his development and they make their presence felt
in his poetry long before 1905 although it is only in the Second Volume
that they dominate. Before the revolution broke out, Blok, "mystically", as
an artist, was in a state of rebellion:

> Quite contrary to the judgement of vulgar criticism, as though "the revolution had
> cast a spell on us", we put forward the opposite conclusion: the revolution took place
> not only in this, but in other worlds.... Just as something broke in us, so something
> broke in Russia. And Russia herself ... turned out to be our own soul.... As before the
> soul of the people arose the blue phantom created by them themselves, so ours rose
> before us. ... We lived through the madness of other worlds, demanding a miracle
> before the time was ripe; the same thing happened with the soul of the people: it
> demanded a miracle prematurely and was reduced to ashes by the lilac worlds of
> revolution....

Written in 1910, in the key article "On the Present State of Russian Symbo-
lism", this is no smug "reactionary" pronouncement. Blok identified himself
with the element of revolution too completely to pronounce judgement. He is
merely stating what he believed to be true. Revolution was an attempt by

* Editor's italics.

man to bring about salvation by his own efforts, "to create the world anew", a theme which echoes through Soviet poetry to this day, lending heroic pathos to the higher flights of Soviet humanism. Blok's temperament and, in part, even his reason were in sympathy with this. But *in experience* it did not work: even as when he refused to await "The Lady" and tried to summon Her, to make an invocation, he was confronted by Another, "the beautiful doll, the blue phantom, the earthly miracle", so mankind, too, payed for its wilful demands by a kind of dance out into emptiness, a descent into Hell from which only Christ could raise it—or this was the theory which Blok worked out with his friend Zhenya Ivanov (see Note 49). But Blok, though ready to imitate, to come down from his mystic heights and to "take on flesh", to accept suffering—

И бережно свой крест несу

(And carefully I bear my cross)

and even death—somehow could not and would not acknowledge the only Christ he seems to have known, the somewhat effeminate, pre-Raphaelite figure of the Russian *art nouveau*, as Redeemer—whether of himself or of the World—and he looked always for "Another", even though, right through his life, from the Mystic Summer of 1901 to "The Twelve", he *knew* with unreasoning certainty that Christ was "with the people".

History, the elements, the Spirit of Music—every higher mystic sanction of Blok's art—were also "with the people": so were common sense and compassion. Blok's attitude to "the people", once he had become aware of their existence, of their equal right to life, was realistic and "religious" in his sense of the word. His attitude to Revolution was, on the contrary, "mystic". Revolution was for him an intoxication, a passion—like his love for Volokhova, like his love for "Carmen" (L. A. Del'mas) and, like all his passions, self-consuming and self-defeating and yet, in some ways, creative and purifying, leaving him clear-sighted, empty, sober, and very wide awake. Blok valued passion and revolution both because they burnt away many evil, choking things and because of an inborn tendency to self-destruction:

> Blok once told me that his doctor had said to him: your physique is remarkably robust, but you have done everything in your power to undermine it. Blok was addicted to tea as black as coffee, to wine, to sleepless nights, to all things sharp or spicy for the one reason that these things were *harmful*....

So Blok was remembered by one of his closest friends, Vladimir Pyast, and Blok himself wrote constantly of the "will to die" of the Intelligentsia as a whole.

Even his final acceptance of the October Revolution, as he expresses it in his "answer" to a bitter letter of reproach from Zinaida Hippius, the poem

"Женщина, безумная гордячка" is, both in its rhythms and its imagery, an act of passionate self-surrender:

Страшно, сладко, неизбежно, надо
Мне бросаться в многопенный вал...

(It is my fear, my joy, my fate, my calling
To fling myself into the foam-flecked wave...)

Blok appears to have considered it his duty as a poet to follow where his passions led: anything else was a betrayal of "the spirit of music". His constant nightmare was to stroll indifferent and insubstantial across the surface of life, to become "empty" like the "mystics" in his play, *The Puppet Show*, written in 1906, or like the terrible walking corpse in the first poem of the Cycle "Dance of Death" (see No. 61). In passion he found an outlet from himself into the suffering of humanity—and into the hell of art; but, as Dante carried the image of Beatrice through Hell, so Blok carried the memory of the Most Beautiful Lady through the Hell of his own and of his country's passions.

Each passion left a desolation more terrible than the last ("*We were reduced to ashes* by the lilac mists of Revolution", Blok wrote and, in the poem "Born in the years of sloth and dull decay" (No. 97) he uses the term испепеляющие годы which means literally "years which reduced to ashes"). But Blok continued to seek passions and to render faithful account of the inferno which they opened up before him:

Как тяжело ходить среди людей
И притворяться непогибшим,
И об игре трагической страстей
Поветствовать ещё не жившим.

И, вглядываясь в свой ночной кошмар,
Строй находить в нестройном вихре чувства,
Чтобы по бледным заревам искусства
Узнали жизни гибельной пожар.

(How hard it is to walk with other men
And to pretend to them one is not dead
And of the tragic game of human passions
Render account to those who have not lived.

And, looking deep into the heart of nightmare,
To find the plan behind the unplanned whirl of sense,
So that, in the pale afterglow of art,
Others should recognize the deadly fire of life.)

Immediately after the 1905 Revolution there came a period of shocked quiet and of spiritual stagnation, symbolized in Blok's poetry by the recurring image of the marshlands (cf. the cycle *Bubbles of the Earth*, written between 1904 and 1905, the long poem *The Night Violet*, November–December 1905, the article *Безвременье*, October 1906, and the terrifying poem *Задебренные лесом кручи*, October 1907–29th August 1914).

Blok himself wrote to his father, on 30th December 1905, when the First Russian Revolution was already slipping away into history:

> My own attitude to "the movement of liberation" found expression, alas, almost solely in liberal conversations and at one time even in sympathy for the Social Democrats. Now I am leaving all that further and further behind me having absorbed everything of which I am capable (in the sphere of "social conscience") and discarded that which the soul does not accept. And it accepts almost nothing of that sort, so let it take its own place, there where it would be: never shall I become either a revolutionary, or a "builder of life", and not because I see no sense in either of these occupations, but simply because of the nature, the quality and the theme of my soul's emotional experiences.

As the sounds of revolution faded from Blok's ears, so his home—the walls of which he had "broken", the door of which he had "left open to the snowstorm" —began to disintegrate around him.

His "mystic" friendship with Andrey Bely and Sergey Solov'ev, founded on a shared cult which they were eager to discuss, analyse and dissect *ad nauseam* but which Blok now felt to belong wholly to the sphere of the inexpressible, was the first part of his idyll to crumble and to dissolve. Having entertained Blok and his wife in Moscow in the winter of 1903–1094 and spent a happy summer with them at Shakhmatovo in 1904, the two young men decided to repeat the visit in the summer of 1905. Because Blok's love for his wife was so evidently and inextricably confused with his poetry of the Eternal Feminine, Solov'ev and Bely, his "spiritual brothers", had, half in play (they were all still students, all under 25), half in earnest, made their own cult of Lyubov' Dmitriyevna. Blok—himself originally responsible for drawing his bride into "the strange world" of his verses, "where everything was singing, everything half-said"—could hardly blame her for acting up to his friends a little, for silently and graciously accepting the tributes of their unconcealed admiration, for submitting to their absurd half-laughing, half-serious attempts to ascribe some higher significance to her every mood, gesture and, even, change of hair-ribbon or parasol. In this way a false situation gradually came into being and young Serezha and Bely, *plus royalistes que le roi*, even considered themselves entitled to take Blok to task for his betrayal, in poetry, of the Most Beautiful Lady. When Blok, with his usual total lack of hypocrisy, confided to Bely that he had already betrayed not only his Muse but his wife—Bely determined to "rescue" Lyubov'. Not unnaturally, he fell desperately in love with her in the process and the affair, hopelessly clouded up for all parties from the very beginning by what for Blok was already in part yesterday's mysticism, very nearly ended in tragedy. The house-party in

Shakhmatovo having broken up over some quite minor incident, Blok, feeling that the whole situation was really his fault in the first place, left the decision entirely up to his wife. She vacillated—for nearly two years. Bely, who, as Mochul'sky, the wise biographer of both poets, most penetratingly observed, was in love with *both* Bloks, almost went out of his mind. He wrote letters of explanation long as short novels to everyone concerned, including Blok's mother who was extremely fond of him, stormed to and fro between Petersburg and Moscow, begging, pleading, analysing, discussing his woes with Zinaida Hippius and her sisters Tata and Nata. Blok's family troubles soon became the property of all literary Petersburg. Advice, sought and unsought, showered down on the young couple's head. Blok was miserable, exasperated and unhelpful. All through the winter of 1906 he buried himself in academic work during the day and began wandering round the town at nights, drinking, brooding, observing the corrupt Petersburg night-life and the night-horror of poverty—always so much more terrible in a cold climate—with aloof fascination, wavering between hushed submission (*The Ring of Suffering*, No. 39), drunken dreams (*The Stranger*, No. 40), and moods of wild romantic irony and savage pathos (cf. the play *The Puppet Show* (1906), the article *Irony* (November 1908), Notes 21 and 34). Eventually, however, Lyubov' Dmitriyevna decided to stay with her husband, Bely went abroad and Blok's life passed into a completely new phase.

The epigraph to the third published collection of Blok's verse, "The Earth in Snow" (1908), is taken from one of his favourite poets—Apollon Grigoriev. It tells how a comet hurtles blazing through the sky, threatening the other stars in their ordered courses. But the comet is indifferent to the chaos and the discord which it leaves in its erratic wake. It has been hurled from the heart of creation "to attain through trial and struggle the goal of purification, the goal of self-creation".

Blok's passion for the actress Nataliya Volokhova was such a comet. Mariya Beketova describes Volokhova's appearance at this time:

> I will say one thing. The poet did not exaggerate the fascination of his "Snow-Maiden". Those who saw her then, at the time of his infatuation for her, know what a spellbinding charm she exercised. A tall, slender figure, fine features, black hair and eyes, truly "winged" eyes, black, wide open, "the poppies of her malicious eyes". And striking too was her smile, glittering with the whiteness of her teeth, a triumphant, victorious smile.

And here is Chukovsky's description of Blok in that same year:

> His entire *façon-d'être* was aristocratic: correct, measured, a little arrogant. When I first met him he seemed indestructibly healthy—broad-shouldered, well-grown, ruddy-lipped, calm; and even the melancholy of his unhurried walk, even the heavy sad-

ness of his greenish, broodingly thoughtful eyes could not destroy the impression of irresistable youthful strength by which, in those far-distant years, he always impressed me.... Neither before nor since have I ever seen a man who so clearly, sensibly and visibly radiated magnetism.

A striking couple, perfectly endowed by nature to play the leading romantic roles in a gloriously talented society of young people who had "lost the borders between the real and the fantastic".

Volokhova was one of the troupe directed by Vera Kommisarzhevskaya and the young Vsevolod Meyerhold who, in the autumn of 1906, were rehearsing Blok's play *The Puppet Theatre*. (Two other plays which Blok had written in the same year, *The King in the Square* and *The Stranger*, were accepted by Meyerhold but forbidden by the theatrical censor—*The Stranger* because the censor, although frankly admitting in his report that he could make neither head nor tail of it, suspected that the author was in some way taking in vain the name of the Holy Virgin, *The King in the Square* for reasons unknown, but probably because it is clearly about the Revolution.) It was Kommisarzhevskaya's policy to steep her whole troupe in the atmosphere of contemporary art—and to this end she encouraged her beautiful and intelligent young actresses to hold receptions for the leading poets, artists and musicians of Petersburg. "We were all very young", Volokhova remembers of that time, "All afire with love of our art: poetry, the theatre, painting. And all of us were head over ears in love with life and art, with the power of life and the might of beauty and truth in art. It was this general state of infatuation which made our meetings so vivid, light and beautiful...." But, for Blok, the "general state of infatuation" soon found a particular object. His dream-woman, "The Stranger", came to life for him in Nataliya Volokhova. One evening, as Valentina Verigina, another actress of Kommisarzhevskaya's troupe, remembered:

... Blok came as usual to call on us in our dressing-room. When the interval was over we accompanied him to the head of the stairs. He began to go down and Volokhova remained standing at the head of the stairs to watch him go. Suddenly, Alexandr Alexsandrovich turned round, took a few indeterminate steps towards her, halted again and, finally, stepping up onto the lowest stair, said shyly and solemnly that just now, in this minute, he had understood the meaning of his premonitions, of the confusion of the last few months. "I have just seen it in your eyes, I have just realized that it is they and nothing else which bring me to this theatre."

This was the beginning of a graciously enacted dream. In reality, Volokhova would have none of Blok, precisely because he was at this time unreal—and so was his feeling for her, however overwhelming the infatuation. Hurt, and considerably astonished, Blok made her his daemonic and unattainable Snow Maiden, transformed their romance into a masquerade of balls and parties and sleigh-rides, of fizzing wine and swirling snow. Verigina shows in her memoirs how every poem of the ethereal *Snow-mask* cycle, which seems to waver between the worlds of pure phantasy and of pure music, was in fact based on some real incident, on Volokhova's actual words (see Note 47 for full reference). This, indeed, was the "transformation of life into art" of which Blok writes in the article *On the Present State of Russian Symbolism*—"A tendency", he noted afterwards, which "runs most vividly through all European decadence...". And, to some extent, this period of undisciplined mysticism was the climax of Blok's Westernism—although the poetry of this winter could have been written nowhere but in St.Petersburg and in no language but Russian, with its almost limitless capacity for liquid alliterations, dissolving assonance and intoxicating internal rhyming. Perhaps it would be truer to say that it was the climax of Blok's Westernism *as he felt it*, perceived through the prism of Petersburg culture, a culture brilliant and irreal, a thread stretched to breaking point between the petrified wisdom of the ages and the sturdy pull of a young nation. "The themes of Europe", Blok once wrote, "Are Art and Death. Russia is life." The themes of Blok's poetry to Volokhova, in her incarnation as the Snow Maiden, are just these: Art and Death. In so far as it is possible to make precise statements about so infinitely complex and sensitive a subject (Stanislavsky, in a letter of condolence to Blok's mother, said quite rightly that it was "only possible to speak of Blok in verse")—it seems that he had to write these themes out of his system by complete self-abandonment to their rhythms before taking up his great and simple themes of Russia, man and history.

To these he came through Volokhova's other incarnation. She was also the "Faina" of his poetry—the wild, untamed spirit of Russia, the circus rider who contemptuously slashed the clown's "white pancake of a face" with her fine whip as she galloped past him. "In the soul of the clown there is a conflagration of laughter, despair and passion. From beneath the red three-cornered brows the blood is pouring—which is why he cannot see his way. He gropes on, staggering and fooling—but don't put out your hand to help and don't try to save him." By her steadfast refusal to take Blok seriously as a "real person", by her very impatience with his inability to distinguish between "dream, life and death", by virtue of her own passionate, melancholy rejection of the superficiality of their lives—Volokhova came to symbolize for Blok not "The Stranger" only, the "beautiful doll" conjured out of nothingness by his own will for his own delight—but also "Faina", the unawakened spirit of his country, the Sleeping Princess awaiting her true Prince, the gipsy singer waiting for a "real" lover and rejecting with cruel laughter the erudite compliments of men of letters. The pain of rejection, even if the wound were to his self-respect rather than to his heart, brought him to life, bewildered still and lost, but angry and determined. For this reason he treasured the pain—for this reason, like the blinded clown, he asked no help. Blok realized that, if he remained as he was, a wandering dreamer "half in love with easeful death"—his country would not take him seriously either. This was his "Second Christening", the moment when he awoke to the knowledge that "there are people and there is work to be done" (Что люди есть, и есть дела).

Towards the end of the autobiographical play, *The Song of Fate* (1907), Faina and the hero are talking—lost together in a snowy wilderness. Faina exclaims impatiently: "There, you're all like that; ...like dead men ... and I am alive!" The hero answers dreamily: "Perhaps I shall die in the snow. It doesn't matter: I might as well die." Faina cries out on him furiously: "Again—words? A fine lot of living you've done to lie down and die! People only die in fairy-tales!" At the end of the play, Faina has gone back to her "old master", but for a while only, and the hero is left alone, lost in the wilderness into which Faina has led him, far from "the quiet white house" where his wife and mother await him and which he left because, there, he was "too comfortable". "All is white", he murmurs. "One thing has remained: my prayer to Thee, Lord: a clear conscience. But there's no road. What can I do—a beggar? Where can I go?" At this moment, against the wailing of the wind, a rough voice uplifted in a well-known folk-song is heard approaching, breaks off and demands: "'Ere, Oo's there? What are you standing about for? Want to freeze?"—"I'll find the way", the hero rejoins stiffly. "Well, keep moving, brother, keep moving", recommends the voice. "A saint might stand there as though there were nothing to it, but that's not for the likes of you an' me. Blizzard'll bury you! And you'll not be the first she's rocked to sleep in her snows...."—"Who are you talking about?"—"Who? Anyone could tell you *that*: Mother Russia, that's who...."—"And do you know the road?"—"Well, if I don't, nobody does. You'll not be a stranger to these parts, then?"—"A stranger." "Well, how could you expect to know the road then? See that light over yonder?"—"No, I can't see it."—"Well, look a bit 'arder and yer will. But where is it you'll be going?"—"That's just it. I don't know myself."—"You don't *know*? You're a queer sort of man, I see. Tramp, I suppose. Well, come on, come on, don't stand still. I'll lead you to the next halt and then you'll go on as you think fit."—"Lead on, Passer-by", agrees the hero, adding, thoughtfully and purposefully, "And then I'll go on as I think fit...".

And so Blok began to grope forward again towards that harmonious future which he had perceived "in his first youth", acknowledging himself a stranger in his own land, accepting the temporary tutelage of "the people" who, like the providential guide of *The Song of Fate*, could at least offer a certain amount of local knowledge and of common sense. Through the blizzards of 1906 and 1907 he came to his great theme: the theme of *Russia and the Intelligentsia.* In a letter of 6th December 1908 Blok wrote to Stanislavsky:

> To this theme I consciously and indeflectibly dedicate my life. I feel more and more vividly that this is—the very first question, the most vital, the most *real*. I have been working up to it for a long time, since the beginning of my thinking life, and I know that my road, in its basic direction, is straight as an arrow and—like an arrow—purposeful.

Eleven years later, Blok published a collection of seven articles,* all dedicated to this his "theme", written over a span of years from 1907 to 1918. In the preface he explained:

> ... I never approached this question from the political angle. My theme, if I may use the expression, is musical (of course, in a peculiar sense of the word). Hence the general title of all these articles—"Russia and the Intelligentsia".
> Russia here is not a state, not a national entity, not the fatherland, but a kind of complex body, constantly changing its outer form, fluid (like Heraclites' world) and yet unchanging somehow in what is most fundamental. The nearest definition for this conception are the words: "The people", "the soul of the people", "the element", but any one of these words on its own still does not exhaust the musical significance of the word *Russia*.
> In exactly the same way, the word "intelligentsia" is not used in its sociological sense: it is not a class, not a political force, not a "classless group", but, again, a kind of complex whole, which, nevertheless, does have a real existence and, by the will of history, has entered into a very significant relationship with the "people", the "element"; that is—into a relationship of conflict.
> The intelligentsia, like Russia, constantly changes its outer forms, but also remains faithful to itself in what is most fundamental. Closely related concepts are the concept of "enlightenment" (at least in the sense which the eighteenth century gave to that word), and of "culture" (not in the ancient but in the modern sense); but, there again, the musical correspondence between these concepts and what I am talking about is not complete; it would be better to say that the antimusicality† of the concept *intelligentsia* forces me to use this word and no other.

"Other people" had at last come alive for Blok—every last man of them, including the "peasants". One, a young man with poetic aspirations and some education who later became famous as the "peasant poet", Nikolay Kluyev, wrote to him from the provinces asking for help in publishing his verse. A correspondence was struck up and, in Kluyev's letters, Blok heard once again the "distant thunder":

> The peasant isn't shy of "you", he just envies you, and hates you and if he puts up with having you about it's only for so long as he can hope to get something out of you. Oh, how painful is the cancer of "your" existence among us; what an ever-present and grievous curse it is to know that—for the moment—we cannot do without "you"... the

---

* "Религиозные искания" и народ (1907) ("Religious Quests" and the People); Народ и Интеллигенция (1908) (The People and the Intelligentsia); Стихия и Культура (1908) (The Element and the People); Ирония (1908) (Irony); Дитя Гоголя (1909) (The Child of Gogol); Пламень (1913) (Flame); Интеллигенция и Революция (1918) (The Intelligentsia and the Revolution).

† "Antimusicality" in Blok's vocabulary means being out of tune with nature and therefore with the underlying harmony of things.

realization that "you" are everywhere, that "you" "may", whereas "we" "must"—
there's all the insurmountable barrier that bars an approach from our side. But what's
to stop you from contacting us? Nothing—but profound contempt and purely physical
revulsion.

Yet Kluyev offered hope of reconciliation:

> To hear you talk, you'd think those of you who have at last seen things as they are
> feel it impossible to alter anything in themselves. This is the lie in your mouth, or so I
> like to think. I feel that you, who know the great examples of martyrdom and glory,
> the great works of the human spirit, have got things wrong. ... To judge from the way
> you go on, all one can suppose is that millions of years of human struggle and suffer-
> ing have passed unnoticed for those who (as you say) "have for several generations be-
> longed to the gentry".

It was in the autumn of 1907 that Blok flung these words at a gathering of
intellectuals met to discuss "Religious Quests and the People"—a popular
topic since the Merezhkovskys had made a special "journey to the interior"
and "discovered" the "sectarians". Blok spoke like a judge and like a pro-
phet—and not unnaturally called down a storm of indignation on his own
head which boiled down to a general cry of "Speak for yourself". Not all
the intelligentsia were decadent aristocrats, his opponents pointed out; not
all wrote incomprehensible poems about wine and women, or obscure symbol-
ists plays in which the characters spent half their time arguing the various
merits of French cheeses. The history of the intelligentsia as a whole, they
said hotly, was one of sobriety and self-sacrifice—and of devoted service to
the people as teachers and healers. There was much truth in this. Blok *was*
exceptionally sophisticated, exceptionally Europeanized—but there was also
much truth in his sombre answer: "My questions are put, not by myself, but
by the history of Russia. It was not I who answered in the affirmative the
question of the inaccessibility of the intelligentsia to the people: the history
of Russia answered." And, indeed, it was not Blok's *thought* which was out
of reach of literate villagers like Kluyev—it was his general knowledge and
vocabulary, which were common currency for all the "intelligentsia". Thus
Kluyev wrote to him in 1910:

> I've read your article on the present state of Russian Symbolism! But in my ignor-
> ance I could not understand one or two words that hadn't come my way before: such
> as theurgist, Baedeker, concretise, thesis and antithesis, Bellini and Beato, Signorelli—
> but still I felt something fateful for symbolists in general about it, a kind of last post
> sounded over a field of bones, and gather from this that there really must be something
> amiss with Russian literature.*

Blok was not given to idealising the People. "We are not savages", he said
at one stage, "to make a God out of the unknown and the frightening". But
he insisted on their "cleverness". If only the intelligentsia could share out its

---

* Letter of 5/XI/1910, ЦГАЛИ, No. 55, Опись No. 3, Ед. Хр. No. 35.

education, not "the poisons" of its education, but all that was great and good in the past of Europe, with the people, in whom were "music", natural spontaneity of action, the "will to live"—then there would be hope for Russia. Blok made no attempt to take up active revolutionary work or to "go to the people" as the intelligentsia had attempted to do in the 1880's; his field was not constructive action and, besides, he already felt it to be too late. The "new men" would take over. They must be helped when the time came. By hastening that time the revolutionary "intelligentsia" was merely sawing off the branch of the tree on which it had been sitting, merely laying faggots at its base to make a merrier blaze. This would have been all right had they been aware of what they were doing: "Culture must be loved so much that it's destruction should not seem terrible...." Blok wrote of his spiritual heritage and, of his own home, his material birthright: "But I love it so much that I wouldn't mind selling it, I would regret nothing. ..."

In 1917, after a terrible outburst against tradition in which "Religion (priests and so forth)", "Romanticism", "Everything which has silted up with dogma, delicate dust, legendary unreality" is dismissed as "filth", Blok adds sternly: "Only he who has loved as I have loved has the right to hate."

In spirit a Greek rather than a Hebrew, Blok disliked the Bible and there is more of the Liturgy than of the Testaments in his poetry, but one text to which he returns again and again, from 1907 onwards, is the line which, in "The Song of Fate", he originally puts in the mouth of his mother:

> Perfect love casteth out fear.

Only once did he begin to sound the rhythms of a lament for the old culture, and here he pulled himself up and wrote no more:

> Есть одно, что в ней скончалось
> Безвозвратно,
> Но нельзя его оплакать
> И нельзя его почтить,
> Потому что там и тут
> В кучу сбившиеся тупо
> Толстопузые мещане
> Злобно чтут
> Дорогую память трупа —
> Там и тут,
> Там и тут ...
>                              (February 1918–8 April 1919)

> (Something there is which has passed with her passing
> Irretrievably;
> But we may not mourn it
> And we may not reverence it
> Because that here and there
> Dully huddling together

Paunchy shop-keepers
Spitefully reverence
The dear memory of the corpse
Here and there,
Here and there. ...)

The old must give way lovingly to the new, and the collapse of the old is inevitable. Such was Blok's message and warning. In his poetry, it sounded obliquely:

Пройдёт весна — над этой новью,
Вспоенная твоею кровью,
Созреет новая любовь.                 (1907)

(Spring will pass—above the virgin soil,
Nurtured by your blood,
A new love will ripen).

Доспех тяжел, как перед боем.
Теперь твой час настал. — Молись!   (1907)

(The armour weighs heavily, as before the battle
Now your hour has come.—To prayer!)

И невозможное возможно,
Дорога долгая легка...                (1908)

(And the impossible is possible
The long road is not hard....)

За твоими тихими плечами
Слышу трепет крыл...
Бьёт в меня светящими очами
Ангел бури — Азраил!                  (1913)

(Behind your quiet shoulders
I hear the quivering of wings...
With blazing eyes he beats his wings at me
The angel of the tempest—Azrael!)

Будьте довольны жизнью своей,
   Тише воды, ниже травы!
О, если б знали, дети, вы,
   Холод и мрак грядущих дней      (1910–14)

(Be happy with your life and ways
Stiller than water, lower than grass
Oh, if you knew what comes to pass
The cold and gloom of coming days)   (Bowra)

Пусть день далёк — у нас всё те ж
Заветы юношам и девам:
Презренье созревает гневом,
И зрелость гнева есть мятеж.          (1910–14)

(And though the day be far—the same
Advice we have for youths and girls;
Contempt will ripen into anger,
And the fruit of anger is—rebellion.)

«Безумный друг! Ты мог бы счастлив быть!...»
«Зачем? Средь бурного ненастья
Мы, всё равно, не можем сохранить
. Неумирающего счастья!»                (1914)

("Oh foolish friend! you might have found content!"
"Wherefor? Amidst the raging of the storm
We cannot keep however we may try,
Immortal happiness")


И пусть над нашим смертным ложем
Взовьётся с криком вороньё, —
Те, кто достойней, боже, боже,
Да узрят царствие твоё!                (1914)

(And let above our death-bed rather
The circling ravens wheel and cry
Thy Heavenly Kingdom, Abba, Father,
Let who is worthier descry   (Kemball).


Он занесён — сей жезл железной —
Над нашей головой. И мы
Летим, летим над грозной бездной
Среди сгущаюшейся тьмы.

Но чем полет неукротимей,
Чем ближе веяние конца,
Тем лучезарнее, тем зримей
Сияние Её лица.                        (1914)


(For it is poised—this iron sword
Above our heads. And we
Fly, fly above the threatening abyss
Amidst the gathering dark

Yet, the more uncontrollable the flight,
The nearer the forefeeling of the End,
The more perceptable, more radiant
Her Haloed Face)


In 1908, however, emerging from utter confusion, Blok had still to earn
the right to speak of such last things, a right which he always used with mod-
esty and discretion, not preaching his opinions but waiting for the symbols
and images to come of themselves, preferring always not to explain, often not
consciously understanding.

Meanwhile life went on. Volokhova left Petersburg in the spring for the
summer season in the provinces. So did Lyubov' Dmitriyevna. Blok was left
to brood over the ashes of his marriage and of his romance. But Lyubov'
Dmitriyevna came back, expecting a child—not Blok's. For a time there

seemed some hope that their private life would make sense for, in their feeling for one another, there was "more than literature". Volokhova was forgotten. The dream remained graven in verse, the real woman went on her own way and she and Blok never met again. But Lyuba, who had forgiven Blok so much, was welcomed and in her turn forgiven and Blok, although he did not give up his vagabond existence in Petersburg, was genuinely happy in the thought of a son, of how they would raise and care for him. But the baby died. After that, nothing really new happened in Blok's personal life. Even the vivid and happy love affair with L. A. Del'mas (the "Carmen" of Blok's verses), who remained a true and faithful friend to the end of his days, was only the most intense and joyous of a series of fleeting relationships which left nothing behind but—poetry...

И выпал снег
И не прогнать
Мне земных чар...
И не вернуть тех нег
И странно вспоминать
Что был пожар.

(And the snow fell
And I can't chase away
These earthly charms...
Nor bring back pleasures, and
It's strange now to recall
That once all was aflame.)

Lyubov' Dmitriyevna and Blok continued as before—unhappy apart, often miserable together, but essential to one another, deeply loving, suffering, always vulnerable in everything that concerned the other. Blok wrote to his wife in 1911:

I wanted to write you that everything "unique" in myself I have already given to you and cannot give it to anyone else even when, at times, I have wished that I could do so. That is what defines the tie between us. All that I have left over for others is, first and foremost, my mind and the feeling of friendship (which is distinguished from love only in that it is multiple and loses nothing by being so); further—merely daemonic sentiments, or indefinable attractions (more and more rarely) or, finally, low instincts.*

In the play, the Song of Fate, the hero's wife follows him after he leaves their "quiet white house", stumbling out into the blizzard carrying a shielded lantern. She has been promised that, at the end of the road, she will again find the soul of her beloved. When Blok read the play to friends, the image of the wife passed unnoticed. Blok noted this in his diary with some surprise and added: "Well, let it be so. My darling will remain hidden from human eyes until the time is ripe."

* Letter of 31/V (11/VI)/1911 (Духов День).

To recuperate from their troubles, the young Bloks—he was still only 28, she 27—went to Italy where they spent the summer of 1909. Here, Blok wrote the magnificent Italian Verses, full of awe for the past, alive with memories of the Renaissance, of the crumbling splendour of Rome and of Blok's favourite sphere of art where Heaven touches earth in the paintings of Bellini and Fra Beato Angelico. Europe sobered Blok and gave him perspective. On his return to Russia he defined his programme as "apprenticeship, spiritual diet, to remain, in life, an ordinary man".

Two more journeys abroad before the outbreak of the First World War (1911, 1913) confirmed Blok in his opinion that Europe was dying—and dying most ungracefully in a fever of senseless activity. The Basque coast gave Blok the background for his exquisite poem *The Nightingale Garden* (1915) which combines the uncanny charm of the story of Oisin in Tir na n-Og with something resembling the moral message of Tennyson's *Palace of Art*. In Brittany, he found inspiration for the play *The Rose and the Cross* (1912). But from Paris he wrote to his mother:

> At times the heat and meaninglessness take on an aspect of sheer genius. Various drinking-houses and café-concerts of almost unadulterated vulgarity. The usual blasphemies, pornography calculated to impress no-one but a third-to-fifth-form school-boy. Sometimes—a really witty vaudeville, or, suddenly—an astonishing song, always old (provençale, for instance), or something that has already been heard a thousand times (one of Yvette Gilbert's, for example).

Strangely, his vision of Paris corresponded not so much to that of his near-contemporaries the post-impressionists as to that of *our* contemporary, Bernard Buffet: "A Sahara—yellow boxes scattered with dead oases, the blue-grey immensities of dead churches and palaces: a dead Notre Dame, a dead Louvre." At Biarritz, he enjoyed wading out through the shoulder-high Atlantic rollers and took a childish delight in exploring the rock-pools for squids and starfish and playing with the crabs who, he discovered with enthusiasm, would carry off his long, Russian cardboard cigarette ends and then settle down to chew the tobacco. Towards his fellow holiday-makers, however, he was less indulgent: "Mama", he wrote, "Biarritz is inundated with the French bourgeoisie—to such an extent that the eye grows weary of contemplating hideous men and women." He also complained of fleas. Antwerp impressed him: "The Scheldt is huge, like the Neva, there are clouds of ships, docks, cranes, scaffolded distances, the smell of the sea, a mass of churches, old houses, fountains, towers...", but the charm of the Netherlands soon wore off: "I travelled right across Zeeland in a Bummelzug ... canals, big steamers ... windmills.... There's not much fun to Holland after all—nice, tidy and watery, nothing to take exception to." For Germany, Blok's feelings were more complex. His first love in foreign literature had been the German romantic poets. Nietzsche and particularly Wagner were important to him till the end of his life. He adored the Gothic in all its manifestations and he appreciated German cleanliness and efficiency. Finally, Blok's impressions of Germany were rather more relaxed and domesticated than those of France or Italy since he had visited a drowsy Kurort, Bad Nauheim, on several occasions alone and as his mother's escort when she travelled there to drink the waters (1897, 1903, 1909), and the place had a muted fascination for him as the scene of his first romantic adventure (see the cycle *Twelve Years Later*). But even Germany soon bored him, and the sight of the German bourgeoisie listening to the evening concert at Bad Nauheim was scarcely less depressing than that of their French counterparts taking their ease on the sands at Biarritz. To return to Russia—to his provincial, poverty-stricken and beloved Russia—was always a profound relief and a refreshing rediscovery.

In the very beautiful series of prose fragments entitled *Lightnings of Art (Молнии Искусства)* (1909), Blok describes his return from Italy to Russia; the flat, wind-swept platforms, where the old women shout their wares and nothing ever happens; the vast, drizzling plain on which the only sign of life is the distant figure of a man, a gun slung over his shoulder, trotting a shabby pony along the edge of a field; the rusty marshlands near Petersburg with their pathetic clumpings of naked, wind-bitten scrub; Petersburg itself—"vast, wet and homely"; "and everywhere the rain is falling, everywhere there is a wooden church, a telegraphist and a policeman". So Blok, the emancipated European returning from Europe, looked his country full in the eyes and recognized in her his kin, his equal, "the laughing-stock of the world": "Здравствуй, Матушка!"

"But ...", Blok goes on, almost as though talking in his sleep, "'I so terribly want to live'—says the Colonel from the *Three Sisters*. ..." Chekhov's *Three Sisters* haunted Blok as a recurring symbol of this huge desire for life—so did the image of people waiting on a railway platform (cf. the tragic poem *On the Railway [На железной дороге]* and Blok's bitter comment that, after the Revolution, the "best people" of Russia were like passengers who had sat and waited too long on a freezing platform so that, when their train at last came in, they had hardly the strength to board it and no desire left to travel). Touched by his country's helplessness, Blok wanted life *for* her. Real life—simple, joyful and free of poverty. The underlying conviction that "happiness is not human", that "those who have approached once, only once, cannot go away and forget, and that cross is already enough to bear", that Salvation is outside the temporal process, continued to exist parallel to this hope for Russia and, indeed, for man in History. If someone you love is hungry and dirty, you feed them and clean them before you pray

for their soul, or at least while you do so. Blok loved Russia very much, and
he wanted to see her fed and spruced up (see *The New America*, No.94
and Note, also Note to No.91). He was acutely aware of her strength which,
he noted for himself in 1916, lay "... in the still almost untapped resources of
the mass of the people and in her underground riches" and, here, *in the possi-
bility of a material renaissance in Russia he perceived the possibility of a spiri-
tual renaissance for European culture*. For Blok believed that the culture of
the "intelligentsia", which was in fact the culture of Europe, had grown too
far from the "musical dampness" from which it had been born, had dried up,
shrivelled and become merely "civilization", "'culture' in the modern sense
of the word". The "people", meanwhile, and especially "Russia" in her mas-
sive provincialism, had preserved the "spirit of music", and culture must be
ploughed back into the masses ("revertitur in terram suam unde erat", he
quoted in the article *The Collapse of Humanism [Хрушение Гуманизма]*).
In resisting this process, "civilization" becomes the enemy of "culture" and
the "people", who have nothing but "the spirit of music", neither science,
nor technical proficiency, nor law, become, paradoxically, the preservers of
culture. This is not to say that Blok thought of Russia as a land of vandals.
There were things which shocked him: the conversation of his cooks, for in-
stance: "such words that the blood runs cold from shame and despair"—he
confided to his diary on 1st December 1911; the shiftiness of his tenants
(there is a wonderful passage in Blok's Notebooks for 11th/12th May 1909,
in which he describes with deeply mixed feelings how, rising from his bed at
four in the morning to watch for a planet, he had instead caught the local
ne'er-do-well Yegor stealing straw from *his* barn and loosing chickens into
*his* newly-sewn oats and sheep onto *his* clover); the brutality, hypocrisy and
sheer money-grubbing greed of the middle classes (cf., for instance, the poem
*To wallow shamelessly in sin*, No.96); the vulgarities and horrors of the
"Terrible World" which he depicts with a kind of spell-bound revulsion in
the poetry of the Third Volume. Even when Blok's wife wrote to him in 1917
of the general lowering of standards, of the insolence and negligence which
she observed all about her, and of her fear of a Leninist victory, he answered
merely:

> I do not feel inclined to quarrel particularly with what you write; I can only say one
> thing: if it is really true (and there is much truth in it, although there are also other
> truths) then it merely intensifies the tragedy of Russia. There is also a terrible truth in
> that which, at the moment, is known as "Bolshevism". If you could only see and know
> that which I see and know, your attitude would be different, in spite of everything;
> your point of view is rather limited, it is essential to rise above it.

But, in spite of his fastidious, indeed almost hypersensitive awareness of
the shortcomings of the *hoi polloi*, Blok really did believe that his people

would show themselves worthy guardians of all that was best in their heritage:

> It is quite impermissible to insult any people with adaptations, popularizations. Vulgarization is not democratization. In time the people will come to appreciate everything and will pronounce their verdict—a cruel, cold verdict—on all those who have considered them inferior to themselves... who have tried to "condescend" to them...

Believing in his own values, which were the values and the hopes of Europe's past, Blok believed also in "Russia", in "the soul of the people":

> Don't be afraid [he exhorted his fellow-intellectuals in 1918]. Surely you don't believe that so much as one grain of that which is truly valuable can be lost? We have loved but little if we are afraid for that which we love. "Perfect love casteth out fear". Do not fear the destruction of Kremlins, palaces, pictures, books. They should be preserved for the people; but, having lost them, the people have not lost everything. A palace destroyed is no palace. A fortress wiped off the face of the earth is no fortress. A Tzar who tumbles off his throne of his own accord is no Tzar. Fortresses are in our hearts, Tzars in our heads. Eternal forms which have been revealed to us can be taken away only together with our hearts and with our heads.

And so Blok remained true to himself—an uncompromising idealist; a man who believed that only the destruction of the worst in the world into which he had been born would make possible the preservation of the best; who believed this from his own inner experience, not from observation, not from abstract conviction; a man with a roaring sound in his ears which grew ever louder and more threatening as his life grew quieter; a courteous misanthrope who went less and less into society but who lived in a state of intense inner concentration, hearkening, not to voices from "other worlds", but to "the music of history"; "a man in bondage", a servant of art; a "mere artist", constantly and painfully conscious of having fallen from a greater calling; a man deliberately confining his art to self-imposed "human" limitations. "Back to the heart, not only to the man but to the whole man with spirit, and heart, and body, and with all the details of his everyday life..."; a man appointed "by the will of fate, to be a witness to a great epoch"; a man who wrote of himself: "by the will of fate and not in my own feeble strength, I am an artist, that is, a witness."

Blok remained true to himself but, until the outbreak of the First World War, his outward fame rested largely on his restaurant lyrics; on the *Harps and Violins* to which he set his occasional love songs; on the masterly and fearful poetry of the "terrible world"; on the Stranger and the black rose in the golden glass of wine; on his Byronic physical beauty, the flower in his button-hole and the passionate gypsy rhythms of *Carmen*; on the easy and suspect sentiment of *The Sugar Angel* and the delicious, unwithstandable music of *The Maiden in the Church Choir Singing*, of *Pipes on the Bridge Struck up to Play*. Blok, for pre-Revolutionary Petersburg, was the poet of the *Nightingale Garden* and of the Gypsy Romance. The society which he pilloried preened itself languorously before the dark mirror of his verse. It was only national tragedy which brought the nation to a full awareness of Blok's tragic simplicity—and perhaps even now it is not fully realized.

The 1914 War entered Blok's listening and attentive universe like a great discord. It seemed to him that this internecine struggle had nothing to do with the main melodies of history. It represented a back-falling into barbarity which promised no regeneration. In a way it was the logical outcome of the "meaninglessness" he had sensed in Paris. His friend Pyast tries to analyse his attitude;

> It wasn't exactly that he was "pro-German", or that he was a convinced pacifist. But he was *against the allies*. He had no love either for the French or for the English, either as individuals or for the national ideas of the people. Belgium was comparatively dearer to him. He had travelled about the country, and also about Holland, and had found the experience rewarding; an unforgettable impression had been produced on him by the forefather of the Netherlands school of painting, Quentin Massys. But I remember how, at the beginning of the war, I was reduced to a state of cold fury by one sentence thrown at me by Blok: "Those toy countries of yours—Belgium and Sweden". ...

At a time when half Europe was mourning the rape of Antwerp, Blok was asked to write a poem on the subject—which he dutifully did. Although much of his verse is a direct reflection of contemporary events, this is the only one quite obviously written to order. "I feel only Russia", he confided to his diary, as he struggled with the reluctant rhythms. But even Russia he still felt only as a passive victim—"the river swelled by one more tear"—

> Идут века, шумит война,
> Встаёт мятеж, горят деревни,
> Но ты всё та ж, моя страна,
> В красе заплаканной и древней. —
> Доколе матери тужить?
> Доколе коршуну кружить?

Time passes. War returns. Rebellion rages.
The farms and villages go up in flame,
My Russia, in her ancient, tear stained beauty,
  Is yet the same,
Unchanged through all the ages. How long will
The mother grieve and the kite circle still?

(Frances Cornford)

It was during the war that Blok's poems about Russia were collected and published in a single collection. "Symbolism" had begun to go out of fashion in the first circles of literature and Blok with it. But these verses re-established him as a leading contemporary poet for all schools (see G. Ivanov's important review in the periodical *Apollo*, 8–9, 1915). Paradoxically, for the year of its publication—1915—marked perhaps the nadir of his patriotism, Blok was at last acclaimed as a *national* poet. For it was found that he wrote not so much of Russia as for Russia and that, in 1910, he had been making no idle claim when he had diffidently asked:

> And indeed, what is so very self-assured in the thought that a writer who believes in his calling ... should identify himself with his country, should be sick with her sicknesses, should suffer with her sufferings, should partake of her crucifixion and, in those minutes when they leave off torturing her poor tormented body even for a moment, should feel himself at rest together with her?

The acclaim of the critics was an accident of recognition. The poems about Russia were in fact written over a period covering the years 1907–1915 and, after the Revolution, when asked to recite something "about Russia", Blok replied sharply: "They are all about Russia."

But the war struck Blok as sheer madness (cf. particularly No. 75 and note). He was called up in 1916 to serve in a sanitary division behind the lines in the Pinsk marshes. The regular discipline, hard riding, and dull office work did wonders for his health, but he was bored and could not write. After the February Revolution, in March 1917, he hastened back to the capital and, with the help of his friend, the Maecenas, sugar millionaire and Minister of Foreign Affairs to the Provisional Government Ivan Tereshchenko, obtained leave from his unit to serve as verbatim reporter to the Special Commission set up to interrogate former dignitaries of the Imperial Court involved in the Rasputin scandal. And so, for the first time, Blok found himself at the centre of his country's political life. On 14th May he wrote to his wife:

> I am now hearing and seeing things which almost no-one else hears or sees, which only a few are fated to observe once in a hundred years ... the time is such, the situation is such that there is no telling what may happen tomorrow; everything is saturated with electricity, I am myself.... All this is about me (as usual, but it is my lot always to begin with myself, it's my nature and part of my plan), but I am still waiting for things to coincide; and it is I who am waiting, who have never yet been mistaken....

While Blok waited for events in the outside world to coincide with the calamitous excitement within him, he worked hard and conscientiously reporting the findings of the Special Commission. The prisoners filled him with a kind of cold pity and he saw the "spirit of Rasputin" not only in them but in himself:

> One should never judge. In misery and humiliation people become like children. Remember Vyrubova, she lies like a child, and how someone must have loved her. Remember how guiltily Protopopov looked at Murav'ev—glancing up at him *like a guilty little boy*, when he was told:—"You, Alexandr Dmitriyevich, have landed yourself in a very complex historical situation." He nodded: "Yes, indeed, quite so". And glanced up from under his brows: I shall never forget.
> Remember how Voeykov, when asked whether he had engaged a defending council (concerning some commercial suit served on him), also looked up like a guilty child and said pitifully: —But I don't know anyone.

The heart is drenched with tears for the pity of it all, and, remember, one should never judge. Remember again, what Klimovich said in his cell and how he said it; how old Kafafov wept; how Beletsky wept at the interrogation, that he was *ashamed* of his children.

Remember more—more, more, weep more, it may cleanse the soul.

The interrogators themselves seemed totally dwarfed by the magnitude of events—clever lawyers seeking a legal formula to condemn something already condemned by history—strangely cultured, talkative and occasionally even facetious instruments of retribution. Not this Special Commission appointed by Parliament in which, as Blok at one stage remarked, the revolution had not so much as spent the night—but the streets of Petrograd and the Workers' and Soldiers' Soviets became the nerve centre of the rapidly changing situation. For some time, Russian troops had been fraternizing with the Germans at the front and it seemed as though the German officers were losing control of their men.

Lyuba, [Blok wrote at this stage] There's nothing new to tell you about myself and if there were it would be impossible to work up any excitement over it because the whole content of life has become the World Revolution, at the head of which stands Russia. We are so young that in a few months we could recover completely from a 300-year-old sickness.... I was at the Union of the Soviets of Soldiers' and Workers' Deputies and, in general, I see my future, although I am still up to my neck in work on a past which has gone without trace.

All this is nothing but a generalization, a summary of anxious thoughts and impressions which are daily rubbing and polishing themselves against other's thoughts and impressions, alas, often the opposite of mine, which keeps me in a constant state of suppressed anger and nerves and sometimes of simple hatred for the "intelligentsia". If the "brain of the country" is going to go on nourishing itself on the same old ironies, the slavish fears, the slavish experience of weary nations, then it will stop being the brain and will be ripped out—quickly, cruelly and authoratively, as everything is done which really does get done nowadays. What right have we to fear our great, clever and good people? And our experience, bought with the blood of children, could be shared with these children....

But, with the reopening of the offensive at the front on 18th June, and with the suppression of the workers' demonstrations on 3rd July, the dream of peaceful reconstruction and of "recovery in a few months" began to fade. This would only have been possible with the co-operation of the old culture. "The people", Blok noted, "have wings. But in skills and knowledge they need our help. Gradually I am coming to understand this. But surely it cannot be that many who could help will not go over to them?" But the clashing discords of nationalism were already threatening to drown the "music" of revolution. The people, "Russia"—wanted peace. The Provisional Government, the "intelligentsia", under pressure from the allies, had decided to continue the war. The Bolsheviki—up to this time a minority even in the Workers' and Soldiers' Soviets—had come to be identified in the popular mind with the refusal to go on getting killed in an unpopular war and had been outlawed by the Provisional Government. General Kornilov was preparing to march on Petersburg, as he thought to aid Kerensky to suppress the Bolsheviki. But Kerensky, fearing a right-wing dictatorship, wavered. The alternative seemed to be between reaction and anarchy—at times, Blok felt that the moderate, intellectually acceptable and eminently sane ideas of the Cadet party would be infinitely preferable. However, even as he noted this in his diary, he added: "but I would be ashamed to support them". His nerves were stretched to breaking point:

> I shall never take power into my own hands, I shall never join any party, I shall never choose, I have nothing to be proud of, I understand nothing.
> I can only whisper, and sometimes cry out: leave me alone, it is no business of mine how reaction sets in after revolution, how people who don't know how to live, who have lost the taste for life, begin by yielding, then grow afraid, then start to frighten and to terrorise people who have not yet "lived", who desperately want to live a little like rich people....
>
> (19th July 1917)

All this time Blok wrote no poetry. His diary is a chronicle of his busy life as editor of the report on the findings of the Special Commission—and of the political life of Petrograd. He has "only eyes, but no voice". The strain shows most vividly in odd moments when the artist glances up from his uncongenial work.

> The moon is on the wane beyond the window over the roofs to the East—a terrible, sharp sickle. And beneath the window a couple is embracing, embracing long and sweetly. The woman is bent back against the man's shoulder in such a long and languorous curve and does not withdraw her lips. How beautiful! And I sit here between two candles....

Or again:

> While I was writing, a little sparrow flew into my room and at once I was overcome by the dreariness of the moment, the governmental filth in which, for some reason, I am sitting up to my ears, and I began to remember Lyuba...

Blok had offered himself as "a witness", and history and Russia had accepted the offer, but the "free spirit" still fluttered against the bars (cf. No. 92). Yet the discipline was useful. Blok formed the firm decision: "If anything really does happen, then I shall retire into life, not private but 'artistic' life, all the wiser for the experience and somewhat chastened...."

Already, he "knew" instinctively what was going to happen. Throughout July and August a heavy smell of smouldering turf lay over Petrograd and ate its way into his very dreams:

> Between two dreams;—"Help, help!"—"Help what?" Russia, The Motherland, The Fatherland, I don't know what to call her; that there may be no grief nor bitterness nor shame before the poor, the embittered, the ignorant, the oppressed! Only help us! The yellowish-brown billows of smoke are already menacing the villages, bushes and grass are flaming up in wide strips, and God sends no rain and the crops

have failed and what there is will burn ... other such yellowish-brown billows, behind which everything is fermenting and smouldering ... are surging over millions of souls; the flames of enmity, barbarity, Tatarshchina, anger, humiliation, oppression, revenge—flare up, now here, now there: Russian bolshevism is on the loose, and there is no rain and God sends none. ...

On awakening, Blok tried to make sense of his nightmares:

But this is the task of Russian culture, to direct that flame onto what must be burnt, to set such limits to the destruction as will not weaken the force of the fire but will organize that force; to organize ungovernable freedom, to direct the slothful fermentation which also secretes the possibility of violence into the Rasputin-dominated corners of the soul and there to blow it up into a sky-high conflagration so that our cunning, slothful, servile sensuality may burn. ...

Already, the refrains of "The Twelve" were beginning to sing themselves in Blok's subconscious mind:

> Злоба, грустная злоба
>      Кипит в груди ...
> Чёрная злоба, святая злоба ...

(Anger, sad anger
     Seethes in the breast ...
Black anger, holy anger ...)

> Мировой пожар в крови —
>      Господи, благослови!

(A World conflagration in the blood
Lord, grant us Thy blessing!)

Then, towards the end of October, "something" really did "happen". The Soviets, under Bolshevik leadership, staged an armed uprising and dissolved the Representative assembly. Blok, all eyes and ears, mixing, as usual, the intimate and the general, wrote in his diary:

This morning Mama was talking very well on the necessity of putting an end to the war: the crassness of the word "dishonour". We have the wealth, the West—the ability. ...

Yesterday, in the Soviet of Workers' and Soldiers' Deputies, there was a violent schism in the ranks of the Bolsheviki. Zinoviev, Trotsky and others thought that the rising of the 20th must take place, whatever the results, but they envisaged these results pessimistically. Only Lenin believes that the take-over of power by the democracy will really liquidate the war and put everything in the country to rights.

In this way, both parties want the rising, but some—from despair, and Lenin—with a feeling that good will come of it. ...

On 25th October a new "Provisional Workers' and Peasants' Government" known as the Council of People's Commissars was established with Lenin at its head. On the night of 26th October the new government adopted the Decree of Peace, calling upon the belligerent countries to conclude an immediate armistice for a period of not less than three months to permit negotiations for peace, and on the workers "of the three most advanced nations of mankind and the largest states participating in the present war, namely, Great Britain, France and Germany", to help "to bring to a successful conclusion the cause of peace, and at the same time the cause of the emancipation of the toiling and exploited masses of the population from all forms of exploitation".

It is against the background of this decree that Blok's support for the Bolshevik party must be understood.

In January 1918 he wrote "The Twelve" and "The Scythians", the fruit of eighteen months' silence and a lifetime of artistic integrity and "mystic" concentration. In January also he wrote the article "The Intelligentsia and the Revolution". In March—"Art and the Revolution"—in which, in explaining Wagner, he formulated the driving force of his own life:

> How can one hate and erect an altar at the same time? How is it possible anyway to love and to hate at the same time? If this attitude is extended to something "abstract" like Christ, then, perhaps, it is possible; but if this becomes the general attitude, if this is the way people will react to everything in the world? To their country; their parents; their "wives" and so on? It will be unbearable, because there will be no peace....
>
> The new age is unsettled, not peaceful. He who understands that the meaning of human life lies in anxiety and concern has already ceased to be a parasite. ...

More articles followed, the most remarkable of which are *Catilina (Катилина)* (April–May 1918), *The Collapse of Humanism (Крущение гуманизма)* (March–April 1919), *Vladimir Solov'ev and our Times (Владимир Соловьев и наши дни)* (August 1920) and *On the Calling of the Poet (О назначении поэта)* (February 1921). Blok wrote virtually no more poetry, but in this last article, he defined his conception of the part poetry had to play in the history of man:

> The poet is a son of harmony; and he has a part to play in world culture. Three tasks are laid on him: in the first place, to release sounds from the timeless womb of the elements in which they have their being; in the second—to make harmony from those sounds, to give them form; in the third—to carry that harmony out into the world. ...
>
> The first obligation laid upon the poet by his service is to leave the "cares of this vain world" in order to raise the outer coverings, to reveal the depths. ...
>
> The second command of Apollo is that the sound which has been brought up from the depths and which remains a foreign body in the world should be clothed in the solid and visible form of the word; sounds and words should make up one single harmony. That is the part of craftmanship. ...
>
> Then it is the turn of the third task of the poet: he must take out into the world these sounds which he has absorbed into his soul and arranged in harmony. This is where the celebrated clash takes place between the poet and the mob. ...
>
> The testing of hearts with harmony is not a peaceful occupation calculated to guarantee the kind of even flow of events in the outside world on which the mob best thrives.*

* A complete translation of this article by Alex Miller was published in *The Poetry Review*, Vol. XLII, No. 6, London, Nov.-Dec., 1951.

There is so much more to tell of Alexander Blok. His last years were lonely
—many of his old friends dropped him from their acquaintance after the
publication of *The Twelve* and those who stayed by him were shell-shocked
by the Revolution. Viktor Shklovsky recalls Petrograd in 1918:

> ... deaf and dumb somehow.
> Like a minefield when all is over, everything has been blown up.
> Like a man whose guts have been blown out, and he goes on talking.
> Imagine a whole society of people like that.
> Sitting around and talking.

In the middle of 1918 Blok remarked to a friend, V. A. Zorgenfrei: "I
don't believe in their socialism; socialism, of course, is impossible; socialism
isn't the point...." Zorgenfrei thought that the "point" was in Blok's "limit-
less hatred for the old world". But this was only half the picture. Blok served
conscientiously on various committees, watching with stern and loving anx-
iety over the birth-pangs of Soviet culture, although a friend of his last
years, E. Knipovich, says that he never realized how eagerly his own poetry
was read by the "new people" whose advent he had so long forseen. His own
fate appears to have worried him not at all. In February 1919 he was arrested,
but released again two days later. The suspicion that he was the author of
Left Social Revolutionary propaganda leaflets called forth only the amused
rejoinder that surely no one could suspect *him* of quite such blatant lapses of
style. He continued to watch events with a deep concern which would scarcely
have been possible for a man animated only by hatred. He blamed the con-
tinuation of the war for the violation "of the spirit of music", but he spoke
out also against abuses at home. "Only music", he said in a speech in honour
of Maxim Gorky in March 1919, "can put an end to this blood-letting
which becomes nothing but a miserable commonplace when it has ceased to
be a sacred madness." The deprivations of the Civil War took their toll of
Blok's health. Deafened by the collapse of the "old world", he had lost the
ability to "release sounds from the timeless womb of the elements". Because
he had identified himself completely with his mission as a poet, he had also
lost his reason for living. The same Zorgenfrei asked him, as his health grew
perceptibly worse, why he didn't seek permission to go abroad. "I'd get
permission all right, I could go", Blok answered, "There's 80,000 marks owing
me in Germany, but no... I've absolutely no wish to go." "And these",
comments his friend, "were difficult days when faith and hope were both on
the wane and all that remained was—love."

Blok died on 7th August 1921, after months of great spiritual and physical
anguish, burnt out by love and hatred, exhausted, at the age of 40, by a life
of self-destruction and of service.

"Everyone is claiming Blok as their own now", his mother wrote to a friend nine days after his death. "The communists, the white guards (that is the most insulting), the priests, the Jews (they are saying that his father was a Jew!)."[*] The undignified sectarian debates continued to rage round the dead poet for some time. Like all controversial figures, Blok was praised and blamed for a great many things which most probably never entered his mind. "He had his detractors", said Zorgenfrei, "but in so far as I observed him he didn't know what it was to bear ill-will."

As time carries us away from him, we can look back and see him more clearly for what he was. A man fated to stand on the very water-shed of history, "in life, an ordinary man", a "failure", a dedicated artist and great poet, a prophet of coming cold and darkness—and a man with a bewilderingly simple message of faith, of hope and of love beyond faith or hope. "It is quite true", he wrote to a nephew on 10th December 1920, "that there is much I wish to 'disintegrate' and that I have many 'doubts', but that is not 'art' for art's sake, but stems from an extremely exacting attitude towards life; from the fact that I think that what cannot be 'disintegrated' will not disintegrate, but will merely be purified. I do not consider myself in the least a pessimist."

---

* Letter of 16/VIII/1921, ЦГАЛИ, Ф. No. 55, Опись No. 1, Ед. Хр. No. 544.

PART I

**JUVENILIA**


PART II

**POEMS FROM VOLUME I**

## 1.

На окне
В тишине
Под-стаканник
Стоит
Позадишь
Позади
Сам стаканник
Лежит.

И стакан говорит
Ведь
Тебя
Я
Люблю.
Под-стаканник
В ответ
Ах мой
Милый сосед
И тебя
Я люблю.

## 2.

Ноч была темная и война била большая. Много ружей сабель штыков рапир сикир писталетов револьверов и барабанов просовывалось через тьму. На конце поля битвы стояла избушка. Старые стены едва держались. Потолок чуть не проваливался. Ржавые окна то есть крючки на окнах тоже едва держались. Но вдруг огромная бомба разорвала избушку.

# VERSES FROM THE COLLECTION "ANTE LUCEM"

## 1.

Пусть светит месяц — ночь темна.
Пусть жизнь приносит людям счастье, —
В моей душе любви весна
Не сменит бурного ненастья.
Ночь распростерлась надо мной
И отвечает мертвым взлядом
На тусклый взор души больной,
Облитой острым, сладким ядом.
И тщетно, страсти затая,
В холодной мгле передрассветной
Среди толпы блуждаю я
С одной лишь думою заветной:
Пусть светит месяц — ночь темна.
Пусть жизнь приносит людям счастье, —
В моей душе любви весна
Не сменит бурного ненастья.

*Январь 1898. С.-Петербург*

## 2. МОЕЙ МАТЕРИ

Друг, посмотри, как в равнине небесной
Дымные тучки плывут под луной,
Видишь, прорезал эфир бестелесный
Свет ее бледный, бездушный, пустой?

Полно смотреть в это звездное море,
Полно стремиться к холодной луне!
Мало ли счастья в житейском просторе?
Мало ли жару в сердечном огне?

Месяц холодный тебе не ответит,
Звезд отдаленных достигнуть нет сил...
Холод могильный везде тебя встретит
В дальней стране безотрадных светил...

*Июль 1898*

## 3. ГАМАЮН, ПТИЦА ВЕЩАЯ

*(Картина В. Васнецова)*

На гладях бесконечных вод,
Закатом в пурпур облеченных,
Она вещает и поет,
Не в силах крыл поднять смятенных...
Вещает иго злых татар,
Вещает казней ряд кровавых,
И трус, и голод, и пожар,
Злодеев силу, гибель правых...
Предвечным ужасом объят,
Прекрасный лик горит любовью,
Но вещей правдою звучат
Уста, запекшиеся кровью!..

*23 февраля 1899*


## 4. DOLOR ANTE LUCEM

Каждый вечер, лишь только погаснет заря,
Я прощаюсь, желанием смерти горя,
И опять, на рассвете холодного дня,
Жизнь охватит меня и измучит меня!

Я прощаюсь и с добрым, прощаюсь и с злым,
И надежда и ужас разлуки с земным,
А наутро встречаюсь с землею опять,
Чтобы зло проклинать, о добре тосковать!..

Боже, боже, исполненный власти и сил,
Неужели же всем ты так жить положил,
Чтобы смертный, исполненный утренних грез,
О тебе тескованье без отдыха нес?..

*3 декабря 1899*

5.                 *О.М.Соловьевой*

Ищу спасенья.
Мои огни горят на высях гор —
Всю область ночи озарили.
Но ярче всех — во мне духовный взор
И Ты вдали... Но Ты ли?
            Ищу спасенья.


Торжественно звучит на небе звездный хор.
Меня клянут людские поколенья.
Я для Тебя в горах зажег костер,
            Но Ты — виденье.
            Ищу спасенья.


Устал звучать, смолкает звездный хор.
Уходит ночь. Бежит сомненье.
Там сходишь Ты с далеких светлых гор.
Я ждал Тебя. Я дух к Тебе простер.
            В Тебе — спасенье!

*25 ноября 1900*

# VERSES FROM THE COLLECTION
# "СТИХИ О ПРЕКРАСНОЙ ДАМЕ"

## (1901–1902)

### 6. ВСТУПЛЕНИЕ

*Отдых напрасен. Дорога крута.*
*Вечер прекрасен. Стучу в ворота.*

*Дольнему стуку чужда и строга,*
*Ты рассыпаешь кругом жемчуга.*

*Терем высок, и заря замерла.*
*Красная тайна у входа легла.*

*Кто поджигал на заре терема,*
*Что воздвигала Царевна Сама?*

*Каждый конек на узорной резьбе*
*Красное пламя бросает к тебе.*

*Купол стремится в лазурную высь.*
*Синие окна румянцем зажглись.*

*Все колокольные звоны гудят.*
*Залит весной беззакатный наряд.*

*Ты ли меня на закатах ждала?*
*Терем зажгла? Ворота отперла?*

*28 декабря 1903*

### 7.

Ты отходишь в сумрак алый,
В бесконечные круги.
Я послышал отзвук малый,
Отдаленные шаги.

Близко ты, или далече
Затерялась в вышине?
Ждать иль нет внезапной встречи
В этой звучной тишине?

В тишине звучат сильнее
Отдаленные шаги.
Ты ль смыкаешь, пламенея,
Бесконечные круги?

*6 марта 1901*

## 8.

Небесное умом не измеримо,
Лазурное сокрыто от умов.
Лишь изредка приносят серафимы
Священный сон избранникам миров.

И мнилась мне Российская Венера,
Тяжелою туникой повита,
Бесстрастна в чистоте, нерадостна без меры,
В чертах лица — спокойная мечта.

Она сошла на землю не впервые,
Но вкруг нее толпятся в первый раз
Богатыри не те, и витязи иные…
И странен блеск ее глубоких глаз…

*29 мая 1901. С. Шахматово*

## 9.

И тяжкий сон житейского сознанья
Ты отряхнешь, тоскуя и любя.
                              *Вл. Соловьев*

Предчувствую Тебя. Года проходят мимо —
Всё в облике одном предчувствую Тебя.

Весь горизонт в огне — и ясен нестерпимо,
И молча жду, — *тоскуя и любя.*

Весь горизонт в огне, и близко появленье,
Но страшно мне: изменишь облик Ты,

И дерзкое возбудишь подозренье,
Сменив в конце привычные черты.

О, как паду — и горестно, и низко,
Не одолев смертельныя мечты!

Как ясен горизонт! И лучезарность близко.
Но страшно мне: изменишь облик Ты.

*4 июня 1901. С. Шахматово*

## 10.

Прозрачные, неведомые тени
К Тебе плывут, и с ними Ты плывешь,
В объятия лазурных сновидений,
Невнятных нам, — Себя Ты отдаешь.

Перед Тобой синеют без границы
Моря, поля, и горы, и леса,
Перекликаются в свободной выси птицы,
Встает туман, алеют небеса.

А здесь, внизу, в пыли, в униженьи,
Узрев на миг бессмертные черты,
Безвестный раб, исполнен вдохновенья,
Тебя поет. Его не знаешь Ты,

Не отличишь его в толпе народной,
Не наградишь улыбкою его,
Когда вослед взирает, несвободный,
Вкусив на миг бессмертья Твоего.

*3 июля 1901*

## 11.

Будет день — и свершится великое,
Чую в будущем подвиг души.

Ты — другая, немая, безликая,
Притаилась, колдуешь в тиши.

Но, во что обратишься — не ведаю,
И не знаешь ты, буду ли твой,

А уж *Там* веселятся победою
Над единой и страшной душой.

*23 ноября 1901*

## 12. ДВОЙНИКУ

Ты совершил над нею подвиг трудный,
Но, бедный друг! о, различил ли ты
Ее наряд, и праздничный и чудный,
И странные весенние цветы?..

Я ждал тебя. А тень твоя мелькала
Вдали, в полях, где проходил и я,
Где и она когда-то отдыхала,
Где ты вздыхал о тайнах бытия...

И знал ли ты, что я восторжествую?
Исчезнешь ты, свершив, но не любя?
Что я мечту безумно-молодую
Найду в цветах кровавых без тебя?

Мне ни тебя, ни дел твоих не надо,
Ты мне смешон, ты жалок мне, старик!
Твой подвиг — мой, — и мне твоя награда:
Безумный смех и сумасшедший крик!

*27 декабря 1901*

## 13.

Брожу в стенах монастыря,
Безрадостный и темный инок.
Чуть брежжит бледная заря, —
Слежу мелькания снежинок.

Ах, ночь длинна, заря бледна
На нашем севере угрюмом.
У занесенного окна
Упорным предаюся думам.

Один и тот же снег — белей
Нетронутой и вечной ризы.
И вечно бледный воск свечей,
И убеленные карнизы.

Мне странен холод здешних стен
И непонятна жизни бедность.
Меня пугает сонный плен
И братий мертвенная бледность.

Заря бледна и ночь долга,
Как ряд заутрень и обеден.
Ах, сам я бледен, как снега,
В упорной думе сердцем беден...

*11 июня 1902. С. Шахматово*

## 14.

Свет в окошке шатался,
В полумраке — один —
У подъезда шептался
С темнотой арлекин.

Был окутанный мглою
Бело-красный наряд.
Наверху — за стеною —
Шутовской маскарад.

Там лицо укрывали
В разноцветную ложь.
Но в руке узнавали
Неизбежную дрожь.

*Он* — мечом деревянным
Начертал письмена.
Восхищенная странным,
Потуплялась *Она.*

Восхищенью не веря,
С темнотою — один —
У задумчивой двери
Хохотал арлекин.

*6 августа 1902*

## 15.

Я вышел в ночь — узнать, понять
Далекий шорох, близкий ропот,
Несуществующих принять,
Поверить в мнимый конский топот.

Дорога, под луной бела,
Казалось, полнилась шагами.
Там только чья-то тень брела
И опустилась за холмами.

И слушал я — и услыхал:
Среди дрожащих лунных пятен
Далёко, звонко конь скакал,
И легкий посвист был понятен.

Но здесь, и дальше — ровный звук,
И сердце медленно боролось,
О, как понять, откуда стук,
Откуда будет слышен голос?

И вот, слышнее звон копыт,
И белый конь ко мне несется...
И стало ясно, кто молчит
И на пустом седле смеется.

Я вышел в ночь — узнать, понять
Далекий шорох, близкий ропот,
Несуществующих принять,
Поверить в мнимый конский топот.

*6 сентября 1902. С.-Петербург*

## 16. RELIGIO

### 1

Любил я нежные слова.
Искал таинственных соцветий.
И, прозревающий едва,
Еще шумел, как в играх дети.

Но, выходя под утро в луг,
Твердя невнятные напевы,
Я знал Тебя, мой вечный друг,
Тебя, Хранительница-Дева.

Я знал, задумчивый поэт,
Что ни один не ведал гений
Такой свободы, как обет
Моих невольничьих Служений.

*18 октября 1902*


2

Безмолвный призрак в терему,
Я — черный раб проклятой крови.
Я соблюдаю полутьму
В Ее нетронутом алькове.

Я стерегу Ее ключи
И с Ней присутствую, незримый,
Когда скрещаются мечи
За красоту Недостижимой.

Мой голос глух, мой волос сед.
Черты до ужаса недвижны.
Со мной всю жизнь — один Завет:
Завет служенья Непостижной.

*18 октября 1902*

# РАСПУТЬЯ

## 17.

Все кричали у круглых столов,
Беспокойно меняя место.
Было тускло от винных паров.
Вдруг кто-то вошел — и сквозь гул голосов
Сказал: «Вот моя невеста».

Никто не слыхал ничего.
Все визжали неистово, как звери.
А один, сам не зная отчего, —
Качался и хохотал, указывая на него
И на девушку, вошедшую в двери.

Она уронила платок,
И все они, в злобном усильи,
Как будто поняв зловещий намек,
Разорвали с визгом каждый клочок
И окрасили кровью и пылью.

Когда все опять подошли к столу,
Притихли и сели на место,
Он указал им на девушку в углу
И звонко сказал, пронизывая мглу:
«Господа! Вот моя невеста».

И вдруг тот, кто качался и хохотал,
Бессмысленно протягивая руки,
Прижался к столу, задрожал, —
И те, кто прежде безумно кричал,
Услышали плачущие звуки.

*25 декабря 1902*

## 18.

Погружался я в море клевера,
Окруженный сказками пчел.
Но ветер, зовущий с севера,
Мое детское сердце нашел.

69

Призывал на битву равнинную —
Побороться с дыханьем небес.
Показал мне дорогу пустынную,
Уходящую в темный лес.

Я иду по ней косогорами
И смотрю неустанно вперед,
Впереди с невинными взорами
Мое детское сердце идет.

Пусть глаза утомятся бессонные,
Запоет, заалеет пыль…
Мне цветы и пчелы влюбленные
Рассказали не сказку — быль.

*18 февраля 1903*

## 19.

Мне снились веселые думы,
Мне снилось, что я не один…
Под утро проснулся от шума
И треска несущихся льдин.

Я думал о сбывшемся чуде…
А там, наточив топоры,
Веселые красные люди,
Смеясь, разводили костры:

Смолили тяжелые челны…
Река, распевая, несла
И синие льдины, и волны,
И тонкий обломок весла…

Пьяна от веселого шума,
Душа небывалым полна…
Со мною — весенняя дума,
Я знаю, что Ты не одна…

*11 марта 1903*

## 20.

Я вырезал посох из дуба
Под ласковый шопот вьюги.
Одежды бедны и грубы,
О, как недостойны подруги!

Но найду, и нищий, дорогу,
Выходи, морозное солнце!
Проброжу весь день ради бога,
Ввечеру постучусь в оконце...

И откроет белой рукою
Потайную дверь предо мною
Молодая, с золотой косою,
С ясной, открытой душою.

Месяц и звезды в косах...
«Входи, мой царевич приветный...»
И бедный дубовый посох
Заблестит слезой самоцветной...

*25 марта 1903*

## 21.

Я был весь в пестрых лоскутьях,
Белый, красный, в безобразной маске.
Хохотал и кривлялся на распутьях,
И рассказывал шуточные сказки.

Развертывал длинные сказанья
Бессвязно, и долго, и звонко —
О стариках, и о странах без названья,
И о девушке с глазами ребенка.

Кто-то долго, бессмысленно смеялся,
И кому-то становилось больно.
И когда я внезапно сбивался,
Из толпы кричали: «Довольно!»

*Апрель 1903*

## 22. ФАБРИКА

В соседнем доме окна жолты.
По вечерам — по вечерам
Скрипят задумчивые болты,
Подходят люди к воротам.

И глухо заперты ворота,
А на стене — а на стене
Недвижный кто-то, черный кто-то
Людей считает в тишине.

Я слышу всё с моей вершины:
Он медным голосом зовет
Согнуть измученные спины
Внизу собравшийся народ.

Они войдут и разбредутся,
Навалят нá спины кули.
И в жолтых окнах засмеются,
Что этих нищих провели.

*24 ноября 1903*

## 23. ИЗ ГАЗЕТ

Встала в сияньи. Крестила детей.
И дети увидели радостный сон.
Положила, до полу клонясь головой,
Последний земной поклон.

Коля проснулся. Радостно вздохнул,
Голубому сну еще рад наяву.
Прокатился и замер стеклянный гул:
Звенящая дверь хлопнула внизу.

Прошли часы. Приходил человек
С оловянной бляхой на теплой шапке.
Стучал и дожидался у двери человек.
Никто не открыл. Играли в прятки.

Были веселые морозные Святки.

Прятали мамин красный платок.
В платке уходила она по утрам.
Сегодня оставила дома платок:
Дети прятали его по углам.

Подкрались сумерки. Детские тени
Запрыгали на стене при свете фонарей.
Кто-то шел по лестнице, считая ступени.
Сосчитал. И заплакал. И постучал у дверей.

Дети прислушались. Отворили двери.
Толстая соседка принесла им щей.
Сказала: «Кушайте». Встала на колени
И, кланяясь, как мама, крестила детей.

Мамочке не больно, розовые детки.
Мамочка сама на рельсы легла.
Доброму человеку, толстой соседке,
Спасибо, спасибо. Мама не могла...

Мамочке хорошо. Мама умерла.

*27 декабря 1903*


## 24.

Мой любимый, мой князь, мой жених,
Ты печален в цветистом лугу.
Павиликой средь нив золотых
Завилась я на том берегу.

Я ловлю твои сны на лету
Бледно-белым прозрачным цветком,
Ты сомнешь меня в полном цвету
Белогрудым усталым конем.

Ах, бессмертье мое растопчи, —
Я огонь для тебя сберегу.
Робко пламя церковной свечи
У заутрени бледной зажгу.

В церкви станешь ты, бледен лицом,
И к царице небесной придешь, —
Колыхнусь восковым огоньком,
Дам почуять знакомую дрожь...

Над тобой — как свеча — я тиха,
Пред тобой – как цветок – я нежна.
Жду тебя, моего жениха,
Всё невеста — и вечно жена.

*26 марта 1904*


## 25.

Вот он — ряд гробовых ступене́й.
И меж нас — никого. Мы вдвоем.
Спи ты, нежная спутница дней,
Залитых небывалым лучом.

Ты покоишься в белом гробу.
Ты с улыбкой зовешь: не буди.
Золотистые пряди на лбу.
Золотой образок на груди.

Я отпраздновал светлую смерть,
Прикоснувшись к руке восковой,
Остальное — бездонная твердь
Схоронила во мгле голубой.

Спи — твой отдых никто не прервет.
Мы — окрай неизвестных дорог.
Всю ненастную ночь напролет
Здесь горит осиянный чертог.

*18 июня 1904. С. Шахматово*

# PART III

# POEMS FROM VOLUME II

## 26. ВСТУПЛЕНИЕ

*Ты в поля отошла без возврата.*
*Да святится Имя Твое!*
*Снова красные копья заката*
*Протянули ко мне острие.*

*Лишь к Твоей золотой свирели*
*В черный день устами прильну.*
*Если все мольбы отзвенели,*
*Угнетенный, в поле усну.*

*Ты пройдешь в золотой порфире —*
*Уж не мне глаза разомкнуть.*
*Дай вздохнуть в этом сонном мире,*
*Целовать излучённый путь...*

*О, исторгни ржавую душу!*
*Со святыми меня упокой,*
*Ты, Держащая море и сушу*
*Неподвижно тонкой Рукой!*

*16 апреля 1905*

# POEMS OF THE 1905 REVOLUTION
# FROM THE COLLECTIONS
# "РАЗНЫЕ СТИХОТВОРЕНИЯ" and "ГОРОД"

## 27.

Поднимались из тьмы погребов.
Уходили их головы в плечи.
Тихо выросли шумы шагов,
Словеса незнакомых наречий.

Скоро прибыли тóлпы других,
Волочили кирки и лопаты.
Расползлись по камням мостовых,
Из земли воздвигали палаты.

Встала улица, серым полна,
Заткалась паутинною пряжей.
Шелестя, прибывала волна,
Затрудняя проток экипажей.

Скоро день глубоко отступил,
В небе дальнем расставивший зори.
А незримый поток шелестил,
Проливаясь в наш город, как в море.

Мы не стали искать и гадать:
Пусть заменят нас новые люди!
В тех же муках рождала их мать,
Так же нежно кормила у груди...

В пелене отходящего дня
Нам была эта участь понятна...
Нам последний закат из огня
Сочетал и соткал свои пятна.

Не стерег исступленный дракон,
Не пылала под нами геенна.
Затопили нас волны времен,
И была наша участь — мгновенна.

*10 сентября 1904*

## 28.

Барка жизни встала
На большой мели.
Громкий крик рабочих
Слышен издали.
Песни и тревога
На пустой реке.
Входит кто-то сильный
В сером армяке.
Руль дощатый сдвинул,
Парус распустил
И багор закинул,
Грудью надавил.
Тихо повернулась
Красная корма,
Побежали мимо
Пестрые дома.
Вот они далёко,
Весело плывут.
Только нас с собою,
Верно, не возьмут!

*Декабрь 1904*

## 29.

Шли на приступ. Прямо в грудь
Штык наточенный направлен.
Кто-то крикнул: «Будь прославлен!»
Кто-то шепчет: «Не забудь!»

Рядом пал, всплеснув руками,
И над ним сомкнулась рать.
Кто-то бьется под ногами,
Кто — не время вспоминать...

Только в памяти веселой
Где-то вспыхнула свеча.
И прошли, стопой тяжелой
Тело теплое топча...

Ведь никто не встретит старость —
Смерть летит из уст в уста...
Высоко пылает ярость,
Даль кровавая пуста...

Что же! громче будет скрежет,
Слаще боль и ярче смерть!
И потом — земля разнежит
Перепуганную твердь.

*Январь 1905*

## 30. ПОВЕСТЬ

*Г. Чулкову*

В окнах, занавешенных сетью мокрой пыли,
Темный профиль женщины наклонился вниз.
Серые прохожие усердно проносили
Груз вечерних сплетен, усталых стертых лиц.

Прямо перед окнами — светлый и упорный —
Каждому прохожему бросал лучи фонарь.
И в дождливой сети — не белой, не черной —
Каждый скрывался — не молод и не стар.

Были как виденья неживой столицы —
Случайно, нечаянно вступающие в луч.
Исчезали спины, возникали лица,
Робкие, покорные унынью низких туч.

И — нежданно резко — раздались проклятья,
Будто рассекая полосу дождя:
С головой открытой — кто-то в красном платье
Поднимал на воздух малое дитя...

Светлый и упорный, луч упал бессменный —
И мгновенно женщина, ночных веселий дочь,
Бешено ударилась головой о стену,
С криком исступленья, уронив ребенка в ночь ...

И столпились серые виденья мокрой скуки.
Кто-то громко ахал, качая головой.
А она лежала на спине, раскинув руки,
В грязно-красном платье, на кровавой мостовой.

Но из глаз открытых — взор упорно-дерзкий
Всё искал кого-то в верхних этажах...
И нашел — и встретился в окне у занавески
С взором темной женщины в узорных кружевах.

Встретились и замерли в беззвучном вопле взоры,
И мгновенье длилось... Улица ждала...
Но через мгновенье наверху упали шторы,
А внизу — в глазах открытых — сила умерла...

Умерла — и вновь в дождливой сети тонкой
Зычные, нестройные звучали голоса.
Кто-то поднял на́ руки кричащего ребенка
И, крестясь, украдкой утирал глаза...

Но вверху сомнительно молчали стекла окон.
Плотно-белый занавес пустел в сетях дождя.
Кто-то гладил бережно ребенку мокрый локон.
Уходил тихонько. И плакал, уходя.

*Январь 1905*

## 31.

Еще прекрасно серое небо,
Еще безнадежна серая даль.
Еще несчастных, просящих хлеба,
Никому не жаль, никому не жаль!

И над заливами голос черни
Пропал, развеялся в невском сне.
И дикие вопли: «Свергни! О, свергни!»
Не будят жалости в сонной волне...

И в небе сером холодные светы
Одели Зимний дворец царя,
И латник в черном не даст ответа,
Пока не застигнет его заря.

Тогда, алея над водной бездной,
Пусть он угрюмей опустит меч,
Чтоб с дикой чернью в борьбе бесполезной
За древнюю сказку мертвым лечь...

*18 октября 1905*

# VERSES FROM THE COLLECTION

## "ПУЗЫРИ ЗЕМЛИ"

### (1904–1905)

### 32. БОЛОТНЫЙ ПОПИК

На весенней проталинке
За вечерней молитвою — маленький
Попик болотный виднеется.

Ветхая ряска над кочкой
  Чернеется
Чуть заметною точкой.

И в безбурности зорь красноватых
Не видать чертенят бесноватых,
   Но вечерняя прелесть
Увила вкруг него свои тонкие руки...
   Предзакатные звуки,
   Легкий шелест.

Тихонько он молится,
Улыбается, клонится,
Приподняв свою шляпу.

И лягушке хромой, ковыляющей,
   Травой исцеляющей
Перевяжет болящую лапу.
Перекрестит и пустит гулять:
«Вот, ступай в родимую гать.
   Душа моя рада
   Всякому гаду
   И всякому зверю
   И о всякой вере».

И тихонько молится,
Приподняв свою шляпу,
За стебель, что клонится,
За больную звериную лапу,
　　　　И за римского папу.


Не бойся пучины тряской —
Спасет тебя черная ряска.

*17 апреля 1905*


## 33. СТАРУШКА И ЧЕРТЕНЯТА

*Григорию Е.*

Побывала старушка у Троицы
И всё дальше идет, на восток.
Вот сидит возле белой околицы,
Обвевает ее вечерок.


Собрались чертенята и карлики,
Только диву даются в кустах
На костыль, на мешок, на сухарики,
На усталые ноги в лаптях.


«Эта странница, верно, не рада нам —
Приложилась к мощам — и свята;
Надышалась божественным ладаном,
Чтобы видеть Святые Места.


Чтоб идти ей тропинками злачными,
На зеленую травку присесть...
Чтоб высóко над елями мрачными
Пронеслась золотистая весть...»


И мохнатые, малые каются,
Умиленно глядят на костыль,
Униженно в траве кувыркаются,
Поднимают копытцами пыль:

«Ты прости нас, старушка ты божия,
Не бери нас в Святые Места!
Мы и здесь лобызаем подножия
Своего, полевого Христа.

Занимаются села пожарами,
Грозовая над нами весна,
Но за майскими тонкими чарами
Затлевает и нам Купина...»

*Июль 1905*

# VERSES FROM THE COLLECTIONS

## "РАЗНЫЕ СТИХОТВОРЕНИЯ"

### (1904–1908)

## and

## "ГОРОД"

### (1904–1908)

## 34. БАЛАГАНЧИК

Вот открыт балаганчик
Для веселых и славных детей,
Смотрят девочка и мальчик
На дам, королей и чертей.
И звучит эта адская музыка,
Завывает унылый смычок.
Страшный чорт ухватил карапузика,
И стекает клюквенный сок.

#### Мальчик

Он спасется от черного гнева
Мановением белой руки.
Посмотри: огоньки
Приближаются слева...
Видишь факелы? видишь дымки?
Это, верно, сама королева...

#### Девочка

Ах, нет, зачем ты дразнишь меня?
Это — адская свита...
Королева — та ходит средь белого дня,
Вся гирляндами роз перевита,
И шлейф ее носит, мечами звеня,
Вздыхающих рыцарей свита.

Вдруг паяц перегнулся за рампу
И кричит: «Помогите!
Истекаю я клюквенным соком!
Забинтован тряпицей!
На голове моей — картонный шлем!
А в руке — деревянный меч!»

Заплакали девочка и мальчик,
И закрылся веселый балаганчик.

*Июль 1905*

## 35.

Девушка пела в церковном хоре
О всех усталых в чужом краю,
О всех кораблях, ушедших в море,
О всех, забывших радость свою.

Так пел ее голос, летящий в купол,
И луч сиял на белом плече,
И каждый из мрака смотрел и слушал,
Как белое платье пело в луче.

И всем казалось, что радость будет,
Что в тихой заводи все корабли,
Что на чужбине усталые люди
Светлую жизнь себе обрели.

И голос был сладок, и луч был тонок,
И только высоко, у царских врат,
Причастный тайнам, — плакал ребенок
О том, что никто не придет назад.

*Август 1905*

## 36.

В голубой далекой спаленке
Твой ребенок опочил.
Тихо вылез карлик маленький
И часы остановил.

Всё, как было. Только странная
Воцарилась тишина.
И в окне твоем — туманная
Только улица страшна.

Словно что-то недосказано,
Что всегда звучит, всегда...
Нить какая-то развязана,
Сочетавшая года.

И прошла ты, сонно-белая.
Вдоль по комнатам одна.
Опустила, вся несмелая,
Штору синего окна.

И потом, едва заметная,
Тонкий полог подняла.
И, как время безрассветная,
Шевелясь, поникла мгла.

Стало тихо в дальней спаленке —
Синий сумрак и покой,
Оттого, что карлик маленький
Держит маятник рукой.

*4 октября 1905*

## 37.

*Евгению Иванову*

Вот он — Христос — в цепях и розах
За решеткой моей тюрьмы.
Вот агнец кроткий в белых ризах
Пришел и смотрит в окно тюрьмы.

В простом окладе синего неба
Его икона смотрит в окно.
Убогий художник создал небо.
Но лик и синее небо — одно.

Единый, светлый, немного грустный —
За ним восходит хлебный злак,
На пригорке лежит огород капустный,
И березки и елки бегут в овраг.

И всё так близко и так далёко,
Что, стоя рядом, достичь нельзя,
И не постигнешь синего ока,
Пока не станешь сам как стезя…

Пока такой же нищий не будешь,
Не ляжешь, истоптан, в глухой овраг,
Обо всем не забудешь, и всего не разлюбишь,
И не поблекнешь, как мертвый злак.

*10 октября 1905*

## 38.

Прискакала дикой степью
На вспенённом скакуне.
«Долго ль будешь лязгать цепью?
Выходи плясать ко мне!»

Рукавом в окно мне машет,
Красным криком зажжена,
Так и манит, так и пляшет,
И ласкает скакуна.

«А, не хочешь! Ну, так с богом!»
Пыль клубами завилась…
По тропам и по дорогам
В чистом поле понеслась…

Не меня ты любишь, Млада,
Дикой вольности сестра!
Любишь краденые клады,
Полуночный свист костра!

И в степях, среди тумана,
Ты страшна своей красой —
Разметавшейся у стана
Рыжей спутанной косой.

*31 октября 1905*

## 39. ПЕРСТЕНЬ-СТРАДАНЬЕ

Шел я по улице, горем убитый.
Юность моя, как печальная ночь,
Бледным лучом упадала на плиты,
Гасла, плелась и шарахалась прочь.

Горькие думы — лохмотья печалей —
Нагло просили на чай, на ночлег,
И пропадали средь уличных далей,
За вереницей зловонных телег.

Господи боже! Уж утро клубится,
Где, да и как этот день проживу?..
Узкие окна. За ними — девица.
Тонкие пальцы легли на канву.

Локоны пали на нежные ткани —
Верно, работала ночь напролет…
Щеки бледны от бессонных мечтаний,
И замирающий голос поет:

«Что́ я сумела, когда полюбила?
Бросила мать и ушла от отца…
Вот я с тобою, мой милый, мой милый…
Перстень-Страданье нам свяжет сердца.

Что́ я могу? Своей алой кровью
Нежность мою для тебя украшать…
Верностью женской, вечной любовью
Перстень-Страданье тебе сковать».

*30 октября 1905*


## 40. НЕЗНАКОМКА

По вечерам над ресторанами
Горячий воздух дик и глух,
И правит окриками пьяными
Весенний и тлетворный дух.

Вдали, над пылью переулочной,
Над скукой загородных дач,
Чуть золотится крендель булочной,
И раздается детский плач.

И каждый вечер, за шлагбаумами,
Заламывая котелки,
Среди канав гуляют с дамами
Испытанные остряки.

Над озером скрипят уключины,
И раздается женский визг,
А в небе, ко всему приученный,
Бессмысленно кривится диск.

И каждый вечер друг единственный
В моем стакане отражен
И влагой терпкой и таинственной,
Как я, смирён и оглушен.

А рядом у соседних столиков
Лакеи сонные торчат,
И пьяницы с глазами кроликов
«In vino veritas!» кричат.

И каждый вечер, в час назначенный
(Иль это только снится мне?),
Девичий стан, шелками схваченный,
В туманном движется окне.

И медленно, пройдя меж пьяными,
Всегда без спутников, одна,
Дыша духами и туманами,
Она садится у окна.

И веют древними поверьями
Ее упругие шелка,
И шляпа с траурными перьями,
И в кольцах узкая рука.

И странной близостью закованный,
Смотрю за темную вуаль,
И вижу берег очарованный
И очарованную даль.

Глухие тайны мне поручены,
Мне чье-то солнце вручено,
И все души моей излучины
Пронзило терпкое вино.

И перья страуса склоненные
В моем качаются мозгу,
И очи синие бездонные
Цветут на дальнем берегу.

В моей душе лежит сокровище,
И ключ поручен только мне!
Ты право, пьяное чудовище!
Я знаю: истина в вине.

*24 апреля 1906. Озерки*

## 41. АНГЕЛ-ХРАНИТЕЛЬ

Люблю Тебя, Ангел-Хранитель, во мгле.
Во мгле, что со мною всегда на земле.

За то, что ты светлой невестой была,
За то, что ты тайну мою отняла.

За то, что связала нас тайна и ночь,
Что ты мне сестра, и невеста, и дочь.

За то, что нам долгая жизнь суждена,
О, даже за то, что мы — муж и жена!

За цепи мои и заклятья твои.
За то, что над нами проклятье семьи.

За то, что не любишь того, что люблю.
За то, что о нищих и бедных скорблю.

За то, что не можем согласно мы жить,
За то, что хочу и не смею убить —

Отмстить малодушным, кто жил без огня,
Кто так унижал мой народ и меня!

Кто запер свободных и сильных в тюрьму,
Кто долго не верил огню моему.

Кто хочет за деньги лишить меня дня,
Собачью покорность купить у меня…

За то, что я слаб и смириться готов,
Что предки мои — поколенье рабов,

И нежности ядом убита душа,
И эта рука не поднимет ножа…

Но люблю я тебя и за слабость мою,
За горькую долю и силу твою.

Что огнем сожжено и свинцом залито —
Того разорвать не посмеет никто!

С тобою смотрел я на эту зарю —
С тобой в эту черную бездну смотрю.

И двойственно нам приказанье судьбы:
Мы вольные души! Мы злые рабы!

Покорствуй! Дерзай! Не покинь! Отойди!
Огонь или тьма — впереди?

Кто кличет? Кто плачет? Куда мы идем?
Вдвоем — неразрывно — навеки вдвоем!

Воскреснем? Погибнем? Умрем?

*17 августа 1906*

## 42. РУСЬ

Ты и во сне необычайна.
Твоей одежды не коснусь.
Дремлю — и за дремотой тайна,
И в тайне — ты почиешь, Русь.

Русь, опоясана реками
И дебрями окружена, .
С болотами и журавлями,
И с мутным взором колдуна,

Где разноликие народы
Из края в край, из дола в дол
Ведут ночные хороводы
Под заревом горящих сел.

Где ведуны с ворожеями
Чаруют злаки на полях,
И ведьмы тешатся с чертями
В дорожных снеговых столбах.

Где буйно заметает вьюга
До крыши — утлое жилье,
И девушка на злого друга
Под снегом точит лезвее.

Где все пути и все распутья
Живой клюкой измождены,
И вихрь, свистящий в голых прутьях,
Поет преданья старины...

Так — я узнал в моей дремоте
Страны родимой нищету,
И в лоскутах ее лохмотий
Души скрываю наготу.

Тропу печальную, ночную
Я до погоста протоптал,
И там, на кладбище ночуя,
Подолгу песни распевал.

И сам не понял, не измерил,
Кому я песни посвятил,
В какого бога страстно верил,
Какую девушку любил.

Живую душу укачала,
Русь, на своих просторах, ты,
И вот — она не запятнала
Первоначальной чистоты.

Дремлю — и за дремотой тайна,
И в тайне почивает Русь,
Она и в снах необычайна.
Ее одежды не коснусь.

*24 сентября 1906*


## 43. СЫН И МАТЬ

*Моей матери*

Сын осеняется крестом.
Сын покидает отчий дом.

В песнях матери оставленной
Золотая радость есть:
Только б он пришел прославленный,
Только б радость перенесть!

Вот, в доспехе ослепительном,
Слышно, ходит сын во мгле,
Дух свой предал небожителям,
Сердце — матери-земле.

Петухи поют к заутрене,
Ночь испуганно бежит.
Хриплый рог туманов утренних
За спиной ее трубит.

Поднялись над луговинами
Кудри спутанные мхов,
Метят взорами совиными
В стаю легких облаков…

Вот он, сын мой, в светлом облаке,
В шлеме утренней зари!
Сыплет он стрелами колкими
В чернолесья, в пустыри!..

Веет ветер очистительный
От небесной синевы.
Сын бросает меч губительный,
Шлем снимает с головы.

Точит грудь его пронзенная
Кровь и горние хвалы:
Здравствуй, даль, освобожденная
От ночной туманной мглы!

В сердце матери оставленной
Золотая радость есть:
Вот он, сын мой, окровавленный!
Только б радость перенесть!

Сын не забыл родную мать:
Сын воротился умирать.

*4 октября 1906*


# В ОКТЯБРЕ

Открыл окно. Какая хмурая
   Столица в октябре!
Забитая лошадка бурая
   Гуляет на дворе.

Снежинка легкою пушинкою
   Порхает на ветру,
И елка слабенькой вершинкою
   Мотает на юру.

Жилось легко, жилось и молодо —
         Прошла моя пора.
Вон — мальчик, посинев от холода,
         Дрожит среди двора.

Всё, всё по старому, бывалому,
         И будет как всегда:
Лошадке и мальчишке малому
         Не сладки холода.

Да и меня без всяких поводов
         Загнали на чердак.
Никто моих не слушал доводов,
         И вышел мой табак.

А всё хочу свободной волею
         Свободного житья,
Хоть нет звезды счастливой более
         С тех пор, как запил я!

Давно звезда в стакан мой канула, —
         Ужели навсегда?..
И вот душа опять воспрянула:
         Со мной моя звезда!

Вот, вот — в глазах плывет манящая,
         Качается в окне...
И жизнь начнется настоящая,
         И крылья будут мне!

И даже всё мое имущество
         С собою захвачу!
Познал, познал свое могущество!..
         Вот вскрикнул... и лечу!

Лечу, лечу к мальчишке малому,
         Средь вихря и огня...
Всё, всё по старому, бывалому,
         Да только — без меня!

*Октябрь 1906*

## 45.

Так окрыленно, так напевно
Царевна пела о весне.
И я сказал: «Смотри, царевна,
Ты будешь плакать обо мне».

Но руки мне легли на плечи,
И прозвучало: «Нет. Прости.
Возьми свой меч. Готовься к сече.
Я сохраню тебя в пути.

Иди, иди, вернешься молод
И долгу верен своему.
Я сохраню мой лед и холод,
Замкнусь в хрустальном терему.

И будет радость в долгих взорах,
И тихо протекут года.
Вкруг замка будет вечный шорох,
Во рву — прозрачная вода...

Да, я готова к поздней встрече,
Навстречу руки протяну
Тебе, несущему из сечи
На острие копья — весну».

Даль опустила синий полог
Над замком, башней и тобой.
Прости, царевна. Путь мой долог.
Иду за огненной весной.

*Октябрь 1906*

## 46.

Зачатый в ночь, я в ночь рожден,
    И вскрикнул я, прозрев:
Так тяжек матери был стон,
    Так черен ночи зев.

Когда же сумрак поредел,
    Унылый день повлек
Клубок однообразных дел,
    Безрадостный клубок.

*Что быть должно — то быть должно,*
　　Так пела с детских лет
Шарманка в низкое окно,
　　И вот — я стал поэт.


Влюбленность расцвела в кудрях
　　И в ранней грусти глаз.
И был я в розовых цепях
　　У женщин много раз.


И всё, *как быть должно,* пошло:
　　Любовь, стихи, тоска;
Всё приняла в свое русло
　　Спокойная река.


Как ночь слепа, так я был слеп,
　　И думал жить слепой...
Но раз открыли темный склеп,
　　Сказали: *Бог с тобой.*


В ту ночь был белый ледоход,
　　Разлив осенних вод.
Я думал: «Вот, река идет».
　　И я пошел вперед.


В ту ночь река во мгле была,
　　И в ночь и в темноту
Та — незнакомая — пришла
　　И встала на мосту.


Она была — живой костер
　　Из снега и вина.
Кто раз взглянул в желанный взор,
　　Тот знает, кто она.


И тихо за руку взяла
　　И глянула в лицо.
И маску белую дала
　　И светлое кольцо.

«Довольно жить, оставь слова,
  Я, как метель, звонка,
Иною жизнию жива,
  Иным огнем ярка».

Она зовет. Она манит.
  В снегах земля и твердь.
Что́ мне поет? Что́ мне звенит?
  Иная жизнь? Глухая смерть?

*12 апреля 1907*

# VERSES FROM THE COLLECTIONS

# "СНЕЖНАЯ МАСКА",

# "ВОЛЬНЫЕ МЫСЛИ" (1907)

# and

# "ФАИНА" (1906–1908)

## 47. СНЕЖНОЕ ВИНО

И вновь, сверкнув из чаши винной,
Ты поселила в сердце страх
Своей улыбкою невинной
В тяжелозмейных волосах.

Я опрокинут в темных струях
И вновь вдыхаю, не любя,
Забытый сон о поцелуях,
О снежных вьюгах вкруг тебя.

И ты смеешься дивным смехом,
Змеишься в чаше золотой,
И над твоим собольим мехом
Гуляет ветер голубой.

И как, глядясь в живые струи,
Не увидать себя в венце?
Твои не вспомнить поцелуи
На запрокинутом лице?

*29 декабря 1906*

## 48. ВТОРОЕ КРЕЩЕНЬЕ

Открыли дверь мою метели,
Застыла горница моя,
И в новой снеговой купели
Крещен вторым крещеньем я.

И, в новый мир вступая, знаю,
Что люди есть, и есть дела,
Что путь открыт наверно к раю
Всем, кто идет путями зла.

Я так устал от ласк подруги
На застывающей земле.
И драгоценный камень вьюги
Сверкает льдиной на челе.

И гордость нового крещенья
Мне сердце обратила в лед.
Ты мне сулишь еще мгновенья?
Пророчишь, что весна придет?

Но посмотри, как сердце радо!
Заграждена снегами твердь.
Весны не будет, и не надо:
Крещеньем третьим будет — Смерть.

*3 января 1907*

## 49. НАСТИГНУТЫЙ МЕТЕЛЬЮ

Вьюга пела.
И кололи снежные иглы.
И душа леденела.
Ты меня настигла.

Ты запрокинула голову в высь.
Ты сказала: «Глядись, глядись,
Пока не забудешь
Того, что любишь».

И указала на дальние города линии,
На поля снеговые и синие,
На бесцельный холод.

И снежных вихрей подъятый молот
Бросил нас в бездну, где искры неслись,
Где снежинки пугливо вились...

Какие-то искры,
Каких-то снежинок неверный полет...
Как быстро — так быстро
Ты надо мной
Опрокинула свод
Голубой...

Метель взвила́сь,
Звезда сорвалась,
За ней другая...

И звезда за звездой
        Понеслась,
            Открывая
Вихрям звездным
Новые бездны.

В небе вспыхнули темные очи
Так ясно!
И я позабыл приметы
Страны прекрасной —
В блеске твоем, комета!
В блеске твоем, среброснежная ночь!

И неслись опустошающие
Непомерные года,
Словно сердце застывающее
Закатилось навсегда.

Но бредет за дальним полюсом
Солнце сердца моего,
Льдяным скованное поясом
Безначалья твоего.

Так взойди ж в морозном инее,
Непомерный свет — заря!
Подними над далью синей
Жезл померкшего царя!

*3 января 1907*


## 50. О СМЕРТИ

Всё чаще я по городу брожу.
Всё чаще вижу смерть — и улыбаюсь
Улыбкой рассудительной. Ну, что же?
Так я хочу. Так свойственно мне знать,
Что и ко мне придет она в свой час.

Я проходил вдоль скачек по шоссе.
День золотой дремал на грудах щебня,
А за глухим забором — ипподром
Под солнцем зеленел. Там стебли злаков
И одуванчики, раздутые весной,
В ласкающих лучах дремали. А вдали
Трибуна придавила плоской крышей
Толпу зевак и модниц. Маленькие флаги
Пестрели там и здесь. А на заборе
Прохожие сидели и глазели.

Я шел и слышал быстрый гон коней
По грунту легкому. И быстрый топот
Копыт. Потом — внезапный крик:
«Упал! Упал!» — кричали на заборе,
И я, вскочив на маленький пенёк,
Увидел всё зараз: вдали летели
Жокеи в пестром — к тонкому столбу.

Чуть-чуть отстав от них, скакала лошадь
Без седока, взметая стремена.
А за листвой кудрявеньких березок,
Так близко от меня — лежал жокей,
Весь в желтом, в зеленях весенних злаков,
Упавший навзничь, обратив лицо

В глубокое ласкающее небо.
Как будто век лежал, раскинув руки
И ногу подогнув. Так хорошо лежал.
К нему уже бежали люди. Издали́,
Поблескивая медленными спицами, ландо
Катилось мягко. Люди подбежали
И подняли его...

                    И вот повисла
Беспомощная желтая нога
В обтянутой рейтузе. Завалилась
Им на́ плечи куда-то голова...
Ландо подъехало. К его подушкам
Так бережно и нежно приложили
Цыплячью желтизну жокея. Человек
Вскочил неловко на подножку, замер,
Поддерживая голову и ногу,
И важный кучер повернул назад.
И так же медленно вертелись спицы,
Поблескивали козла, оси, крылья...

Так хорошо и вольно умереть.
Всю жизнь скакал — с одной упорной мыслью,
Чтоб первым доскакать. И на скаку
Запнулась запыхавшаяся лошадь,
Уж силой ног не удержать седла,
И утлые взмахнулись стремена,
И полетел, отброшенный толчком...
Ударился затылком о родную,
Весеннюю, приветливую землю,
И в этот миг — в мозгу прошли все мысли,
Единственные нужные. Прошли —
И умерли. И умерли глаза.
И труп мечтательно глядит наверх.
Так хорошо и вольно.

Однажды брел по набережной я.
Рабочие возили с барок в тачках
Дрова, кирпич и уголь. И река
Была еще сине́й от белой пены.
В отстегнутые вороты рубах

Глядели загорелые тела,
И светлые глаза привольной Руси
Блестели строго с почерневших лиц.
И тут же дети голыми ногами
Месили груды желтого песку,
Таскали — то кирпичик, то полено,
То бревнышко. И прятались. А там
Уже сверкали грязные их пятки,
И матери — с отвислыми грудями
Под грязным платьем — ждали их, ругались
И, надавав затрещин, отбирали
Дрова, кирпичики, бревёшки. И тащили,
Согнувшись под тяжелой ношей, вдаль.
И снова, воротясь гурьбой веселой,
Ребятки начинали воровать:
Тот бревнышко, другой — кирпичик…


И вдруг раздался всплеск воды и крик:
«Упал! Упал!» — опять кричали с барки.
Рабочий, ручку тачки отпустив,
Показывал рукой куда-то в воду,
И пестрая толпа рубах неслась
Туда, где на траве, в камнях булыжных,
На самом берегу — лежала сотка.
Один тащил багор.


                    А между свай,
Забитых возле набережной в воду,
Легко покачивался человек
В рубахе и в разорванных портках.
Один схватил его. Другой помог,
И длинное растянутое тело,
С которого ручьем лилась вода,
Втащили нá берег и положили.
Городовой, гремя о камни шашкой,
Зачем-то щеку приложил к груди
Намокшей, и прилежно слушал,
Должно быть, сердце. Собрался́ народ,
И каждый вновь пришедший задавал
Одни и те же глупые вопросы:

Когда упал, да сколько пролежал
В воде, да сколько выпил?
Потом все стали тихо отходить,
И я пошел своим путем, и слушал,
Как истовый, но выпивший рабочий
Авторитетно говорил другим,
Что губит каждый день людей вино.

Пойду еще бродить. Покуда солнце,
Покуда жар, покуда голова
Тупа, и мысли вялы...

        Сердце!
Ты будь вожатаем моим. И смерть
С улыбкой наблюдай. Само устанешь,
Не вынесешь такой веселой жизни,
Какую я веду. Такой любви
И ненависти люди не выносят,
Какую я в себе ношу.

        Хочу,
Всегда хочу смотреть в глаза людские,
И пить вино, и женщин целовать,
И яростью желаний полнить вечер,
Когда жара мешает днем мечтать
И песни петь! И слушать в мире ветер!

## 51. ОСЕННЯЯ ЛЮБОВЬ

### 1

Когда в листве сырой и ржавой
Рябины заалеет гроздь, —
Когда палач рукой костлявой
Вобьет в ладонь последний гвоздь, —

Когда над рябью рек свинцовой,
В сырой и серой высоте,
Пред ликом родины суровой
Я закачаюсь на кресте, —

Тогда — просторно и далеко
Смотрю сквозь кровь предсмертных слез,
И вижу: по реке широкой
Ко мне плывет в челне Христос.

В глазах — такие же надежды,
И то же рубище на нем.
И жалко смотрит из одежды
Ладонь, пробитая гвоздем.

Христос! Родной простор печален!
Изнемогаю на кресте!
И челн твой — будет ли причален
К моей распятой высоте?

2

И вот уже ветром разбиты, убиты
Кусты облетелой ракиты.

И прахом дорожным
Угрюмая старость легла на ланитах.

Но в темных орбитах
Взглянули, сверкнули глаза невозможным...

И радость, и слава —
Всё в этом сияньи бездонном,
И дальном.

Но смятые травы
Печальны,
И листья крутятся в лесу обнаженном...

И снится, и снится, и снится:
Бывалое солнце!
Тебя мне всё жальче и жальче...

О, глупое сердце,
Смеющийся мальчик,
Когда перестанешь ты биться?

## 3

Под ветром холодные плечи
Твои обнимать так отрадно:
Ты думаешь — нежная ласка,
Я знаю — восторг мятежа!

И теплятся очи, как свечи
Ночные, и слушаю жадно —
Шевелится страшная сказка,
И звездная дышит межа...

О, в этот сияющий вечер
Ты будешь всё так же прекрасна,
И, верная темному раю,
Ты будешь мне светлой звездой!

Я знаю, что холоден ветер,
Я верю, что осень бесстрастна!

Но в темном плаще не узнают,
Что ты пировала со мной!..

И мчимся в осенние дали,
И слушаем дальние трубы,
И мерим ночные дороги,
Холодные выси мои...

Часы торжества миновали —
Мои опьяненные губы
Целуют в предсмертной тревоге
Холодные губы твои.

*3 октября 1907*

## 52. СНЕЖНАЯ ДЕВА

Она пришла из дикой дали —
Ночная дочь иных времен.
Ее родные не встречали,
Не просиял ей небосклон.

Но сфинкса с выщербленным ликом
Над исполинскою Невой
Она встречала легким вскриком
Под бурей ночи снеговой.

Бывало, вьюга ей осыпет
Звездами плечи, грудь и стан, —
Всё снится ей родной Египет
Сквозь тусклый северный туман.

И город мой железно-серый,
Где ветер, дождь, и зыбь, и мгла,
С какой-то непонятной верой
Она, как царство, приняла.

Ей стали нравиться громады,
Уснувшие в ночной глуши,
И в окнах тихие лампады
Слились с мечтой ее души.

Она узнала зыбь и дымы,
Огни, и мраки, и дома —
Весь город мой непостижимый —
Непостижимая сама.

Она дарит мне перстень вьюги
За то, что плащ мой полон звезд,
За то, что я в стальной кольчуге,
И на кольчуге — строгий крест.

Она глядит мне прямо в очи,
Хваля неробкого врага.
С полей ее холодной ночи
В мой дух врываются снега.

Но сердце Снежной Девы немо
И никогда не примет меч,
Чтобы ремень стального шлема
Рукою страстною рассечь.

И я, как вождь враждебной рати,
Всегда закованный в броню,
Мечту торжественных объятий
В священном трепете храню.

*17 октября 1907*

## 53. ЗАКЛЯТИЕ ОГНЕМ И МРАКОМ

За всё, за всё тебя благодарю я:
За тайные мучения страстей,
За горечь слез, отраву поцелуя,
За месть врагов и клевету друзей;
За жар души, растраченный в пустыне.

*Лермонтов*

1

О, весна без конца и без краю —
Без конца и без краю мечта!
Узнаю тебя, жизнь! Принимаю!
И приветствую звоном щита!

Принимаю тебя, неудача,
И удача, тебе мой привет!
В заколдованной области плача,
В тайне смеха — позорного нет!

Принимаю бессонные споры,
Утро в завесах темных окна,
Чтоб мои воспаленные взоры
Раздражала, пьянила весна!

Принимаю пустынные веси!
И колодцы земных городов!
Осветленный простор поднебесий
И томления рабьих трудов!

И встречаю тебя у порога —
С буйным ветром в змеиных кудрях,
С неразгаданным именем бога
На холодных и сжатых губах...

Перед этой враждующей встречей
Никогда я не брошу щита...
Никогда не откроешь ты плечи...
Но над нами — хмельная мечта!

И смотрю, и вражду измеряю,
Ненавидя, кляня и любя:
За мученья, за гибель — я знаю —
Всё равно: принимаю тебя!

*24 октября 1907*

9*

Гармоника, гармоника!
Эй, пой, визжи и жги!
Эй, желтенькие лютики,
Весенние цветки!

Там с посвистом да с присвистом
Гуляют до зари,
Кусточки тихим шелестом
Кивают мне: смотри.

Смотрю я — руки вскинула,
В широкий пляс пошла,
Цветами всех осыпала
И в песне изошла...

Неверная, лукавая,
Коварная — пляши!
И будь навек отравою
Растраченной души!

С ума сойду, сойду с ума,
Безумствуя, люблю,
Что вся ты — ночь, и вся ты — тьма,
И вся ты — во хмелю...

Что душу отняла мою,
Отравой извела,
Что о тебе, тебе пою,
И песням нет числа!..

*9 ноября 1907*

### 54.

Она пришла с мороза,
Раскрасневшаяся,
Наполнила комнату
Ароматом воздуха и духов,
Звонким голосом
И совсем неуважительной к занятиям
Болтовней.

---

\* Blok's numeration retained.

Она немедленно уронила нá пол
Толстый том художественного журнала,
И сейчас же стало казаться,
Что в моей большой комнате
Очень мало места.

Всё это было немножко досадно
И довольно нелепо.
Впрочем, она захотела,
Чтобы я читал ей вслух «Макбéта».

Едва дойдя до *пузырей земли*,
О которых я не могу говорить без волнения,
Я заметил, что она тоже волнуется
И внимательно смотрит в окно.

Оказалось, что большой пестрый кот
С трудом лепится по краю крыши,
Подстерегая целующихся голубей.
Я рассердился больше всего на то,
Что целовались не мы, а голуби,
И что прошли времена Пáоло и Франчески.

*6 февраля 1908*


## 55.

Когда вы стоите на моем пути,
Такая живая, такая красивая,
Но такая измученная,
Говорите всё о печальном,
Думаете о смерти,
Никого не любите
И презираете свою красоту —
Что же? Разве я обижу вас?

О, нет! Ведь я не насильник,
Не обманщик и не гордец,
Хотя много знаю,
Слишком много думаю с детства
И слишком занят собой.
Ведь я — сочинитель,
Человек, называющий всё по имени,
Отнимающий аромат у живого цветка.

Сколько ни говорите о печальном,
Сколько ни размышляйте о концах и началах,
Всё же, я смею думать,
Что вам только пятнадцать лет.

И потому я хотел бы,
Чтобы вы влюбились в простого человека,
Который любит землю и небо
Больше, чем рифмованные и нерифмованные
Речи о земле и о небе.

Право, я буду рад за вас,
Так как — только влюбленный
Имеет право на звание человека.

*6 февраля 1908*

# PART IV
# POEMS FROM VOLUME III

# VERSES FROM THE COLLECTION

## "СТРАШНЫЙ МИР"

### (1909–1916)

## 56. К МУЗЕ

Есть в напевах твоих сокровенных
Роковая о гибели весть.
Есть проклятье заветов священных,
Поругание счастия есть.

И такая влекущая сила,
Что готов я твердить за молвой,
Будто ангелов ты низводила,
Соблазняя своей красотой...

И когда ты смеешься над верой,
Над тобой загорается вдруг
Тот неяркий, пурпурово-серый
И когда-то мной виденный круг.

Зла, добра ли? — Ты вся — не отсюда.
Мудрено про тебя говорят:
Для иных ты — и Муза, и чудо.
Для меня ты — мученье и ад.

Я не знаю, зачем на рассвете,
В час, когда уже не было сил,
Не погиб я, но лик твой заметил
И твоих утешений просил?

Я хотел, чтоб мы были врагами,
Так за что ж подарила мне ты
Луг с цветами и твердь со звездами —
Всё проклятье своей красоты?

И коварнее северной ночи,
И хмельней золотого аи,
И любови цыганской короче
Были страшные ласки твои…

И была роковая отрада
В попираньи заветных святынь,
И безумная сердцу услада —
Эта горькая страсть, как полынь!

*29 декабря 1912*

## 57.

Поздней осенью из гавани
От заметенной снегом земли
В предназначенное плаванье
Идут тяжелые корабли.

В черном небе означается
Над водой подъемный кран,
И один фонарь качается
На оснеженном берегу.

И матрос, на борт не принятый,
Идет, шатаясь, сквозь буран.
Всё потеряно, всё выпито!
Довольно — больше не могу…

А берег опустелой гавани
Уж первый легкий снег занес...
В самом чистом, в самом нежном саване
Сладко ли спать тебе, матрос?

*14 ноября 1909*


## 58. В РЕСТОРАНЕ

Никогда не забуду (он был или не был,
Этот вечер): пожаром зари
Сожжено и расдвинуто бледное небо,
И на желтой заре — фонари.

Я сидел у окна в переполненном зале.
Где-то пели смычки о любви.
Я послал тебе черную розу в бокале
Золотого, как небо, аи.

Ты взглянула. Я встретил смущенно и дерзко
Взор надменный и отдал поклон.
Обратясь к кавалеру, намеренно резко
Ты сказала: «И этот влюблен».

И сейчас же в ответ что-то грянули струны,
Исступленно запели смычки...
Но была ты со мной всем презрением юным,
Чуть заметным дрожаньем руки...

Ты рванулась движеньем испуганной птицы,
Ты прошла, словно сон мой легка...
И вздохнули духи, задремали ресницы,
Зашептались тревожно шелка.

Но из глуби зеркал ты мне взоры бросала
И, бросая, кричала: «Лови!..»
А монисто бренчало, цыганка плясала
И визжала заре о любви.

*19 апреля 1910*

## 59. УНИЖЕНИЕ

В черных сучьях дерев обнаженных
Желтый зимний закат за окном.
(К эшафоту на казнь осужденных
Поведут на закате таком).


Красный штоф полинялых диванов,
Пропыленные кисти портьер ...
В этой комнате, в звоне стаканов,
Купчик, шулер, студент, офицер ...


Этих голых рисунков журнала
Не людская касалась рука ...
И рука *подлеца* нажимала
Эту грязную кнопку звонка ...


Чу! По мягким коврам прозвенели
Шпоры, смех, заглушенный дверьми ...
Разве дом этот — дом в самом деле?
Разве *так* суждено меж людьми?


Разве рад я сегодняшней встрече?
Что ты ликом бела, словно плат?
Что в твои обнаженные плечи
Бьет огромный холодный закат?


Только губы с запекшейся кровью
На иконе твоей золотой
(Разве *это* мы звали любовью?)
Преломились безумной чертой ...


В желтом, зимнем, огромном закате
Утонула (так пышно!) кровать ...
Еще тесно дышать от объятий,
Но ты свищешь опять и опять ...


Он не весел — твой свист замогильный ...
Чу! опять — бормотание шпор ...
Словно змей, тяжкий, сытый и пыльный,
Шлейф твой с кресел ползет на ковер ...

Ты смела! Так еще будь бесстрашней!
Я — не муж, не жених твой, не друг!
Так вонзай же, мой ангел вчерашний,
В сердце — острый французкий каблук!

*6 декабря 1911*

## 60. АВИАТОР

Летун отпущен на свободу.
Качнув две лопасти свои,
Как чудище морское в воду,
Скользнул в воздушные струи.

Его винты поют, как струны...
Смотри: недрогнувший пилот
К слепому солнцу над трибуной
Стремит свой винтовой полет...

Уж в вышине недостижимой
Сияет двигателя медь...
Там, еле слышный и незримый,
Пропеллер продолжает петь...

Потом — напрасно ищет око:
На небе не найдешь следа:
В бинокле, вскинутом высоко,
Лишь воздух — ясный, как вода...

А здесь, в колеблющемся зное,
В курящейся над лугом мгле,
Ангары, люди, всё земное —
Как бы придавлено к земле...

Но снова в золотом тумане
Как будто — неземной аккорд...
Он близок, миг рукоплесканий
И жалкий мировой рекорд!

Всё ниже спуск винтообразный,
Всё круче лопастей извив,
И вдруг... нелепый, безобразный
В однообразьи перерыв...

И зверь с умолкшими винтами
Повис пугающим углом...
Ищи отцветшими глазами
Опоры в воздухе... пустом!

Уж поздно: на траве равнины
Крыла измятая дуга...
В сплетеньи проволок машины
Рука — мертвее рычага...

Зачем ты в небе был, отважный,
В свой первый и последний раз?
Чтоб львице светской и продажной
Поднять к тебе фиалки глаз?

Или восторг самозабвенья
Губительный изведал ты,
Безумно возалкал паденья
И сам остановил винты?

Иль отравил твой мозг несчастный
Грядущих войн ужасный вид:
Ночной летун, во мгле ненастной
Земле несущий динамит?

*1910 – январь 1912*


## 61. ПЛЯСКИ СМЕРТИ

### 1

Как тяжко мертвецу среди людей
Живым и страстным притворяться!
Но надо, надо в общество втираться,
Скрывая для карьеры лязг костей...

Живые спят. Мертвец встает из гроба,
И в банк идет, и в суд идет, в сенат...
Чем ночь белее, тем чернее злоба,
И перья торжествующе скрипят.

Мертвец весь день трудится над докладом.
Присутствие кончается. И вот —
Нашептывает он, виляя задом,
Сенатору скабрезный анекдот…

Уж вечер. Мелкий дождь зашлепал грязью
Прохожих, и дома, и прочий вздор…
А мертвеца — к другому безобразью
Скрежещущий несет таксомотор.

В зал многолюдный и многоколонный
Спешит мертвец. На нем — изящный фрак.
Его дарят улыбкой благосклонной
Хозяйка — дура и супруг — дурак.

Он изнемог от дня чиновной скуки,
Но лязг костей музыкой заглушон…
Он крепко жмет приятельские руки —
Живым, живым казаться должен он!

Лишь у колонны встретится очами
С подгругою — она, как он, мертва.
За их условно-светскими речами
Ты слышишь настоящие слова:

«Усталый друг, мне странно в этом зале». —
«Усталый друг, могила холодна». —
«Уж полночь». — «Да, но вы не приглашали
На вальс NN. Она в вас влюблена…»

А там — NN уж ищет взором страстным
Его, его — с волнением в крови…
В ее лице, девически прекрасном,
Бессмысленный восторг живой любви…

Он шепчет ей незначащие речи,
Пленительные для живых слова,
И смотрит он, как розовеют плечи,
Как на плечо склонилась голова…

И острый яд привычно-светской злости
С нездешней злостью расточает он...
«Как он умен! Как он в меня влюблен!»

В ее ушах — нездешний, странный звон:
То кости лязгают о кости.

*19 февраля 1912*

## 2

Ночь, улица, фонарь, аптека,
Бессмысленный и тусклый свет.
Живи еще хоть четверть века —
Всё будет так. Исхода нет.

Умрешь — начнешь опять сначала,
И повторится всё, как встарь:
Ночь, ледяная рябь канала,
Аптека, улица, фонарь.

*10 октября 1912*

## 3

Пустая улица. Один огонь в окне.
Еврей-аптекарь охает во сне.

А перед шкапом с надписью *Venena,*
Хозяйственно согнув скрипучие колена,

Скелет, до глаз закутанный плащом,
Чего-то ищет, скалясь черным ртом...

Нашел... Но ненароком чем-то звякнул,
И череп повернул... Аптекарь крякнул,

Привстал — и на другой свалился бок...
А гость меж тем — заветный пузырек

Сует из-под плаща двум женщинам безносым
На улице, под фонарем белёсым.

*Октябрь 1912*

4

Старый, старый сон. Из мрака
     Фонари бегут — куда?
     Там — лишь черная вода,
     Там — забвенье навсегда.

     Тень скользит из-за угла,
     К ней другая подползла.
     Плащ распахнут, грудь бела,
Алый цвет в петлице фрака.

Тень вторая — стройный латник,
     Иль невеста от венца?
     Шлем и перья. Нет лица.
     Неподвижность мертвеца.

     В воротáх гремит звонок,
     Глухо щелкает замок.
     Переходят за порог
Проститутка и развратник...

Воет ветер леденящий,
     Пусто, тихо и темно.
     Наверху горит окно.
          Всё равно.

     Как свинец, черна вода.
     В ней забвенье навсегда.
     Третий призрак. Ты куда,
Ты, из тени в тень скользящий?

*7 февраля 1914*

5

     Вновь богатый зол и рад,
     Вновь унижен бедный.
     С кровель каменных громад
     Смотрит месяц бледный,

Насылает тишину,
Оттеняет крутизну
Каменных отвесов,
Черноту навесов...

Всё бы это было зря,
Если б не было царя,
    Чтоб блюсти законы.

Только не ищи дворца,
Добродушного лица,
    Золотой короны.

Он — с далеких пустырей
В свете редких фонарей
    Появляется.

Шея скручена платком,
Под дырявым козырьком
    Улыбается.

*7 февраля 1914*

## 62. ДЕМОН

Иди, иди за мной — покорной
И верною моей рабой.
Я на сверкнувший гребень горный
Взлечу уверенно с тобой.

Я пронесу тебя над бездной,
Ее бездонностью дразня.
Твой будет ужас бесполезный —
Лишь входновеньем для меня.

Я от дождя эфирной пыли
И от круженья охраню
Всей силой мышц и сенью крылий
И, вознося, не уроню.

И на горах, в сверканьи белом,
На незапятнанном лугу,
Божественно-прекрасным телом
Тебя я странно обожгу.

Ты знаешь ли, какая малость
Та человеческая ложь,
Та грустная земная жалость,
Что дикой страстью ты зовешь?

Когда же вечер станет тише,
И, околдованная мной,
Ты полететь захочешь выше
Пустыней неба огневой, —

Да, я возьму тебя с собою
И вознесу тебя туда,
Где кажется земля звездою,
Землею кажется звезда.

И, онемев от удивленья,
Ты у́зришь новые миры —
Невероятные виденья,
Создания моей игры ...

Дрожа от страха и бессилья,
Тогда шепнешь ты:отпусти...
И, распустив тихонько крылья,
Я улыбнусь тебе: лети.

И под божественной улыбкой,
Уничтожаясь на лету,
Ты полетишь, как камень зыбкий,
В сияющую пустоту...

*9 июня 1916*

## 63. ГОЛОС ИЗ ХОРА

Как часто плачем — вы и я —
Над жалкой жизнию своей!
О, если б знали вы, друзья,
Холод и мрак грядущих дней!

Теперь ты милой руку жмешь,
Играешь с нею, шутя,
И плачешь ты, заметив ложь,
Или в руке любимой нож,
    Дитя, дитя!

Лжи и коварству меры нет,
А смерть — далека.
Всё будет чернее страшный свет,
И всё безумней вихрь планет
          Еще века, века!

И век последний, ужасней всех,
          Увидим и вы и я.
Всё небо скроет гнусный грех,
На всех устах застынет смех,
          Тоска небытия...

Весны, дитя, ты будешь ждать —
          Весна обманет.
Ты будешь солнце на небо звать —
          Солнце не встанет.
И крик, когда ты начнешь кричать,
          Как камень, канет...

Будьте ж довольны жизнью своей,
          Тише воды, ниже травы!
О, если б знали, дети, вы,
          Холод и мрак грядущих дней!

*6 июня 1910 – 27 февраля 1914*

# VERSES FROM THE COLLECTION
## "ВОЗМЕЗДИЕ"*
### (1908–1913)

## 64.

О доблестях, о подвигах, о славе
Я забывал на горестной земле,
Когда твое лицо в простой оправе
Передо мной сияло на столе.

Но час настал, и ты ушла из дому.
Я бросил в ночь заветное кольцо.
Ты отдала свою судьбу другому,
И я забыл прекрасное лицо.

Летели дни, крутясь проклятым роем...
Вино и страсть терзали жизнь мою...
И вспомнил я тебя пред аналоем,
И звал тебя, как молодость свою...

Я звал тебя, но ты не оглянулась,
Я слезы лил, но ты не снизошла.
Ты в синий плащ печально завернулась,
В сырую ночь ты из дому ушла.

Не знаю, где приют своей гордыне
Ты, милая, ты, нежная, нашла...
Я крепко сплю, мне снится плащ твой синий,
В котором ты в сырую ночь ушла...

Уж не мечтать о нежности, о славе,
Всё миновалось, молодость прошла!
Твое лицо в его простой оправе
Своей рукой убрал я со стола.

*30 декабря 1908*

* Not to be confused with the long poem of the same title, from which an extract is printed on pp. 167-9.

129

## 65. ШАГИ КОМАНДОРА

*В. А. Зоргенфрею*

Тяжкий, плотный занавес у входа,
    За ночным окном — туман.
Что́ теперь твоя постылая свобода,
    Страх познавший Дон-Жуан?

Холодно и пусто в пышной спальне,
    Слуги спят, и ночь глуха.
Из страны блаженной, незнакомой, дальней
    Слышно пенье петуха.

Что́ изменнику блаженства звуки?
    Миги жизни сочтены.
Донна Анна спит, скрестив на сердце руки,
    Донна Анна видит сны...

Чьи черты жестокие застыли,
    В зеркалах отражены?
Анна, Анна, сладко ль спать в могиле?
    Сладко ль видеть неземные сны?

Жизнь пуста, безумна и бездонна!
    Выходи на битву, старый рок!
И в ответ — победно и влюбленно —
    В снежной мгле поет рожок...

Пролетает, брызнув в ночь огнями,
    Черный, тихий, как сова, мотор,
Тихими, тяжелыми шагами
    В дом вступает Командор...

Настежь дверь. Из непомерной стужи,
    Словно хриплый бой ночных часов —
Бой часов: «Ты звал меня на ужин.
    Я пришел. А ты готов?..»

На вопрос жестокий нет ответа,
    Нет ответа — тишина.
В пышной спальне страшно в час рассвета,
    Слуги спят, и ночь бледна.

В час рассвета холодно и странно,
        В час рассвета — ночь мутна.
Дева Света! Где ты, донна Анна?
        Анна! Анна! — Тишина.

Только в грозном утреннем тумане
        Бьют часы в последний раз:
*Донна Анна в смертный час твой встанет.*
        *Анна встанет в смертный час.*

*Сентябрь 1910 – 16 февраля 1912*

# VERSES FROM THE COLLECTION

## "ЯМБЫ"

### (1907–1914)

Fecit indignatio versum.*

Juvenal, Satires, I.79

### 66.

О, я хочу безумно жить:
Всё сущее — увековечить,
Безличное — вочеловечить,
Несбывшееся — воплотить!

Пусть душит жизни сон тяжелый,
Пусть задыхаюсь в этом сне, —
Быть может, юноша веселый
В грядущем скажет обо мне:

*Простим угрюмство — разве это
Сокрытый двигатель его?
Он весь — дитя добра и света,
Он весь — свободы торжество!*

*5 февраля 1914*

### 67.

Тропами тайными, ночными,
При свете траурной зари,
Придут замученные ими,
Над ними встанут упыри.
Овеют призраки ночные
Их помышленья и дела,
И загниют еще живые
Их слишком сытые тела.
Их корабли в пучине водной

* Verse is born of indignation.

Не сыщут ржавых якорей,
И не успеть дочесть отходной
Тебе, пузатый иерей!
Довольных сытое обличье,
Сокройся в темные гроба!
Так нам велит *времен величье*
И *розоперстая судьба!*
Гроба, наполненные гнилью,
Свободный, сбрось с могучих плеч!
Всё, всё — да станет легкой пылью
Под солнцем, не уставшим жечь!

*3 июня 1907*

## 68.

Да. Так диктует вдохновенье:
Моя свободная мечта
Всё льнет туда, где униженье,
Где грязь, и мрак, и нищета.
Туда, туда, смиренней, ниже, —
Оттуда зримей мир иной...
*Ты видел ли детей в Париже,*
*Иль нищих на мосту зимой?*
На непроглядный ужас жизни
Открой скорей, открой глаза,
Пока великая гроза
Всё не смела в твоей отчизне, —
Дай гневу правому созреть,
Приготовляй к работе руки...
Не можешь — дай тоске и скуке
В тебе копиться и гореть...
Но только — лживой жизни этой
Румяна жирные сотри,
Как боязливый крот, от света
Заройся в землю — там замри,
Всю жизнь жестоко ненавидя
И презирая этот свет,
Пускай грядущего не видя, —
Дням настоящим молвив: *нет!*

*Сентябрь 1911 – 7 февраля 1914*

## 69.

Земное сердце стынет вновь,
Но стужу я встречаю грудью.
Храню я к людям на безлюдьи
Неразделенную любовь.

Но за любовью — зреет гнев,
Растет презренье и желанье
Читать в глазах мужей и дев
Печать забвенья, иль избранья.

Пускай зовут: *Забудь, поэт!*
*Вернись в красивые уюты!*
Нет! Лучше сгинуть в стуже лютой!
Уюта — нет. Покоя — нет.

*1911 – 6 февраля 1914*

# VERSES FROM THE COLLECTION

# "ИТАЛЬЯНСКИЕ СТИХИ"

## (1909)

Sic finit occulte sic multos decipit aetas
Sic venit ad finem quidquid in orbe manet
Heu heu praeteritum non est revocabile tempus
Heu propius tacito mors venit ipsa pede.*

Inscription under the clock of the Church
of Santa Maria Novella (Florence)

## 70. РАВЕННА

Всё, что минутно, всё, что бренно,
Похоронила ты в веках.
Ты, как младенец, спишь, Равенна,
У сонной вечности в руках.

Рабы сквозь римские ворота
Уже не ввозят мозаик.
И догорает позолота
В стенах прохладных базилик.

От медленных лобзаний влаги
Нежнее грубый свод гробниц,
Где зеленеют саркофаги
Святых монахов и цариц.

Безмолвны гробовые залы,
Тенист и хладен их порог,
Чтоб черный взор блаженной Галлы,
Проснувшись, камня не прожег.

* As imperceptibly as the years work their destruction, So all that is in the world come[s]
to an end; Alas, alas! The re is no recalling time that is gone, Alas, death hurries towards
us with silent footfall.

Военной брани и обиды
Забыт и стерт кровавый след,
Чтобы воскресший глас Плакиды
Не пел страстей протекших лет.

Далёко отступило море,
И розы оцепили вал,
Чтоб спящий в гробе Теодорих
О буре жизни не мечтал.

А виноградные пустыни,
Дома и люди — всё гроба.
Лишь медь торжественной латыни
Поет на плитах, как труба.

Лишь в пристальном и тихом взоре
Равеннских девушек, порой,
Печаль о невозвратном море
Проходит робкой чередой.

Лишь по ночам, склонясь к долинам,
Ведя векам грядущим счет,
Тень Данта с профилем орлиным
О Новой Жизни мне поет.

*Май – июнь 1909*

## 71. ФЛОРЕНЦИЯ

### 1

Умри, Флоренция, Иуда,
Исчезни в сумрак вековой!
Я в час любви тебя забуду,
В час смерти буду не с тобой!

О, Bella, смейся над собою,
Уж не прекрасна больше ты!
Гнилой морщиной гробовою
Искажены твои черты!

Хрипят твои автомобили,
Твои уродливы дома,
Всеевропейской желтой пыли
Ты предала себя сама!

Звенят в пыли велосипеды
Там, где святой монах сожжен,
Где Леонардо сумрак ведал,
Беато снился синий сон!

Ты пышных Ме́дичей тревожишь,
Ты топчешь лилии свои,
Но воскресить себя не можешь
В пыли торговой толчеи!

Гнусавой мессы стон протяжный
И трупный запах роз в церквах —
Весь груз тоски многоэтажный —
Сгинь в очистительных веках!

*Май – июнь 1909*

### 2

Флоренция, ты ирис нежный;
По ком томился я один
Любовью длинной безнадежной,
Весь день в пыли твоих Кашин?

О сладко вспомнить безнадежность:
Мечтать и жить в твоей глуши;
Уйти в твой древний зной и в нежность
Своей стареющей души…

Но суждено нам разлучиться,
И через дальние края
Твой дымный ирис будет сниться,
Как юность ранняя моя.

*Июнь 1909*

3

Страстью длинной, безмятежной
Занялась душа моя,
Ирис дымный, ирис нежный,
Благовония струя,
Переплыть велит все реки
На воздушных парусах,
Утонуть велит навеки
В тех вечерних небесах,
И когда предамся зною,
Голубой вечерний зной
В голубое голубою
Унесет меня волной…

*Июнь 1909*

4

Жгут раскаленные камни
Мой лихорадочный взгляд.
Дымные ирисы в пламени,
Словно сейчас улетят.
О, безысходность печали,
Знаю тебя наизусть!
В черное небо Италии
Черной душою гляжусь.

*Июнь 1909*

5

Окна ложные на́ небе черном,
И прожектор на древнем дворце.
Вот проходит она — вся в узорном
И с улыбкой на смуглом лице.

А вино уж мутит мои взоры
И по жилам огнем разлилось…
*Что мне спеть в этот вечер, синьора?*
*Что мне спеть, чтоб вам сладко спалось?*

*Июнь 1909*

6

Под зноем флорентийской лени
Еще беднее чувством ты:
Молчат церковные ступени,
Цветут нерадостно цветы.

Так береги остаток чувства,
Храни хоть творческую ложь:
Лишь в легком челноке искусства
От скуки мира уплывешь.

*17 мая 1909*

7

Голубоватым дымом
Вечерний зной возносится,
Долин тосканских царь...

Он мимо, мимо, мимо
Летучей мышью бросится
Под уличный фонарь...

И вот уже в долинах
Несметный сонм огней,
И вот уже в витринах
Ответный блеск камней,
И город скрыли горы
В свой сумрак голубой,
И тешатся синьоры
Канцоной площадной.

Дымится пыльный ирис,
И легкой пеной пенится
Бокал Христовых Слез...

Пляши и пой на пире,
Флоренция, изменница,
В венке спаленных роз!..

Сведи с ума канцоной
О преданной любви,
И сделай ночь бессонной,
И струны оборви,
И бей в свой бубен гулкий,
Рыдания тая!
В пустынном переулке
Скорбит душа твоя...

*Август 1909*

# VERSES FROM THE COLLECTION
## "РАЗНЫЕ СТИХОТВОРЕНИЯ"
### (1908–1916)

### 72. ДРУЗЬЯМ

> Молчите, проклятые струны!
>
> *А. Майков*

Друг другу мы тайно враждебны,
Завистливы, глухи, чужды,
А как бы и жить и работать,
Не зная извечной вражды!

Чтó делать! Ведь каждый старался
Свой собственный дом отравить,
Все стены пропитаны ядом,
И негде главы приклонить!

Чтó делать! Изверившись в счастье,
От смеху мы сходим с ума
И, пьяные, с улицы смотрим,
Как рушатся наши дома!

Предатели в жизни и дружбе,
Пустых расточители слов,
Чтó делать! Мы путь расчищаем
Для наших далеких сынов!

Когда под забором в крапиве
Несчастные кости сгниют,
Какой-нибудь поздний историк
Напишет внушительный труд...

Вот только замучит, проклятый,
Ни в чем не повинных ребят
Годами рожденья и смерти
И ворохом скверных цитат...

Печальная доля — так сложно,
Так трудно и празднично жить;
И стать достояньем доцента,
И критиков новых плодить...

Зарыться бы в свежем бурьяне,
Забыться бы сном навсегда!
Молчите, проклятые книги!
Я вас не писал никогда!

*24 июля 1908*


## 73. СОН

*Моей матери*

Я видел сон: мы в древнем склепе
Схоронены; а жизнь идет
Вверху — всё громче, всё нелепей;
И день последний настает.

Чуть брежжит утро Воскресенья.
Труба далекая слышна.
Над нами — красные каменья
И мавзолей из чугуна.

И он идет из дымной дали;
И ангелы с мечами — с ним;
Такой, как в книгах мы читали,
Скучая и не веря им.

Под аркою того же свода
Лежит спокойная жена;
Но ей не дорога свобода:
Не хочет воскресать она...

И слышу, мать мне рядом шепчет:
«Мой сын, ты в жизни был силен:
Нажми рукою свод покрепче,
И камень будет отвален». —

«Нет, мать. Я задохнулся в гробе,
И больше нет бывалых сил.
Молитесь и просите обе,
Чтоб ангел камень отвалил».

*20 июня 1910*

## 74. ХУДОЖНИК

В жаркое лето и в зиму метельную,
В дни ваших свадеб, торжеств, похорон,
Жду, чтоб спугнул мою скуку смертельную
Легкий, доселе не слышанный звон.

Вот он — возник. И с холодным вниманием
Жду, чтоб понять, закрепить и убить.
И перед зорким моим ожиданием
Тянет он еле приметную нить.

С моря ли вихрь? Или сирины райские
В листьях поют? Или время стоит?
Или осыпали яблони майские
Снежный свой цвет? Или ангел летит?

Длятся часы, мировое несущие.
Ширятся звуки, движенье и свет.
Прошлое страстно глядится в грядущее.
Нет настоящего. Жалкого — нет.

И, наконец, у предела зачатия
Новой души, неизведанных сил, —
Душу сражает, как громом, проклятие:
Творческий разум осилил — убил.

И замыкаю я в клетку холодную
Легкую, добрую птицу свободную,
Птицу, летевшую смерть унести,
Птицу, летевшую душу спасти.

Вот моя клетка — стальная, тяжелая,
Как золотая, в вечернем огне.
Вот моя птица, когда-то веселая,
Обруч качает, поет на окне.

Крылья подрезаны, песни заучены.
Любите вы под окном постоять?
Песни вам нравятся. Я же, измученный,
Нового жду — и скучаю опять.

*12 декабря 1913*

## 75.

Ты твердишь, что я холоден, замкнут и сух,
Да, таким я и буду с тобой:
Не для ласковых слов я выковывал дух,
Не для дружб я боролся с судьбой.

Ты и сам был когда-то мрачней и смелей,
По звездам прочитать ты умел,
Что грядущие ночи — темней и темней,
Что ночам неизвестен предел.

Вот — свершилось. Весь мир одичал, и окрест
Ни один не мерцает маяк.
И тому, кто не понял вещания звезд, —
Нестерпим окружающий мрак.

И у тех, кто не знал, что прошедшее есть,
Что грядущего ночь не пуста, —
Затуманила сердце усталость и месть,
Отвращенье скривило уста...

Было время надежды и веры большой —
Был я прост и доверчив, как ты.
Шел я к людям с открытой и детской душой,
Не пугаясь людской клеветы...

А теперь — тех надежд не отыщешь следа,
Всё к далеким звездам унеслось.
И к кому шел с открытой душою тогда,
От того отвернуться пришлось.

И сама та душа, что, пылая, ждала,
Треволненьям отдаться спеша, —
И враждой, и любовью она изошла,
И сгорела она, та душа.

И остались — улыбкой сведенная бровь,
Сжатый рот и печальная власть
Бунтовать ненасытную женскую кровь,
Зажигая звериную страсть...

Не стучись же напрасно у плотных дверей,
Тщетным стоном себя не томи:
Ты не встретишь участья у бедных зверей,
Называвшихся прежде людьми.

Ты — железною маской лицо закрывай,
Поклоняясь священным гробам,
Охраняя железом до времени рай,
Недоступный безумным рабам.

*9 июня 1916*

# VERSES FROM THE COLLECTION

## "АРФЫ И СКРИПКИ"

### (1908–1916)

### 76.

Свирель запела на мосту,
        И яблони в цвету.
И ангел поднял в высоту
        Звезду зеленую одну,
И стало дивно на мосту
Смотреть в такую глубину,
        В такую высоту.

Свирель поет: взошла звезда,
        Пастух, гони стада …
И под мостом поет вода:
        Смотри, какие быстрины́,
Оставь заботы навсегда,
Такой прозрачной глубины
        Не видел никогда …
Такой глубокой тишины
        Не слышал никогда …

Смотри, какие быстрины,
Когда ты видел эти сны?..
*22 мая 1908*

### 77.

И я любил. И я изведал
Безумный хмель любовных мук,
И пораженья, и победы,
И имя: *враг;* и слово: *друг.*

Их было много … Что́ я знаю?
Воспоминанья, тени сна …
Я только странно повторяю
Их золотые имена.

Их было много. Но одною
Чертой соединил их я,
Одной безумной красотою,
Чье имя: страсть и жизнь моя.

И страсти таинство свершая,
И поднимаясь над землей,
Я видел, как идет другая
На ложе страсти роковой...

И те же ласки, те же речи,
Постылый трепет жадных уст,
И примелькавшиеся плечи...
Нет! Мир бесстрастен, чист и пуст!

И, наполняя грудь весельем,
С вершины самых снежных скал
Я шлю лавину тем ущельям,
Где я любил и целовал!

*30 марта 1908*

## 78.

*Вл. Пясту*

Май жестокий с белыми ночами!
Вечный стук в ворота: выходи!
Голубая дымка за плечами,
Неизвестность, гибель впереди!
Женщины с безумными очами,
С вечно смятой розой на груди! —
Пробудись! Пронзи меня мечами,
От страстей моих освободи!

Хорошо в лугу широком кру́гом
В хороводе пламенном пройти,
Пить вино, смеяться с милым другом
И венки узорные плести,
Раздарить цветы чужим подругам,
Страстью, грустью, счастьем изойти, —
Но достойней за тяжелым плугом
В свежих росах по́утру идти!

*28 мая 1908*

## 79.

Я пригвожден к трактирной стойке.
Я пьян давно. Мне всё — равно.
Вон счастие мое — на тройке
В сребристый дым унесено...

Летит на тройке, потонуло
В снегу времен, в дали веков...
И только душу захлестнуло
Сребристой мглой из-под подков...

В глухую темень искры мечет,
От искр всю ночь, всю ночь светло...
Бубенчик под дугой лепечет
О том, что счастие прошло...

И только сбруя золотая
Всю ночь видна... Всю ночь слышна...
А ты, душа... душа глухая...
Пьяным пьяна... пьяным пьяна...

*26 октября 1908*


## 80.

Бывают тихие минуты:
Узор морозный на стекле;
Мечта невольно льнет к чему-то,
Скучая в комнатном тепле...

И вдруг — туман сырого сада,
Железный мост через ручей,
Вся в розах серая ограда,
И синий, синий плен очей...

О чем-то шепчущие струи,
Кружащаяся голова...
Твои, хохлушка, поцелуи,
Твои, гортанные слова...

*Июнь 1909*

## 81.

Была ты всех ярче, верней и прелестней,
Не кляни же меня, не кляни!
Мой поезд летит, как цыганская песня,
Как те невозвратные дни...

Что было любимо — всё мимо, мимо,
Впереди — неизвестность пути...
Благословенно, неизгладимо,
Невозвратимо... прости!

*31 августа 1914*

## 82.

За горами, лесами,
За дорогами пыльными,
За холмами могильными —
Под другими цветешь небесами...

И когда забелеет гора,
Дол оденется зеленью вешнею,
Вспоминаю с печалью нездешнею
Всё былое мое как вчера...

В снах печальных тебя узнаю
И сжимаю руками моими
Чародейную руку твою,
Повторяя далекое имя.

*30 сентября 1915*

# VERSES FROM THE COLLECTION

## "КАРМЕН"

### (1914)

### 83.

Есть демон утра. Дымно-светел он,
Золотокудрый и счастливый.
Как небо, синь струящийся хитон,
Весь — перламутра переливы.

Но как ночною тьмой сквозит лазурь,
Так этот лик сквозит порой ужасным,
И золото кудрей — червонно-красным,
И голос — рокотом забытых бурь.

*24 марта 1914*

### 84.

Среди поклонников Кармен,
Спешащих пестрою толпою,
Ее зовущих за собою,
Один, как тень у серых стен
Ночной таверны Лиллас-Пастья,
Молчит и сумрачно глядит,
Не ждет, не требует участья,
Когда же бубен зазвучит
И глухо зазвенят запястья, —
Он вспоминает дни весны,
Он средь бушующих созвучий
Глядит на стан ее певучий
И видит творческие сны.

*26 марта 1914*

## 85.

Ты — как отзвук забытого гимна
В моей черной и дикой судьбе.
О, Кармен, мне печально и дивно,
Что приснился мне сон о тебе.

Вешний трепет, и лепет, и шелест,
Непробудные, дикие сны,
И твоя одичалая прелесть —
Как гитара, как бубен весны!

И проходишь ты в думах и грезах,
Как царица блаженных времен,
С головой, утопающей в розах,
Погруженная в сказочный сон.

Спишь, змеею склубясь прихотливой,
Спишь в дурмане и видишь во сне
Даль морскую и берег счастливый,
И мечту, недоступную мне.

Видишь день беззакатный и жгучий
И любимый, родимый свой край,
Синий, синий, певучий, певучий,
Неподвижно-блаженный, как рай.

В том раю тишина бездыханна,
Только в куще сплетенных ветвей
Дивный голос твой, низкий и странный,
Славит бурю цыганских страстей.

*28 марта 1914*

## 86.

*О да, любовь вольна, как птица,*
    *Да, всё равно — я твой!*
*Да, всё равно мне будет сниться*
    *Твой стан, твой огневой!*

*Да, в хищной силе рук прекрасных,*
    *В очах, где грусть измен,*
*Весь бред моих страстей напрасных,*
    *Моих ночей, Кармен!*

Я буду петь тебя, я небу
    Твой голос передам!
Как иерей, свершу я требу
    За твой огонь — звездам!

Ты встанешь бурною волною
    В реке моих стихов,
И я с руки моей не смою,
    Кармен, твоих духов...

И в тихий час ночной, как пламя,
    Сверкнувшее на миг,
Блеснет мне белыми зубами
    Твой неотступный лик.

Да, я томлюсь надеждой сладкой,
    Что ты, в чужой стране,
Что ты, когда-нибудь, украдкой
    Помыслишь обо мне...

За бурей жизни, за тревогой,
    За грустью всех измен, —
Пусть эта мысль предстанет строгой,
    Простой и белой, как дорога,
    Как дальний путь, Кармен!

*28 марта 1914*

## 87.

Нет, никогда моей, и ты ничьей не будешь.
Так вот что так влекло сквозь бездну грустных лет,
Сквозь бездну дней пустых, чье бремя не избудешь.
Вот почему я — твой поклонник и поэт!

*Здесь* — страшная печать отверженности женской
За прелесть дивную — постичь ее нет сил.
*Там* — дикий сплав миров, где часть души вселенской
Рыдает, исходя гармонией светил.

Вот — мой восторг, мой страх в тот вечер в темном зале!
Вот, бедная, зачем тревожусь за тебя!
Вот чьи глаза меня так странно провожали,
Еще не угадав, не зная... не любя!

Сама себе закон — летишь, летишь ты мимо,
К созвездиям иным, не ведая орбит,
И этот мир тебе — лишь красный облак дыма,
Где что-то жжет, поет, тревожит и горит!

И в зареве его — твоя безумна младость...
Всё — музыка и свет: нет счастья, нет измен...
Мелодией одной звучат печаль и радость...
Но я люблю тебя: я сам такой, *Кармен*.

*31 марта 1914*

## 88.

### ПЕРЕД СУДОМ

Чтó же ты потупилась в смущеньи?
Погляди, как прежде, на меня.
Вот какой ты стала — в униженьи,
В резком, неподкупном свете дня!

Я и сам ведь не такой — не прежний,
Недоступный, гордый, чистый, злой.
Я смотрю добрей и безнадежней
На простой и скучный путь земной.

Я не только не имею права,
Я тебя не в силах упрекнуть
За мучительный твой, за лукавый,
Многим женщинам сужденный путь...

Но ведь я немного по-другому,
Чем иные, знаю жизнь твою,
Более, чем судьям, мне знакомо,
Как ты очутилась на краю.

Вместе ведь по краю, было время,
Нас водила пагубная страсть,
Мы хотели вместе сбросить бремя
И лететь, чтобы потом упасть.

Ты всегда мечтала, что, сгорая,
Догорим мы вместе — ты и я,
Что дано, в объятьях умирая,
Увидать блаженные края...

Что же делать, если обманула
Та мечта, как всякая мечта,
И что жизнь безжалостно стегнула
Грубою веревкою кнута?

Не до нас ей, жизни торопливой,
И мечта права, что нам лгала. —
Всё-таки, когда-нибудь счастливой
Разве ты со мною не была?

Эта прядь — такая золотая
Разве не от старого огня? —
Страстная, безбожная, пустая,
Незабвенная, прости меня!

*11 октября 1915*

# VERSES FROM THE COLLECTION

## "РОДИНА"

### (1907–1916)

### 89.

В густой траве пропадешь с головой.
В тихий дом войдешь, не стучась…
Обнимет рукой, оплетет косой
И, статная, скажет: «Здравствуй, князь.

Вот здесь у меня — куст белых роз.
Вот здесь вчера — повилика вилась.
Где был, пропадал? что за весть принес?
Кто любит, не любит, кто гонит нас?»

Как бывало, забудешь, что дни идут,
Как бывало, простишь, кто горд и зол.
И смотришь — тучи вдали встают,
И слушаешь песни далеких сел…

Заплачет сердце по чужой стороне,
Запросится в бой — зовет и манит…
Только скажет: «Прощай. Вернись ко мне» —
И опять за травой колокольчик звенит…

*12 июля 1907*

## 90. НА ПОЛЕ КУЛИКОВОМ

### 1

Река раскинулась. Течет, грустит лениво
    И моет берега.
Над скудной глиной желтого обрыва
    В степи грустят стога.

О, Русь моя! Жена моя! До боли
    Нам ясен долгий путь!
Наш путь — стрелой татарской древней воли
    Пронзил нам грудь.

Наш путь — степной, наш путь — в тоске безбрежной,
    В твоей тоске, о, Русь!
И даже мглы — ночной и зарубежной —
    Я не боюсь.

Пусть ночь. Домчимся. Озарим кострами
    Степную даль.
В степном дыму блеснет святое знамя
    И ханской сабли сталь...

И вечный бой! Покой нам только снится
    Сквозь кровь и пыль...
Летит, летит степная кобылица
    И мнет ковыль...

И нет конца! Мелькают версты, кручи...
    Останови!
Идут, идут испуганные тучи,
    Закат в крови!

Закат в крови! Из сердца кровь струится!
    Плачь, сердце, плачь...
Покоя нет! Степная кобылица
    Несется вскачь!

*7 июня 1908*

## 2

Мы, сам-друг, над степью в полночь стали:
Не вернуться, не взглянуть назад.
За Непрядвой лебеди кричали,
И опять, опять они кричат...

На пути — горючий белый камень.
За рекой — поганая орда.
Светлый стяг над нашими полками
Не взыграет больше никогда.

И, к земле склонившись головою,
Говорит мне друг: «Остри свой меч,
Чтоб недаром биться с татарвою,
За святое дело мертвым лечь!»

Я — не первый воин, не последний,
Долго будет родина больна.
Помяни ж за раннею обедней
Мила друга, светлая жена!

*8 июня 1908*

## 3

В ночь, когда Мамай залег с ордою
    Степи и мосты,
В темном поле были мы с Тобою, —
    Разве знала Ты?

Перед Доном темным и зловещим,
    Средь ночных полей,
Слышал я Твой голос сердцем вещим
    В криках лебедей.

С полунóчи тучей возносилась
    Княжеская рать,
И вдали, вдали о стремя билась,
    Голосила мать.

И, чертя круги, ночные птицы
    Реяли вдали.
А над Русью тихие зарницы
    Князя стерегли.

Орлий клёкот над татарским станом
    Угрожал бедой,
А Непрядва убралась туманом,
    Что княжна фатой.

И с туманом над Непрядвой спящей,
    Прямо на меня
Ты сошла, в одежде свет струящей,
    Не спугнув коня.

Серебром волны блеснула другу
　　На стальном мече,
Освежила пыльную кольчугу
　　На моем плече.

И когда, наутро, тучей черной
　　Двинулась орда,
Был в щите Твой лик нерукотворный
　　Светел навсегда.

*14 июня 1908*

### 4

Опять с вековою тоскою
Пригнулись к земле ковыли.
Опять за туманной рекою
Ты кличешь меня издали́...

Умчались, пропали без вести
Степных кобылиц табуны,
Развязаны дикие страсти
Под игом ущербной луны.

И я с вековою тоскою,
Как волк под ущербной луной,
Не знаю, что делать с собою,
Куда мне лететь за тобой!

Я слушаю рокоты сечи
И трубные крики татар,
Я вижу над Русью далече
Широкий и тихий пожар.

Объятый тоскою могучей,
Я рыщу на белом коне...
Встречаются вольные тучи
Во мглистой ночной вышине.

Вздымаются светлые мысли
В растерзанном сердце моем,
И падают светлые мысли,
Сожженные темным огнем...

«Явись, мое дивное диво!
Быть светлым меня научи!»
Вздымается конская грива...
За ветром взывают мечи...

*31 июля 1908*


### 5

И мглою бед неотразимых
Грядущий день заволокло.

*Вл. Соловьев*

Опять над полем Куликовым
Взошла и расточилась мгла,
И, словно облаком суровым,
Грядущий день заволокла.

За тишиною непробудной,
За разливающейся мглой
Не слышно грома битвы чудной,
Не видно молньи боевой.

Но узнаю тебя, начало
Высоких и мятежных дней!
Над вражьим станом, как бывало,
И плеск и трубы лебедей.

Не может сердце жить покоем,
Недаром тучи собрались.
Доспех тяжел, как перед боем.
Теперь твой час настал. — Молись!

*23 декабря 1908*


## 91. РОССИЯ

Опять, как в годы золотые,
Три стертых треплются шлеи,
И вязнут спицы росписные
В расхлябанные колеи...

Россия, нищая Россия,
Мне избы серые твои,
Твои мне песни ветровые —
Как слезы первые любви!

Тебя жалеть я не умею
И крест свой бережно несу...
Какому хочешь чародею
Отдай разбойную красу!

Пускай заманит и обманет, —
Не пропадешь, не сгинешь ты,
И лишь забота затуманит
Твои прекрасные черты...

Ну что ж? Одной заботой боле —
Одной слезой река шумней,
А ты всё та же — лес, да поле,
Да плат узорный до бровей...

И невозможное возможно,
Дорога долгая легка,
Когда блеснет в дали дорожной
Мгновенный взор из-под платка,
Когда звенит тоской острожной
Глухая песня ямщика!..

*18 октября 1908*


## 92.

Русь моя, жизнь моя, вместе ль нам маяться?
Царь, да Сибирь, да Ермак, да тюрьма!
Эх, не пора ль разлучиться, раскаяться...
Вольному сердцу на что твоя тьма?

Знала ли что? Или в бога ты верила?
Что там услышишь из песен твоих?
Чудь начудила, да Меря намерила
Гатей, дорог да столбов верстовых...

Лодки да грады по рекам рубила ты,
Но до Царьградских святынь не дошла...
Соколов, лебедей в степь распустила ты —
Кинулась и́з степи черная мгла...

Зá море Черное, зá море Белое
В черные ночи и в белые дни
Дико глядится лицо онемелое,
Очи татарские мечут огни...

Тихое, долгое, красное зарево
Каждую ночь над становьем твоим...
Чтó же маячишь ты, сонное марево?
Вольным играешься духом моим?

*28 февраля 1910*

## 93.

Приближается звук. И, покорна щемящему звуку,
    Молодеет душа.
И во сне прижимаю к губам твою прежнюю руку,
    Не дыша.

Снится — снова я мальчик, и снова любовник,
    И овраг, и бурьян,
И в бурьяне — колючий шиповник,
    И вечерний туман.

Сквозь цветы, и листы, и колючие ветки, я знаю,
    Старый дом глянет в сердце мое,
Глянет небо опять, розовея от краю до краю,
    И окошко твое.

Этот голос — он твой, и его непонятному звуку
    Жизнь и горе отдам,
Хоть во сне твою прежнюю милую руку
    Прижимая к губам.

*2 мая 1912*

## 94. НОВАЯ АМЕРИКА

Праздник радостный, праздник великий,
Да звезда из-за туч не видна...
Ты стоишь под метелицей дикой,
Роковая, родная страна.

За снегами, лесами, степями
Твоего мне не видно лица.
Только ль страшный простор пред очами,
Непонятная ширь без конца?

Утопая в глубоком сугробе,
Я на утлые санки сажусь.
Не в богатом покоишься гробе
Ты, убогая финская Русь!

Там прикинешься ты богомольной,
Там старушкой прикинешься ты,
Глас молитвенный, звон колокольный,
За крестами — кресты, да кресты...

Только ладан твой синий и росный
Просквозит мне порою иным...
Нет, не старческий лик и не постный
Под московским платочком цветным!

Сквозь земные поклоны, да свечи,
Ектеньи, ектеньи, ектеньи —
Шопотливые, тихие речи,
Запылавшие щеки твои...

Дальше, дальше... И ветер рванулся,
Черноземным летя пустырем...
Куст дорожный по ветру метнулся,
Словно дьякон взмахнул орарем...

А уж там, за рекой полноводной,
Где пригнулись к земле ковыли,
Тянет гарью горючей, свободной,
Слышны гуды в далекой дали...

Иль опять это — стан половецкий
И татарская буйная крепь?
Не пожаром ли фески турецкой
Забуянила дикая степь?

Нет, не видно там княжьего стяга,
Не шеломами черпают Дон,
И прекрасная внучка варяга
Не клянет половецкий полон...

Нет, не вьются там пó ветру чубы,
Не пестреют в степях бунчуки...
Там чернеют фабричные трубы,
Там заводские стонут гудки.

Путь степной — без конца, без исхода,
Степь, да ветер, да ветер, — и вдруг
Многоярусный корпус завода,
Города из рабочих лачуг...

На пустынном просторе, на диком
Ты всё та, что была, и не та,
Новым ты обернулась мне ликом,
И другая волнует мечта...

Черный уголь — подземный мессия,
Черный уголь — здесь царь и жених,
Но не страшен, невеста, Россия,
Голос каменных песен твоих!

Уголь стонет, и соль забелелась,
И железная воет руда...
То над степью пустой загорелась
Мне Америки новой звезда!

*12 декабря 1913*

## 95.

*Моей матери*

Ветер стих, и слава заревая
    Облекла вон те пруды.
Вон и схимник. Книгу закрывая,
    Он смиренно ждет звезды.

Но бежит шоссейная дорога,
    Убегает вбок...
Дай вздохнуть, помедли, ради бога,
    Не хрусти, песок!

Славой золотеет заревою
    Монастырский крест издалека.
Не свернуть ли к вечному покою?
    Да и что за жизнь без клобука?..

И опять влечет неудержимо
Вдаль из тихих мест
Путь шоссейный, пробегая мимо,
Мимо инока, прудов и звезд...

*Август 1914*

## 96.

Грешить бесстыдно, непробудно,
Счет потерять ночам и дням,
И, с головой от хмеля трудной,
Пройти сторонкой в божий храм.

Три раза преклониться долу,
Семь — осенить себя крестом,
Тайком к заплеванному полу
Горячим прикоснуться лбом.

Кладя в тарелку грошик медный,
Три, да еще семь раз подряд
Поцеловать столетний, бедный
И зацелованный оклад.

А воротясь домой, обмерить
На тот же грош кого-нибудь,
И пса голодного от двери,
Икнув, ногою отпихнуть.

И под лампадой у иконы
Пить чай, отщелкивая счет,
Потом переслюнить купоны,
Пузатый отворив комод,

И на перины пуховые
В тяжелом завалиться сне...
Да, и такой, моя Россия,
Ты всех краев дороже мне.

*26 августа 1914*

## 97.

*З. Н. Гиппиус*

Рожденные в года глухие
Пути не помнят своего.
Мы — дети страшных лет России —
Забыть не в силах ничего.

Испепеляющие годы!
Безумья ль в вас, надежды ль весть?
От дней войны, от дней свободы —
Кровавый отсвет в лицах есть.

Есть немота — то гул набата
Заставил заградить уста.
В сердцах, восторженных когда-то,
Есть роковая пустота.

И пусть над нашим смертным ложем
Взовьется с криком воронье, —
Те, кто достойней, боже, боже,
Да узрят царствие твое!

*8 сентября 1914*


## 98. КОРШУН

Чертя за кругом плавный круг,
Над сонным лугом коршун кружит
И смотрит на пустынный луг. —
В избушке мать над сыном тужит:
«На́ хлеба, на́, на́ грудь, соси,
Расти, покорствуй, крест неси».

Идут века, шумит война,
Встает мятеж, горят деревни,
А ты всё та ж, моя страна,
В красе заплаканной и древней. —
Доколе матери тужить?
Доколе коршуну кружить?

*22 марта 1916*

## 99.

(Extract from "Ответ Мережковскому")

Родина — это огромное, родное, дышащее существо, подобное человеку, но бесконечно более уютное, ласковое, беспомощное, чем отдельный человек; человек — маленькая монада, состоящая из веселых стальных мышц телесных и душевных, сам себе хозяин в этом мире, когда здоров и здрав, пойдет куда захочет, и сделает, что пожелает, ни перед кем, кроме бога и себя, не отвечает он за свои поступки. Так пел человека еще Софокл, таков он всегда, вечно юный.

Родина — древнее, бесконечно древнее существо, большое, потому неповоротливое, и самому ему не счесть никогда своих сил, своих мышц, своих возможностей, так они рассеяны по матушке-земле. Родине суждено быть некогда покинутой, как матери, когда сын ее, человек, вырастает до звезд и найдет себе невесту. Эту обреченность на покинутость мы всегда видим в больших материнских глазах родины, всегда печальных, даже тогда, когда она отдыхает и тихо радуется. Не родина оставит человека, а человек родину. Мы еще дети и не знаем сроков, только читаем их по звездам; но, однако, читаем уже, что близко время, когда границы сотрутся и родиной станет вся земля, а потом и не одна земля, а бесконечная вселенная, только мало крыльев из полотна и стали, некогда крылья Духа понесут нас в объятия Вечности. Время близко, потому что мы читаем о нем в звездах, но оно бесконечно далеко для нашего младенческого духа, так далеко, как звезды от авиатора, берущего мировой рекорд высоты. И земная родина еще поит нас и кормит у груди, мы ей обязаны нашими силами и вдохновениями и радостями.

*Ноябрь 1910*

# AN EXTRACT FROM THE LONG POEM

## "ВОЗМЕЗДИЕ"

### ПЕРВАЯ ГЛАВА

Век девятнадцатый, железный,
Воистину жестокий век!
Тобою в мрак ночной, беззвездный
Беспечный брошен человек!
В ночь умозрительных понятий,
Матерьялистских малых дел,
Бессильных жалоб и проклятий
Бескровных душ и слабых тел!
С тобой пришли чуме на смену
Нейрастения, скука, сплин,
Век расшибанья лбов о стену
Экономических доктрин,
Конгрессов, банков, федераций,
Застольных спичей, красных слов,
Век акций, рент и облигаций,
И малодейственных умов,
И дарований половинных
(Так справедливей — пополам!),
Век не салонов, а гостиных,
Не Рекамье, — а просто дам...
Век буржуазного богаства
(Растущего незримо зла!).
Под знаком равенства и братства
Здесь зрели темные дела...
А человек? — Он жил безвольно:
Не он — машины, города,
«Жизнь» так бескровно и безбольно
Пытала дух, как никогда...
Но тот, кто двигал, управляя
Марионетками всех стран, —

Тот знал, что делал, насылая
Гуманистический туман:
Там, в сером и гнилом тумане,
Увяла плоть, и дух погас,
И ангел сам священной брани,
Казалось, отлетел от нас:
Там — распри кровные решают
Дипломатическим умом,
Там — пушки новые мешают
Сойтись лицом к лицу с врагом,
Там — вместо храбрости — нахальство,
А вместо подвигов — «психоз»,
И вечно ссорится начальство,
И длинный громоздко́й обоз
Воло́чит за собой команда,
Штаб, интендантов, грязь кляня,
Рожком горниста — рог Роланда
И шлем — фуражкой заменя...
Тот век немало проклинали
И не устанут проклинать.
И как избыть его печали?
Он мягко стлал — да жестко спать...

Двадцатый век... Еще бездомней,
Еще страшнее жизни мгла
(Еще чернее и огромней
Тень Люциферова крыла).
Пожары дымные заката
(Пророчества о нашем дне),
Кометы грозной и хвостатой
Ужасный призрак в вышине,
Безжалостный конец Мессины
(Стихийных сил не превозмочь),
И неустанный рев машины,
Кующей гибель день и ночь,
Сознанье страшное обмана
Всех прежних малых дум и вер,
И первый взлет аэроплана
В пустыню неизвестных сфер...
И отвращение от жизни,
И к ней безумная любовь,

И страсть и ненависть к отчизне...
И черная, земная кровь
Сулит нам, раздувая вены,
Все разрушая рубежи,
Неслыханные перемены,
Невиданные мятежи...
Чтó ж, человек? — За ревом стали,
В огне, в пороховом дыму,
Какие огненные дали
Открылись взору твоему?
О чем — машин немолчный скрежет?
Зачем — пропеллер, воя, режет
Туман холодный — и пустой?

# VERSES FROM THE COLLECTION

## "О ЧЕМ ПОЕТ ВЕТЕР"

### (1913)

### 101.

Поет, поет...
Поет и ходит возле дома...
И грусть, и нежность, и истома,
Как прежде, зá сердце берет...

Нетяжко бремя,
Всей жизни бремя прожитой,
И песнью длинной и простой
Баюкает и нежит время...

Так древни мы,
Так древен мира
Бег,
И лира
Поет нам снег
Седой зимы,
Поет нам снег седой зимы...

Туда, туда,
На снеговую грудь
Последней ночи...
Вздохнуть — и очи
Навсегда
Сомкнуть,
Сомкнуть в объятьях ночи...

Возврата нет
Страстям и думам...
Смотри, смотри:
С полночным шумом
Идет к нам ветер от зари...
Последний свет
Померк. Умри.
Померк последний свет зари.

*19 октября 1913*


## 102.

Милый друг, и в этом тихом доме
    Лихорадка бьет меня.
Не найти мне места в тихом доме
    Возле мирного огня!


Голоса поют, взывает вьюга,
    Страшен мне уют...
Даже за плечом твоим, подруга,
    Чьи-то очи стерегут!


За твоими тихими плечами
    Слышу трепет крыл...
Бьет в меня светящими очами
    Ангел бури — Азраил!

*Октябрь 1913*

# 103. ДВЕНАДЦАТЬ

## 1

Черный вечер.
Белый снег.
Ветер, ветер!
На ногах не стоит человек.
Ветер, ветер —
На всем божьем свете!

Завивает ветер
Белый снежок.
Под снежком — ледок.
Скользко, тяжко,
Всякий ходок
Скользит — ах, бедняжка!

От здания к зданию
Протянут канат.
На канате — плакат:
«Вся власть Учредительному Собранию!»
Старушка убивается — плачет,
Никак не поймет, что значит,
На что такой плакат,
Такой огромный лоскут?
Сколько бы вышло портянок для ребят,
А всякий — раздет, разут…

Старушка, как курица,
Кой-как перемотнулась через сугроб.
— Ох, Матушка-Заступница!
— Ох, большевики загонят в гроб!

Ветер хлесткий!
Не отстает и мороз!
И буржуй на перекрестке
В воротник упрятал нос.

А это кто? — Длинные волосы
И говорит вполголоса:
　　— Предатели!
　　— Погибла Россия!
Должно быть, писатель —
　　Вития...

А вон и долгополый —
Сторонкой — за сугроб...
Что нынче невеселый,
　　Товарищ поп?

Помнишь, как бывало
Брюхом шел вперед,
И крестом сияло
Брюхо на народ?..

Вон барыня в каракуле
К другой подвернулась:
— Ужь мы плакали, плакали...
　　Поскользнулась
И — бац — растянулась!

　　　Ай, ай!
　　Тяни, подымай!

Ветер веселый
И зол, и рад.
Крутит подолы,
Прохожих косит,

Рвет, мнет и носит
Большой плакат:
«Вся власть Учредительному Собранию»...
И слова доносит:

...И у нас было собрание...
...Вот в этом здании...
　...Обсудили —
　　Постановили:
На время — десять, на́ ночь — двадцать пять...
　...И меньше — ни с кого не брать...
　　...Пойдем спать...

Поздний вечер.
Пустеет улица.
Один бродяга
Сутулится,
Да свищет ветер...

Эй, бедняга!
    Подходи —
Поцелуемся...

Хлеба!
Что впереди?
Проходи!

Черное, черное небо.

Злоба, грустная злоба
    Кипит в груди...
Черная злоба, святая злоба...

Товарищ! Гляди
    В оба!


2

Гуляет ветер, порхает снег.
Идут двенадцать человек.

Винтовок черные ремни,
Кругом — огни, огни, огни...

В зубах — цыгарка, примят картуз,
На спину б надо бубновый туз!

Свобода, свобода,
    Эх, эх, без креста!

Тра-та-та!

Холодно, товарищи, холодно!

— А Ванька с Катькой — в кабаке...
— У ей керенки есть в чулке!

— Ванюшка сам теперь богат...
— Был Ванька наш, а стал солдат!

— Ну, Ванька, сукин сын, буржуй,
Мою, попробуй, поцелуй!

        Свобода, свобода,
     Эх, эх, без креста!
     Катька с Ванькой занята —
     Чем, чем занята?..

        Тра-та-та!

Кругом — огни, огни, огни...
Оплечь — ружейные ремни...

Революцьонный держите шаг!
Неугомонный не дремлет враг!

Товарищ, винтовку держи, не трусь!
Пальнем-ка пулей в Святую Русь —

        В кондову́ю,
        В избяну́ю,
     В толстозадую!

     Эх, эх, без креста!


                3

     Как пошли наши ребята
     В красной гвардии служить —
     В красной гвардии служить —
     Буйну голову сложить!

     Эх ты, горе-горькое,
     Сладкое житье!
     Рваное пальтишко,
     Австрийское ружье!

Мы на горе всем буржуям
Мировой пожар раздуем,
Мировой пожар в крови —
Господи, благослови!


4

Снег крутит, лихач кричит,
Ванька с Катькою летит —
Електрический фонарик
    На оглобельках...
    Ах, ах, пади!..

Он в шинелишке солдатской
С физиономией дурацкой
Крутит, крутит черный ус,
    Да покручивает,
    Да пошучивает...

Вот так Ванька — он плечист!
Вот так Ванька — он речист!
    Катьку-дуру обнимает,
    Заговаривает...

Запрокинулась лицом,
Зубки блещут жемчугóм...
    Ах ты, Катя, моя Катя,
    Толстоморденькая...


5

У тебя на шее, Катя,
Шрам не зажил от ножа.
У тебя под грудью, Катя,
Та царапина свежа!

    Эх, эх, попляши!
    Больно ножки хороши!

В кружевном белье ходила —
Походи-ка, походи!
С офицерами блудила —
Поблуди-ка, поблуди!

Эх, эх, поблуди!
Сердце ёкнуло в груди!

Помнишь, Катя, офицера —
Не ушел он от ножа...
Аль не вспомнила, холера?
Али память не свежа?

   Эх, эх, освежи,
   Спать с собою положи!

Гетры серые носила,
Шоколад Миньон жрала,
С юнкерьем гулять ходила —
С солдатьем теперь пошла?

   Эх, эх, согреши!
   Будет легче для души!

## 6

...Опять навстречу несется вскачь,
Летит, вопит, орет лихач...

Стой, стой! Андрюха, помогай!
Петруха, сзаду забегай!..

Трах-тарарах-тах-тах-тах-тах!
Вскрутился к небу снежный прах!..

Лихач — и с Ванькой — наутек...
Еще разок! Взводи курок!..

Трах-тарарах! Ты будешь знать,
. . . . . . . . . . . . . . . . .
Как с девочкой чужой гулять!..

Утек, подлец! Ужо, постой,
Расправлюсь завтра я с тобой!

А Катька где? — Мертва, мертва!
Простреленная голова!

Что, Катька, рада? — Ни гу-гу...
Лежи ты, падаль, на снегу!

Революцьонный держите шаг!
Неугомонный не дремлет враг!


## 7

И опять идут двенадцать,
За плечами — ружьеца.
Лишь у бедного убийцы
Не видать совсем лица...

Всё быстрее и быстрее
Уторапливает шаг.
Замотал платок на шее —
Не оправиться никак...

— Что, товарищ, ты не весел?
— Что, дружок, оторопел?
— Что, Петруха, нос повесил,
Или Катьку пожалел?

— Ох, товарищи, родные,
Эту девку я любил...
Ночки черные, хмельные
С этой девкой проводил...

— Из-за удали бедовой
В огневых ее очах,
Из-за родинки пунцовой
Возле правого плеча,
Загубил я, бестолковый,
Загубил я сгоряча... ах!

— Ишь, стервец, завел шарманку,
Что ты, Петька, баба что ль?
— Верно, душу наизнанку
Вздумал вывернуть? Изволь!
— Поддержи свою осанку!
— Над собой держи контроль!

— Не такое нынче время,
Чтобы няньчиться с тобой!
Потяжеле будет бремя
Нам, товарищ дорогой!

И Петруха замедляет
Торопливые шаги...

Он головку вскидавáет,
Он опять повеселел...

   Эх, эх!
Позабавиться не грех!

Запирайте етажи,
Нынче будут грабежи!

Отмыкайте погреба —
Гуляет нынче голытьба!


    8

Ох ты, горе-горькое!
  Скука скучная,
   Смертная!

 Ужь я времячко
 Проведу, проведу...

 Ужь я темячко
 Почешу, почешу...

 Ужь я семячки
 Полущу, полущу...

 Ужь я ножичком
 Полосну, полосну!..

Ты лети, буржуй, воробышком!
 Выпью кровушку
 За зазнобушку,
 Чернобровушку...

Упокой, господи, душу рабы твоея...

  Скучно!

## 9

Не слышно шуму городского,
Над невской башней тишина,
И больше нет городового —
Гуляй, ребята, без вина!

Стоит буржуй на перекрестке
И в воротник упрятал нос.
А рядом жмется шерстью жесткой
Поджавший хвост паршивый пес.

Стоит буржуй, как пес голодный,
Стоит безмолвный, как вопрос.
И старый мир, как пес безродный,
Стоит за ним, поджавши хвост.

## 10

Разыгралась чтой-то вьюга,
Ой, вьюга́, ой, вьюга́!
Не видать совсем друг друга
За четыре за шага!

Снег воронкой завился,
Снег столбушкой поднялся...

— Ох, пурга какая, спасе!
— Петька! Эй, не завирайся!
От чего тебя упас
Золотой иконостас?
Бессознательный ты, право,
Рассуди, подумай здраво —
Али руки не в крови
Из-за Катькиной любви?
— Шаг держи революцьонный!
Близок враг неугомонный!

Вперед, вперед, вперед,
Рабочий народ!

## 11

...И идут без имени святого
Все двенадцать — вдаль.
Ко всему готовы,
Ничего не жаль...

Их винтовочки стальные
На незримого врага...
В переулочки глухие,
Где одна пылит пурга...
Да в сугробы пуховые —
Не утянешь сапога...

В очи бьется
Красный флаг.

Раздается
Мерный шаг.

Вот — проснется
Лютый враг...

И вьюга́ пылит им в очи
Дни и ночи
Напролет...

Вперед, вперед,
Рабочий народ!

## 12

...Вдаль идут державным шагом...
— Кто еще там? Выходи!
Это — ветер с красным флагом
Разыгрался впереди...

Впереди — сугроб холодный,
— Кто в сугробе — выходи!..
Только нищий пес голодный
Ковыляет позади...

— Отвяжись ты, шелудивый,
Я штыком пощекочу!
Старый мир, как пес паршивый,
Провались — поколочу!

… Скалит зубы — волк голодный —
Хвост поджал — не отстает —
Пес холодный — пес безродный…
— Эй, откликнись, кто идет?

— Кто там машет красным флагом?
— Приглядись-ка, эка тьма!
— Кто там ходит беглым шагом,
Хоронясь за все дома?

— Всё равно, тебя добуду,
Лучше сдайся мне живьем!
— Эй, товарищ, будет худо,
Выходи, стрелять начнем!

Трах-тах-тах! — И только эхо
Откликается в домах…
Только вьюга долгим смехом
Заливается в снегах…

    Трах-тах-тах!
    Трах-тах-тах…

… Так идут державным шагом —
Позади — голодный пес,
Впереди — с кровавым флагом,
И за вьюгой невиди́м,
И от пули невредим,
Нежной поступью надвьюжной,
Снежной россыпью жемчужной,
В белом венчике из роз —
Впереди — Исус Христос.

*Январь 1918*

# 104. СКИФЫ

Панмонголизм! Хоть имя дико,
Но мне ласкает слух оно.

*Владимир Соловьев*

Мильоны — вас. Нас — тьмы, и тьмы, и тьмы.
    Попробуйте, сразитесь с нами!
Да, скифы — мы! Да, азиаты — мы,
    С раскосыми и жадными очами!

Для вас — века, для нас — единый час.
    Мы, как послушные холопы,
Держали щит меж двух враждебных рас
    Монголов и Европы!

Века, века ваш старый горн ковал
    И заглушал грома́ лавины,
И дикой сказкой был для вас провал
    И Лиссабона, и Мессины!

Вы сотни лет глядели на Восток,
    Копя и плавя наши перлы,
И вы, глумясь, считали только срок,
    Когда наставить пушек жерла!

Вот — срок настал. Крылами бьет беда,
    И каждый день обиды множит,
И день придет — не будет и следа
    От ваших Пестумов, быть может!

О, старый мир! Пока ты не погиб,
    Пока томишься мукой сладкой,
Остановись, премудрый, как Эдип,
    Пред Сфинксом с древнею загадкой!

Россия — Сфинкс. Ликуя и скорбя,
    И обливаясь черной кровью,
Она глядит, глядит, глядит в тебя,
    И с ненавистью, и с любовью!..

Да, так любить, как любит наша кровь,
    Никто из вас давно не любит!
Забыли вы, что в мире есть любовь,
    Которая и жжет, и губит!

Мы любим всё — и жар холодных числ,
    И дар божественных видений,
Нам внятно всё — и острый галльский смысл,
    И сумрачный германский гений...

Мы помним всё — парижских улиц ад,
    И венецьянские прохлады,
Лимонных рощ далекий аромат,
    И Кельна дымные громады...

Мы любим плоть — и вкус ее, и цвет,
    И душный смертный плоти запах...
Виновны ль мы, коль хрустнет ваш скелет
    В тяжелых, нежных наших лапах?

Привыкли мы, хватая под уздцы
    Играющих коней ретивых,
Ломать коням тяжелые крестцы,
    И усмирять рабынь строптивых...

Придите к нам! От ужасов войны
    Придите в мирные объятья!
Пока не поздно — старый меч в ножны,
    Товарищи! Мы станем — братья!

А если нет, — нам нечего терять,
    И нам доступно вероломство!
Века, века — вас будет проклинать
    Больное позднее потомство!

Мы широко по дебрям и лесам
    Перед Европою пригожей
Расступимся! Мы обернемся к вам
    Своею азиатской рожей!

Идите все, идите на Урал!
    Мы очищаем место бою
Стальных машин, где дышит интеграл,
    С монгольской дикою ордою!

Но сами мы — отныне вам не щит,
    Отныне в бой не вступим сами,
Мы поглядим, как смертный бой кипит,
    Своими узкими глазами.

Не сдвинемся, когда свирепый гунн
    В карманах трупов будет шарить,
Жечь города, и в церковь гнать табун,
    И мясо белых братьев жарить!..

В последний раз — опомнись, старый мир!
    На братский пир труда и мира,
В последний раз на светлый братский пир
    Сзывает варварская лира!

*30 января 1918*

PLATE 1    Alexander L'vovich Blok (1852–1909) and Alexandra Andreyevna Beketova
(1860–1923), the poet's father and mother.

PLATE 2    A road near Shakhmatovo.

PLATE 3    Alexander Blok as a boy at Shakhmatovo.

PLATE 4   Alexander Blok out riding with his groom near Shakhmatovo.

PLATE 5   The chapel near Shakhmatovo, scene of Blok's marriage in 1903.

PLATE 6    Lyubov' Dmitriyevna as Sophie in
Griboyedov's *Woe from Wit*.

PLATE 7    Lyubov' Dmitriyevna as Ophelia.

PLATE 8   Sergey Mikhailovich Solov'ev
(1885–1941).

PLATE 9   Boris Nikolayevich Bugayev (Andrey Bely)
(1880–1934).

PLATE 10   Lyubov' Dmitriyevna Mendeleyeva (1881–1939), Blok's wife.

PLATE 11    The Bronze Horseman—statue of Peter the Great which dominates Blok's
poetry about the 1905 Revolution.

**Actresses of Vera Kommisarzhevskaya's
theatre during the winter seasons
1906–7 and 1907–8**

PLATE 12   E. M. Hunt.

PLATE 13   V. V. Ivanova.

PLATE 14    Nataliya Nikolayevna Volokhova,
heroine of the cycles "Snezhnaya Maska"
and "Faina".

PLATE 15    Valentina Petrovna Verigina.

Plate 16    Lyubov' Alexandrovna Del'mas
("Carmen", 1913).

Plate 17    Alexander Blok in St. Petersburg.

Plate 18    Alexander Blok at Shakhmatovo.

PLATE 19   A typical courtyard on the "Islands".

PLATE 20   The railings of the "Summer Garden".

PLATE 21    The house on the corner of Offitserskaya Street where Blok spent the last
nine years of his life.

**Persistent images: a childhood drawing** (PLATE 22) . . .

... and a page from the first draft of "The Twelve" (PLATE 23).

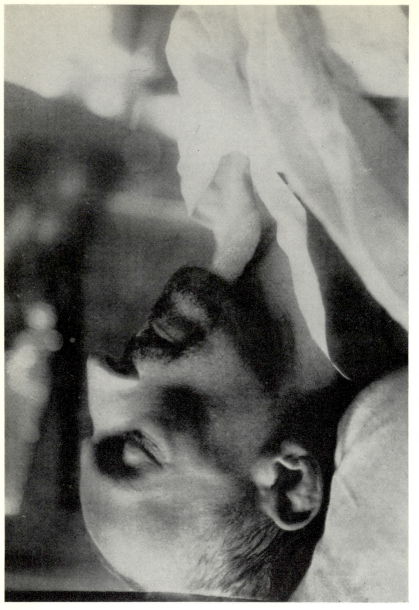

PLATE 24   Alexander Blok on his deathbed, August 1921.

# NOTES

### Abbreviations used in Notes

*Соч. в двух томах:*

Александр Блок. *Сочинения в двух томах, Государственное Издательство Художественной Литературы*, Москва, 1955.

*С.С.:*

Александр Блок. *Собрание Сочинений в восьми томах.* под общей редакцией В. Н. Орлова, А. А. Суркова, К. И. Чуковского. Государственное Издательство Художественной Литературы Москва–Ленинград, 1960 et seq.

(In spite of the publication of a ninth volume, this edition is still known as The Complete Works in Eight Volumes.)

| *Собр. Стих. 1911–1912:* | *Собрание стихотворений в трех книгах, Изд.* Мусагет, Москва. 1911–1912. |
| *Переписка:* | "Александр Блок и Андрей Белый. Переписка." Летописи Государственного Литературного Музея. *Изд.Гос.Лит. Музей,* Москва, 1940. |
| *Юношеский Дневник:* | Until recently available only in *Литературное Наследство,* 27/28, Журнальногазетное Общество, Москва, 1937, pp. 229–370. Now republished in Vol. 7 of *C. C.* |

## Juvenilia 1

This poem was originally "published" in a collection of Blok's juvenilia entitled "The Ship" (Корабль), Institute of Literature, Pushkin House, Архив А. А. Блока, Ф. 654, оп. I, No. 162. The "collection" is in the form of a double-lined exercise book, painstakingly filled by a shaky, unformed hand. The style throughout is a curious mixture of unaffected childishness and the literary turn of phrase Blok must have borrowed from his grandmother, mother and aunts, all of whom wrote. The complete serenity of this poem, the sense of active charity between inanimate objects re-create something of the rarified harmony of Blok's childhood. "He is a child of light and goodness", he was to write later of himself. "All that he is the triumph of freedom." (Cf. No. 66.)

"Позадишь"—evidently a childhood variation of "Позади". Either invented especially for the poem, or else a family word. In the autobiographical poem "Retribution" Blok writes of his family:

> Свои словечки и привычки,
> Над всем чужим — всегда кавычки.

His letters to his wife and mother are full of family misspellings, jokes, special words.

For Blok's family background and childhood see Мария Бекетова, *Александр Блок,* Петербург, 1922 and *Александр Блок и его мать,* Ленинерад — Москва, 1925.

## Juvenilia 2

This "prose" passage is from the same exercise book as the preceding poem—and in complete contrast to it. Apart from the schoolboy pleasure in enumerating the various weapons used in the field of battle, the piece is entirely original and contains no plagiarisms (much of Blok's juvenilia is patently borrowed from Robinson Crusoe, Jules Verne, Fenimore Cooper and Sherlock Holmes). Here, Blok's writing, if not grammatical, is graphic. The image of the broken home was to haunt his poetry always. So was the sense of elation in the face of catastrophe.

1(I.3) Пусть светит месяц — ночь темна
       First pub.: *Собр. стих.* I, 1911.

Blok's adolescent poetry is pessimistic in tone. In this, it reflected the intellectual climate of the late nineteenth century, dominated by Schopenhauer, Maeterlink's *Blind,* Ibsen's *Ghosts* and the pearly clarity of Chekhovian tragi-comedy [cf. A. Bely, *Воспоминания об Александре Блоке,* Эпопея, I, 1922, p. 133]. It also reflected Blok's own mood of which he was to write later in his brief "Autobiography": "At 15 I was first troubled by thoughts of love and by onsets of despair and irony." (Автобиография, *Соч. в двух томах,* p. 208.)

The manner is derivative and still very much of the nineteenth century. (For nineteenth-century influences on Blok see the chapter "О поэтике Блока" in L. Timofeyev's *Александр Блок,* М., 1957.)

Two features of this poem were, however, to remain constants of Blok's poetry throughout his life. The use of the ring form of repetition (here achieved by a straightforward repeat of the first four lines at the end of the poem), and the use of strong contrast in the first line or first two lines—not only a technical trick but, for Blok, an essential of self-expression.

For Blok's increasingly subtle use of repetition see Fookhed-Stoyanova "О композиционных повторах у Блока", Dutch Contribution to the Fourth International Congress of Slavists, Moscow, September 1958, Monton et Cie, The Hague, 1958, pp. 175–203. Blok's use of contrasting and contradictory forms ("Ты в поля отошла безвозвратно / Да святится имя Твое". "Черный вечер / Белый снег". "Милый друг, и в этом тихом доме / Лихорадка бьет меня". "Миллионы Вас, нас тьмы, и тьмы, и тьмы", "В небе — день, всех ночей суеверней", "В огне и холоде тревог", etc., *ad infinitum*) has been remarked by most students of his poetry and is well illustrated by L. I. Timofeyev in an article "Стих, Слово, Образ", *Вопросы Литературы,* 6, pp. 76–89.

2(I.7) Моей матери (Друг, посмотри' как в равнине небесной)
       First pub.: *Записки Мечтателей,* 1919, No. 1.

Blok's greatest friend Evgeniy Ivanov records that the poet's mother, Alexandra Andreyevna Kublitskaya-Piottukh (1860–1923), did not give the impression of "parental seniority" but was always on the side of the "children" against established authority. Perhaps because the family had never known a real father, Blok's attitude to her was responsible, protective. It is always he who points the way, she who follows. Blok tells us that she understood him "in everything". Ivanov—that, when she listened to her son's poetry, it was evident that she was able to follow him into "the whirlwinds, mists and illusions" which constituted "the aerial battle-field" of his inspiration. But Blok himself always returned to earth; he sought the earth in the women he loved ("elemental women", his mother complained in a letter to a friend); he sought it in his poetry and in his life—and here he calls his mother back from the empty abstract spheres whose terrors he already knew too well—but in which he, also, was perhaps most truly at home. Commenting on her son's homesick longing for "life", Alexandra Andreyevna wrote: "Sasha keeps on saying lately that he loves *life*. But what have we made of it? It bears no resemblance to life..." (letter of 3/XI/1913 to M.P. Ivanova, Ф No. 55, опись No. 1, Ед. Хр. 546. АН СССР (П II) Отдел Рукописей). However, mother and son united in loving life as it should be: "I am in love with the World, with Beauty, Truth and the Coming Glory of the Light... I feel my love for Sasha through this, because he is another such lover, and in this is the greatest tie between us, not counting the blood-tie" (letter of 20/XI/1908, *ibid.*).

3(I.19)  Гамаюн, птица вещая (На гладях бесконечных вод)
First pub.: *Киевские Вести*, 27th April 1908.
Trans.: A.L.Basham, "Hamayun the Prophet Bird", *SEER*, Vol. XVI, 1938, p.288.

Blok records in his autobiography that, as an unknown student, he offered this poem for publication to V.P.Ostrogorsky, the editor of the mildly liberal journal *Мир Божий*, at a time when the universities were in a state of political uproar. Ostrogorsky told him to be ashamed of himself for writing such abstract nonsense when "God knows what is going on at the University" ("Автобиография", *Соч. в двух томах*, Vol.II, p.209).

Blok was at this time quite oblivious of politics in general and arrogantly sceptical of student politics in particular (see D.E.Maksimov, "Александр Блок и революция 1905 года", *Революция 1905 года и русская литература*, Moscow–Leningrad, 1956, pp.246–79). His opinions, in so far as he had any, were much more conservative than those of his grandfather, who lost his position as Rector of Petersburg University for championing disaffected students. Yet this poem is not a product of the "ivory tower" mentality, but a prelude to Blok's verses about Russia, a foreshadowing of his role as compassionate prophet of his country's fate. (Cf. V.Lvov-Rogachevsky, *Поэт—пророк*, М., 1921, and Б. Я. Брайна, "Право на жизнь (I-ая книга А.Блока)", *О Блоке*, М., 1929, p. 291).

Гамаюн: a mythical bird of ill-omen with a human face.
V.Vasnetsov (1848–1926). No great artist, but one whose work contributed much to

Russian intellectual society's revived interest in their own pre-nineteenth century art and literature, a revival which was furthered by the first generation of "modernist" writers. Vasnetsov excelled in themes from Russian folk-lore executed in the heroic style.

4(I.33)  Dolor Ante Lucem (Каждый вечер, лишь только погаснет заря)
    First pub.: *Собр. стих.* I, 1911, under the title "Dolor ingens ante lucem".

This poem—"Sorrow before the dawn"—is typical of Blok's mood in the autumn of 1899. Compare particularly with another poem to his mother "Сгустилась мгла, туманами чревата" (*С.С.*, Vol. I, p. 31), in which Blok again takes up the lament for Paradise Lost:

> И нашим-ли умам поверить, что когда-то
> За чей-то грех на нас наложен гнет?

From the beginning, Blok is coldly resentful of this loss, cannot comprehend it's origin and is sceptical of the idea of redemption.

5(I.68)  Ищу спасенья
    First pub.: *Русь*, 30th July 1907.
    Trans.: V. de S. Pinto, "I seek salvation", *Book of Russian Verse*, p. 66.

Here Blok strikes the first major chord in honour of the Most Beautiful Lady. The poem marks the beginning of what he describes as a period of "submission to God and Plato" ([Комментарии А. А. Блока к "Стихам о Прекрасной Даме"] *Дневник, 1917–1921*, 17(30) / VIII / 1918). Although this poem is dedicated to Olga Solov'ev, the sister-in-law of the philosopher Vladimir Solov'ev and a cousin of Blok's mother, Blok had yet to discover Solov'ev's poetry to the Divine Sophia. His original perception of Salvation in the form of the "Eternal Feminine" or the "World Soul" was a profound personal experience, not the product of literary fashion.

For Solov'ev's influence on Blok see D. E. Maksimov, "Материалы из библиотеки Ал. Блока (к вопросу об Ал. Блоке и Вл. Соловьеве)", *Ученые записки Ленинградского государственного педагогического института*, том 184, 1958, факультет языка и литературы, выпуск 6, pp. 351–86, a detailed article based on published and unpublished sources. Briefly, Blok found confirmation of his own intuitive experience in the lyric poetry of Vladimir Solov'ev, which he began to read in the spring of 1901, and then became interested in his philosophic writings. Later, these bored him, but he always felt Solov'ev as a cultural fact of immense importance. (See the articles "Владимир Соловьев и наши дни", *С.С.*, Vol. VI, pp. 154–9, and "Рыцарь-Монах", *С.С.*, Vol. V, pp. 446–54.)

6(I.74) Вступление (Отдых напрасен. Дорога крута)

First pub.: *Стихи о Прекрасной Даме*, Петербург, 1905.

Trans.: R. Kemball "Rest unavailing. The road steep and straight", *Russian Review*, January 1958, p. 56.

Blok wrote of his poems to the Most Beautiful Lady that they represented a diary in verse and should be read in chronological order. However, he himself chose this purely evocative, typically elusive poem written towards the end of December 1903 to be the introduction to the whole cycle, the rest of which was composed between the years 1901 and 1902.

Although the Most Beautiful Lady is Herself a spirit, an Eternal and Immutable reality which, like God Himself, can never be totally perceptible to man, Blok believed that Her image could be fleetingly perceived in the real everyday world: in the face of a beloved woman "in repose"; in nature; in the wavering light of candles glowing before dark ikons; in the skies; in the sails of approaching ships. Blok glorified Her in this fashion most often in the features of the daughter of a country neighbour, Lyubov' Mendeleyeva, the girl who, in November 1902, agreed to become his wife. After this date Blok continued to write of the Most Beautiful Lady but, in later editions of his work, he included the new verses in another book entitled—"The Parting of the Ways".

The "manifestations" of the Most Beautiful Lady were associated with the landscape of Blok's childhood: the fir and birch woods, the white-wavering barley fields, the winding, undulating roads and the enormous, bird-wracked skies of Middle Russia.

Russia, childhood, love, earthly happiness and Paradise Regained are images and concepts which blend and fuse in this poetry. Russia is seen as a pastoral country: Blok's imagination carries him easily back into the Middle Ages. Not difficult—since the real setting of his romance was wonderfully secluded from the modern world. The weary ride through the woods to his Lady's home, the high window of her room, the "Princess" Herself dressed in simple, timeless clothes, her long hair braided thick as Rapunzel's, and the carved wooden horses glowing in the evening sun all really existed. But, for Blok, their secret and enchantment lay in the fact that they and the real feelings they inspired created an atmosphere in which he became aware of the existence of a deeper reality, of a kind of Eternal Joy underlying the distorted temporal "appearance" of the world in which we live.

Терем: The women's quarters of medieval Russian houses. Following the long years of occupation by the "Golden Horde", Muscovite women were kept in almost oriental seclusion until the end of the seventeenth century.

7(I.81)  Ты отходишь в сумрак алый
         First pub.: *Альманах Гриф* (1904).
         Trans.: Deutsch, B. and Yarmolinsky, A., "Into Crimson Dark",
         *Russian Poetry, an Anthology*, New York and London, 1927, p.61.

"From the beginning", Blok wrote of his Most Beautiful Lady, "she is felt
to be moving away from the individual poet to manifest Herself in history."
And elsewhere, in an attempt to write a commentary on these verses under-
taken many years later: "Already She is in the day, that is beyond the night
from which I am looking at Her. That is, She is already set in some definite
course and 'flying away', whereas to me it is given only to watch and to call
down blessings on Her departure."
(Комментарии А.А.Блока к "Стихам о Прекрасной Даме", *Дневник
1917–1921*, 17(30)/VIII/1918.)

This poem—all echoes and circles and "sounding silences"—shows Blok's
growing mastery of music, the effect here being achieved through repetition
of single words and combinations of words—"круги" "шаги", "беско-
нечные", "отдаленные", "звучная тишина", "в тишине звучат". The in-
cantatory effect is heightened by the use of assonance, particularly of the
long-drawn "*е*": "бесконечные", "далече", "встречи", "сильнее", "пла-
менея", "бесконечные".

At the same time, the extremely vague, ethereal language already demon-
strates the practical impossibility of writing of the Lady. Not to be described
in the terms of our experience, she is literally beyond words.


8(I.91)  Небесное умом не измеримо
         First pub.: *Собр. Стих.* I (1911)

The first impulses of Blok's evolution from the esoteric and individual to
the general are illustrated in this lovely and statuesque evocation of the
Russian Venus. "Lyricism, broken in the prism of History, took on monu-
mental proportions" was the verdict of one critic, E. Lundberg, on Blok's
poetry as a whole. The phrase seems to apply particularly to this poem, in
which the Lady is already foreseen "manifesting Herself in history" (see
Note 7). It is neither allegory nor the description of "a vision" (Blok stated
expressly in a letter to Andrey Bely, that he "never had any visions")—but
true symbolist poetry. The thing is seen "as in a glass, darkly": the soul of
Russia, seen where the temporal country touches on the Eternal and the
Universal (always the border-line when the "Most Beautiful Lady" shines
through the actual object of contemplation), and the "new men", although
here they are still clad in legendary splendour, foreshadow Blok's poetry of
1905 (see Nos. 27, 28 and notes).

9(I.94)   Предчувствую Тебя. Года проходят мимо
          First pub.: *Новый путь*, 1903, No.3.
          Trans.: H. MacDiarmid, "I ha'e forekennt Ye", *A Drunk Man Looks
          at the Thistle*, Edinburgh, 1926, p.10. B. Deutsch and A. Yarmolinsky,
          "The unknown woman" (I have foreknown Thee), *Russian Poetry*,
          1927. C. M. Bowra, "I have forebodings of Thee", *A Book of Russian
          Verse*, London, 1943, p.97. R. Kemball, "Presentiments of Thee",
          *Russian Review, January* 1958, p.57.

This is perhaps the most-quoted, certainly the most-translated, of Blok's
poems to the Beautiful Lady. It foreshadows a change in Blok's muse and
the appearance of a new heroine, "The Stranger", first mentioned by name
in a letter from Blok to Bely of 3rd February 1903 (Переписка, p.18). Many
have taken it as a presentiment of change in the Most Beautiful Lady herself.
Yet Blok states clearly that this is impossible:

> I still sometimes meet with debates on the "transformation" of the Beautiful Lady
> into the images of my later books: the Stranger, the Snow-mask, Russia, etc. As if the
> transformation of one image into another were something simple and natural! And,
> particularly, as though an essence possessed of an independent existence could change
> itself into a ghost, an image, an idea, a dream! (Набросок предисловия к нео-
> существленному изданию сборника "Стихи о Прекрасной Даме", 15/VIII/
> 1918, *C.C.*, Vol. I, p. 560.)

The Most Beautiful Lady was a religious concept and Blok, as Ilya
Ehrenburg has said, was not, in the last analysis, a religious poet (*Портреты
русских поэтов*, Berlin, 1922, p.36). "True art", Blok noted in his diary in
1906, "does not correspond in its impulses with religion" (*Записные книж-
ки*, 18/I/1906) and, in 1919: "All culture, whether scientific or artistic, is
daemonic" (*Дневник, 1917–1921*, 6/I/1919). "It is my fate," he wrote in his
first letter to Bely, "to explore (the nature of) the 'Whore of Babylon' and
only 'to live in white', not 'to create white'" (*Переписка*, letter of 3/I/1903,
p.4).

From the beginning, Blok the poet could not endure prayerfully to await
inspiration. He could not resist weaving spells and conjuring with his own
imagination. When he did this, he was liable to perceive not the Most
Beautiful Lady, whose chief attribute was "immutability", but a creature of
his own dark and tainted dreams, whose "aura" was "stormy and dark at
the centre" (*Переписка*, letter of 18/VI/1903, pp.35–36), "a dead doll with
a face reminiscent of that other one glimpsed among the heavenly roses"
("О современном состоянии русского символизма", *C.C.*, Vol. V, p.429).
This creature, whom Blok identified with "the Apocalyptic Whore of Baby-
lon" and with the Moon-Goddess Astarte, shared the qualities of the moon
in that she was changeable and shone only with reflected light. The Most

Beautiful Lady, the Immutable, he identified with the "Woman clothed with the Sun" of the Apocalypse. In this poem, therefore, the poet foresees not a change in the nature of the Most Beautiful Lady, but his own fall from "religion", which he defined as "standing watch" into "mysticism", which he defined as "the Bohemian element of the soul" (*Записные Книжки*, 18/I/1906).

Unable to hold a steady course in the supernatural spheres "beyond good and evil" where, he knew, his Lady reigned in God ("perhaps She is the Holy Spirit", he once suggested and, again, more definitely, "She has something to do with the end of the World" [*Переписка*, letter of 18/VI/1903, p.35]), Blok was destined to pass through a stage of allegiance to "Astarte" and then, in despair, to limit his poetry to the purely human. Yet so important to him was the experience of his youth that he is said to have told his mother towards the end of his life: "Do you know what?—I wrote only the First Volume. All the rest are trifles" (V. Pyast, "О первом томе Блоке", *Об Александре Блоке*, Petersburg, 1921, p.213).


10(I.107)  Прозрачные, неведомые тени
      First pub.: *Русская Мысль*, 1914, No.10.

Requires little commentary. A hymn of adoration to the Most Beautiful Lady as the World Soul, the material Universe redeemed. It is given to the poet to perceive and adore, but there is no communication. The link between sinful man and Salvation is missing. Of this Blok wrote to Bely: "... for me the most important difference between you and me: you love Christ more than Her. I cannot. *I know that you are ahead—without doubt.* But I cannot.... For this reason I do not know Her as you do..." (*Переписка*, letter of 1/VIII/1903, p.45).

And in another letter, that *something* he "knew for certain", but that this *something* was the "what" and not the "how" of salvation (*ibid.*, letter of 14 or 15/X/1905, p.158).


11(I.142)  Будет день — и свершится великое
      First pub.: *Золотое Руно*, 1908, No.1.

Blok himself explains that in the autumn of 1901 his feeling of the imminence of the Lady was cut off short by "the limit of the knowability of God" (see also "Ты уходишь от земной юдоли", *С.С.*, Vol.I, p.129).

His feeling for Lyubov' Dmitriyevna, his earthly love, wavered correspondingly and lost some of its sacramental magic: "In November", he writes, "began my open sorcery, for I invoked doubles: ("Зарево белое", "Ты другая, немая") "(Комментарии А.А. Блока к "Стихам о Прекрасной Даме", *Дневник 1917–1921*, 17 (30)/VIII/1918).

безликая — «лик»: Old Russian word for face usually applied to the faces of saints and the Holy Family as depicted on icons. Thus "безликий" means more than face-less: it means that the thing described has lost its higher identity, God's image or re-flection.

12(I.152) Двойнику (Ты совершил пад нею подвиг трудный)
First pub.: *Собр. Стих.* I (1911).

On 27th December 1901 Blok noted in his diary: "I have split into two... for I invoked doubles" (cf. last note). From now on the double is a constant theme of his poetry. Sometimes it is broken into the recurring themes of Pierrot and Harlequin, of monk and knight-errant. In the play *The Rose and the Cross*, as in some of Dostoyevsky's novels, there is a whole plethora of doubles. Most often the poet simply talks to himself, mocking false sanctity, as here, weeping over broken sacraments, passionately seeking to accept and to comprehend the sensual world yet sceptical of "the seeming", "the appearance"—corrosively ironic, yet racked by the memory of a lost har-mony. "As to mysticism, I know, that it is REAL and terrible, and that it will punish me. But how can it punish me more than I am punished, and what can it take from me when I am beggared?" (*Переписка*, letter of 14 or 15/X/1905, p.158).

13(I.198) Брожу в стенах монастыря
First pub.: *Стихи о Прекрасной Даме*, 1908.

The image of the "dark monk" is a favourite of Blok's. In 1916 he obtained a copy of the φιλοκαλία (in Russian "Добротолюбие") and discovered in the writings of Father Evgariy on "demons" an affinity with Strindberg and with his own preoccupation with "doubles" (*Письма к родным*, Vol. II, letter 530, pp.293–4). Of this, Blok writes to his mother: "As you know, the invariable technique of monks is to expound texts from the Holy Scriptures on the basis of their personal experience. I retain a very strange impression from this: the texts—every single one of them—remain dead, but the experi-ence is alive" (*ibid.*). In the note to this letter on p.475 reference is made to Blok's copy of the φιλοκαλία in the possession of N.A. Pavlovich. N.A. Pavlovich was kind enough to show me the volume containing the "life" and writings of Abbot Evgariy, against which Blok had marked the following passage, noting in the margin "NB. Знаю, все знаю".

There is a thought which can suitably be called the wanderer. It mostly comes to the brethren towards the end of the night and leads the mind from town to town, from village to village, from house to house. At first the mind conducts simple conversations, but later, drawn into long talks with some old acquaintances, it lets its state be corrupted according to the qualities of those it meets. Thus, little by little, it falls away from the consciousness of God and virtue, and forgets its calling and its vow. Therefore a hermit must watch this demon, observing whence he comes and what he touches, for it is not for nothing that he makes such a wide circuit. He does this to disturb the hermit's state in order that the mind, inflamed by it all and intoxicated by many conversations, should at once fall under the demon of fornication, or anger, or discontent.

A double pencil-mark in the margin draws attention to Evgariy's observations on the symptoms of those who have overcome this demon. "Such a conquest of the demon is followed by great sleepiness, deadening of the eyelids, a feeling of coldness, excessive yawning and drooping shoulders; but with diligent prayers the Holy Spirit disperses it all." (Translation from E. Kadlouborsky and G. E. H. Palmer, *Early Fathers from the Philokalia*, Faber Ltd., London, 1954, pp. 119–20.)

This passage—presumably unknown to Blok in the summer of 1902—exactly mirrors the mood of this and many other "devotional" poems to the Most Beautiful Lady. Complete religious concentration is a perpetual struggle for the artist and victory leaves him heavy, cold and uninspired.

Against Evgariy's notes on the Demon of despondency, which the Abbot compares to a poison, useful in small doses as an antidote but deadly if taken "without measure", Blok's note reads: "This demon is essential to the artist."

заутреня: Matins.
обедня: Mass, Communion Service.


14(I.210) Свет в окошке шатался
          First pub.: *Альманах Гриф* (1904).

Again the double theme. This is the first appearance of the Harlequin-double, whose function is usually to deride false, romantic mysticism. Blok wrote of this poem that it was an attempt to "thin down" the "dense, lightning-filled atmosphere" of his poetry by the introduction of a "cruel Harlequinade" (letter to Z. N. Hippius of 14th September 1902, 1937, N. 27/28, p. 352). Blok loved to picture himself as a true knight-errant, but here he is only a fancy-dress knight, a ridiculous figure with a cardboard sword. His Lady—her hand trembling from the simplest of emotions, but her face hidden by the "many-coloured falsity" of her mask—sits dumbly, fascinated by his "strange" talk. But Blok is also the Harlequin, who sees through them both and laughs.

Typical of Blok's elusive manner at this time is the transferred epithet "у задумчивой двери"—it is, of course, the Harlequin, not the door, who is thoughtful, but perhaps he is thoughtful because the door between him and the masquerade imposes thought, because the door symbolizes the fact that he is outside in the dark, an observer, not an actor. Like all true symbols, Blok's accord with Vyacheslav Ivanov's definition and are "multi-significant, multi-faceted, and always dark in their last depths".

See Orlov's note on this poem (*C.C.*, Vol. I, p. 609) for its connection with the verse play *Балаганчик*. Cf. also No. 34 and note.

бело-красный наряд: the Harlequin's traditional costume is made from a diamond-patterned print in brilliant colours — often white and red.

письмена: Archaic plural of письмо, meaning a letter, in both English senses of the word, a script or, simply, writing. The archaic plural would suggest the translation "characters".

15 (I. 215)  Я вышел в ночь—узнать, понять
         First pub.: *Альманах "Северные цветы"* (1908).

With the help of Blok's letters, diaries and recorded comments, we have seen that many of the poems to the Most Beautiful Lady are much simpler and more explicable than they first appeared to his contemporaries. This is not of their number. Blok's friend, E. P. Ivanov, tells us: "In answer to my direct question as to who it was who sat laughing in the empty saddle, he didn't know 'how' to find a straight-forward reply but answered on a note of semi-interrogation: 'Probably, Antichrist'." (Quoted from Ivanov's unpublished memoirs by Vl. Orlov, *C.C.*, Vol. I, p. 610.) The poem is a masterpiece of music, of a kind of surrealistic impressionism. It is deliberately vague and rather terrifying. A brilliant analysis of this deliberate exploitation of the indefinite, particularly of the pronouns "someone" and "something", is given in the opening pages of K. Chukovsky's *Книга об Александре Блоке*, Эпоха, Петербург, 1922 ("Кто-то", "Без подлежащего", "Туманы", "Сны", "Криптограммы", "Тайны").

16 (I. 230)  Religio (Любил я нежные слова. Безмолвный призрак в терему)
         First pub.: "Любил я нежные слова", *Золотое Руно*, 1908, Ио. 1. *"Безмолвный призрак в терему"*, Альманах Северные Цветы, 1903.

Still the poet is struggling to preserve his "one thought" (see No. 14 and note). He is exhausted, empty, old before his time. But both parts of the poem end in triumphant affirmations of the glories of "the service of the Unattainable".

*Religio*: piety (Lat.).

Соцветие: botanical term: the floscule or raceme of a flower. Blok's grandfather was a distinguished botanist and the old man and the boy loved to wander through the woods in search of specimen plants. They were great friends and, at midsummer, the grandfather would enchant the child by taking him out at night to search for the "paporotnik"—the magic fern which, according to legend, only flowers at midnight on Midsummer's Eve. Blok remained an excellent naturalist all his life and knew the Latin names of most Russian grasses and wild flowers.

Терем: see Note 6.

Нетронутый альков: again a transferred epithet and one of Blok's very rare lapses of taste. The word "alcove" in Russian has all the connotations of plushy Edwardian romance. It is out of keeping with the medieval decor of the rest of the poem—still more with the truly "immaculate" image of the Lady.

17 (I.252) Все кричали у круглых столов
First pub.: *Стихи о Прекрасной Даме*, 1905.

This poem is very much in Blok's later manner. The scene—no longer the quiet, open landscape of Shakhmatovo, but a crowded Petersburg pub. In August 1902 Blok wrote to his father of his "disenchantment" with the "fairytale quality" of his mysticism. He still believed in his mystic intuitions, in the possibility of coming upon "a sudden twist in the road, destined to lead us out from the depths (albeit from the 'Universal' depths) into 'God's good day'", but he wished to find a more objective and realistic expression for such intuitions. "In general", he adds, quoting Dostoyevsky, "my realism borders, yes, and will evidently continue to border, on the fantastic" (*Письма к родным*, Vol. I, pp. 76–77).

In a letter to his fiancée, dated 25th December 1902, Blok wrote of this poem:

> I have written some good verses, but I won't send them to you now. They are of quite a new type—from Dostoyevsky, and so Christian that I could only have written them under your influence. Often, now, I feel like forgiving everyone. Things which last year filled me with pain and anger now seem purer and less murky. Such strong and supple shoots are springing from my heart that it often seems as though I am standing on the Threshold of some revelation of sheer joy—and I want to say: "Come unto me, all ye that are weary and heavy laden, and I will give you rest. For my yoke is easy." Life is full of light, easy, beautiful (Архив А. А. Блока, Ф. Ио. 55, опись Ио. I, Ед. хр. Ио. 97, ЦГАЛИ).

But when, two days later, Blok does send her the poem, he is more nervous about it:

> What do you think of it? There's decadence, if you like—isn't it? There's formlessness for you. It is quite simple and happens in life in those outlying districts where Stavrogins

go biting generals' ears. But it is "Scorpionism" and will have to go to Bryusov. They [the editors of Merezhkovsky's journal *Novyy Put'*, A.P.] wouldn't like it here. But perhaps it's rubbish? Write me about it, all that matters is what you think (letter of 27/XII/1902: as above).

18(I.265) Погружался я в море клевера
        First pub.: *Новый Путь*, 1904, No.6.

The wind, the road and the pilgrim's staff are symbols which haunt Blok's poetry in this period of transition from the "fairy-tale" hymns to the Most Beautiful Lady to the more "realistic" poetry of his second and third volumes. Here, the poet is called away from idyllic dreams and spiritual delights to attempt the hard pilgrimage through a world which previously frightened and disgusted him. Like Germann, the hero of Blok's most auto-biographical play *The Song of Fate*, he is called away by the song of the wind. He is bound to go or his mysticism itself will become suspect and corrupt as in his verse, though not in his mind, it already has done. Already, in 1902, Blok became doubtful of the validity of myth-making as a way to truth: "Absolute emancipation from the earthly idol can come to pass only by way of complete παθος in earthly form (the theme of Dostoyevsky which penetrates his whole philosophy of life)…" (*Юношеский Дневник*, 26/VI/1902).

Nevertheless, he always remembers that the *substance* if not the *manner* of his mystical devotion to the Most Beautiful Lady was not a fairy-tale—but a reality.

быль: a true story.

19(I.271) Мне снились веселые думы
        First pub.: *Журнал для всех*, 1904, No.5.

In the early months of his Devotion to the Most Beautiful Lady, Blok had guarded Her possessively for himself, not feeling "… that the *people* or society have any part in Her Grace…" (*Переписка*, letter of 1/VIII/1903, p.44). Now, as he condescends towards the ugly, broken life around him, he suddenly, joyously feels that neither he nor She is alone. The Spring is a recurrent symbol of delight and of affirmation of life in Blok's poetry (see R. Triomphe's article "Sous le signe de Printemps", *Revue des Etudes Slaves*, Vol.38, Paris, 1961, pp.197–206). This is a Petersburg landscape with figures: workmen melt tar over great bonfires to paint the boats which will soon be afloat again on an ice-free river. Blok, who loved all physical work and was strong and skilled with his hands, finds himself aglow in unaccustomed communion with their labour and laughter. This was a rare mood, but one he

treasured intensely. Much evidence for this side of Blok's character is mar-
shalled in Vladimir Orlov's popular study of "The Twelve" (Поэма Алек-
сандра Блока "Двенадцать", страница из истории советской литературы,
Moscow, 1962, pp. 13–14).

челны: boats (poetical).

20 (I. 273)  Я вырезал посох из дуба
            First pub.: *Новый Путь*, 1904, No. 5.

Again the pilgrim theme. Again the wind—this time "the caressing whisper
of the snowstorm". But, here, Blok's new thought is poured into the old
bottles of "fairy-tale" mysticism. It is the stylized Russian Princess of folk-
lore who will open the door to him at the end of the road—and Her welcome
will transform the poor pilgrim into a legendary Prince, his staff of oak into
a sceptre tipped by a crystal tear (compare the poem "Последнее напут-
ствие" (*C. C.*, Vol. III, p. 272).

> И опять — коварство, слава,
> Злато, лесть, всему венец —
> Человеческая глупость,
> Безысходна, величава,
> Бесконечна... Что ж, конец?
>
> Нет... еще леса, поляны,
> И проселки, и шоссе,
> Наша русская дорога,
> Наши русские туманы,
> Наши шелести в овсе...
>
> А когда пройдет все мимо,
> Чем тревожила земля,
> Та, кого любил ты много,
> Поведет рукой любимой
> В Елисейские поля                    (14th May 1914)

And the yearning entry in Blok's diary:

There is much still to come. But Thou—come back, come back, come back—when
the trials appointed for us are at an end. We will pray to Thee amidst the future terror
and passion which is our lot. I shall wait again—always Thy slave, having betrayed
Thee but, again and again,—returning.

Leave me the piercing memory, as it is now. Do not lull my sharp uneasiness. Do
not break off my torments. Let me see Thy dawn. Come back (*Записные Книжки*,
8/VII/1909).

Самоцвет: semi-precious stone.

21 (I.277)  Я был весь в пестрых лоскутьях
          First pub.: *Альманах Гриф*, 1904.

Again—the double theme, again—the harlequin or wandering jester.
Self-doubt tormented Blok as greatly when he "set forth on pilgrimage"
as when he attempted cloistered devotion. Perhaps he was not setting out on
pilgrimage at all—but merely betraying his ideal? He was to write later that he
"had long wished secretly for perdition" (*Дневники, 1917–1921*, 15th August,
1917). In 1908 Blok wrote an article on the sickness of the age, "Irony", in
which his vision of the poet is almost the same as in this poem:

> I know people who are ready to choke themselves with laughter as they tell you that
> their mother is dying, that they themselves are starving, that their fiancée has betrayed
> them ... and it seems funny to me too. ... We are drunk on irony, on laughter, as if on
> vodka; in this way everything is devalued, everything "dishonoured", everything—
> adds up to the same. ...
>   Do not believe our laughter, believe the pain which is behind it. ... Do not make of
> our searchings—fashionable diversions, of our souls—fairground puppets dragged
> around the street for the amusement of the public.... (*C. C.*, Vol.V, pp. 345, 347,
> 349.)

22 (I.302)  Фабрика (В соседнем доме окна жолты)
          First pub.: *Альманах Гриф*, 1905. In 1904 the poem was forbidden
          by the censor.
          Trans.: C. Kisch, "The Factory", *Alexander Blok, Prophet of
          Revolution*, London, 1960, p.34.

Blok's home at this time was on the most historical of Petersburg's
"Islands", the Petrogradskaya Storona, in the officers' quarters of the bar-
racks of the Grenadier Regiment of Life Guards. The barracks face across
a wide backwater—the Bolshaya Nevka—to a vista of huge industrial chim-
neys rising to abrupt heights from the flat shore of the next island—the
Vyborgskaya Storona (immortalized by Maxim Gor'ky in his reminiscences
of his youth as an industrial worker). But the "neighbouring house" with the
"yellow windows" was a grim Victorian factory right alongside the barracks.
Blok must have been able to see into it as he sat in his own clean and orderly
room. For him, it seems to have embodied the whole horror of the nineteenth
century "which drew down over the living face of man the lacquered veil of
mechanics, positivism and economic materialism, which drowned the voice
of man in the roaring of machines" ("Ирония", *C. C.*, Vol.5, p.347).

Not yet a poem of social protest, this is the first poem to connect Blok's
passionate rejection of every ugly or evil aspect of life with a definite social
group of people—those who, as Blok was to say in a later poem, "had to sell
their day for money" (No.41).

The Russian word for yellow usually spelt "желтый" is here deliberately written – "жолтый". For Blok "жолтый", "чорный" were different colours from "желтый", "черный"—in the same way as for a certain English poet "gray" is between beige and grey: "grey"—between blue and grey. When Blok uses "o" instead of "e" the connotation is peculiarly sinister.

Note clever use of repetition—like a working piston rather than a refrain: "По вечерам—по вечерам", "а на стене—а на стене".

кули (sing. куль): a mat bag or sack.

23(I.308) Из газет (Встала в сияньи. Крестила детей)
      First pub.: *Журнал для всех*, 1904, No.4.

One way by which Blok grew nearer to people was to read about them in the daily papers—again like Dostoyevsky. This poem was inspired by a *fait du jour*: the widowed mother of a family who threw herself under a train because she could no longer feed her children. Blok tells the story without sentimentality—from the point of view of the children, who don't really understand what has happened. The style is laconic, impressionistic, subdued.

The effect—in spite of the gentleness of the neighbour, the soothing words of comfort—is one of fierce compassion. The poet refrains from comment. The poem says: "this is happening to me. It is impossible. It should not be."

человек с оловянной бляхой на теплой шапке: a policeman with the tin badge of his office on his warm winter cap.
Святки: The twelve days of Christmas.

24(I.315) Мой любимый, мой князь, мой жених
      First pub.: *Стихи о Прекрасной Даме*, 1905.

Blok's wife does not yet accompany him into this terrible world where children are left comfortless and grown men enslaved. She is still "on the far bank", as it were in sanctuary but, even though in his weariness he threatens to drag her down from her sublime security and "trample her immortality", she will pray for him, wait for him, true to her function for him as his only true love. In the manuscript, Blok first entitled the poem "Вечно" (Eternally), but then crossed the word out. Possibly because of the impression made on him by the first revolution, increasing maturity of vision soon made Blok suspicious of such aestheticization of suffering. In October 1906 he was already writing with a certain wry contempt of his own mystic quietism and of the image of the wandering horseman on his weary mount:

    We will set our ear to our beloved, native earth: is the heart of our mother still beating? No, the beauty of stillness has come down upon her and we are warmed through and through, cradled by her tenderly lowered wings: it is as though the prophecy of the Friend and Comforter had already come true, for we have nothing left to regret; we will give up everything, we have no regrets and, it would seem, no fears. We are wise, for we are poor in spirit; voluntarily, we go forth from our families, voluntarily, we take up the pilgrim's staff and bundle and drag our weary way across the great Russian plains. And will a wanderer hear anything of the Russian revolution, of the cries of the hungry and of the oppressed, of capital cities, of decadence, of the government? No, for the earth is wide and the sky is high and the water is deep and the works of man will pass by unheeded and will be replaced by other works ... We, the Wanderers, will hear only Stillness.

But what if this earthly, Russian stillness, all our aimless freedom and our joy—is woven from the web of the spider? If the fat She-Spider weaves and weaves the web of our happiness, of our life, of our reality,—who will break the web?

The most terrible of all demons is whispering in our ear the sweetest of speeches; may the violet eyes of the Bride, of the Night Violet, gaze ever through the mist which rises from the marshes. May the happiness of the horseman circling the marshes on his weary steed under one great, green star, soundlessly run its course.

May this not be so. ("Безвременье", *С.С.*, Vol. V, p. 282.)

In 1904 this poem was offered to the journal *Новый Путь* but for some reason it was struck out by the censor (see Orlov's notes, *С.С.*, Vol. 1, p. 627)—probably as the result of previous trouble with the Ecclesiastical censor (to which *Новый Путь*, which dealt in religion as well as in literature, had to be subjected) on account of the doubtful orthodoxy of Blok's cult of the Most Beautiful Lady (cf. P. Pertsov, *Ранний Блок*, М., 1922, pp. 21–22).


25 (I. 323)  Вот он — ряд гробовых ступеней
             First pub.: *Стихи о Прекрасной Даме*, 1905.

In this poem, which is the last of Blok's First Volume in all editions of his work, the poet seems to abandon all attempt to perceive the Most Beautiful Lady through his wife. He takes leave of her using the old high manner—the steps, the white coffin enveloped in a shaft of radiant light.

Yet the grave is the grave only of the Divine. The human girl sleeps on, smiling in her sleep. There is tenderness and renunciation in the poem. From the beginning, she had wanted only to be herself: "You have imagined all sorts of fine things about me", Lyubov' Dmitriyevna had written to Blok two years earlier in a letter, which she only showed to him after they had become engaged, "and behind that fantastic fiction which lived only in your imagination you have overlooked and failed to notice *me*—a live human being with a living soul. ... I am a live human being and that is what I want to be even with all my imperfections." (Published by D. E. Maksimov, "Из архивных материалов об А. Блоке', *Ученые записки Ленинградского Государственного Педагогического Института*, Фак. языка и литературы, выпуск 5, 1956, pp. 242–51.)

Now, the poet resolves to trouble her no more with his "mystic" imaginings. Yet he always felt that, in her refusal to live on his mystic "heights", where, she protested, she was "cold, frightened and bored", it was, in a sense, she who slept—and he who "kept watch" for them both. At the same time, he knew that he had somehow failed her as "a live human being". The first sketch for this poem differs considerably from the published version. Orlov gives it in full together with variant readings for three lines and for the whole of the first verse (*C. C.*, Vol. I, p. 632).

окрай: on the threshhold of.

26 (II. 7) Вступление (Ты в поля отошла без возврата)
    First pub.: *Нечаянная радость**, 1907.
    Trans.: R. Kemball, "Thou art far in the fields—and forever", *Russian Review*, January 1958, p. 59.

Blok will write no more of the Most Beautiful Lady. She is gone—but only for him. She continues to hold the world in the hollow of her hand. This poem, in manuscript entitled "Молитва" (Prayer), was used by Blok as an introduction to his second volume in the 1916 edition and thereafter.

Да святится имя Твое: direct quotation from the Lord's Prayer: "And hallowed be Thy name".
Уста: Old Russian word for lips.
* Нечаянная Радость: The subdivision of Blok's early poetry into such titles as "The Parting of the Ways", "The Town", "Various Verses", etc., was made only when Blok was preparing his first *Collected Works* for publication in 1911. His first book, which comprised poems from the cycles "Verses about the Most Beautiful Lady", "The Parting of the Ways" and even some verses later included in the Second Volume, was published under the title "Стихи о Прекрасной Даме" in 1905; his second, which comprised verses from "Bubbles of the Earth", "The Night Violet", "Various Verses" and "The Town"—under the title "Нечаянная Радость"—in 1907. This is the title given to a Russian icon depicting the Virgin, Her Child in Her Arms, turning in forgiveness towards a kneeling sinner. The meaning—"Joy beyond Hope".

27 (II. 153) Поднимались из тьмы погребов
    First pub.: *Нечаянная Радость*, 1907, under the title "Пришлецы" (The Newcomers).

Increasing disaffection triggered off by the disastrous Russo-Japanese War brought the still half-peasant industrial workers out from the obscurity of the industrial suburbs in procession through the intensely formal, exclusive, eighteenth-century centre of Petersburg. The intelligentsia, the aristocracy, the new enlightened bourgeoisie, had all been brought up to "love the Russian people". Many had worked selflessly for years to mend their bodies and to enlighten their minds. Some had long been spreading the idea of rebellion. It was nevertheless a shock to see this same people not as an object of pity, but as a force, relentlessly powered by the huge dignity of a common humanity, as a grey, unexpectedly alien flood engulfing *their* part of the town, *their* statued symbol of order and civilization. Many suppressed their first reaction of startled panic. Blok, whose elements were catastrophe and perfection, seems to have perceived at once the enormity of the challenge, its elemental quality and potential destructiveness. He felt that, in establishing their own full humanity, these people were fated to destroy him and his.

As ever, his motivation in accepting the doom of his generation—"Пусть заменят нас новые люди"—was dual, at once daemonic and religious, suicidal and gloriously hopeful. The Intelligentsia, he wrote, after he had had time to meditate the subject, was not fit to lead the people because it was possessed by "the will to die", whereas the people have "ever carried in themselves 'the will to live'" ("Народ и интеллигенция", *C. C.*, Vol. 5, p. 327). Blok's passions were normally self-destructive, and Revolution was his great passion. But his acceptance of Revolution sprang also from the simple and sober recognition of the common humanity of man, and from the anguished awareness that the best things in his own cultural heritage had been created and could be enjoyed only by the select few. So that this heritage might become the portion of all, Blok was truly willing to sacrifice not only his privileges and possessions, but life itself.

This was where he differed radically from other prophets of the twilight of the Western world, particularly, perhaps, from Friedrich Nietzsche whose enthusiasm for the qualities of "will and masculinity" Blok appears to have shared and whose work influenced his whole generation (cf. particularly R. Labry, "Alexandre Blok et Nietzsche", *La Revue des Etudes Slaves*, No. XXVII, Paris, 1951, pp. 201-8). Nietzsche, like Blok, was, in the words of his own Zarathustra, "one of those heavy drops, falling singly from the dark cloud which hangs over humanity and falling, as precursors, to annihilation". But Blok's thought could never have led to the apotheosis of the "Blond Beast" or to the glorification of strength for its own sake. Twenty-two years after Blok's death, forty-three years after Nietzsche's, this difference in thought, which is still being worked out in the movement of history, was expressed with Gallic clarity by a French resistance worker from Morocco with a passion for Russian literature in "Letters to a German Friend". "The difference between us", wrote Albert Camus, "is that I have never made my peace with despair."

Словеса: old form of plural for слово (word). Cf. similar use of archaic plurals письмена (Note 14) and каменья (Note 73). These forms lend dignity and mystery to everyday words, in this particular context transforming the rough (but surely perfectly comprehensible) speech of the workers into an "unfamiliar dialect" of high significance.

28 (II. 161)  Барка жизни встала

> First pub.: *Наша жизнь*, 26th November 1905.
>
> Trans.: O. Elton, "Life our bark has stranded", *Verses from Pushkin and Others*, London, 1935. C. Kisch "The ship of life rose", *Alexander Blok, Prophet of Revolution*, p. 71.

All his life Blok loved ships. In his poetry, they are almost always harbingers of change and joy, as in the play ("The King in the Square"), and as in the unforgettable lines which end his long poem "The Night Violet".

> Но ночная фиалка цветет,
> И лиловый цветок ее светел.
> И в зеленой ласкающей мгле,
> Слышу волн круговое движенье,
> И больших кораблей приближенье,
> Будто вести о новой земле.
> Так заветная прялка прядет
> Сон живой и мгновенный,
> Что нечаянно Радость придет
> И пребудет она совершенной.
> И ночная фиалка цветет.   (*С. С.*, Vol. II, p. 34)

Here, the shock of Revolution has momentarily grounded the ship of life, and it is the "new people" of the last poem who are destined to push her safely off again and to sail her masterfully and merrily away on her long quest. "Only", adds the poet, looking longingly after them, "they will hardly take us along with them." Some ultra-bolshevik critics say that the helmsman in the grey jacket should have been leading "The Twelve", but there, as here and as always, Blok wrote of what he "saw"—and, though prepared to listen with courteous interest to the explanations of others, never altered that which had once been seen and recorded.

The number of the journal which first published "Барка жизни" was confiscated by the police.

мель: shoal.
армяк: peasant's cloth coat or jacket.
багор: boat-hook.

29(II.59) Шли на приступ. Прямо в грудь

> First pub.: *Наша Жизнь*, 26th November 1905 (see preceding
> Note).

Blok has not yet learnt to write convincingly of revolution and the date of
the poem—January 1905—is undoubtedly the most remarkable thing about it.
Andrey Bely remembers how he arrived in Petersburg and went directly from
the station to Blok's home on 9th January—the day known as Bloody
Sunday. Workers' processions were known to be converging on the Winter
Palace under the leadership of a priest named Gapon. It was a peaceful
demonstration, the participants bearing icons and church banners, marching
to the sturdy singing of sacred songs and carrying petitions to the Tsar,
confident that they would receive a hearing. Instead, the administration
panicked, the procession was met with gun-shot, unarmed men, women and
children were killed and wounded, and the Slavophile myth of the mystic
oneness of the Tsar and his people—founded not in constitutions but in
mutual love and trust—shattered for ever. It was perhaps on this day more
than on any other that the iron entered into the soul of Russia. Bely describes
Blok's reaction to the tragedy:

> I have never seen him in such a state; chain smoking as he strode up and down the
> room he would pause every now and again at the windows, staring out fixedly at the
> great, desolate expanse of frozen river, as though he were trying to work up some indom-
> itable determination.
> There were a great many things I had wanted to talk to him about. But it was im-
> possible. Events had reduced words to insignificance. (A. Bely, "Воспоминания о
> Блоке", *Эпопея*, II, Berlin, 1922, p.165.)

твердь: firmament.


30(II.163) Повесть (В окнах занавешенных сетью мокрой пыли)
           First pub.: *Вопросы жизни*, 1905, No.415.

A *fait du jour*, like No.24, but this time with a new, revolutionary undertone.
Two worlds meet for a moment as the woman seated at the window looks
into the eyes of the other woman in the red dress, lying broken on the blood-
stained pavement.

> And the moment spun itself out ... the street waited...
> But the next moment the shutters came down over
> the upstairs window
> And below—in the wide open eyes—the power died.

The woman who dies is not a victim of the actual massacre described in the
last poem, although it is probably significant that these verses, too, were
written in January 1905—but merely a prostitute with a baby who can no

longer support the life of a world in which the people in the street are only "grey illusions of damp boredom" and other women live in security behind "suspiciously silent window panes" and "opaque white curtains".

G. I. Chulkov, to whom this poem is dedicated, was the editor of the journal in which it was first published, and a close companion of Blok's—to some extent his *âme damné*—during the years 1905–1907 (cf. Note 50 for literature on Blok's association with Chulkov).

31 (II.176)  Еще прекрасно серое небо
First pub.: *Нечаянная Радость*, 1907.

The moment of choice was over. The revolution had fizzled out with the October Manifesto, a document which granted a form of constitution and certain civic rights. This poem, together with the one directly preceding it (*C. C.*, Vol. II, p.175), was Blok's immediate reaction to the publication of the Manifesto—both were written on the same day. Many moderate liberals were at first delighted with this outcome, but to Blok it was no outcome at all (see particularly "Поэты", *C. C.*, Vol. III, p. 12). He was not concerned with parliamentary representation on a system of limited suffrage, but with the hopeless indifference of man towards the misery of man. Where there is no understanding there will be conflict: Blok understood, or rather intuitively *felt*, both sides. His contradictory nostalgia for a hierarchic and ordered past and his joyful acceptance of the inevitability of an equalitarian and, for a while at least, chaotic future is vividly expressed in the image of "the armed man in black", one of the great statues which overlooks the Neva and the Islands from the roof of the Winter Palace (see Blok's letter to E. P. Ivanov of 16th October 1905, *Письма Ал. Блока к Е. П. Иванову*, Leningrad, 1936, p.43) preparing to lay down his life "for an old legend" in a last doomed stand against "the wild rabble".

It is noteworthy that Blok saw nothing worth troubling about between the "old legend" and the "rabble". The bourgeois, the gentry, the moderate liberals—he dismissed gently but firmly in the poem "Сытые", written in the same month:

> Пусть доживет свой век привычно —
> Нам жаль их сытость разрушать.
> Лишь чистым детям — неприлично
> Их старой скуке подражать.   (*C. C.*, Vol. II, p. 180)

Blok once said of himself: "I was born in the Middle Ages. That is why I find the Renaissance red and terrifying" (*Записные книжки*, 4th December 1910). Yet, in 1917, Blok supported the Bolsheviks and, already in 1905, his sympathies were with the extreme left. This becomes less surprising if we look at the French communist Louis Aragon, another democratic devotee of chivalry, who also believed that "man was born to be happy and free", but that the very process of auto-liberation involves a total commitment of man's willpower—for the communist as for the medieval knight. Both these men found the world into which they were born unworthy of itself. Since both were extremely cultured animals, they looked for reasons in history. Blok, at least, found the seeds of that indifference of man towards man which permitted the enslavement of many to dull, mechanical jobs for the benefit of the few, in the individualism and the humanism of the Renaissance, where man is glorified for what he is rather than for what he might become. He had been brought up in the aristocratic ideal of work performed freely as "duty"—and this he recognized: the idea of work as a way of gaining bread— the original curse of Adam—horrified him. Post-Renaissance society had come to terms with the curse, and for this, as much as for anything else, Blok rejected it.

32(II.14)  Болотный попик (На весенней проталинке
            First pub.: *Весы*, 1906, No.5.

In his article "On the present state of Russian Symbolism" Blok declared that: "Quite contrary to the judgement of vulgar criticism that 'we got carried away by the revolution,' we offer a directly contrary explanation: the revolution took place not only in this, but in other worlds..." ("О современном состоянии русского символизма", *C.C.*, Vol.V, p.431).

Blok's own metaphysical rebellion against the spiritual discipline which he had been fighting a losing battle to impose on his "Verses about the Most Beautiful Lady" caused him not only to feel an extraordinary, lyrical sympathy with rebellious and anarchistic forces in society—it led to a new and riotous release of "mystical" energy. The epigraph to the first book of his second volume, "Пузыри Земли", is taken from Macbeth:

> The earth has bubbles, as the water hath
> And these are of them.

Having shaken off religious restraint, Blok allowed his imagination to run riot amongst these "bubbles", which his fantasy conjured up among the wreathing mists and rusty waters of the marshy country around Petersburg. With newly acquired—or perhaps newly released—technical virtuosity, he brings to life a host of little demons, will-o'-the-wisps, watersprites and jaunty hooded imps.

One of the most charming of these "bubbles" is the little Priest of the Marshes—something between St. Francis and Dr. Doolittle—dressed in a rusty black cassock and standing knee-high to a grasshopper.

Безбурность: Lit. stormlessness.

Прелесть: like its English equivalent "charm", this word has largely lost its meaning in modern Russian. Blok uses it in the sense reserved for it by the peasantry and by medieval ecclesiastic writers to mean at once "enchantment" and "temptation".

33(II.20) Старушка и чертенята (Побывала старушка у Троицы)
      First pub.: *Слово*, 2nd April 1906.

Blok did not like the Orthodox Christian tradition which he considered too "metaphysical", by which he meant too divorced from the earth. Here, with his tongue in his cheek, he represents the little shaggy demon children and imps of the marshes humbly putting their case to the pilgrim-woman, whose asceticism and holiness impresses but rather frightens them. They, too, have their "pastoral Christ" and their "Most Beautiful Lady". However, like all the "Bubbles-of-the-Earth" poems, this one is a slippery enchantment, a poetic and philosophic sleight of hand, all done with mirrors and not to be analysed too closely, or the worthy reader will soon find himself firmly stuck in the bog with the will-o'-the-wisps and the echoes of Blok's fantasy mocking him from every side.

Григорий Е: a pet hedgehog (see M. Beketova, *Александр Блок и его Мать*, Л.–М., 1925, pp. 87–91, for the full story of Grigory and Blok's love of all animals).

у Троицы: at the Troitse–Sergeyevsky Monastery at Zagorsk.

Купина: a bush—the word used in the Bible for "the burning bush" in which God appeared to Moses: "неопалимая купина". The symbolic meaning is "something which burns but does not burn away", "something invested with the presence of God". Blok and Andrey Bely both used the term to describe the Most Beautiful Lady.

34(II.67) Балаганчик (Вот открыт балаганчик)
      First pub.: *Нечаянная Радость* (1907)

One of a series of bitter-sweet fairy-tales (cf. "Поэт" and "У моря", *С.С.*, Vol. II, pp. 67, 71)—all on the same theme of childhood, illusion and disillusion. Blok's self-abandonment to his own fantasy entailed a corresponding increase in self-consciousness and self-doubt, which is reflected in these poems and in the whole theme of the Puppet Theatre. "Балаганчик" is a product of a time in Blok's life of which he wrote: "I cannot distinguish between life, dream and death, this world and other worlds" ("О современном состоянии русского символизма", *С.С.*, Vol. V, p. 429). Gifted with a child's capacity for immersing himself completely in his own imaginings, Blok was also distinguished by a child's ruthlessness in exposing comfortable pretence. Here, identifying himself completely with the children watching the puppet show, he suffers bitter disillusion when what he had thought to be the approach of the Queen turns out to herald nothing but the entrance of a train of devils: yet, at the same time, he is aware that even disillusionment is false—that, like the clown, he is "bleeding to death with Cranberry Juice".

These words are repeated in a verse-play of the same name as this brief and poignant poem (see Blok's commentary in the 1912 edition of his Second Volume quoted *C.C.*, Vol. II, p. 398). The "props"—the wooden swords and cardboard helmets—are common to both. But the play *The Puppet Show* belongs entirely to the half-world of the footlights, whereas in the poem the little girl still remembers that the True Queen—whose eagerly awaited coming in the poems and plays of Blok's "Second Volume" is so often accomplished amid a storm of bathos—walks only "in the full light of day".

35 (II. 79) Девушка пела в церковном хоре
      First pub.: *Наша жизнь*, 18th February 1906.
      Trans.: Anon., "A maiden's song in the choir", *A Book of Russian Verse*, p. 97. F. Cornford and E. Salaman, "In the cathedral choir", *Poems from the Russian*, p. 53. R. Kemball, "A young girl stood in a church choir singing", *Poetry Review*, Vol. XLVI, No. 1, 1955, p. 30. G. F. Cunningham, "From the choir her girlish treble blesses", *Lyrics from the Russian*, p. 65.

F. Stepun ("A. Bloks Weg von Solovyev zu Lenin", *Eckart*, 20/21 Jahrgang, Dez. 51/Jan. 52, Witten–Berlin, 1951–2, pp. 111–22) tells us that, before 1917, this poem was known by heart by every village schoolmistress and was copied into the autograph albums of 16-year-old misses from select seminaries. It is, nevertheless, a terrible poem. The sweetness of the melody, the lovely and surprising image of the white dress singing in the shaft of sun, the "sweet" voice, the "radiant" life, the "white" shoulder, the "slender" sunbeam and the "quiet" harbour all convey overwhelmingly the soaring joy brought to the listening people by the girl singing. The thin wailing of the infant which, according to the custom of the Orthodox Church, has been carried up to the gates of the iconostas to receive Communion, passes almost unnoticed. But it is the child who has just received the Sacraments and who knows: the quiet havens may indeed await the great ships, but they are ports of no return. Olga Forsch gives an eerie description of how Blok recited this poem at his last public appearance in Leningrad in her lyrical reminiscences

*Сумашедший Корабль*, pp. 122–4 and Roman Jacobson makes it the subject of a detailed linguistic study in *Orbis Scriptus*, München, 1966, pp. 385–401.

Царские врата: Holy gates: in an Orthodox church the altar is wholly screened off from the rest of the church by the iconostas, in which are three "gates" through which the officiating priests and deacons pass in and out. The central gates are called the royal or holy gates.

36 (II. 83)  В голубой далекой спаленьке
            First pub.: *Весы*, 1906, No. 5.

This poem is a magnificent illustration of Blok's love of the indefinite and the half-said: "Что-то недосказано", "нить какая-то" (cf. Note 15 for reference to Chukovsky). Who is the "Thou", all "sleepy-pale"? Who is the dwarf? Who the little boy? Why does the dwarf catch the pendulum of the clock and stop time, so that, perhaps, the darkness will go on for ever? Is this all a profound, roundabout, symbolic way of saying the little boy has died?

A vivacious young actress once asked Blok this last question in the hush which followed his recital of the poem. "His mother smothered him", answered Blok. "Impossible," exclaimed his interlocutor, "there's no murder in that poem!" Alexsandr Alexandrovich's face broke into a smile. "All right, then, he just died, it can be read like that." Without doubt—the memorist adds—in this case some story from the newspapers had got mixed up in the world of Blok's poetry and had been reflected in this way. (V. Verigina, "Воспоминания об Александре Блоке", *Труды по Русской и Славянской Филологии*, IV, Tartu, 1961, p. 313.)

37 (II. 84)  Вот он—Христос—в цепях и розах
            First pub.: *Весы*, 1906, No. 5.

The dedication to Blok's friend E. Ivanov points the way to the understanding of this poem. Blok's mother, who was as truthful as her son, writes of Ivanov in a letter to his sister Mariya Pavlovna' "Zhenya is the best person I have ever met" (7.2.1913, Цгали, Ф.55, Оп. No.1, ед. хр. No.539). Ivanov was a Christian of no worldly distinction—not unlike some such character from Russian fiction as Prince Myshkin or Alyosha Karamazov. In many ways he was the opposite of Blok—a self-avowed "pagan" ("Исповедь Язычника", *С. С.*, Vol. VI, pp. 38–39), beautiful, daemonic, renowned. Yet there was no inequality in the lifelong friendship between these two men which, in Blok's own estimate, resembled the friendship between Dante and Virgil on their pilgrimage through Hell (letter to G. Chulkov quoted by N. Chulkov in her unpublished memoirs of her husband).

Blok was no Dr. Johnson: Ivanov no Boswell. There was between them a real love and genuine exchange of ideas. It was Ivanov's theory that Christ would enter into the town (in the widest sense of modern urban civilization)—from the Russian fields, a theory bound up with the Platonic and Christian neo-Platonic philosophies most dear to Blok and, as ever, with the idea of the World Soul or the Earth redeemed, for Christ was imagined literally growing from the earth and coming into ear like corn in the fields, awaiting the moment to re-enter the modern world. This poem was Blok's reaction to a long evening spent discussing his friend's theory. The continuity between this vision of Christ and the Apparition at the end of the Twelve is evident. The incongruous crown of roses was already there. Blok's visual image of Christ was distinctly pre-Raphaelite and even effeminate, which may account for much of the spiritual antipathy he felt towards the "gentle Jesus meek and mild" in which so many children of the late nineteenth century were brought up to believe. It is as though Blok's Christ had just stepped out of a picture by M. V. Nesterov, an artist who lived from 1862 to 1942 and whose pre-revolutionary work is that of a Russian pre-Raphaelite, depicting a series of dreamy-eyed saints against the delicate and tender background of the central Russian landscape. Blok himself acknowledged Nesterov's influence on this poem (*Собр. Стих.*, II, 1912 quoted *C. C.*, Vol. II, p. 402).

Yet, if the poem illustrates Blok's essential antipathy to the figure of Christ as he saw Him, it also shows an understanding of Christianity much deeper and simpler than that of the occultists, theosophists and other exotic mystics who abounded in Western and Russian literary circles during the early years of the twentieth century. The meaning of the poem is simply this: Christ can be "seen", but not comprehended nor possessed from behind the "prison bars" of the world of appearances; although He stands close up against the bars, the only way to touch Him, to get to Him—is to renounce everything and, like the fabled ear of corn, to fall into the earth and die.

For further literature on Evgeny Ivanov and his relationship with Blok see *Письма Александра Блока к Е. П. Иванову*, ред. и предисловие Ц. Вольпе, подготовка текста и комментарии А. Костана, АН. СССР, Moscow–Leningrad, 1936, and A. Ugryumov, "А. А. Блок и семья Ивановых", *Русская Мысль*, Nos. 887, 888, 890, Paris, 17th, 19th and 24th April 1956, and M. Dikan's remarks in her afterword to the Eighth Volume, *C. C.*, pp. 546–7 and "Воспоминания и записки Евгения Иванова об Александре Блоке" (пуб. Е. П. Гомберг и Д. Е. Максимова), *Блоковский сборник*, Тарту, 1962, pp. 344–424!

стезя: path, way.

38 (II. 86)  Прискакала дикой степью
       First pub.: *Нечаянная Радость*, 1907. Reworked in 1915.

The wild, galloping rhythm of this poem is in complete contrast to the lovely formality of No. 37. That was an exercise for the spirit, this—the song of the blood. For Blok, there was nothing between these two extremes but weariness, duty, barren thought, dull debauch and—sometimes—a great tenderness and compassion which itself was of the spirit and of the passions rather than of the heart.

"Sasha lives by passions and by the spirit", his mother once wrote to a friend. "This has been so since his earliest years. Sentiments have always been foreign to him" (letter of 18/IV/1912 to Evgeny Pavlovich Ivanov, Ф. 662, No. 62, Архив Иванова Е. П., АН. СССР, П. Д.). Blok does not tell us who the gypsy girl with the tangled red braid is. Perhaps he does not yet know himself. But, if Christ walks meekly in "chains and roses", this girl mocks at the poet for "dragging his chains". She is Revolution. Revolution against the ordered spiritual life; against domesticity; against the social order; against civilization itself. Blok looks for no kindness, no favours from her; it is not him she loves; but she is "terrible in her beauty", her wild freedom is in itself a challenge and the very fact that she does not stay to woo increases the desire to follow.

Млада: young one—a form of address taken from folk-lore.

39 (II. 179)  Перстень-Страданье (Шел я по улице, горем убитый)
       First pub.: *Нечаянная Радость*, 1907—final text, somewhat abbreviated, 1915.

Another heroine—neither gipsy nor stately princess nor apocalyptic whore—just a defenceless human being whose only answer to the cursed condition of humanity is suffering accepted as love. Perhaps she, too, is, in fact, a pale reflection of the "World Soul". Certainly, she is an aspect of Russia—human, patient and sorrowful. In his introduction to the collection *Нечаянная Радость* (dated August 1906, *C. C.*, Vol. II, p. 369) Blok writes of the horrors of life in the great towns, where people fall dead in the streets and only "the red wine..."

> deafens, that the ears may not hear the murders, blinds, that the eyes may not see death.
> And the silent girl behind the narrow window weaves me my Ring of Suffering all through the night; her work calls forth in me soft songs of despair, songs of Submission.

In Blok's rough draft the poem ends with two further verses:

Сердце мое, приживальщик убогий!
Слушай же девичью песню, вникай!
После, коль можешь, зловонной дорогой
Снова шататься и плакать ступай.
Только не смей разрыдаться у окон.
Здесь тишина. Здесь святыня жива.
Низко спустился задумчивый локон. ...
Нищий! Не смей нарушать Торжества!

40 (II.185) Незнакомка (По вечерам над ресторанами)
First pub.: *Нечаянная Радость*, 1907.
Trans.: H. Macdiarmid, "As darknin' hings above the hough",
*A Drunk Man looks at the Thistle*, Edinburgh, 1926, p.7.
B. Deutsch and A. Yarmolinsky, "The Lady Unknown", *Russian Poetry, an Anthology*, New York and London, 1927, p.143.
F. Cornford and E. Salaman, "The Stranger", *Poems from the Russian*, London, 1943, p.54. C. Kisch, "*The Unknown Lady*", *Alexander Blok, Prophet of Revolution*, 1960, p.43.

After "The Twelve"—perhaps the best known of all Blok's poems. It is sheer magic; the terrifyingly successful result of Blok's undisciplined sorcery. Blok saw the Stranger in the window of a station buffet where he was sitting alone, drinking red wine. She took shape amid the billowing smoke of a passing train:

> Life has become art and I have made an invocation and before me has arisen that which I (personally) call "The Stranger": the beautiful doll, the blue phantom, the earthly miracle.
> That is the crown of the antithese [The "Thesis" being the revelation of the Most Beautiful Lady, A.P.]. And the light, winged enthusiasm before one's own creation lasts for a long time. The violins praise it in their own language.
> The Stranger. It is not in the least just a lady in a black dress with ostrich feathers in her hat. It is a devilish alloy of many worlds. ...
> That which has been created in this way—by the invocation and will of the artist with the help of the many little demons which are at the beck and call of every artist—has neither beginning nor end; it is neither alive nor dead ("О Современном Состоянии Русского Символизма", *С.С.*, Vol. V, p. 430).

"The Stranger" is a succuba. Blok never calls her so, but she is surely Lilith. By Blok's contemporaries she was taken for a prostitute, and Annenkov even tells us that the Petersburg prostitutes took to dressing exactly like her, even to borrowing her name, so often did they hear tipsy students reciting Blok's tipsy verses (Yu. Annenkov, "Об Александре Блоке", *Новый Журнал*, кн. XV, New York, 1956, pp. 108–32). Blok himself, perhaps, evoked Her in prostitutes—as well as simply from the mists and shadows of his native city. Yet, essentially, she was a thing without substance—"a dead doll with a face faintly reminiscent of that other one glimpsed among the heavenly roses…" (*C. C.*, Vol. V, p. 429), the Moon-Goddess, shining with reflected splendour (see Note 9).

Озерки: a kind of pleasure park surrounded by suburban holiday houses just outside Petersburg. In his notes to "The Stranger" (*C. C.*, Vol. II, p. 423), Vl. Orlov quotes from E. P. Ivanov's unpublished diary on how Blok took his friend to this place and showed him all the objects evoked in his poem: "the baker's sign", the lakes with their "squeaking rowlocks" and "female squealing", the "level crossings"—and the station buffet. Orlov, however, refrains from quoting Ivanov's comment when he woke up the following morning with a bad hangover: "Для кого как, а для меня еще истины в вине нет." ("For others, perhaps, but for me there's no veritas in vino as yet.")

Крендель булочный: a gilded croissant was the baker's trade sign in Tsarist Russia.

41 (II. 102) Ангел-Хранитель (Люблю Тебя, Ангел-Хранитель, во мгле)
First pub.: *Трудовой путь*, 1907, No. 6—excluding the fourth verse.

The interest of this poem is, perhaps, primarily biographical. Blok himself was obviously dissatisfied with its form (see *C. C.*, Vol. II, p. 405, for the history of the many changes he made in the printed versions before returning to the full original text in the 1918 edition of his works).

In the spring of 1906, when Blok wrote "The Stranger", he had returned home drunk with the verses scribbled in pencil on a crumpled wine-list to find his friend Andrey Bely with his wife, Lyubov'. This he had expected. Ever since Blok had given up writing of the Most Beautiful Lady and had taken to looking for Truth in life, wine and debauch, Bely had been trying to "rescue" his wife, to persuade her to leave his friend, in whom he was bitterly disappointed, for himself. This poem, written on the third anniversary of their marriage, tells us much about their relationship and much about Blok. (Vladimir Orlov is not so sympathetic a biographer as he is thorough a scholar. Nevertheless, Orlov's "История одной любви", based on Lyubov' Dmitriyevna's unpublished memoirs and the still largely unpublished correspondence between Blok and his wife, is the best-documented work in print on Blok's marriage. In the same book—*Пути и Судьбы*, М.-Л., 1963, pp. 579–667—Orlov gives a detailed study of Blok's relations with Andrey Bely—"История одной дружбы-вражды", pp. 446–578.)

The original numbers of the journal in which the poem was published was confiscated by the police and the editors called to answer before the law for "incitement to weighty and criminal deeds". The censors considered the lines "За то, что хочу и не смею убить" to be " in essence, although in a somewhat obscure form, written in praise of political assassination" (cf. O. Tsekhovitser, "Символизм и Царская Цензура", *Ученые Записки Ленинградского Государственного Университета*, No. 76, Leningrad, 1941, p. 293).

42 (II. 106) Русь (Ты и во сне необычайна)
       First pub.: *Золотое Руно*, 1907, No. 6.

For the first time Blok names his other great and lasting earthly love. She is the Gypsy and the Princess and the Seamstress of "Перстень-Страданье". She is Wife and Mother. Sometimes, she may catch and reflect the light of the Most Beautiful Lady, who is in part her Soul as she is the Soul of the Creation. But Russia herself is not transcendent (see No. 99)—but alive with earthly life. And, because she was alive, Russia was to Blok, who frequently doubted his own ability "to take on flesh" (cf. Z. Hippius, *Живые Лица*, Prague, 1925, pp. 7–70, and [in French] *Mercure de France*, No. 596, Vol. CLXI, Paris, 1923, pp. 289–326), an object of reverence and mystery.

This poem is a young man's love poem—a song of headlong passion and high chivalry.

It is also a remarkable ethnographical, geographical and historical evocation of a huge country: "girdled with rivers", "encircled by wild forests", inhabited by peoples of various races, flickered over by the light of burning villages, snow-covered, abandoned—where only "The wind whistling through naked reeds sings legends of the Olden Days".

In a sense, this is still Pobedonostsev's Russia which Blok evokes—"A frozen waste over which there staggers a drunk man"—as that rather macabre statesman once told Dmitry Merezhkovsky, an author whose ideas influenced Blok considerably, particularly before 1905 (cf. Z. Hippius, *D. S. Merezhkovsky*, Paris, 1952). But Blok looks at the huge, sleeping expanses with the eye of love and perceives the variety, the colour, the abundance of human tragedy and hope. When the poem was reprinted in 1908 in the collection *Земля в снегу*, Blok gave it the following epigraph from Tyutchev:

> Не поймет и не заметит
> Гордый взор иноплеменный
> Что сквозит и тайно светит
> В наготе твоей смиренной.

Seeing himself as a wandering, homeless poet, an outcast from Paradise, he warms himself in the rags which is all his country's tattered poverty has to offer him and, rocked to sleep in her spacious wastes, sees her in dreams as a Sleeping Beauty on a ragged couch, so wonderful, so pure in sleep that he

dare not even touch the hem of her garment. For this idea of Russia as a
Sleeping Beauty see also the poem "Сны", not included in this anthology—
C.C., Vol.V, III, No.266, trans. by R.Kemball, "Dreams", *Russian Review*,
October 1959, p.309, and the play *Песня Судьбы*, C.C., Vol.IV, pp.143–5.

погост: graveyard.

43(II.108) Сын и мать (Сын осеняется крестом)
      First pub.: in the Almanac *Белые Ночи*, 1907.
      Trans.: F.Cornford and E.Salaman, "Son and Mother", *Poems
      from the Russian*, London, 1943, p.56.

The idea of the quest, of the knight-errant or the pilgrim turning his back
on home and security, here reaches a fuller note of tragic foreboding. For
the original text see C.C., Vol.II, pp.46–47.

луговины: meadow lands.
чернолесье: deciduous woods.

44(II.193) В октябре (Открыл окно. Какая хмурая)
      First pub.: *Перевал*, 1907, No.7.

In "Русь" Blok contemplates his country's poverty, mystery and far-flung
loveliness. Here, the specific and much less romantic poverty of his native
city—Petersburg. After the Revolution, everything is going on as before.
Of his circle, literary and social, he alone is haunted by the fate of the dis-
possessed and the degraded.

Blok's "lucky star" has long since fallen from the sky into his wineglass
but—in a passion of compassion for a little boy trembling with cold in the
courtyard and a small, brown, much-beaten horse—he finds new life and
winged purpose.

A similar mood is expressed in "Холодный День" (C.C., Vol.II, p.191)
and in several other poems written in the autumn of 1906. As usual, these
poems have a precise setting in time and space. Blok and his wife were
living alone, away from Blok's mother and stepfather, for the first time, and
their tiny flat looked down into one of the almost unbelievably uncared-for
and desolate Petersburg back-yards (cf. "Окна во двор", C.C., Vol.II, p.198,
and other poems written this autumn).

45(II.115) Так окрыленно, так напевно
> First pub.: in the Almanac *Белые Ночи*, 1907, with two additional verses (see *C.C.*, Vol.II, p.409).

Having taken leave of his mother, Blok now bids farewell to his wife. In fact, he left neither, but in spirit he was becoming more and more the homeless wanderer. He wrote this inner drama out of his system in the play *The Song of Fate*, where the hero, who shares a cottage in the mountains with his wise mother and sweet young wife, is suddenly overcome by restlessness and a kind of shame. Before setting out, he prays:

> Lord, I can't go on. I am too comfortable in my quiet white house. Give me strength to leave it and to see what life in the world is like. Only preserve the ardours of my young soul and living conscience, Lord. I ask nothing more of you. ("Песня судьбы", *C.C.*, Vol. IV, pp. 110–11.)

Some images from this poem are borrowed from Victor Hugo's "Légende du beau Pécopène et de la belle Baldoure" and echoes of the same theme are to be found in the article "Девушка розовой калитки и муравьиный царь" (*C.C.*, Vol. V, pp. 83–94) in the poem "В густой траве пропаду с головой" (*C.C.*, Vol.III, p.247) and, simplified and russified, in the Bride's aria which Blok wrote at the request of the composer Yuri Shaporin for Shaporin's cantata on the theme of Kulikovo Pole (*C.C.*, Vol.III, p.374).
ров: moat.

46(II.130) Зачатый в ночь, я в ночь рожден
> First pub.: *Золотое Руно*, 1907, No.6.

One of Blok's earliest "black" poems foreshadowing the predominant tonality of the third volume. His adventures in search of "life in the world" bring him, as he had foreseen, strife and despair—but this is his Fate, and Blok, like Nietzsche, clung both by temperament and conviction to the devise "Amor Fati" (Love of Fate)—"Что быть должно, то быть должно".

K. Chukovsky recalls almost enviously that Blok's rendering of the lines

> Влюбленность расцвела в кудрях
> И в ранней грусти глаз.
> И был я в розовых цепях
> У женщин много раз

was resigned and plaintive (K. Chukovsky, "Александр Блок", *Современники*, Moscow, 1962, p.441). Women were part of Blok's fate. They happened to him.

Again this poem, in contrast with the two previous "farewells", marks Blok's dualism. There he is setting forth on a hero's quest, here he is yielding to temptation, plunging blindly after the "Stranger". In the play—*The Song of Fate*—he is doing both.

For the numerous variants of this poem see *C.C.*, Vol.II, pp.411–13.

47(II.211) Снежное вино (И вновь, сверкнув из чаши винной).
First pub.: *Снежная Маска*, 1907.

Dated 29th December 1906, this is the first poem of a cycle dedicated to the actress Nataliya Volokhova. During the next fortnight Blok was to write twenty-nine more, sometimes at the rate of six poems in one day. It is outside the scope of these notes to probe deeply into the biographical background of Blok's inspiration. For those who are interested, both Nataliya Volokhova and her friend and contemporary, another actress from Vera Kommissarzhevskaya's troupe, Valentina Verigina, have published delightful memoirs of Blok at this period (*Труды по русской и славянской филологии*, IV, Tartu, 1961, pp. 310–78). The memoirs are published by E. G. Minz and D. E. Maksimov, who contributes an important introductory article "Театральные воспоминания о Блоке В. П. Веригиной и Н. Н. Волоховой". See also Mochulsky's well-documented account of Blok's life and poetry at this time (*Александр Блок*, Paris, 1948, pp. 175–80) and the introduction to this volume. Suffice it to say here that Volokhova's dark, tragic beauty and gracious, melancholy "style" (she herself told the author of these notes that, having been endowed by nature with a tragic appearance, she had "far too good taste" to cultivate a cheerful personality) exactly suited Blok's mood in the winter of 1906–7. Like Blok, Volokhova was young, brilliant, beautiful, successful. Like Blok, she suffered quite genuinely from that high sorrow which has no specific object but the generally unsatisfactory state of the world (although in them both at this time—Volokhova says, and Blok confirms in a letter to E. Ivanov, 15/X/1906—there was an element of pose and self-admiration). Like Blok, Volokhova possessed to a rare degree the gift of enthusiasm—the Russians call it "азарт". All his life Blok was subject to violent crazes. As a child it was games of the imagination, then serious acting—from time to time gardening or building. At 31 he developed a *passion* for switchback-riding—at other times for sea-bathing, bicycle-riding, chopping trees, gymnastics, aviation, even, after the Revolution, for laying fires and cleaning rooms. Almost in the same way, his preoccupation with the theatre (the troupe in which Volokhova played was responsible for Meyerhold's first brilliant staging of Blok's verse play *The Puppet-Theatre*) resolved itself into a *passion* for Volokhova—for her beauty, her lovely, "silver" voice, her company. And she fell under the spell of his personality as completely as he under hers: except that she remained coolly, basically aware that she did not love him; that this was a game; that Blok saw her as a daemon-woman—in some sense as the Faina of his "Song of Fate", who is the wild, wayward and unawakened spirit of Russia—whereas she was, in fact, a lyrical, serious and gently bred young lady who wanted to love, and to be loved not by a "poet" but by a "real person". And so the complete absorption in Volokhova, which transformed the soft, snowy winter of 1906/7 into a whirlwind of poetry, was not, as some of Blok's verses have led biographers to believe (cf. N. Berberova, *Alexandre Blok et son temps*, Paris, 1947; Sir Cecil Kisch, *Alexander Blok, Prophet of Revolution*, London, 1960), a carnal Bacchanalia. It was rather, as Valentina Verigina describes it:

> the enchanted circle of play in which we whirled away our youth... the centre of that circle was Blok's "Snow-Maiden", who had her being not only in Nataliya Volokhova, but in us all... even Meyerhold succumbed to the enchantment of the dancing masks and often fell under the spell of Blok's wild whirligig and, like the rest of us, lived a double life: one in reality, the other—in the silver of Blok's swirling blizzards. Here, there was nothing real—neither heart-break nor longing, nor jealousy, nor fear, only the carefree circles woven by the dancing masks on the white snow under the stormy sky.... These two theatre seasons were an unforgettable, wonderful dream for all those initiated into Blok's snowy, dazzling visions. ... (V.P. Verigina, "Воспоминания об Александре Блоке", *Ученые Записки Тартуского Гос. Университета, Труды по русской и славянской филологии,* IV, 1961, pp. 325–7.)

With regard to the last verse of this poem, here is Volokhova's own account of how Blok first read it to her:

> ... he looked up and, seeing the utter astonishment on my face, he looked somewhat disconcerted and, with a shamefaced smile, began to explain that, in the realm of poetry, a little exaggeration is permissible. "As the poets say: 'sub specie aeternitatis', which means literally", he said, smiling, "sauced up in eternity" (N.N. Volokhova, "Земля в снегу", *ibid.*, pp. 374–5).

48 (II.216)  Второе Крещенье (Открыли дверь мою метели)
             First pub.: *Снежная Маска,* 1907.
             Trans.: C. Kisch, "Second Christening", *Alexander Blok, Prophet of Revolution*, London, 1960, p. 79.

The idea of departure expressed in Nos. 44, 45 now finds new expression in the idea of the door thrown open to the blizzard; of the "Second Christening" in the "font of snows". Here is the final acceptance of Blok's earlier foreboding:

«В моей душе любви весна / Не сменит бурного ненастья».

(Cf. No. 1.)

The spring of Blok's life was over, although faint recollections of its glowing expectancy lingered on in his poetry—above all in his constant, heartbreaking tenderness for his wife. But from now on he goes grimly forward through the dark, grey depth of winter. Bely describes the change brought about in his friend by this "Second Christening", playing on the star-theme which rings icily through all Blok's wintry passions:

> He was simpler, more thoughtful; his manliness more pronounced; there was now a stern, tempered quality about him. ... Stars are of the night, of the night of tragedy; that night I felt Blok from within the night of tragedy... and understood that in him the period of shadows and evil spirits, of "Joy beyond Hope", was at an end; for in the dark of the night there are no shadows—only a calm, uniform darkness, set with stars; the Blok who sat before me had already crossed the dividing line of the "Snow-mask". (Andrey Bely, "Воспоминания об А. А. Блоке", *Эпопея,* III, Berlin, 1922, pp. 290–1.)

In the archives of the Pushkin House in Leningrad are many books from Blok's private library, among them his own copy of this book, *Снежная Маска,* in which Volokhova had written beneath the dedication "To the tall woman in black with the winged eyes enamoured of the lights and darkness of my snowy city": "Joyfully I accept this strange book, joyfully, and with fear—in it there is so much beauty, poetry, death. I await the accomplishment of your task."

When asked, in Moscow, in 1960, what she had meant by his "task", Volokhova thought for a moment, her fine silver head slightly on one side, then queried with a little laugh in her voice: "Didn't I say 'miracle'? Blok and I often talked of a 'miracle', of the possibility of his becoming a real, live human being. I suppose that is what I meant." She paused, the chiselled, hollow-cheeked face and the dark "tragic" brows still and concentrated, "He avoided me after 1908—but of course I read his poetry—later on, after he died, mostly. I think, in the Third Volume, he achieved his miracle."

Volokhova spoke of death in her acceptance of the book. "The Second Christening" involves a death and looks towards death as the third and final baptism. The "winged trochees" (Bely's expression), which make up two-thirds of the poems of this cycle, were, for Blok, the metre of death (cf. entry in diary for 4th March 1918: "Толстопузые мещане злобно чтут дорогую память трупа (у меня непроизвольно появляются хореи, значет, может-быть погибну)", (I am breaking into trochees without meaning to, which means, perhaps, I shall perish). In the midst of this brilliant winter season of gaiety and make-believe, Blok wrote to E. Ivanov: "My dear, trust me, I have the right to ask that of you just now. Most important is that you should accept *that I am in a state of terror and that there is no more firm ground\**" (letter to E. P. Ivanov of 18/II/1907). The last poems of the Second Volume, like the last poems of the Third, are of death and—hope.

горница: room, chamber (archaic).

* Editor's italics.

49 (II. 217)  Настигнутый метелью (Вьюга пела)
            First pub.: *Снежная Маска*, 1907.

This poem is a kind of quintessence of the whole cycle. Note the curious
correspondence between "Вот Он — Христос":

> … Стоя рядом достичь нельзя,
>
> . . . . . . . . . . . .
>
> Пока такой же нищий не будешь,
> Не ляжешь, истоптан, в глухой овраг,
> *Обо всем не забудешь и всего не разлюбишь,** 
> И не поблекнешь, как мертвый злак.

and the second verse of this poem:

> Ты запрокинула голову в высь.
> Ты сказала: «Глядись, глядись,
> *Пока не забудешь*
> *Того, что любишь.»** 
> И указала на дальние города линии,
> На поля снеговые и синие,
> На бесцельный холод.

Only that the first call—which Blok refused—contains a covenant of new life:
the second—which he accepted—premises the "aimless cold" of tragic Nordic
mythology. In his reminiscences of Blok, E. Ivanov has left a full record of
their discussions about "The Daemon" (neither Devil nor Angel, in Blok's
view, but a suffering man, empty and desolate, finding comfort neither in
God nor in the world, loved by woman for his suffering and loving her in
return only for her compassion). They spoke of how, when man feels
completely cut off from God, he requires something in the nature of "a
tarantella"—a "descent into hell". Of this, only the Daemon or Christ are
capable. The Revolution is such a tarantella, such a descent. Only the Son of
Man can help the Daemon to rise again. Such was the theory Ivanov dis-
cussed with Blok on 30th March 1905. The "Snow-mask" may be likened to
the beginning of Blok's daemonic descent. His "tarantellas" were the infatua-
tion for Volokhova which helped him to break the last ties with domesticity
and the security of his environment after the 1905 Revolution: the passion
for L. A. Del'mas, in which he touched new heights of emptiness and ecstasy
in the spring before the outbreak of the First World War (see the cycle
"Carmen" and notes—also the poem "Daemon", No. 62); and the Revo-
lution, when, in January 1918, he "surrendered to the elements for the last
time" (see "The Twelve", "The Scythians" and notes).

снежные иглы: snow needles. Petersburg is low-lying and its climate damp. Often in
    winter splinters of humidity will freeze in the air and dance around the street lamps.

* Editor's italics.

50 (II. 295) О смерти (Всё чаще я по городу брожу)
> First pub.: In the Almanac *Факелы*, III, 1908, from the cycle *Вольные Мысли*.

The dedication is to George Chulkov, the boon companion of Blok's aimless, often tipsy wanderings about the outskirts of Petersburg during the spring and summer of 1907 and the originator, together with the poet Vyacheslav Ivanov, of the theory of "Mystic Anarchism" with which Blok's name was linked for a short season after the Revolution before, at the instigation of Andrey Bely, he formally disassociated himself from it in print (see Andrey Bely, "Воспоминания об А. А. Блоке", *Эпопея*, III, Berlin, 1922, pp. 250–80; G. Chulkov, *Годы Странствия*, Moscow, 1930, pp. 121–44, 360–98, "Александр Блок и его время", *Письма Александра Блока*, Leningrad, 1925, pp. 91–120; also Blok's letters to Chulkov in the same volume, pp. 121–50).

The blank iambs of the cycle "Free Thoughts" are in complete contrast to the tumbling trochees and dancing mixed metres of "The Snow-Mask". So is the whole artistic approach. White, Apollonian clarity succeeds the Dionysian mists and music, even as the northern sun ruthlessly illumines the race-course, the pleasure-parks, the river-bound "islands" and the shallow, sandy coast of the Gulf of Finland which form the objects of Blok's contemplation on his idle summer jauntings about the capital. It is as though, having at last torn his slow but immensely powerful concentration away from the contemplation of Nature and Eternity, he had at first perceived the town and its citizens through a shimmering haze and had here, for the first time, achieved sharp focus. In "The Stranger" and "The Snow-Mask" the real dissolves always into the fantastic and the fantastic—suddenly turning round to face you—displays a visage of the most blatant vulgarity. "Free Thoughts", on the contrary, have been compared to Pushkin in their chiselled, classical descriptive realism (K. Chukovsky, "А. А. Блок" in the book *Современники*, Moscow, 1962, p. 440). Possibly, however, this assessment should be modified by Blok's own description of Pushkin: "Everything is clear to the point of terror, like the lines of the hand under a microscope. Not mysterious, it would seem, and yet, perhaps, in a different way, 'suicidally' mysterious... possibly Pushkin is infinitely more lonely and more 'deadly' (Merezhkovsky) than Tyutchev..." (*Записные Книжки*, 10th December 1913–9th January 1914).

Certainly, the lyrical hero of this cycle is not only more detached but also more isolated than in Blok's early poetry, where he is at once alone and universal, or than in his later works, in which he succeeds in "organically introducing the new and the general into the equally organic, individual experience which forms the content of the first four books" (*Записные Книжки*, 3/VI/1916). The peasant poet Klyuyev, in 1907 still an unknown provincial songster who had made himself to some extent the mentor of Blok's social conscience, objected strongly to Blok's latest role of idle looker-on:

> "Free Thoughts" are the thoughts of a gentleman on holiday, amusing himself, drinking, chasing the girls "for a bit of a change" and, in general, taking his ease in the bosom of nature. They are of no use to anyone, except to Chulkov, to whom these "thoughts" are dedicated. (Letter No. 5, Письма Клюева Николая Алексеевича Блоку Александру Александровичу, ЦГАЛИ, Ф. No. 55, Опись No. 3, Ед. хр. No. 35.)

Vl. Orlov, on the other hand, considers "Free Thoughts" to be "one of the most important milestones on Blok's road to emancipation from decadent aestheticism", a first essay in "satire", "clarity", "epic sweep" and dramatic tension" (Александр Блок, *Стихотворения и поэмы*, Библиотека поэта, Малая серия, Изд. 3, Leningrad, 1961, Introduction, pp. 36–37).

A third opinion of these verses might be that they are interesting and necessary formal experiments in exact observation and objectivity, which Blok was later to combine with his unique gift for "music" in the great poetry of the Third Volume. Where they lapse into lyricism, however, they are still wholly linked with the spiritual ambivalence and self-destructive pathos of the Second Volume rather than with the "social" themes of Blok's later works.

щебень: broken brick or metal.
рейтузы: breeches.
сотка: a small bottle.


51 (II. 263–5) Осенняя любовь
        First pub.: *Весы*, 1907, No. 12.
        Trans.: C. M. Bowra, "Autumn Love", *A Book of Russian Verse*, London, 1943, p. 99.

The autumn of 1907 found Blok again at the feet of his "Snow-Maiden", Volokhova. This strange poem in three parts tells us much of his confused state of soul. In the first part, he sees himself crucified before the eyes of his "stern Motherland" and, in his death-throes, it seems to him that a small boat is approaching his "crucified heights", and that in the boat is seated Christ, who gave Himself to be crucified "in the same hopes". He does not know whether or not the boat will draw in to land beneath *his* cross. Some critics (notably B. Zaitsev in his article "Побежденный", *Современные Записки*, кн. XXV, Paris, 1925, pp. 250–61, and Sophie Bonneau in her book

*L'Univers poétique d'Alexandre Blok*, Paris, 1946) use this poem as one of the arguments in favour of the theory that Blok identified Christ with the Russian people or at least saw Him as a specifically Russian, "unresurrected" Christ. I agree rather with Vl. Weidle (review of S. Bonneau's book, *Critique*, Vol. IV, No. 20, Paris, 1948, pp. 80–82) that this is an over-simplification. There is undoubtedly a connection between Christ and Russia in Blok's thought, but probably largely because "He came down to Earth from Heaven" and, of all the Earth, Blok "felt" in his blood and flesh and bones "only Russia" (cf. *Записные Книжки* 6th October 1914). In his letters to Bely, Blok definitely connects his lack-love attitude to Christ with his individualism and his youthful contempt for "the masses" (cf., for instance, the letter of 1/VIII/1903, *Переписка*, p. 41). But Blok's feeling for Jesus of Nazareth was certainly more personal and more complex. Haunted by Him, he resisted to the end the idea that Christ would have the final shaping of Salvation— either in history, or in his own soul. A friend of Blok's last years, N. A. Pavlovich, told me that he "disliked humility", hence the famous comment on his own vision of Christ at the head of the Twelve Red Guards: "Unfortunately—Christ!"

In the second part of the poem, Blok, employing a broken, tonic rhythm the use of which in modern Russian poetry he canonized and which here seems to have been invented especially to suggest the capricious eddying of falling leaves, harks back to his own happy and glorious youth—before he had so irrevocably turned his back upon the Spring.

In the third part, he returns to his cold and fatal passion—and to the daemonic element of rebellion:

> Ты думаешь — нежная ласка,
> Я знаю — восторг мятежа.

ланиты: cheeks (archaic).


52 (II. 267) Снежная дева (Она пришла из дикой дали)
        First pub.: *Весы*, 1907, No. 12.

Petersburg has always fascinated Russian authors and Blok continued the tradition of Pushkin, Gogol and Dostoyevsky as one of the greatest singers of this beautiful and phantasmagorical city. (See Vl. Orlov's preface to the collection of Blok's verse, *Город мой*, Leningrad, 1957, pp. 5–48; A. M. Dokusov's article in the collection *Литературно-памятные места Ленинграда*, Leningrad, 1959, pp. 435–58; N. Antsiferov, "Непостижимый город" in the collection *Об Александре Блоке*, Petersburg, 1921, pp. 285–325; and for another artist's impression, Yevtushenko's poem "Когда я думаю о Блоке".)

Volokhova's memoirs tell us of the background to this poem:

> Often, after the play, we would go for long walks; then Aleksandr Aleksandrovich would show me "his town" as he called it. He showed me all the places bound up with his play "The Stranger": the bridge where the Astrologer stood and where he met the Poet, the very spot on which the Stranger came down to Earth, and the alley of street-lamps into which she disappeared. We visited the restaurant with painted walls. ... Reality was so intermingled with the imagination, with the dreams of the poet, that, unwittingly, I lost the boundaries of the real and, with awe and with enchantment, entered into the unknown world of poetry. I felt as though I were receiving as a gift from the hands of the poet this strange, fantastic town, all woven from subtlest blues and bright golden stars (N. Volokhova, *op. cit.*, p. 373).

Сфинкс с выщербленным ликом: two Theban Sphynxes face each other across a broad double sweep of stone stairs down to the broad, grey waters of the Neva. The sphynxes are surprisingly situated, some way from the courtly confluence of rivers on which stand the Winter Palace and other great buildings—further down river towards the cranes and masts of the docks and the cosy, murky labyrinth of canals known as New Holland. Blok loved to play with the idea that Volokhova was a reincarnation of Cleopatra whose waxen image in the Petersburg Panoptikum held a strong fascination for him (cf., for instance, *C.C.*, Vol. II, p. 207) and this is why, in the poem, she meets the exiled sphynx with "a little cry" of recognition.

53 (II. 272) From the cycle: Заклятие огнем и мраком

О' весна без конца и без краю

First pub.: *Весы*, 1908, No. 3, under the title "Заклятие огнем и мраком и пляской метелей" and with a dedication to N. N. Volokhova, "И вновь посвящаю эти стихи — Тебе". In the rough draft this first poem of the cycle is also dedicated to her as to "A woman, poisoned by her own beauty".

The epigraph from Lermontov is important, for the inspiration of this cycle, as of much of Blok's poetry, is akin to Lermontov's inspiration. D. Maksimov, in his all-too-brief article "Lermontov and Blok" (*Поэзия Лермонтова*, Leningrad, 1959, pp. 309–25), maintains that Lermontov's fascination for Blok lay in his positive conception of the daemonic; in his combination of extreme individualism with a profound, loving and exacting commitment to Russia in all her poverty; and, above all, in Lermontov's "unrelieved uneasiness of spirit" (p. 318). Even before meeting Blok, Andrey Bely declared him the successor of Lermontov "as though by the laying on of hands" (letter from Bely to Blok of 4/I/1903, *Переписка*, p. 7). N. Pavlovich writes of Blok:

Как долг хранил он вечный непокой

and further, remembering Blok's own words:

А в юности казалось в глубине,
Что наделен я лермонтовской силой,
И чувство непреложно говорило,
Что светлый подвиг был завещан мне.

(N. Pavlovich, *Воспоминания о Блоке,* Moscow, 1966, 2nd ed., p. 24).

For Blok on Lermontov see the articles "Безвременье" (*C.C.*, Vol.V, pp. 66–82), "Педант о поэте" (*ibid.*, pp.25–30), a brief but important reference in the article "Народ и интеллигенция" (*ibid.*, p.321), etc. Unfortunately, the manuscript of Blok's original introduction to Lermontov's *Collected Works* (*Всемирная литература*, 1919) is lost; the published version is purely informative and throws no light on Blok's attitude to Lermontov in his later years.

To return to the first poem of this cycle: Blok later came to regard it with a certain irony, as he regarded most of the verses written during the transitional years of 1904–8. "I can't stand people who like the Second Volume best", he remarked irritably towards the end of his life (V.Pyast, "О первом томе Блока", in the collection *Об Александре Блоке*, Petersburg, 1921, pp.213–14). There is, perhaps, a certain lushness about Blok's work in this period which accords ill with his later severity and simplicity. Yet this time of "intoxicated dream" was an essential lap on his tragic pilgrim's progress: he "set out" in style, infatuated with his own youth and strength as much as with the unattainable, almost hostile "Snow-Maiden" who had become his muse. This poem resembles nothing so much as a horn sounded in challenge from the castle walls before a warrior sets forth to battle.

Веси: hills. Usually only in the expression "*по допям и весям*", "over hill and dale".

53 (II.280) From the cycle: Заклятие Огнем и Мраком
Гармоника, гармоника!
First pub.: *Земля в снегу*, 1908 under the title "Пляска".

It has been said by many critics that the great power of Blok's poetry lay in its "music", which lent his verse an immediate emotional impact akin to that of the sentimental romance, the street ballad, the gipsy song or the factory "chastushka" whose rhythms and elan he exploited to dance his reader resistless away on surge upon surge of rhythm. The sophisticated critic Viktor Shklovsky wrote of him:

> This man had not the make-up of an aesthete; the foundation of his craft was the revival of the gypsy romance. He wrote employing the banal image.
> Blok's strength lies in the fact that he is wedded to the very simplest lyric forms ...
> (*Сентиментальное путешествие*, Moscow, 1929, p. 282.)

In such poems as this, Blok borrows his songs almost "straight" from the *café-chantant*. Later, he was to use his ear for the rhythms of the street to lend a startling verisimilitude to "The Twelve". Perhaps it was this quality of Blok's which earned the remarkable tribute from Boris Pasternak that, when he wrote of the city, it was "... as if the doors had been flung open and let in the noises of the street.... as if the town itself were making its presence felt through his lips" (B. Pasternak, *Автобиография*).

For the true aesthete, however, this complete surrender to the choppy swing of folk-rhythm can prove a stumbling block:

> Blok's verses are full of all kinds of lapses which "he could not bring himself to sacrifice". ... Why could he not bring himself? Because "it sung itself that way", because that was the way he saw it, however irrationally, disconnectedly and, frequently, in defiance of the laws of metrics, etymology and syntax and, still more important – of the precise meaning of verbs and adverbs (his definitions are almost always "approximate", seeking only after originality).
> In that is Blok's greatest misfortune. ... (C. K. Makovsky, *На Парнасе Серебряного Века*, Munich, 1962, p. 154.)

54 (II. 290)  Она пришла с мороза
>           First pub.: *Земля в снегу* 1908, under the title "Знакомое".
>           Trans.: A. Miller, "She came in out of the frost", *Stand*, Winter
>           1956/7, p. 1.

This essay in free verse shows a certain sobering up: the details are exactly observed, the tone—one of rueful amusement rather than of intoxication.

Volokhova remembers that the poem was based on a real incident: only the cat among the pigeons was the product of Blok's imagination. In fact, entering his room after a long sleigh ride in 20 degrees of frost, she had been tucked up under a rug to thaw out—and had dropped off to sleep as he read. Blok's poetic imagination almost invariably began with some real sensual impression—visual, oral—more rarely tactile. Beginning from such intensely experienced sensation, the creative process would take over, suggesting associations, ascribing to the thing seen or heard its part in some Universal Harmony.

It is not by chance that Blok returns to the theme of the "Bubbles of the Earth". In a letter to a friend of Andrey Bely (the poet Ellis— L. L. Kobylinsky) dated 5/III/1907, Blok writes of Shakespeare: "I love him deeply; and perhaps, most deeply of all—in the whole of world literature— Macbeth" (unpublished letter, quoted in note to this poem by Vl. Orlov, *C. C.*, Vol. II, p. 436).

Паоло и Франческа: medieval lovers who, in Dante's inferno, are allowed to leave the perpetual whirlwind in which adulterous lovers are caught up in Hell, to tell the poet how they fell in love over a book which they were reading together.

55(II.288) Когда вы стоите на моем пути

First pub.: *Земля в снегу*, 1908, under the title "*Письмо*" and with an epigraph from A.A.Fet:

В чужой восторг переселяться
Заране учится душа

Trans.: A.Miller, "Whenever you stand before me", *Stand*, Winter 1956/7, p.2.

Written on the same evening as the preceding poem, these lines were addressed to quite another heroine—to a determined schoolgirl of 14 who, having seen Blok reading his poetry at various literary gatherings, had decided that he would understand and be able to help her to resolve her adolescent miseries—loss of faith in God and a corrosive hatred of Petersburg—Blok's Petersburg. Her first impression of Blok: "In my soul—an immense attention. This man had such a distant, indifferent, beautiful face, not in the least like the others. I was confronted with something that I had never met before, head and shoulders above anything that I had previously known, something marked of Fate."

The man of 27, whose life and poetry were at that time the scandal and delight of literary Petersburg, received the unknown schoolgirl (who had gate-crashed his flat with no introduction) with courteous attention. She left him feeling that he was perhaps more lost even than she, that she was in some way the older. A few days later the poem "When you stand in my path" arrived through the post. The little girl later achieved as full a life as Blok could have wished for her. Twice married, the mother of three children, she became a nun in the Paris emigration, helped Jews to hide from the Nazis during the occupation and ended her days in the gas chambers of Dachau. By surviving fellow prisoners she is still honoured as a fearless embodiment of the Orthodox principle of "Active Love". For her reminiscences of Blok see Мон. Мария, "Встречи с Блоком", *Современные Записки*, LXII, Paris, 1936, pp.211–28, republished with an introduction by D.E.Maksimov and footnotes by Z.G. Minz in *Ученые записки Тартуского Государственного Университета, Труды по русской и славянской филологии*, XI, Литературоведение, Tartu, 1968, pp. 257–78.

56(III.7)  К Музе (Есть в напевах твоих сокровенных)
　　　　　　First pub.: *Русская Мысль*, 1913, No.11.
　　　　　　Trans.: R.Kemball, "To the Muse", *Russian Review*, October
　　　　　　1959, p.307.

In the poetry of the Third Volume it is clear that Blok has chosen—irrevocably— "The Hell of art". He had become a great artist and his muse gave
him everything except the one thing he had experienced, however transiently,
in his youth—Spiritual Joy; and the thing which he had himself rejected as
an unworthy substitute—human happiness.

In Blok's first draft the poem is dated "Autumn – 29.XII.1912". On
11th October for the same year he noted in his diary a conversation with his
friend and patron M.I.Tereshchenko, which is certainly reflected in this
poem.

> Tereshchenko was saying that art makes people equal (the only thing that does so in
> all the world), that it gives joy and something which can't even be called joy; that he
> cannot understand people who can take any interest in—say—politics—if they have
> ever experienced (really felt) what art is; and that he doesn't understand people who
> can fall in love after "Tristan". With all that I argued and failed to argue, as I am so
> often constrained to do; that is:—I argued, because once I had known something
> greater than art; i.e. not infinity, but the End, not worlds, but the World; I failed to
> argue because that I have lost, probably for ever; I have fallen, betrayed, and am now
> indeed "an artist", living not by that which is the substance of life, but by that which
> makes life black and terrible and thrusts it away. I failed to argue also because I am a
> "pessimist" "universally acknowledged as such", and because there, where for me
> there is despair and horror, for others there is joy, and perhaps—even—Joy. I don't
> know.

> ay: a type of champagne (town in France).

57(III.19)  Поздней осенью из гавани
　　　　　　First pub.: *Новая Жизнь*, 1910, No.1.
　　　　　　Trans.: Francis Cornford, "The Sailor", *Poems from the Russian*,
　　　　　　London, 1943, p.53. J.Hornstein, "The winter day is cold and
　　　　　　snowy", *Poems*, Dorking, undated, p.9.

A wonderful example of the multi-dimensional manner of Blok's Third
Volume which enabled him, while remaining always himself, to become "the
greatest and most exact recorder of the heartbeat of his decade" (Olga Forsh,
*Сумасшедший корабль*, Leningrad, 1931, p.99). Blok "listened" for his
poetry. By deliberate self-discipline he trained himself to "listen" not only
to the "music of the spheres"—but to the sounds of every day life as well.
He won this almost mediumistic gift through the strangest form of asceticism:
through night-wanderings, drunkenness, brothel-haunting, vagabondage. It
was surely with Blok in mind that E.Lundberg wrote:

They are right, from their own point of view, when they say that the failure of Christianity is a human, not a divine failure. All the more stubborn should be the determination to destroy the existing order of things, to build everything up again from the beginning. Or, possibly, not even to build. To have the courage to keep silence, to wait, to listen to oneself and to the world. A kind of asceticism. Inaction as a form of service. Even—blasphemy as a form of service. (*Записки писателя 1917–1920*, Л, 1930, p. 104).

For Lundberg understood the tragic intensity of Blok's experience:

Once upon a time Blok thought *ecstatically* not only of the Most Beautiful Lady but also of Russia. But Fate decoyed him onto a thorny road, into the midst of drunken and ragged Rus', to the beggar, to someone's mocking grin from a prison window—into regions where we lose *the right to judge* and *to choose*, where all is deserted, tattered, hopeless, where the pot-house is *higher* in the scale of values than noble suffering or ecstasy ... (*Ibid.*, p. 132.)

When Blok writes of the sailor left sleeping drunkenly on the dockside, the sailor is Blok and is himself, and the weight of tragedy the poem carries is the intolerable weight of the universal tragedy of all those whose ships have sailed without them.

58 (III.25) В песторане (Никогда не забуду, он был или не был)
      First pub.: *Русская Мысль*, 1910, No. II.

The sheer hypnotic enchantment of this poem is reminiscent of "The Stranger"—but the detail is as precisely observed and recorded as the river and racecourse scenes in "Вольные мысли".

E. M. Nelidova, the heroine of the incident, recalled the occasion many years later:

We were sitting at one of the little tables. "Look", my sister-in-law said, "Blok can't take his eyes off you" (he was sitting quite near us). I turned away so that he could not see my face. He sent me across a glass of wine and in it—a red rose. I took this for an impertinence and, not wanting to stay any longer, got up and left. (Quoted from notes taken in 1948 by A. G. Lebedeva, by Vl. Orlov, *C. C.*, Vol. III, p. 504.)

ау: see Note 56.

смычок: bow, fiddle-stick.

монисто: necklace (usually made from coins, of the type worn by gipsies).

59 (III.31) Унижение (В черных сучьях дерев обнаженных)
      First pub.: *Северные записки*, 1913, No. 2.
      Trans.: C. Kisch, "Humiliation", *Alexander Blok, Prophet of Revolution*, London, 1960, p. 90.

Blok impressed other people as a creature of almost inhuman purity. Valentina Verigina found it almost impossible to believe that the headily sensual notes in some of Blok's poetry could have been sounded by the man she knew. Ivanov wrote of him: "He was pure and reflected in himself all pure things with a still greater purity, as transparent waters reflect their surroundings." Gor'ky has left us the story of Blok's brotherly tenderness for a prostitute, so tired and cold that she could only sleep in his arms (*My Diaries*, Penguin Books, 2nd ed., 1940, pp. 178–80).

Yet Blok looked on himself as "dark". He had inherited from his father some element of erotic daemonism, an essentially cruel sensuality (see the cycle "Черная кровь", *C.C.*, vol. III, pp. 54–58, also Blok's diary for 27th December 1911 and the lines about his father in the poem "Retribution"). There was also a strong tendency towards self-destruction. A friend, the poet Pyast, remembers how Blok once told him:

> ... when you see all that on every side, all that poverty and horror in which you are stifling and the impossibility of changing anything whatsoever in it all; when you know that with a fifty-rouble note like this one here you could do some one person a good, a really good turn—and that in the general way everything will remain exactly as it was—well, then, you go and spend not fifty but one hundred, two hundred roubles with luxurious delight on debauchery which is of no possible use to anyone—least of all to yourself... (V. Pyast, *Воспоминания о Блоке,* Petersburg, 1923, p. 66.)

To his mother Blok once wrote: "The worse you live the better you can write, but this profession does not allow for life" (letter of 29/X/1907, *Письма к родным*, p. 178).

Yet Blok did not visit brothels in search of journalist's copy. The appalling scene described in this poem is not "seen" but "experienced"—as is all Blok's poetry with the possible exception of "Вольные мысли"; and the disgust, which finds its very embodiment in the image of the prostitute's discarded train, trailing from the chair over the carpet like a snake, "heavy, replete and dusty", is self-disgust.

кисть: tassel.

портьера: door-curtain.

шулер: card-sharper.

плат: from the more usual diminutive form "платок" (shawl or kerchief).

на иконе твоей золотой: "on your golden (precious) face (which is made in the image of God)". Note also the use of лик in the preceding verse and cf. Note 11.

60 (III. 33) Авиатор (Летун отпущен на свободу)
    First pub.: *Заветы*, 1912, No. I.
    Trans.: Payson Loomis, "The Aviator", *One Hundred Modern Poems*, selected by Selden Rodman, p. 35.

Watching the first experimental flights at the Kolomyazhsky aerodrome was one of Blok's "crazes". In 1910 he wrote to his mother that in flight

"there is something ancient and predestined for man, and therefore high"
(letter of 24/IV/1910, *Письма к родным*, II, p. 75). In 1911 he saw one of the
first Russian pilots, V. F. Smit, crash to his death before a large crowd of
spectators. The propeller, Blok said, had introduced "a new sound into the
world" (V. Pyast, *Воспоминания о Блоке*, Petersburg, 1923, p. 51). Sounds
were important to him. The poem "Don Juan", for instance, is built around
the sound of a distant motor-horn (see note to No. 65). The prologue to the
long poem "Retribution" (see No. 100) is full of unexplained but significant
sounds. With characteristic concentration Blok went again and again to the
air-shows to make out the meaning of the "new sound" of the propeller. In
this poem, his innate distrust of machinery and his clear-sighted misanthrope
lead him to foresee horrors. But, in the prose passage with which I have
chosen to conclude the selections from "The Motherland" (No. 99), the same
image of the aviator attempting "the world record of flight" leads his pro-
phetic spirit into our present era of terror and achievement—and beyond to
a future in which man's wisdom will match his technical proficiency and "our
motherland will become the whole Earth, and then not the Earth alone, but
the infinite Universe" ("Ответ Мережковскому", *С. С.*, Vol. V, p. 444).

The futurists, who, in the person of V. V. Kamensky, boasted at least one
trained pilot among their company, complained that Blok, who was certainly
more at home on horseback than in any mechanical form of conveyance, had
neither the vocabulary nor the technique to write of twentieth-century ma-
chines. N. Aseyev even went so far as to say of this poem that "Blok saw no-
thing in the coming wings of man but the soullessness of those wings", and
that his approach to the aeroplane bordered on medieval obscurantism
(N. Aseyev, *Работа над стихом*, Leningrad, 1929, p. 63). This assessment of
Blok's attitude is more revealing for futurist iconoclasm than for Blok's
approach to the modern world, but a real discrepancy between style and sub-
ject in this poem *does* serve to emphasize Blok's unique position as a link
between nineteenth- and twentieth-century culture—a position brilliantly
delineated by N. Otsoupe ("Лицо Блока", *Собрание Сочинений*, Vol. IV,
Paris, 1961, pp. 55–77). This poem creates the impression that Blok is contem-
plating a phenomenon essentially alien to his own world and struggling to
find the place of this phenomenon in relation to the whole destiny of Man.
Typically, he makes no attempt to explain the thing according to any logical
system, even to himself, but waits listening for something "from outside"
which in an early letter to Bely he calls simply "the breath of life" (letter of
3/II/1903, *Переписка*, p. 17).

мгла: here (verse 5) a dust-cloud. In the last verse the meaning is the usual one of "dark-
ness".

61 (III. 36–40)  Пляски смерти

> First pub.: (1) *Современник*, 1912, No. 11, under the title "Totentanz". (2 and 3) *Русская Мысль*, 1914, No. 3—together, also under the title "Totentanz". (4) *Биржевые ведомости*, 4th October 1915. (5) *Русская Мысль*, 1915, No. 12, under the title "Пляски смерти".
>
> Trans.: M. Bowra, "Dance of Death", *A Second Book of Russian Verse*, London, 1947, p. 72 et seq.

Although the macabre theme is reminiscent of Poe and Baudelaire, Blok did not suffer from necrophilia. He is evoking forces of decomposition working within his own society and his face is stiff with horror. The first poem was immediately suggested by the personality of one Arkady Rumanov, "an astute and soulless newspaper-man with a talent for simulating passionate sincerity and generous poetic fire" (K. Chukovsky, "А. Блок" in the book *Современники*, Moscow, 1962, p. 439). The rest of the cycle seems to have been inspired by Blok's insomniac wanderings through Petersburg, when:

> Тихая тоска сожмет так нежно горло
>     Ни охнуть, ни вздохнуть,
> Как будто ночь на все проклятие простерла,
>     Сам дьявол сел на грудь,
> Ты вскочишь и бежишь на улицы глухие,
>     Но некому помочь:
> Куда ни повернись, – глядят в глаза пустые
>     И провожает – ночь.
>
> (From "Жизнь моего приятеля", *С. С.*, Vol. III, p. 47.)

In a plan for a play which never came to be written Blok left us a startling self-portrait, which throws some light on these moods:

> But he has been seen not only at receptions, in his study, among piles of books, proud and self-willed. Not only flying past with that other woman. Not only the mysterious renown of woman's love surrounds him.
>
> He has been seen at night—on the wet snow—staggering helplessly under the moon, homeless, bent, weary, despairing of everything. He himself knows the sickness of melancholy which is eating him away, and secretly loves it and torments himself with it. Sometimes he thinks of suicide. Some people he listens to, others he trusts—but most of the time he knows nothing... (*Записные книжки*, 19–20/II/1908.)

The last poem in the series was originally published without the third and fourth verses, which were considered subversive. It is an excellent example of Blok's use of a thoroughly common rhythm to convey rebellious, irresponsible fury.

Присутствие: the presence of an important official in his office: thus "working" or "reception hours".

*Venena*: poison (Lat.).

ненароком: inadvertently, by mistake (slang).

козырек: peaked cap.

62 (III. 60)  Демон (Иди, иди за мной—покорной)
> First pub.: In the Almanac *Творчество*, I, 1917.
> Trans.: C. M. Bowra, *A Book of Russian Verse*, London, 1943, p. 104.

This is the theme which shows, most immediately and unambiguously, Lermontov's influence on Blok (cf. also the other poem of the same title, *C. C.*, Vol. III, p. 26, and Note 53). Blok's muse—less richly romantic than Lermontov's—evokes a less human daemon. We cannot feel pity for this cosmic spirit, as we can and do for Lermontov's outcast wanderer. In this poem Blok transports us to heights of pure spirit—above space, outside time—and there, calmly, almost tenderly, he lets us fall into "a shining emptiness". But perhaps it is the poet's own soul which the daemon lets fall, for he is, after all, only the greatest and most powerful of Blok's doubles.

63 (III. 62)  Голос из Хора (Как часто плачем—вы и я)
> First pub.: *Любовь к трем апельсинам*, 1916, No. 1.
> Trans.: M. Bowra, "Voice from the Chorus", *A Book of Russian Verse*, London, 1943, p. 104. C. Kisch, "A voice from the chorus", *Alexander Blok, Prophet of Revolution*, London, 1960, p. 82.

One of those "inspired" poems, which Blok himself, when he came to re-read them, intensely disliked. "Most unpleasant verses", he is reported to have said. "I don't know why I wrote them. It would have been better for those words to have been left unsaid. But I had to say them. The difficult must be overcome. And beyond it will be clear day" (Vs. Rozhdestvensky, "Александр Блок", *Страницы жизни*, Moscow–Leningrad, 1962, p. 238). Cf. also the first (1910) draft of the poem in Orlov's note (*C. C.*, Vol. III, p. 515), which shows that Blok originally attempted to express this hope of a light "beyond hope".

> Я крылатым рожден и веселым,
> Это ныне лишь …
> Лишь до времени камнем тяжелым
> Вход завален, и дух мой в гробу.

In the first printed version, only the apocalyptic intensity of the darkness suggests the possibility, implicit but unexpressed in all Blok's mature poetry, of "a sudden twist in the road … leading out into God's good day" (letter to A. L. Blok, 5/VIII/1902, *Письма к родным*, I, p. 76). Mother Mariya (see Note 55) remembers that, when he was asked by a periodical publication to contribute a "patriotic" poem during the First World War, Blok, who looked on the war as a symptom of the aimless convulsions of a dying civilization, sent them "Voice from the Chorus". Needless to say, the periodical in question did not consider it suitable for publication.

64(III.64)  О доблестях, о подвигах, о славе
First pub.: *Новый Журнал для Всех*, 1910, No.1.
Trans.: C.M.Bowra, "Glory and gallant deeds and fame forgetting", *A Second Book of Russian Verse*, London, 1947, p.67.
C.Kisch, "Valor, prowess and glory", *Alexander Blok, Prophet of Revolution*, London, 1960, p.94. G.F.Cunningham, "I care not for brave deeds of fame or fable", *Lyrics from the Russian*, Edinburgh, 1961.

Looking back on his life nine years after this poem was written, Blok noted:

> Hardly had my fiancée become my wife when the lilac worlds of revolution enveloped us and swept us into the whirlpool. I, first, as one who had long wished secretly for perdition, was swept into the grey purple, the silver stars, the mother-of-pearls and amethysts of the blizzard. After me followed my wife, for whom the transition (from the difficult to the easy, from the impermissible to the permissible) was a torment harder than for me. (*Дневник*, 15/VIII/1917.)

Blok had opened his own doors to the snow-storm. Even his mother wrote to a friend that his wife's subsequent betrayals were the direct result of "Sasha's lack of domesticity" (несемейственность) (letter to E.P. Ivanov, 17/XI/1908, Архив Е.П.Иванова, П.Д., Ф.662, №.61). Lyubov' Dmitrievna refused Andrey Bely, with whom alone, she believed, she could have betrayed her special relationship with Blok, but she did later seek comfort with other men and independence in her career as an actress. Blok was not indifferent, but felt he had no right to interfere. As in the poems to Volokhova, there is, biographically speaking, much exaggeration in these verses. Blok never withdrew from his marriage, nor was there any final break between him and his wife at this or at any other time. Nevertheless, they were much apart, never sure of one another—and Blok suffered acutely both from the situation itself and from his own feeling of responsibility for the way things had turned out.

The original draft of this poem (given in full by Orlov, *C.C.*, Vol.III, pp.516–17) was written on 1st August 1908 and included material for two other poems. Blok whittled out the present text in December 1908 and, in February 1914, the poems "Забывшее тебя" and "Когда замрут отчаянье и злоба" (*C.C.*, Vol.III, pp.66 and 129).

аналой: a movable lectern on which the Scriptures or the icon pertinent to the festival of the day are set out during the Orthodox Church Service. During the Wedding Service, bride and groom are led three times round this pedestal by the priest.

65(III.80) Шаги Командора (Тяжкий, плотный занавес у входа)
        First pub.: *Русская Мысль*, 1912, No.II.
        Trans.: C.M.Bowra, "The Steps of the Commander", *A Book of Russian Verse*, London, 1943, p.101. C.Kisch, "The Steps of the Commander", *Alexander Blok, Prophet of Revolution*, London, 1960, p.100.

As throughout this cycle—the theme is of betrayal and retribution. Betrayal of the Ideal, betrayal of the Beloved. The last lines promise the terror of judgement and, perhaps, that Joy beyond Hope ("Нечаянная Радость") by which hope Blok had hallowed his first poems of betrayal (cf. footnote to Note 26). For V.P.Burenin's parody of this poem which, at the time it was published in the newspaper *Новое Время*, 23/II/1912, amused Blok considerably, see F.D.Reeve, *Alexander Blok, Between Image and Idea*, New York, 1962, pp. 241–2.

As the poem "The Pilot" (No.60) was suggested by the sound of the propeller (echoed in the prologue to Blok's long autobiographical poem "Retribution"), so "The Steps of the Commander" was inspired by the sound of the horn of a distant car (V.A.Zorgenfrei, "А.А. Блок (по памяти за 15 лет)", *Записки Мечтателей*, 1922, No.6, p. 139). Compare also the short poem dated 11th February 1910:

        Седые сумерки легли
        Весной на город бледный.
        Автомобиль пропел вдали
        В рожок победный.

        Глядись сквозь бледное окно,
        К стеклу прижавшись плотно …
        Глядись. Ты изменил давно,
        Бесповоротно.

Here, Blok avoids the word "мотор" (which grates less on an English than on a Russian ear) for which he failed to find a substitute in the main poem (cf. *C.C.*, Vol.III, p.520). However, the sound, and the accompanying image of the "Quiet black car" with its headlamps "gushing into the night", fully justifies the awkward word. How else would a modern Ulloa arrive to dinner? The scene foreshadows the black motor-cyclists of Cocteau's *Orpheus*; yet it is, perhaps, typical of Blok that one of the most-read, most-marked books in his library is—the nineteenth-century *Don Juan* of George Lord Byron.

66 (III. 85)  О, я хочу безумно жить
        First pub.: *Русское Слово*, 22nd March 1915.

These verses, dedicated to the memory of Blok's half-sister, a deeply reli-
gious, sensitive girl whom he met only after his father's death in December
1909 and who died of typhus at the age of 25 in February 1918, are full of
memories and hopes. In them, Blok reaches beyond the "iron day" to some
deeply hidden promise of Paradise Regained. In spite of all his doubts and
betrayals, in spite of his temperamental inability to create a religious art, the
mainspring of Blok's poetry, whether in affirmation or negation, was "good-
ness and light". He might flee Christ and retain an agnostic attitude to God
but:

> "Another matter is the briefly glimpsed unopened 'flower of the covenant' without
> which 'we' could not exist. Such an experience of 'the moment' is within the range
> of our possibilities, as is quite clear from the teachings and creative works of ancient
> and modern seekers after God" (*Юношеский Дневник*, 26/VI/1902).

67 (III. 87)  Тропами тайными, ночными
        First pub.: *Ямбы*, 1919.

The fact that "The Twelve" took almost all literate Russia completely by
surprise is probably largely attributable to the circumstance that Blok's
most violent post-1905 poetry was not published until after the 1917
Revolution.

This poem has much in common with "Сытие", "Вновь богатый зол и
рад", and with "Двенадцать": the same savage satire on the "old world"
(not for nothing did Blok choose his epigraph to "Iambs" from Juvenal); the
same sarcasm at the expense of the "paunchy priest", who will not even have
time to say the prayers for the dying over his expiring world. Only the hopes
of the future are brighter here than in "The Twelve". There, Christ leads the
twelve men into the distance through blinding snow and wind ("Come unto
me, all ye that are weary and heavy-laden"); here, the old world collapses at
the bidding of "the greatness of the times and rosy-fingered fate". Again,
Blok is thinking back to his "flower of the covenant", this time in its histori-
cal application.

> In our first youth we were given a true covenant. Of the soul of the people and of ours,
> together with theirs reduced to ashes, it is necessary to say in simple, courageous
> accents: "may they rise again". Perhaps we ourselves will die, but the dawn of that
> *first* love will remain. ("О современном состоянии русского символизма",
> *C. C.*, Vol. V, p. 435.)

68 (III.93) Да. Так диктует вдохновенье

> First pub.: *Биржевые ведомости*, 8th November 1915 under the title Современнику, slightly modified for the benefit of the censor (see *C.C.*, Vol. III, p. 524).

> In most cases people live for the present, that is to say, they have nothing to live for – they exist. It is only possible to live for the future (*Дневник*, 24/III/1912).
> *A friend* is someone who does not speak of that which has happened or is happening, but of that which might and should happen to the other person (*Дневник*, 8/II/1913).

Here is Blok's case for "the rejection of life". In the spring of 1911 Blok had been horrified to find Angelina rhapsodizing over a quietist children's book by Marie Corelli—"a sentimental English story, caressing the soul—comfortably cheap..." He wondered whether he should interfere: "I am weak for the task of leading Angelina out of the darkness which surrounds her. If only there was somebody who believed *honestly* and *religiously* without tearfulness, without parasitism. But is there such a person in this world?" *Записные книжки* (6/V/1911).

And the following day, after a careful reading of the offending book, from which Blok concludes that the author's chief aim is to discredit science and the love of freedom (which she identifies with Henrik Ibsen):

> Should Angelina be saved, or not? And who is to save her? Or perhaps it might be better for her to live out her life like that, without learning anything, either of God, or of the world, or of love, or of freedom?
> Soon after that, Angelina came to see me with her mother, so tender, so sensitive, so nervous and believing, that—she must not be left that way (*ibid.*, 7/V/1911).

Whether or not Blok really did introduce his half-sister to his "terrible world" through these poems we do not know, but he must surely have had these thoughts in mind when he dedicated the cycle to her memory. The reference to the children in Paris is explained by a letter which Blok wrote from Paris to his mother on 4th September 1911:

> In the burnt-out squares there are masses of children – pale, with the English sickness. All the faces are either horrifying (the bourgeois) or heart-rending in their strained intensity and weariness (*Письма к родным*, Vol. II, p. 173).

Horrified references to the Russian poor abound in his diaries:

> Evening strolls... through dark places, where hooligans break the street-lamps, a little puppy tries to attach itself to you, the lights are dim behind the curtains. A little girl, walking along, breathing heavily just like a horse: obviously consumption; she can hardly get her breath for the quiet little cough, bends right forward every few paces... Terrible world (*Дневник*, 19/VI/1912).

Or again

> The night is white. I am just going to the station to meet Lyuba. Suddenly I see from the balcony:—a tramp, walking, slinking furtively, obviously not wanting to be seen by anyone, he keeps stooping to the ground. Suddenly he drops down over what looks like a pot hole, now he has raised the lid of the sewage hole, *he drank the water*, wiped his lips ... A MAN (*Дневник*, 19/VI/1912).

As in "Голос из хора", Blok originally tried to express even in this poem that there was hope for man beyond the horror, but subsequently deleted the more optimistic lines; another version of the poem included in the rough draft of the prologue to the third chapter of "Возмездие" reads:

Читатель, ты жестоко судишь,
Ты с оправданьем незнаком,
И знаю, злобствовать ты будешь
Над мертвым, грязным стариком. *
Но так велит мне вдохновенье:
Моя свободная мечта
Все льнет туда, где униженье,
Где грязь, и мрак, и нищета,
И я люблю сей мир ужасный:
За ним виднее мир иной —
Обетованный и прекрасный,
Непредставимый и простой...†
А если ты не жнешь, не сеешь,
Коль ты «так просто — человек»,
То что ты знаешь? Что ты смеешь
Судить в безумный этот век?
Ты был ли жалок и унижен
Болезнью, голодом, тоской?
Ты видел ли детей в Париже
Иль нищих на мосту зимой?
На непроглядный ужас жизни
Открой скорей, открой глаза,
Пока великая гроза
Все не смела в твоей отчизне!
И пусть он зреет, правый гнев,
Не там, где жизни тяжко бремя...
Чудак мой злое сеял семя,
Но не бесплоден был посев...
Он прав хоть тем, что жизни этой
Румяна жирные отверг,
И, как пугливый крот, от света
Зарылся в землю — и померк,
Всю жизнь жестоко ненавидя
И проклиная этот свет,
Пускай — грядущего не видя,
Но сущему сказавши: «Нет»!

* Blok is here referring to his father, who died alone and in squalor as a result of his own eccentricity.

† Variant reading:

Но ты прости мне эту шалость:
Поэта вольная мечта
Все льнет туда, где горе, жалость,
Где грязь, и мрак, и нищета,
И я люблю сей мир ужасный,
За ним сквозит мне мир иной,
Неописуемо прекрасный
И человечески-простой...
Пускай — грядущего не видя,
Но сущему сказавши: «Нет»!

Against the last four lines Blok has scribbled in the margin: "O!o!o!
Трескотня. Мист. анархизм!" (*C. C.*, Vol. III, pp. 524–5).

69 (III. 95) Земное сердце стынет вновь
>First pub.: *Русское Слово*, 22nd March 1915. Originally intended
>to form part of the third chapter of "Возмездие".

Blok was not naturally a wild, self-sufficient Bohemian. He was a method-
ical, tidy, exactingly affectionate man of simple tastes who loved peace and
comfort and never fully emancipated himself from his happy family circle.
He was also a man who loved life—women, sport, nature, art, beauty, in all
its forms—and who was splendidly equipped by nature and circumstance to
enjoy life in all its aspects. But he rejected content, and once wrote that, if he
could chose his epitaph, it would be:

>There was once a man who ... thought more of truth than of happiness. I sought
>pleasures, but never hoped for happiness. It passed by of itself and coming, as always,
>became something other than itself. I don't expect it now, either, God be with it, it's—
>not human (*Дневник*, 13/I/1912).

70 (III. 98) Равенна (Всё, что минутно, всё, что бренно)
>First pub.: Аполлон, 1910, No. 4.
>Trans.: O. Elton, "Ravenna", originally *The Slavonic and East
>European Review*, Vol. III, 1925, p. 750; then in the collection
>*Verses from Pushkin and Others*, London, 1935, p. 182; also in
>*A Second Book of Russian Verse*, ed. C. M. Bowra, London, 1947,
>p. 70. R. Kemball (unpublished).

Blok spent the summer months of the year 1909 in Italy. It was his first
journey abroad since before his marriage in 1903. Previously, he had been
only to Germany, where he felt very much at home, and to Italy as a small
child. This second visit to Italy made a profound impression and moulded, to
some extent, his whole attitude to Europe, the love–hatred so vividly ex-
pressed in "The Scythians". In Italy, Blok was no gawking tourist. His training
at school and university had made him a sound classical scholar. Dante he
regarded as a spiritual brother, perhaps closer to him in inspiration than any
other poet. He was also a worshipper at the shrine of Italian painting and at
home in the history of the Renaissance and of Rome.

Blok's first reaction to Europe was a sense of emancipation from the polit-
ical and literary commitments forced upon him by the mere fact of living in
Russia. He experienced a refreshing sobriety, an immense desire to work and
to study; here, as never before, he felt the solemnity of his own cultural tradi-

tion; on his return he wrote that he was obliged to the West for arousing in
him "the spirit of curiosity and the spirit of modesty" (*Записные Книжки*,
2/VII/1909). At the same time, he felt that modern Italy was dead. "Europe
(her theme)", he was to write years later, "is art and death. Russia is life"
(*Дневник*, 11/I/1918).

In this most lovely classic poem Blok takes land-locked Ravenna as a sym-
bol of the receding tide of history. The town is a rose-hung graveyard—
only:

> The lettered brass, the sovereign Latin,
> Rings like a trumpet from the stone.
> (Elton's trans.)

Only in some timeless dimension of the Ideal, in Dante's dreams of the
New Life—the Vita Nuova—does Ravenna still hold a living message for the
living poet.

Галла/Плакида: one and the same person: Galla Placidia, the sister of the Emperor
Honorius. During Honorius' reign Rome was sacked by the Barbarian Alaric and
Galla taken in marriage by Alaric's brother-in-law, Ataulphus, King of the Visigoths.
After Ataulphus' assassination Galla married the Roman general Constantius, who
defeated Alaric and became co-Emperor with Honorius. To Constantius Galla bore a
son, Valentinian, who, in his turn, became Emperor of the West until his assassina-
tion in A.D. 455. The fate of Galla "Thrown up from the shame of being dragged in
triumph at the chariot wheel of a barbarian onto the throne of the Western Roman
Empire" (A. Blok, *C. C.*, Vol. III, pp. 527–8, from a commentary to the poem "Raven-
na" published in *Собр. Стих.* III, 1912) continued to haunt Blok after he left Italy
(*Записные Книжки,* 8/VII/1909; letter to V. Ya. Bryusov, 2/X/1909; *Дневник*,
14/XI/1911). He saw her not as a Roman matron but rather as an Egypto-Byzantine
type with arched black brows—on eof "his" faces, full of significance for "his" time.

Теодорих: Theodoric the Great, King of the Ostrogoths, who conquered Ravenna in 493
and died there in 526.

Новая Жизнь: "The New Life", Dante's "Vita Nuova".


71 (III. 106–9) Флоренция

> First pub.: (1) "Ночные Часы", 1911. (2) *Собр. Стих.* III,
> 1912. (3) *Русская Мысль*, 1914, No. 5. (4) *Русская Мысль*,
> 1914, No. 5. (5) *Русская Мысль*, 1914, No. 5. (6) *Русская Мысль*,
> 1914, No. 5. (7) *Ночные Часы*, 1911.
> Trans.: R. Kemball (unpublished).

In this curious, many-faceted reverie in seven parts Blok gives full reign to
the contradictory feelings aroused in him by the old world. Blok really loved
only classical, medieval and future Europe. The Renaissance he found
"frightening"—the eighteenth century "repugnant". His own age—vulgar,
mercantile and soulless.

Like Florence's own Savanarola, the "holy monk" whom she burnt, Blok denounces the complaisant amorality of the modern city. As he sees it, the town of Leonardo and Fra Beato has betrayed her heritage. The original denunciation was more violent, including two verses which Blok later referred to as "really ill-tempered" and refrained from printing:

> В Palazzo Vechio впуская
> Своих чиновников стада,
> Ты, словно девка площадная,
> Вся обнажилась без стыда!
>
> Ты ставишь, как она, в хоромы
> Свою зловонную постель,
> Пред пышным, многоцветным Дуомо
> Взнося публичный дом — отель!

L. Vogel in the article "Blok in the Land of Dante", *Russian Review*, vol. 26, No. 3, Hanover, 1967, pp. 251–63, maintains that Blok sees Florence as a Judas first and foremost because she betrayed and exiled her own greatest poet—Dante.

The aesthete journal *Аполлон* refused to print the poem even without these verses and in spite of Blok's plea for it in the letter to the editor which accompanied the manuscript: "I am particularly concerned to put in a word in advance for the first 'Florence', of which most probably no one will approve. But, indeed, it is not blasphemy, but a really deeply felt and 'suffered' experience…" (letter to S. K. Makovsky, 3/XI/1909).

In the second part of the poem, another, softer mood insinuates itself into the poet's meditation. Florence becomes his own youth, and he sees himself as growing old and foresees how, from far away, he will dream of this town as of the "smoky iris" of his own first youth. He feels himself dissolving in the warmth of the evening, floating away in wave upon caressing wave of palest blue, then the mood darkens and he stares hopelessly, himself black-hearted, into the hot, black Italian sky. The rhythms of an intoxicated sensuality beat up through the measured verse and the words go dancing of themselves into a cheap serenade:

> Что мне спеть в этот вечер, синьора?
> Что мне спеть, чтоб вам сладко спалось?

(Blok first heard the song in Florence's "Square of the Signoras". Cf. *Записные Книжки*, 16th–17th May 1909.)

But the heat and sloth of Florence are empty—even of passion. Only the mirage of art offers illusory salvation from the black *tedium vitae* which the Russian poet carried in his soul and which he felt in Europe's very stones.

Blok does not so much disassociate himself from Europe as denounce in her his own world-weariness. The poem was indeed "a deeply felt" and "suffered" experience (Выстраданное переживание). It is significant that the first two lines of the second part originally read:

> Флоренция — ты ирис нежный
> Страны, *где я когда-то жил.* *

Медичей (gen. plur. Медичи): the Medicis—enormously rich and powerful family who ruled Renaissance Florence.

Кашины: Cascine—a park in the suburbs of Florence, famous for its irises.

бокал Христовых Слез: the Italian wine Lachrima Christi.


72(III.125) Друзьям (Друг другу мы тайно враждебны)
    First pub.: *Русская Мысль*, 1909, No.1.

Written in 1908, as Blok was beginning to emerge from his infatuation with Volokhova and from the wildest excesses of his daemonic mysticism, the poem reflects a feeling which runs through Blok's whole creative life: the feeling that poetry should be taken down from the bookshelf and thrown onto the highway of life.

It also gives a vivid picture of the symbolist milieu, with its vanities, its squabbles, its rivalries in romance and poetry, its wild irony and its self-destructive way of life—and with its selfless dreams of a happier world to come.

Against the first draft of the second verse Blok scribbled "Filth" (Мерзость).

Somewhat similar in sentiment is "Поэты" (*C.C.*, Vol.III, p.127).


73(III.134) Сон (Я видел сон: мы в древнем склепе)
    First pub.: in the Almanac *Аполлон*, 1911.

In Blok's notebooks we have the first lines from which this poem was taken:

> Я мертв. Века. И воскресенья
> Чуть брежжит утро. Он идет.
> А надо мной. . . . . . . .
> . . . . . . . . . . . . .
> Идет, как в книгах мы читали...

and Orlov gives the original variant of the first verse as:

> Мать и жена, и я — мы вместе
> Мертвы. — А жизнь вверху идет
> Все непонятней, все нелепей...
> И день последний настает.   (*C.C.*, Vol. III, p. 544.)

The poem was founded on a real dream and seems to be psychologically connected with "The Twelve". All his life, Blok sought salvation from the "noise" and "stupidity" of life independently of Christ: as a youth the qual-

* Editor's italics.

ity he most coveted was "will-power" (M. A. Beketova, *Ал. Блок и его мать*, Leningrad–Moscow, 1925, p. 68) and he looked for some strength in himself or in others which would mend the world (*Записные Книжки*, 5/III/1916). He looked for a new era, "a great Renaissance which would come about under the sign of courage and will" (*Зап. Книжки*, 5/XI/1915). Yet, always, it seemed, he came back with astonishment and regretful incredulity to the inescapable image of Christ: "Just as we read in books—bored and unbelieving." In this boredom with the New Testament, Blok was again completely at one with his mother who once wrote to a Christian friend: "The Gospel is quite foreign to me, boring and incomprehensible, and it always seems to me that some enormous and—according to our lights—insurmountable obstacle has yet to be overcome in order that afterwards we might be able to return to it afresh" (letter to E. P. Ivanova, 18/VI/1914, Ф. №. 55, Опись №. I, ед. хр. №. 541). For Blok's dislike of the Bible, cf. also his letter to his mother of 16th June 1916 (*Письма к Родным*, II, p. 294) and V. Verigina's "Воспоминания об Александре Блоке", *op. cit.*, pp. 319–20.

Каменья: old form of plural for stones (i.e. "Каменья на камне не оставить").

74 (III. 145) Художник (В жаркое лето и в зиму метельную)

First pub.: Almanac *Сирин*, III, 1914.

Trans.: C. M. Bowra, "Artist", *A Book of Russian Verse*, London, 1943, p. 105. C. Kisch, "The Artist", *Alexander Blok, Prophet of Revolution*, London, 1960, p. 105.

One of Blok's most perfect poems. It tells of the process of creation—and of the life of the poet. Blok believed that the artist should never worry or strain to produce a great work. The great work is born naturally and without effort of his "secret labour". But this "secret labour" is a permanent feature of the artist's life which unfits him for conventional relationships and society. Perhaps the best commentary to the line "In the days of your weddings, triumphs, funerals" is to be found in an incident which occurred three years later, and which is recounted in full in P. Medvedev's publication of a letter from Blok to his cousin S. N. Tutolmina (*Красная Газета*, №. 215, Вечерний выпуск, 1928, letter of 6/I/1916. Cf. also *С. С.*, Vol. VIII, pp. 453–5.) In this letter, Blok apologizes to the bride for having demonstratively walked out on a merry family wedding-party between the Church and the reception:

> For a thousand reasons my life has fallen out in such a way that, with a few exceptions, I find it very hard to be together with people, so that I look on life gloomily, as they say (though I don't myself consider my attitude gloomy), and so that I have no feeling for the ties of kinship; at the same time, I know that the work I have to do (whether for good or ill—as you know, I'm not in the least pleased with myself) demands that I should be as I am and not otherwise....

This did not mean that Blok shut himself away from life, but rather that he lived at an extraordinary pitch of intensity which simply did not tolerate conventional attitudes and relationships. He once told a younger poet:

> You can't "make" verses. You have to live them. What is best in them comes from life, and from life alone. The rest dies and there's no point in regretting it. Real verses come only out of that which really happened, which has been filtered through one's consciousness, one's heart, one's liver, if you like. And in general, one should only write those verses which it is impossible not to write. And then, of course, talk about them as little as possible. (Vs. Rozhdestvensky, *op. cit.*, p. 232.)

Сирины (plural of Сирин): mythical birds symbolical of Joy and Happiness in Russian folk-lore and Russian medieval literature.

Жалкого нет: when a Russian says "мне не жаль" he means not only "I am not sorry" or "I feel no pity", but also "I don't grudge it". In this sense Blok uses the words when he is contemplating parting with his family estate: "А я люблю его так, что мне не жалко продать, ничего не жалко", adding, in brackets, a name which has become a world-wide symbol of fearless, disinterested, ruthless love—"Cordelia". (*Записные Книжки*, 23/X/1915.)

> Птицу, хотевшую смерть унести,
> Птицу, летевшую душу спасти.

These lines originally read:

> Птицу, хотевшую мир обновить,
> Птицу, летевшую жизнь воскресить.

(See *C. C.*, Vol. III, p. 551.)

75 (III. 156) Ты твердишь, что я холоден, замкнут и сух
　　　　First pub.: *Седое утро*, 1920.
　　　　Trans.: C. M. Bowra, "You say I am frozen", *A Book of Russian Verse*, London, 1943, p. 107.

Vl. Orlov points to this poem as to the lowest ebb of Blok's spirits between the revolutions. It echoes notes already struck in "Voice from the Choir" (No. 63), but here, although Blok has for once allowed his hope for a paradise beyond the horrors to come to remain evident in the published text, there is a note of personal despair—and no trace of the tenderness of the earlier poem.

The war, now that Blok had had time "to look into it", to listen for its music, seemed to him utterly devoid of greatness or high purpose: "prosaic", "just a huge mobile factory". "The substance", "the salt" of history—and the real enemy—he felt to be somewhere outside the present struggle—and therefore the struggle itself appeared boring, unheroic (*Записные Книжки*, 6/III/1916). Russia was losing her identity. On Easter night the sight of the 1916 equivalent of Teddy-boys swarming over and under the statue of the Bronze Horseman—smoking, the lack of solemnity in the crowds, and a curious "lightening of the atmosphere"—made him note: "Petersburg—finis"

(*Записные Книжки*, 9–10/IV/1916). In the summer he wrote: "This senseless war will lead to nothing" (*Записные Книжки*, 28/VI/1916). As a result of all the pointless brutality involved in fighting without just cause, humanity as a whole appeared to him to be "going savage". "Every extra day of war is sweeping away culture" (*Записные Книжки*, 17/IV/1917). "Весь мир одичал", Blok says in this poem, and the word "одичал"—applied not only to others but even to himself—recurs constantly throughout Blok's wartime diaries (*Записные Книжки*, 10/XI/1915; 14/IV/1917; 18/IV/1917; 7/VI/1918). He owed the word to D. S. Merezhkovsky—"boorish, timid Merezhkovsky"—as he noted with considerable surprise the first time he used it: "Why did he find it? Because he is the only one who has really *worked*, whereas Andreyev and the like—troo-la-la, got stuck up. Gor'ky worked, but got confused (?). Why? Because—he has no 'culture'." (*Записные Книжки*, 10/XI/1915.)

The addressee of the poem is unknown but it was originally entitled—probably on the suggestion of Blok's mother—"Другу" (To a friend). (Cf. letter of 10/VI/1916, *Письма к родным*, II, p. 290 and note on p. 274.)

76(III.158)  Свирель запела на мосту
  First pub.: *Золотое Руно*, 1908, No. 11/12, under the title and the subtitle.
  Trans.: O. Elton, "Pipes on the Bridge struck up to play", *Slavonic and East European Review*, Vol. VII, 1929, p. 393; also *A Second Book of Russian Verse*, ed. C. M. Bowra, London, 1947, p. 68. Y. Hornstein, "Over the rapids on the bridge", *Poems*, Dorking, undated, p. 8.

One of Blok's rare excursions into the realms of "pure poetry". For the subtitle "Romance" and the link between Blok's poetry and simple song see Note 53. This link is particularly in evidence throughout the cycle "Harps and Violins"—as the title suggests. For a list of Blok's poetry which has actually been set to music see K. Chukovsky, *Книга об Александре Блоке*, Эпоха, Петербург, 1922, pp. 95–96, and *Александр Блок в песнях и романсах советских композиторов*, *Музгиз*, Moscow–Leningrad, 1946.

77(III.160)  И я любил. И я изведал
  First pub.: *Образование*, 1908, No. 7 under the title "Анархист".
  Trans.: C. M. Bowra, "Yes, I have loved", *A Book of Russian Verse*, London, 1943, p. 101.

Strindbergian misogyny (cf. "Женщина", *С. С.*, Vol. III, p. 149 and note; also N. A. Nilsson, "Strindberg, Gorky and Blok", *Scandoslavica*, Vol. IV,

1958, pp. 23–42). In the first draft, the verses of this poem are entangled with two others: "Их было много дев прекрасных" and "Душа! Когда устанешь верить?" (*C. C.*, Vol. II, p. 337 and Vol. III, p. 159). Against the three is Blok's comment: "There's cynicism for you! It is called 'Anarchist'!" Blok seems to have been genuinely burdened by his own sensuality (cf. *Записные Книжки*, 3/VI/1916) and, beyond reasonable doubt, to have related it to the evils of society as a whole, as he related his whole lyrical experience of life to the Common Weal or Woe of Russia and of Humanity. Trying to differentiate between religion and mysticism, he once defined the first as "an alliance with people against the world as distortion" and the second as "an alliance with the world against people", explaining that everything "which is of the world but *not* distorted (which may include everything)" immediately becomes the object of religion, and adding "the simple and banal illustration" that "a depraved attitude to women is distortion (and may, perhaps, be mysticism), a pure attitude is religion" (*Записные Книжки*, 18/I/1906). In a moment of great foreboding, shortly before the Bolshevik coup in October 1917, when he already sensed the inevitability of violence, Blok noted for himself that the task of Russian culture was to direct the flames of revolution "into the Rasputin-dominated corners of the soul and there to blow it up into a sky-high conflagration so that our cunning, slothful, servile sensuality may burn..." (*Дневник*, 7/VIII/1917).

In this poem, Blok retains a youthful bravura: he is not yet weighed down by "the terrible world", has not yet been forced to the conclusion that "all this horror is beyond the power of individuals to mend, however well they might live" (letter dated 6th January 1916 to S. N. Tutolmina, *C. C.*, Vol. VIII, p. 454). Here, it is as though the poet expects to rid himself of the very memory of his unwanted loves by one glorious daemonic gesture—yet, strangely, the poem, like No. 63 (The Daemon), is a hymn of passion rather than of penitence. The violence of rejection, the long climb into loneliness and emptiness—are merely the other side of the medal. To return to the first quotation in this note, the poem is mystic rather than religious: the poet is in alliance *with* the world *against* people. This is still more evident in the unpublished last verse:

И слушать стоны и проклятья
И видеть кровь, и боль, и смерть, –
Чтоб мог, жестокий, обладать я –
Тобой одной, Пустая Твердь!

(Cf. *C. C.*, Vol. III, p. 555, for other variant readings.)

78 (III. 161) Май жестокий с белыми ночами!

> First pub.: *Золотое Руно*, 1908, No. 11/12, under the title "Родина".
>
> Trans.: C. Kisch, "May's white nocturne is with fury tainted", *Alexander Blok, Prophet of Revolution*, London, 1960, p. 96.

The proper place for this poem, as will be seen by the date, is at the end of the second volume. It marks the realization—explained in detail in Blok's article "On the Present State of Russian Symbolism"—that:

> ... The way to prepare for the task which demands our service is—first and foremost—apprenticeship, self-improvement, steadiness of watch, "spiritual" diet. ... The artist should be reverent even in boldness itself, knowing the cost of the confusion of art and life and remaining, in life, an ordinary man. ("О Современном Состоянии Русского Символизма", *C. C.*, Vol. V, p. 436.)

This realization was bound up with a reappraisal of contemporary Russian literature, particularly of the so-called "realists" who wrote for the periodical *Знание*, and of Lev Tolstoy. A phrase in Blok's article "Солнце над Россией" written in September 1908 echoes the last lines of this poem:

> So long as Tolstoy still lives, still strides along the furrow behind the plough following his little white horse—the morning is still dewy, fresh, unfrightening, the vampires sleep, and thank God for it. Tolstoy strides along—and it is the sun who is striding. But if the sun goes down, Tolstoy dies, *the last genius takes his departure*—what then? (*C. C.*, Vol. V, p. 303.)

The poem was originally somewhat longer (see *C. C.*, Vol. III, p. 556) passing from the symbol of the plough to the symbol of a sail. Blok rejected this continuation with the scribbled remark: "The boat is beside the point"—(Корабль не при чем).

белые ночи: White nights: Petersburg is far enough north to enjoy roughly six weeks of the year when it never grows completely dark. The effect, as sunset lingers on into sunrise, is uncanny and, to those who are sensitive to climate and light, thoroughly disturbing.

79 (III. 168) Я пригвожден к трактирной стойке

> First pub.: *Новое Образование*, 1910, No. 1/2.
>
> Trans.: G. Shelley, "I'm nailed to the bench of a tavern", *Modern Poems from the Russian*, London, 1942, p. 82.

One of Blok's best drunken poems. The maudlin sentiment, the lurching rhythms verge on the vulgar but honest self-pity of the cheap romance—only the astringent star-dust which illumines the whole sodden night marks the poem as Blok's.

In Blok's notebook, however, the rough draft of this poem is followed by a prose exposition of the troika-theme which links the poem with such articles as "Вопросы, вопросы и вопросы" (*C.C.*, Vol. V, p.229); "Народ и Интеллигенция" (*C.C.*, Vol. V, p.318); "Стихия и Культура" (*C.C.*, Vol. V, p.350) and "Дитя Гоголя" (*C.C.*, Vol. V, p.376).

> And so the quiet curtain of our doubts, contradictions, falls and lunacies rises: do you hear the breathless rush of the troika? Do you see it plunging through the drifts of a dead and desolate plain? It is Russia, hurtling, no man knows whither, into the blue-azure depth of the ages, in her decorated and beribboned troika. Do you see the starry eyes fixed on us with the prayer: "Love me! Love my beauty!" But we are separated from her by this endless stretch of time, by this blue darkness, by this snowy, starry net.—Who of us will prove able to find his way by secret paths of wisdom to meet the hurtling troika, to bring the lathered horses to a halt with a gentle word, to unseat the demon-driver with a bold hand and.... (Cf. *C.C.*, Vol. III, p.560 and *Записные Книжки,* 26/X/1908.)

темень: darkness (normally only used in spoken language).

## 80 (III. 184) Бывают тихие минуты
First pub.: *Новое Слово*, 1912, No. 12.

The cycle "Через Двенадцать Лет" from which this poem is taken is dedicated to K. M. Sadovskaya—Blok's first love, a Ukrainian lady some years his senior. He met her when escorting his mother and aunt to Bad Nauheim in the summer of 1897 and they seemed to have regarded the affair as a charming boyish pastime (cf. Beketova, *Александр Блок*, Petersburg, 1922, p.56). For Blok, it was more than that. It was something he pushed to the back of his mind when he fell in love with Lyubov' Mendeleyeva and which occasionally returned to haunt him—sweetly, as here, or with a suggestion of nightmare as in his *Notebooks*, 5th December 1910.

Хохлушка (masc. Хохол): affectionately familiar Russian term for a Ukrainian—roughly corresponding to English "Taffy", "Aussie", "Yankee".

## 81 (III. 221) Была ты всех ярче, верней и прелестней
First pub.: *Вершины*, 1914, No.1.

On 30th May 1915 Blok noted in his diary: "I have not possessed 100, 200, 300 (or more?) women, but only two: one is Lyuba; the other—all the rest, yet each was different, and I myself different..."

The whole cycle "Harps and Violins" is about "all the rest". All the passions end like this one, all are beautiful, empty, alike—and different.

The first draft of this poem was made in the summer of 1910, but the final version was inspired by Lyubov' Alexandrovna Delmas (see Notes to "Carmen" cycle).

82 (III. 226) За горами, лесами
First pub.: *Ежемесячный Журнал*, 1917, No. 1.

Written for the poet's wife when, at the beginning of the war, she was work-
ing as a nursing sister in Galicia, this poem alone, the last of the book *Harps
and Violins*, is about the One (see Note 81). Not only the sentiment, the choice
of words is different. "За другими цветешь небесами" might be a line from
the "Poems about the Most Beautiful Lady". The poet's sorrow is "not of
here", the hand he caresses is a hand which can work magic, the name is
"distant".

83 (III. 230) Есть демон утра. Дымно-светел он
First pub.: *Дневник писателя*, 1914, No. 2.

The "Carmen" cycle, dedicated to the singer Lyubov' Alexandrovna Del'-
mas, is the apotheosis of Blok's daemonic love poetry and contains many of
his best lyrics. Blok himself relates the cycle to "The Snow Mask" and "The
Twelve": these volcanic peaks of his poetic creation were thrown up in mo-
ments of blind surrender to the elements (see note on "The Twelve"). Dae-
monic rebellion, passion and revolution are inextricably interwoven in Blok's
poetry in a way which had little or nothing to do with his genuine capacity for
affection and compassion or with the reasoned desire for a better world. Blok
distrusted reason and put all his faith in "music". Carmen's "singing body"
and the "music of history" are related concepts. "The Snow Mask" (thirty
poems) was written in the course of two weeks; the "Carmen" cycle (ten
poems) between 4th and 28th March 1914; "The Twelve" (a long poem in
twelve cantos) substantially in two days (27th/29th January 1917) (although
it appears to have been first conceived on 8th January and finally revised on
4th February).

Хитон: tunic.

84 (III. 232) Среди поклонников Кармен
First pub.: *Любовь к трем апельсинам*, 1914, No. 4/5.

Blok's passion for Delmas seems to have been lived more than half within
the world of Bizet's opera. It is Carmen who fascinates him (C. M. Beketova,
Александр Блок, Petersburg, 1922, p. 192). The real Delmas was a woman of
sunny and vital charm who loved Blok, gave him much happiness and re-
mained his friend until his death.

Other poems inspired by her outside the "Carmen" cycle are: "Петер-
бургские сумерки снежные", "Я помню нежность ваших плеч", "Та жизнь

прошла", "Была ты всех ярче, верней и прелестней" (No. 81 of this book), "От знающего почерк ясный...", "Превратила все в шутку сначала..." (*С.С.*, Vol. III, pp. 216, 369, 220, 221, 371, 219, 375) and, possibly, "Перед Судом" (see No. 88 and Note).

Таверна Лиллас-Пастья: Lillas Pastia's Tavern. A scene-setting of the opera.

85 (III. 236)  Ты, как отзвук забытого гимна
         First pub.: *Любовь к трем апельсинам*, 1914, No. 4/5.
         Trans.: C. Kisch, "You have entered my fate dark with passion",
         *Alexander Blok, Prophet of Revolution*, London, 1960, p. 107.

Written on the day Blok first made L. A. Del'mas' acquaintance. The next day he wrote in his notebook "Everything is singing" (29th March 1914).

Кущь: tangle from "кущение" (lit. "bushing out").

86 (III. 237)  *О да, любовь вольна, как птица*
         First pub.: *Любовь к трем апельсинам*, 1914, No. 4/5.

The first line is a quotation from the libretto of Bizet's opera.

Треба: religious rite.

87 (III. 239)  Нет, никогда моей, и ты ничьей не будешь
         First pub.: *Любовь к трем апельсинам*, 1914, No. 4/5.

Blok noted on the day this poem was written (31st March 1914): "Important verses" (Vl. Orlov's notes, *С.С.*, Vol. III, p. 579). Cf. the last two lines with Fate's bequest to the minstrel Gaetan in the play *The Rose and the Cross:*

> Мира восторг беспредельный
> В сердце твое я вложу!
> Песням внимай океана,
> В алые зори глядись!
> Людям будешь ты зовом бесцельным!
> Быть может, тронешь ты
> Сердце девы земной,
> Но никем не тронется
> Сердце твое...
> Оно — во власти моей...
> Странником в мире ты будешь!
> В этом — твое назначенье,
> Радость — Страданье твое!    (*С. С.*, Vol. IV, p. 203.)

Also Gaetan's song (*ibid.*, pp. 232–3).

избудешь: Blok uses the rare verb "избыть" instead of the more usual "изжить", the sense of which is something between "to get rid of", "to grow out of" and "to live down".

88 (III. 151) Перед судом (Что́ же ты потупилась в смущеньи?)
First pub.: *Русская Мысль*, 1916, No. I.

In June 1916 Blok noted that this poem should end the "Carmen" cycle (*Записные Книжки*, 28/VI/1916). However, he did not alter the position of the poem when re-editing the last edition of the Third Volume in 1921. The latest eight-volume collection of his work naturally preserves the order of Blok's 1921 edition, and, in the notes, the editor, Vl. Orlov, records Blok's entry in his notebook, but states that the poem is addressed "beyond question" to Lyubov' Dmitriyevna Blok (p. 552), a statement he repeats in his "История одной любви", *Пути и Судьбы*, Moscow–Leningrad, 1963, p. 652. Presumably there are grounds for making such a categorical assertion, but Del'-mas herself is said to believe the verses are addressed to her and the author of these notes has found nothing to suggest that, at this particular time, Blok would have addressed *such* verses to Lyubov' Dmitriyevna. He was quite capable of delivering a biting scold even to his wife, complains frequently that she is "asleep", earth-bound, unworthy of herself. But: "страстная"? "безбожная"? "пустая"? And why should Blok describe his wife, from whom he had no intention of parting, as "Unforgettable"? More important, in all his poetry it was Blok himself who had betrayed the *unique* dream he had dreamt with his wife (cf. the whole cycle "Возмездие", for instance). Why, in this one poem, should this dream have betrayed *them*, "like every other dream"? See also Notes 81 and 82 for the difference in Blok's vocabulary when he writes of his wife.

However that may be, the poem provides an excellent final chord on which to leave the "harps and violins" of Blok's love poetry for the more ascetic and sober lyricism of his poems about Russia.

89 (III. 247) В густой траве пропадешь с головой
First pub.: Under the title "На родине" in *Трудовой Путь*, 1907, No. 12.

In the poem "On the Field of Kulikovo" Blok exclaims:

О Русь, моя, жена моя. . . .

In other places he speaks of Russia as "mother". In either case, if he is thinking of a person, he is probably thinking of Lyuba: so much more motherly than his real mother, whom he thought of as his "conscience", whose love for him was "anxious", who once wrote to a friend: "If only you knew, Manya dear, how well, how selflessly Lyuba loves Sasha. I could not love like that. Only mothers can. There is such a profound spiritual beauty in her feeling for him" (letter to M.P.Ivanova, 25/I/1912, Архив Блока А.А.Ф. №.55, опись №.34, хр. №.83).

Blok calls Lyuba his "native Galilee": having left her, "he knows not where to lay his head" (cf. "Ты отошла, и я в пустыне", *C.C.*, Vol. III, p. 246, trans.: R.Kemball, "Thou art afar and I have laid me", *Russian Review*, Vol.21, No.2, April 1962). This, of course, is not to say that Blok identified his wife with Russia any more than, at the time he was writing *The Song of Fate*, he identified Volokhova with Russia. Russia, in Blok's poetry, is many-faceted as life itself.

In this poem, the "quiet house" is Lyuba's special realm, as in the play *The Song of Fate*. It was to seek Russia that Blok left them—Lyuba and her home. Yet she is home, and home is Russia; and Russia, in some mysterious way, is at once his battlefield *and* his home; his home when the presence of the World Soul, the Most Beautiful Lady informs her—his battlefield when she lapses into sullen indifference or when she, like he, conjures "The Stranger", "The Blue Phantom", "demanding a miracle before the time is ripe". And when her soul, like his, is "reduced to ashes by the lilac worlds of revolution", he and she are one. (Cf. "О Современном Состоянии Русского Символизма", *C.C.*, Vol. V, p.431.)

After the Revolution Blok gave many public readings of his poetry. At one of these there were shouts from the audience for his poems "about Russia". "They are all about Russia", Blok answered. (V.A.Zorgenfrei, Александр Александрович Блок (По памяти 15 лет, 1906–21 *г.г.*), *Записки Мечтателей*, Petersburg, 1922, p.147).

90(III.249) На Поле Куликовом
    First pub.: In the Almanac *Шиповник*, X, 1909.
    Trans.: R.Kemball, "On the Field of Kulikovo", *Russian Review*, January 1954, p.33. C.Kisch, "On the Field of Kulikovo", *Alexander Blok, Prophet of the Revolution*, London, 1960, p.124. Alex Miller, unpublished.

The Battle of the Field of Kulikovo took place in 1380 between the Mongol Khan Mamay and the Muscovite Prince Dimitry of the Don. It was the first decisive Russian victory since 1237, when the land of Russia had begun to crumble before the expanding might of the Mongol Empire under the leadership of Batu, the grandson of Ghengis Khan. The victory of Kulikovo was celebrated in one of the most famous "Tales" of medieval Russian literature—"The Zadonshchina"—and was recounted in the Chronicles as "The

Tale of the Mamay Battle". Blok's poem is rung through with echoes of these older works, which give a curious and immediate feeling of continuity, of a slipping control over time, as though the poet himself were Russia speaking in the style of a "stream of consciousness" novel. Blok believed the battle of Kulikovo to have been one of those "symbolic events in Russian history" which are "fated to repeat themselves". (Blok's own note on this poem published in the 1912 edition of his collected works and quoted in Orlov's Notes, *C.C.*, Vol. III, p. 587.)

The bruit of this battle that has been and is and is to come rumbles on in Blok's article "The People and the Intelligentsia" (*C.C.*, Vol. V, pp. 323–4) and in the play *The Song of Fate*, in which the hero imagines himself to be a soldier of the reserve, waiting his hour to join the fateful struggle, "as though in these days I am living the life of all the ages, as though I am experiencing in myself all the agonies of my motherland" (*C.C.*, Vol. IV, pp. 148–9). Vaguely, gropingly Blok identifies his own age with that other age of popular awakening which resulted in a Russian victory so decisive that Russia began at last to shake off the "Tartar yoke". In Blok's Russia, the people had different overlords—of their own race, but also of another culture. True, there was a no-man's land between the "intelligentsia" (by which Blok seems to have meant quite simply all the educated classes who put their faith in civilization and "progress" rather than the "intelligentsia" in the more specifically Russian sense [see his preface to the Collection "Россия и Интеллигенция", *C.C.*, Vol. VI, pp. 453–4]) and "the people"; a no-man's land on which those few who realized the importance of bringing the two cultures together were working desperately against time. Between the Tartars and the Russians there had been no such possible meeting ground. Yet Blok felt that, in modern Russia, the vast majority in both camps were as oblivious of one another as human beings as the Tartars and the Russians had been oblivious of one another at the time of Kulikovo.

Even as early as 1908, Blok saw little hope of surmounting this "insurmountable barrier" before battle was joined (cf. his article "Религиозные искания и народ", *C.C.*, Vol. V, p. 214, published under the title "Литературные итоги 1907 года"). The battle would result in a New Russia—perhaps. Yet much of Blok's poetry about Russia, like this poem, is a keening prophecy of coming slaughter, echoing the folk-laments for past sorrows and muted by the heavy expectancy of the present hour.

... Покой нам только снится: The image of someone being borne on and on by a
    runaway horse was taken from a recurrent nightmare suffered by Blok's mother.
сам друг: all alone with each other.
Непрядва: the river on which the battle was fought.
лебеди кричали: both the chronicle and the Zadonshchina mention the crying of swans.

горючий белый камень: the white standing-stone by the roadway is always a sign of ill omen in Russian sagas and ballads.

поганая орда: lit. "the vile horde". In many old tales and ballads the enemies of the Russians are referred to simply as "поганые": the connotation is probably religious since the word is applied only to opponents of other faiths. It means also "unclean". A "поганка", for instance, is a poisonous mushroom.

татарвою (nom. case татарва): collective for Tartar.

"ночные птицы", "тихие зарницы": images borrowed from the medieval accounts of battle.

А Непрядва убралась туманом: another detail from the medieval sources.

нерукотворный: some icons are said not to have been made with hands (нерукотворные): they are "явленные" or "revealed". Here, Blok is, of course, writing of the Most Beautiful Lady, whose image is "revealed" mirrored in his shield at the hour of battle.


91 (III.254)  Россия (Опять, как в годы золотые)
          First pub.: *Новое Слово*, 1910, No.II.
          Trans.: C.Kisch, "Again as in the Golden Days", *Alexander Blok, Prophet of the Revolution*, London, 1960, p.126.
          Jon Stallworthy and Peter France, "Russia", *Times Literary Supplement*, No.3491, 23/1/1969, p.76.

The first printed version of this poem, which is given in full in the notes to the Third Volume (*C.C.*, Vol.III, pp.590–1), is much longer and foreshadows the picture of Russia the guardian of unsuspected riches which Blok was later to paint in "The New America". The barren marshlands, Blok says, are deceptive: they hide coal and precious stones.

          Сулишь ты горы золотые,
          Ты дразнишь дивным мраком недр.
          Россия, нищая Россия,
          Обетованный край твой щедр.

In the final version of the poem, however, Blok left only the lines devoted to the pastoral, poverty-stricken Russia which he loved ...

     ... without making a divinity out of her, exactingly and severely, as the people love, as one can love a mother, a sister or a wife in the single person of the motherland—Russia. There is a concrete and, if the expression is allowable—a "limited" love for native rags, for that "which the proud glance of the foreigner will neither notice nor understand." This love was familiar to Lermontov, Tyutchev, Khomyakov, Nekrasov, Uspensky, Polonsky, Chekhov. ("Народ и Интеллигенция", *C.C.*, Vol. V, p.321 [of Maxim Gorky's love for Russia].)

From the artistic point of view, Blok was undoubtedly right to confine his presentiment of a richer, more joyous Russia to the elusive hints of the last verse. However, the rough draft is extremely interesting as it connects the poem not only with the New America but with the prose extract, which, in this book, concludes the cycle "Родина", and also with the long poem "Retribution", introducing the idea of Russia, captured and subdued at last, giving birth to a son, "in whom she has invested all her freedom", a "mysterious" son over whose cradles she watches, humbly waiting (cf. also the introduction to "Retribution", *C. C.*, Vol. III, pp. 297–9). Blok never fully formulated this idea of "the son". As he had always suspected, he himself died, like Lermontov, without fulfilling all that he might have done (cf. A. Vetlugin, "Жизнь без начала и конца", in the newspaper *Общее Дело*, No. 392, Paris, 19/VIII/1921).

плат — платок: (kerchief) cf. Note 59.

острожный: adjective formed from the noun острог—jail.

92(III. 259)  Русь моя, жизнь моя, вместе ль нам маяться?
        First pub.: *Ночные Часы* (1911) under the title "Родине".
        Trans.: M. Bowra, "Russia, my life!", *A Book of Russian Verse*,
        London, 1943, p. 108.

It was difficult for Blok, the product of two centuries of division "which began under Peter and Catherine", to yoke his "inborn daemonism" to the service of his slow-moving, amorphous Motherland:

> Knowledge of the countryside ... can change a man in two possible directions: either it can kill him, that is destroy all will-power, making a man Russian in the Chekhovian sense (or in Rudin's if you prefer); or—it can give him ten-fold strength, that is, it can intensify his will-power, tune it in, perhaps, to a *super* European form. (Letter to V. Pyast, 6th June 1911; cf. Vl. Pyast, *Воспоминания о Блоке*, Petersburg, 1923, pp. 93–94, and *C. C.*, Vol. VIII, p. 346.)

Russia's provincialism, fatalism, her Chekhovian love of sitting and talking, her Dostoyevskian tendency to wallow in degradation—exasperated Blok beyond all measure—as only the faults of a man's nearest and dearest *can* exasperate him. Returning from a holiday in Germany, for instance, he wrote to his mother:

> I made the journey through Germany at night and slept splendidly in a first-class compartment for which I slipped the Prussian guard 3 marks. In Russia, on the other hand, I spent the whole day and part of the night in one of those absorbing and heart-rending conversations which no-one abroad ever goes in for. Our native land lost no time in showing her hoggish—and her divine countenance. (Letter of 7/IX/1911, *Письма к Родным*, II, p. 184.)

And, a month later:

> All these dear good Russian people with no idea of times or seasons who drop in for a chat and enjoy "going into something rather deep ...". All that is terrible because— for no good reason and with the very best intentions—one exhausts one's last energy, last nerves and ability to work (*Дневник, 1911–13*, 26th December 1911).

Travelling through Germany he was even attacked by a fleeting wish to see the Germans "take over" Russia and "bring in some organization". (Letter of 25/VI/1909, *Письма к Роднымъ*, I, p.269; *Записные Книжки*, note for 25th June 1909.)

During his stay in Italy, Blok went so far as to indulge a dream of "ivory tower" individualism: "I should like to think much and quietly, to live retired, to see as few people as possible, to work and to study. Surely that can't be impossible? If only I could keep out of any sort of politics" (*Записные Книжки*, night of 11th–12th June 1909).

But this he could not do. In spite of the fact that, on his return, Russia seemed to him a vast expanse of "cosy, quiet, slow slush", he still felt in her yearning provincialism (which he compared to that of Chekhov's *Three Sisters*) "a tremendous desire to live" (*Записные Книжки*, 2/VII/1909).

> "Our earthly motherland still feeds us at the breast, and we owe her our strength, our inspiration and our joys. ... We writers, released from all duties except those of common humanity, must play the part of her finest and most important sensory organs. We are not her blind instincts, but her heart's sorrows, her reveries and thoughts, the impulses of her will... ("Ответ Мережковскому", *C.C.*, Vol. V, p. 444).

Nevertheless, there were moments (as, when dying, he wrote with gloomy irony that "Mother Russia" had devoured him "like a sow one of her piglets" [letter to K.Chukovsky of 26th May 1921, *C.C.*, Vol.VIII, p.537]) when Blok rebelled against this service. This poem, written during the winter after his Italian journey, commemorates one such moment. Like Pushkin's famous remark "It must have been the Devil's own idea to have had me born in Russia with brains and talent", Blok's outburst cannot be taken to detract from his great love of his country or from the steadfast chivalry of a life spent in her service.

Ермакъ: (d. 1584) Cossack Ataman and conqueror of Siberia (1581–4) under Ivan the Terrible; hero of many folk-songs, half-brigand, half-soldier.

чудь/меря: old Slavonic tribes who inhabited Central Russia.

грады: old Russian form of города (towns).

Царьград: Constantinople—which, to medieval Russia, was as Rome to medieval Europe, at first an object of covetous ambition and, subsequently, of veneration as centre of the faith. After "The City of Tsars" fell to the Turks in 1453, Russian Orthodox ecclesiastical thinkers declared Moscow "The Third Rome".

становье: archaic form of the word стан (camp).


93(III.265) Приближается звук. И, покорна щемящему звуку
First pub.: *Русская Мысль*, 1913, No. 4.
Trans.: R.Kemball, "Ever nearer the call", *Russian Review*, October 1959, p.308.

Blok at his most romantic. Set to music by Yu. Shaporin (who also composed a cantata on the theme of Kulikovo Pole which was performed at the

Queen's Hall in London under the direction of Albert Coates in 1935), this poem makes a typical nineteenth-century drawing room "romance". Yet it was written by Blok, the prophet of Revolution and the poet of the "Terrible World", two years before the outbreak of the First World War, five years before the October Revolution. Retrospectively, pathos deepens into tragedy against the background of the sack of "the old house" which, in this poem, looks so nostalgically into the heart of the poet. At the time, Blok justified the sacking of his home, which he had in a sense foreseen, even forestalling the shock by relinquishing the very idea of "birthright" (cf. *Дневники, 1917–21*, 6th January 1919). However, in another sense, the pain of loss which had been with him all his life grew no less after the event: "Why was my face all drenched with tears tonight when I was dreaming about Shakhmatovo?" (*Записные Книжки*, 12/XII/1918.)

The theme of happy memories of love and home (cf. also Note 89), together with an intense Alexandrine awareness of the beauty and the expendability of civilization, form, as it were, an essential, recurrent counterpoint to the tragic, heroic, sombre and bedazzled main themes of Blok's work.

94(III.268)  Новая Америка (Праздник радостный, праздник великий)
First pub.: *Русское Слово*, 25th December 1913, under the title "Россия".
Trans.: G. Reavey and M. Slonim, "New America", *Soviet Literature*, London, 1933, p.336. V. de S. Pinto, "The New America", *A Second Book of Russian Verse*, ed. C. M. Bowra, London, 1947, p.74.

Cf. Note 91. When asked, in the difficult years just before the Second World War, what her husband would have thought of the development of the Soviet Union since the Revolution, Blok's widow is said to have thought deeply before replying: "I don't know. Perhaps—he would have got enthusiastic about construction" (Не знаю – может быть, он бы увлекся строительством.). In a sense, Blok felt Russia *economically* very much more acutely than he felt her *politically*. This may seem incongruous in so mystic a poet: in fact, it is not. The true mystic is one who seeks to grasp the fundamentals of reality, the very opposite of the escapist daydreamer (Soviet criticism of Blok would be made much easier if this simple and ancient truth were to be more freely admitted). Politics—to Blok—were words and theories, essentially unmusical ("square", in the modern idiom). Economics, where they touch the fundamentals of life and death, sickness and health, human strength and joy and achievement, were musical ("hip")—a part of the basic rhythms of existence. In his reminiscences of Blok, Pyast writes of the years between the revolutions—

> ... On our expeditions, walks, sittings and wanderings the favourite subject of conversation was Russia. "Look", Blok would say, "There is no effective constitution; they have undermined the parliament in record time.... Yet, all the same, you know, over the last five or six years Russia has been transfigured. As soon as the first breath of freedom came—invisibly, but none the less powerfully and effectively—her own powers awoke. If a foreigner who had visited us in 1903 were to come again now, eight years later—he would see a completely different country. Neither you, nor anyone else can imagine how much the people have been giving out of themselves over this period, how much, that is, of real and tangible value—how many undertakings have been built up, extended, how much productive energy has been released...."
>
> Blok said all this in rather different words, not so stiffly; I didn't note his words, but can guarantee to have conveyed the exact meaning. (V. Pyast, *Воспоминания о Блоке,* Petersburg, 1923, pp. 60–61.)

In 1915 Blok noted for himself that "the future of Russia lies in the almost untapped strength of the mass of the people and in her underground treasures" (*Записные Книжки,* 5/XI/1915).

He even tried to write a play on the theme of the "Industrial Renaissance of Russia" (cf. Vl. Orlov, "Неосуществленный замысел Александра Блока — драма "Нелепый Человек", *Ученые Записки Ленинградского Государственного Педагогического Института Им. А. В .Герцена,* Т. 67, Leningrad, 1948, pp. 234–41, and A. Blok, *Записные Книжки* 23/X/1915; 8/I and 6/VI/1916).

Of course, the title and the last line do not mean that Blok thought or wished that Russia would model herself exactly on the United States. The word "new" is one he uses solemnly—usually in the sense of "transfigured" or "transformed" (as in the Apocalyptical concept of the "New Jerusalem" or in Dante's "Vita Nuova"), and he insists on this word both in this poem and in the preface to the long unfinished poem "Retribution" which should have described "how coal changes into diamonds, Russia—into a new America; a new, not the old America" (*C. C.,* Vol. III, p. 298). Pyast tells us that this poem, which was quoted in the Russian journal *Горнозаводское Дело,* was also translated into English in an article on the economic state of Russia in a "British business magazine" (*op. cit.,* pp. 18–19).

Ектенья: a part of the Russian Orthodox Liturgy.

орарь: surplice band (part of a deacon's vestment).

крепь: here in the sense of stronghold (крепость). Normally—a prop (particularly pit-prop).

феска: fez.

Не щеломами черпают Дон: an echo from the medieval chronicles. A prince, wishing to capture a river, would say he wished to drink its waters from his helmet.

И прекрасная внучка Варяга: an echo of the Lay of the Host of Igor, believed to be the earliest-written Russian narrative poem to have survived the years of the Tartar yoke.

чубы: locks of hair worn over the forehead by South Russians.

бунчук: horse's tail attached to a stick. The symbol of authority of the Ukrainian Hetman, as of the Turkish Pasha.

Нет, не видно там княжьего стана: the technique of making comparisons or introducing similes by the words "No, that is not … it is …" is in the manner of old Russian poetry. As Georgy Ivanov pointed out in a brilliant contemporary review, Blok's poetry about Russia is innocent of clumsy stylization, of the Russian equivalents of such expressions as "yea, I'faith" and "Hail, fair knight". "Yet they contain the Russia of the sagas and of the Tartar Yoke, the Russia of Lermontov and Nekrasov, of the Volga hermitages, of the year 1905" (G. Ivanov, "'Стихи о России' Александра Блока", *Аполлон,* No. 8–9, 1915, p. 99).

The effect is achieved as much by the form as by the content of the verse (see A. Pyman, "Об Английских переводах стихотворений А. Блока", *Международные связи Русской Литературы,* АН СССР, Moscow–Leningrad, 1963, pp. 426–8).

лачуга: shanty.

95 (III. 271) Ветер стих, и слава заревая
First pub.: *Ежемесячный Журнал,* 1914, No. 16.
Cf. Note 13.

Another poem which points to the constancy of Blok's theme and underlines the inverted ascetism of his life: the quiet retreat that in some way is Russia is abandoned *for* Russia, life, the world. In this connection there seems to be a direct line of descent from Gogol (whose words "Our Monastery is Russia" Blok quoted in his 1908 article "The People and the Intelligentsia" [*C. C.*, Vol. V, p. 326]), through Dostoyevsky (Alyosha Karamazov sent out into the world by his spiritual father, the idea, as Blok put it, of complete $\pi\alpha\varphi o\varsigma$ in earthly form) to Blok, with his passionate search "for life in books, for the life of today and for life as it ought to be [жизни настоящей (в обоих смызлах)]". ("Что надо запомнить об Аполлоне Григорьеве", *C. C.*, Vol. VI, p. 28.)

схимник: monk.
клобук: monk's head-dress.

96 (III. 274) Грешить бесстыдно, непробудно
First pub.: *Русское Слово,* 21st September 1914, under the title "Россия".
Trans.: B. Deutsch and A. Yarmolinsky, "Russia", *Russian Poetry, and Anthology,* New York and London, 1927.

Francis Cornford, one of Blok's most distinguished translators, says of him that he describes his country's weaknesses "with careful and clairvoyant hatred" (*Poems from the Russian,* London, 1949, p. 74). I can think of no better description of this poem, but would qualify it by another of Blok's quotations from Gogol:

How can we love our brothers? How can we love people? The soul wants to love only the beautiful, and people, poor things, are so imperfect and there is so little that is beautiful in them! How can we do it? First of all, thank God that you are a Russian. For the Russian there is a way opening up now—and that way is Russia itself. If only the Russian will learn to love Russia—to love everything about Russia. To that love we are being led by God himself. Without the sickness and sorrows which are bottled up in her in such a vast quantity and for which we ourselves are guilty, none of us would feel compassion with her. And compassion is already "the beginning of love"....
(Quoted by Blok in the article "Народ и Интеллигенция", *C. C.*, vol. V, pp. 325–6.)

And, looking forward to the Revolution when Blok deliberately welcomed the forcible destruction of the Russia described in this poem, by Blok's own words: "Only those who have loved as I have loved have the right to hate" (*Дневник, 1917–1921*, 20/II/1918).

купоны: banknotes.

97(III.278) Рожденные в года глухие
First pub.: *Аполлон*, No. 10, 1914.
Trans.: C. M. Bowra, "Those who were born in years of quiet", *A Book of Russian Verse*, London, 1943, p. 109. F. Cornford and E. Salaman, "Born in the years of sloth and dull decay", *Poems from the Russian*, London, 1943, p. 58. C. Kisch, "Born in years of dreariness", *Alexander Blok, Prophet of Revolution*, London, 1960, p. 129.

In his notebook, Blok describes Zinaida Hippius, to whom this poem is dedicated, as близ души—a kindred spirit (*Записные Книжки*, 28/VI/1915). They were, first and foremost, children of the same moment of time—singularly wide-awake children whose nature was to listen to "the music of history" rather than to try to shape events. The two most important historical events of their lifetime were the revolutions of 1905 and 1917, and it is the Japanese war and the 1905 Revolution which Blok calls "days of war and days of freedom" in this poem. The two poets reacted differently to both revolutions, but it is enough to compare their diaries from the beginning of the 1914 war to see how similar was their feeling for events: only the conclusions they drew were diametrically opposed. For instance, on 3rd October 1914, less than a month after Blok had penned the lines:

Есть немота — то гул набата
Заставил заградить уста

(If there is a dumbness—it is the tocsin
which has taught men to guard their lips)

Hippius, who was even more vigorously opposed to the war than Blok, notes: "No-one is in any doubt at all that there will be a revolution. No-one knows of what kind it will be or when it will come and—is it not terrible?—no-one is thinking about it. We have gone numb" (Z. N. Hippius, *Синяя Книга, 1914–18*, Belgrade, 1926, p. 51); and, a few weeks later: "I can change nothing, I only know it's *going to happen*. And those who could do something don't realize for one moment that it's *going to happen*" (*ibid.*, p. 64).

In 1917 Hippius realized at once, as Blok, in fact, only realized more slowly (cf. the letter to his wife of 21st June 1917 in which he says: "I was at the Union of the Soviets of Soldiers' and Workers' Deputies and in general I see my future"), that the Parliament was too timid and too conservative to gain control of the Revolution. On 28th February she was already noting:

> In the Manifesto of the Soviets of Workers' Deputies there is the will to action and to power; and this is set over against the tender lack of authority of the Duma deputies....
> They are foreigners, but those others, the left-wingers—are masters in their own home. Just now they are destroying their own goods (no-one can blame them, they have been out on their own for so long)—but still they are the masters. There will be more fighting. Lord! Save Russia! Help, help, help" (*ibid.*, p. 85).

It was months later that Blok woke up "between two dreams" with the same cry ringing in his ears:

> —Help! Help!
> —Help who?
> —"Russia", "the motherland", "the fatherland", I don't know what to call her....
> (*Дневник, 1917–1921*, 6th August 1917.)

Yet Hippius rejected the October Revolution absolutely and broke off all public relations with Blok, noting furiously: "He walks 'on the steps of eternity' and in 'eternity' we are all 'bolsheviki' (But then, in that Eternity there's not so much as a whiff of Trotsky, oh no!)" (*ibid.*, pp. 211–12).

On 31st May 1918 Blok wrote her a letter in which he tried to make her understand his point of view and to clarify their positions.

> There is "a catastrophic emptiness" in both me and you. It is either something very big, and in that case it is not for us to reproach one another with it; it is not our own opinions we are expressing; or it is very small, ours, private, "decadent"—and in that case it is not worth talking about in the face of approaching events.
> I want only to remind you briefly of our personal relations: we are divided not only by 1917, but even by 1905, when I had still seen little and understood little about life....
> I don't know (or—I know) why you did not see the greatness of October behind the grimaces of October, which were *very few*—there might have been many times more.
> Can it be that you don't know that "there will be no Russia", just as there was already no Rome—not in the V century after the birth of Christ, but in the first year of the I century? In the same way there will be no England, Germany, France. That the world has already been remade? That the "old world" is already at melting point?

(Cf. also the poem "Женщина, безумная гордячка", *С. С.*, Vol. III, p. 372.)

Blok was more pessimistic about individual man and the power of reason than Hippius, more optimistic about the virtues of his "good, great and clever people" and about the purposes of history. He was also the more attractive personality, being quite free of petty spite, and incomparably the greater poet. But, in affirmation and in denial, the two remained "kindred souls". For variant readings of this poem see *C. C.*, Vol. III, p. 599.

98 (III. 281)  Коршун (Чертя за кругом плавный круг)
            First pub.: *Русское Слово*, 10th April 1916.
            Trans.: M. Bowra, "The Vulture", *A Book of Russian Verse*, London, 1943, p. 109. F. Cornford, "The Kite", *Poems from the Russian*, London, 1943, p. 58. S. Kisch, "The Kite", *Alexander Blok, Prophet of Revolution*, London, 1960, p. 130.

Written at a moment when Blok was most depressed about the pointless slaughter of the war. The perfect, epic simplicity justifies the long apprenticeship which enabled Blok not so much to write about Russia as to let her speak through his poetry.

99 (V. 443–4)  From "Ответ Мережковскому"
            First pub.: *Русский Современник*, 1924, No. 3.

This is an extract from an unfinished article not published in Blok's lifetime intended as an answer to D. S. Merezhkovsky's attack on Blok's article "The present state of Russian Symbolism" (cf. *Русское Слово*, 14/IX/1910). It has been included here because it is too long to quote in its entirety in the notes to the "Poems about Russia", because it is beautiful and because it shows so clearly the *kind* of love which Blok bore his country. So much that has been written about Blok gives the impression of a melancholy Chauvinist who practises some mystic cult of the land of his birth. Blok believed that Russia had an historical duty to fulfil, as he believed that he as a poet had a duty to fulfil. When revolution finally broke over Russia, it did indeed seem to him that "Russia had infected humanity with health" (*Дневник, 1917–21*, 20/II/1918), but this was in the immediate context of the Soviet Peace Treaty with Germany, a treaty which filled every Russian "patriot" with profound shame and reduced even Blok's wife to tears—she had, after all, spent some time nursing the wounded behind the front and Blok himself had worn the Tsar's uniform and, in spite of his theoretical disapproval of the war, rather enjoyed the experience. Yet Blok, noting all this, went on categorically: "Patriotism is filth.... Russia has infected humanity with health" (*ibid.*). The new era which he believed the Russian Revolution to have ushered in was "already under the sign of Internationalism" (see Note 104).

100 (III. 304–6)  Extract from "Возмездие" (Первая глава)
First pub.: *Русская Мысль*, 1917, No. I.
Trans.: Sir Cecil Kisch, "Retribution—from Chapter One", *Alexander Blok, Prophet of Revolution*, London, 1960, pp. 165–7.

For the story of Blok's work on this long poem see Notes in *C.C.*, vol. III, pp. 602–25: recent special studies in English are the chapters devoted to "Retribution" by the poem's only English translator, the late Sir Cecil Kisch (as above, pp. 155–85), and by F. D. Reeve (*Alexander Blok: Between Image and Idea*, Columbia U.P. 1962, pp. 175–201, and the notes on this chapter, pp. 244–7) and an article by the Polish scholar W. Lednicki entitled "Blok's Polish Poem" (published in the book *Russia, Poland and the West*, London, 1954, pp. 349–99 and, in Russian, in *Новый Журнал*, Nos. II and III, New York, 1942, pp. 309–24, 260–87). Blok's own foreword to the poem is translated into French by J. Gauvain and E. Beckert ("Alexandre Blok, Poète de la Tragédie Russe [1880–1921]", *Nova et Vetera*, No. 3, Fribourg, 1943) and is printed in Russian before the poem itself in *C.C.*, Vol. III, pp. 295–300, as in most editions of Blok's collected works. In Russian, Blok's biographer V. Mochul'sky devotes a whole chapter to the poem in his book *Александр Блок* (Paris, 1948, pp. 263–300); L. Dolgopolov, who has made a special study of Blok's longer poems, gives us an article based on sound knowledge of manuscript sources ("'Возмездие', поэма А. Блока", *Русская Литература*, 1959, No. 4, pp. 146–70) and G. Remenik a thoughtful analysis in his *Поэмы Александра Блока* (Moscow, 1959, pp. 39–104). An interesting sidelight on "Blok, the hero of Retribution" is thrown by his own cousin, the late Georgiy Blok (*Русский Современник*, 1924, No. 3). There are, of course, other studies but these, being mainly of recent publication, are perhaps the most readily available—with the exception of Georgiy Blok's article which is mentioned because it gives a unique insight into Blok's family background on his father's side.

In this poem, at which he worked from 1910 until the end of his life, Blok tried to pass from the "particular to the general", to introduce "organically" new, general themes into the "equally organic" but individual inspiration "which formed the content of my first four books" (*Записные Книжки*, 3rd June 1915). In these evocations of the two centuries which formed his

poetry and our lives, Blok succeeds in overstepping the bonds not only of
personality, but of nationality; yet the voice remains, unmistakably and "or-
ganically", that of the Russian poet Alexander Blok.

сплин: spleen.

спич: speech.

Рекамье: Madame Recamier, famous early-nineteenth-century hostess.

Роланд: medieval French hero.

Он мягко стлал — да жестко спать: Russian idiom to describe a person or thing
    which gives a deceptively comfortable first impression. Not quite the same as the iron
    hand in the velvet glove. Lit: "It makes up softly—but is hard to sleep on" (as of
    bed).

Мессина: Messina was destroyed by earthquake in 1908. This event—as also the partial
    destruction of Lisbon and the sinking of the *Titanic*—impressed Blok as an omen of
    more general catastrophe.

стихийных сил: Blok associated "elemental" force with popular revolution. "Demo-
    cracy", he said, quoting Carlyle, "comes girded with storms" (*C.C.*, Vol. VI, p. 9).

пропеллер: see note to Авиатор (No. 60).

101 (III. 284)  Поёт, поёт
            First pub.: *Русская Мысль*, 1915, No. 2.
            Trans.: R. Kemball, "It sings, it sings", *Russian Review*, vol. 21,
            No. 2, April 1962, p. 150.

Written a year before the outbreak of the First World War, on the eve of
the encounter with "Carmen", this is an autumn cycle in a minor key. Blok's
old theme of the wind, not calling now but evoking memories and thoughts
of death and mutability in a world which seems hushed and grey. Cf. Notes 19
and 20; also Boris Pasternak's lovely evocation of the Wind theme in Blok's
poetry:

                Этот ветер повсюду. Он — дома,
                В деревьях, в деревне, в дожде,
                В поэзии третьего тома,
                В «Двенадцати», в смерти, везде.

    (B. Pasternak, *Стихотворения*, Moscow, 1961, p. 245, from cycle "Когда разгул-
яется".)

102 (III. 286)  Милый друг, и в этом тихом доме
            First pub.: *Русская Мысль*, 1915, No. 2.

Like many of Blok's quietest and most lyrical poems—among his most
eerie and terrifying. In the margin of the rough draft Blok has noted: "This
was written more than a year before the war."

103 (III. 347–59) Двенадцать

First pub.: *Знамя Труда*, 3 /III (18/II)/1918.

Trans.: C. Bechofer, *The Twelve*, London, 1920. B. Deutsch and A. Yarmolinsky, *The Twelve*, New York, 1920, reprinted in *SEER*, Vol. VIII, London, 1930. G. Reavey and M. Slonim, "The Twelve" (extracts), *Soviet Literature*, London, 1933, p. 338. G. Shelley, "The Twelve", *Modern Poems from the Russian*, London, 1942, p. 70. C. M. Bowra, "The Twelve", *A Second Book of Russian Verse*, 1947, p. 76. A. Miller, "The Twelve", *Stand*, Winter 1955–6, p. 11. C. Kisch, "The Twelve", *Alexander Blok, Prophet of Revolution*, London, 1960, p. 142. A. Hollo, "The Twelve", *Evergreen Review*, No. 19, Vol. 5, 1961, p. 31.

I remember [wrote Vladimir Mayakovsky] during the first days of the revolution I walked past a thin stooping figure in uniform warming itself at the bonfire in front of the Winter Palace. Someone called after me. It was Blok. We walked on to the *Detsky* Gates.

I asked: "How do you like it?"—"Fine", answered Blok, but then added: "My library in the country has been burnt." This "fine" and this "my library's been burnt" were two ways of feeling the revolution which were fantastically combined in his poem "The Twelve". Some saw the poem as a satire on the revolution, others as its glorification. (Vl. Mayakovsky, "Умер Александр Блок", *Полное Собрание Сочинений*, Vol. XII, Moscow, 1937, pp. 31–32.)

The argument has gone on ever since. But the portrait painted of Blok by Mayakovsky in his strangely unsympathetic obituary does not do justice to the older poet, just as argumentative critics have failed to do justice to the poem. Yuriy Annenkov, the first illustrator of "The Twelve", tells us that Blok "never complained" (Ю. Анненков, "Смерть Блока", *Жизнь Искусства*, No. 804, August 1921). On the other hand, he also—invariably—told the truth: he was telling Mayakovsky a fact about the Revolution, which, for him, was important. People were burning libraries—not just anyone's libraries, but the workshops of their own revolutionary poets. Mayakovsky could not have known about the long passage in Blok's diary which justifies the sack of his home (*Дневник, 1917–1921*, 6 January/4 December 1919), although he might have realized that Blok would bear no resentment against the destroyers from his article "The Intelligentsia and the Revolution", published a month before "The Twelve" in the same newspaper.

But, if Mayakovsky misunderstood the essence of Blok's remark about his library, he is uncannily right in his assessment of its importance to the poem. "Fine" was the "music of the Revolution", the roaring sound—"most probably, the sound of the collapse of the Old World"—which Blok heard—physically heard—as he wrote "The Twelve". "Fine" the first months of the Revolution when it seemed that: "... Custom was no more, or rather the tempest had become customary. Soon Germany would fall—England—and the plough would cut across the needless boundaries. And heaven would unroll like a sheet of parchment" (V. Shklovsky, *Сентиментальное путешествие*, Moscow, 1939, pp. 284–5).

At this moment Blok was content "to surrender himself to the elements" no less blindly than at the height of his passions for Volokhova and Del'mas, in January 1907 or in March 1914, "for it was

> ... that exceptional and invariably brief moment, when the revolutionary cyclone produces a tempest in every sea—in nature, in life and in art; in the life of man there is a little backwater, something like the Marquisa's puddle [the Gulf of Finland, A.P.] which is called politics. And there was a storm in that tea-cup too,—it's easy to talk; they were talking of doing away with diplomacy, of a new order of law, of ending the war, then already four years old! The seas of nature, life and art had risen, the spray was playing over them like a rainbow. I was looking into the rainbow when I wrote "The Twelve", and therefore a drop of politics has remained in the poem.
>
> Let's wait and see what time will make of it. Possibly all politics are so dirty that one drop will dim and disintegrate all the rest; perhaps it will not kill the sense of the poem; perhaps, in the last analysis—who knows!—it may prove the ferment thanks to which "The Twelve" will be read in some time not our own. I myself can only speak of that now with irony; but—don't let us take it upon ourselves to decide definitely just yet. ("Из записки о Двенадцати", 1st April 1920, here translated from *С. С.*, Vol. III, pp. 474–5. Originally published in full in the collection *Памяти Александра Блока*, Petersburg, 1922, and, rather more fully than in *С. С.*, Vol. III, in Vol. 5 (1933) of the *XII Volume Collected Works*, pp. 132–4.)

"With all your body, with all your heart, with all your mind—listen to the Revolution", Blok had exhorted his fellow intellectuals. "The Twelve" is the result of *his* listening: "He condemned humanism, parliament, the civil servant and the intellectual. He condemned Cicero and acclaimed Catalina. He accepted the Revolution. Blok accepted the Revolution with blood. For him, born in the precincts of Petersburg University, to do that was difficult" (V. Shklovsky, *op. cit.*, p. 283).

It was difficult: but it was made easier by the fact that, since 1905, Blok had felt blood to be inevitable. What astonished him was the indignation of his fellow intellectuals. He considered them unfit to rule, for they had lost the will to live, never mind the will to govern (cf. Notes 27, 28, 31, 67, 90 and 97 and the collection of articles *The Intelligentsia and the Revolution**). But, to Blok's mind, they were in duty bound to help (Может ли интеллигенция работать с большевиками? Ответ на анкету, *С. С.*, Vol. VI, p. 8). It was difficult to relinquish the old, but Blok's favourite quotation from Plato, constantly in his thoughts in the days of Revolution, was χαλεπά τα καλά ("The Beautiful is always difficult"). The "new people" were at last taking over—and this was "fine".

---

* Translated by L. Freiman, *The Spirit of Music*, with an introduction by Elizabeth Hill, Lindsay Drummond, London, 1946.

But what shook Blok right from the beginning was the helplessness of these new people: "Even now I am the stronger... All culture, whether scientific or artistic, is daemonic... But daemonism is strength. And strength—is to triumph over the weak..." (*Дневник*, 6/I/1919).

Blok felt that, in some way, the excesses of the Revolution were the people's incoherent revenge for their own helplessness. The peasants might burn his library but "... even now I am the stronger, and that strength I owe to the fact that someone, some ancestor of mine, had leisure, money and independence... I have not the right to judge."

At the time, the Bolsheviks reproached Blok for showing the Red Guard as a disorganized rabble, for glorifying anarchy. He was inclined to agree with them.

> The Marxists are the cleverest of the critics, and the Bolsheviks are quite right to be afraid of "The Twelve". But the "tragedy" of the artist remains a tragedy. Besides: if there existed a proper priesthood in Russia, and not just a class of morally dull people of ecclesiastical calling, they would long since "have taken into account" the circumstance "that Christ is with the Red Guards". It is hardly possible to dispute this truth, so simple to those who have read the Gospel and thought about it. But here, instead of that, they are "excommunicated", and this storm in a tea-cup confuses still further the already sufficiently confused (monstrously confused) understanding of the upper and lower middle classes and of the intelligentsia.
>
> "The Red Guard"—is water on the mill of the Christian Church (as are the Sectarians and all the others they have been so busy persecuting). (As wealthy Jewry was water on the mill of Autocracy, something not one "monarch" ever brightened to before it was too late.)
>
> This is where the "horror" lies (if people would only understand). In this is the weakness of the Red Guard itself: children in an iron age: a waifish wooden church in the middle of a drunken and debauched market place.
>
> Did I "glorify"? (Kameneva) [one of Blok's "marxist critics", see *Записные Книжки*, 9th March 1918, A. P.]. I simply stated a fact: if you look into the snow-columns of the blizzard on *that road*, you will see "Jesus Christ". But sometimes I myself deeply hate that feminine phantom. (*Дневник, 1917–21*, 10th March (25th February) 1918.)

On the margin of the first draft of "The Twelve" Blok had scribbled the words и был с разбойником, remembering Christ's crucifixion "between two thieves", and—misquoting from Nekrassov's famous poem about the repentant brigand who sought to redeem himself by the murder of a rich oppressor—"Жило двенадцать разбойников".

In Blok's mind, Christ had always been somehow opposed to art, culture and the exercise of the individual will. At the same time, he had never quite been able to envisage individual salvation without Him (cf. also the other poems about Christ in this volume and Notes 37, 49, 51 and 73).

Endless articles have been written seeking to explain what Blok "meant" by Christ in the Twelve. But Blok himself answered this question when Nikolay Gumilev first objected to the image—"I was surprised myself", he answered, "Why Christ? Wherefore Christ?"

Blok "meant" nothing. He was "stating a fact". He "saw". What he saw he tried to describe in a letter of 12th August 1918 to Yuriy Annenkov:

> Do you know (I have felt this all my life), how when a flag is flapping in the wind (through rain and snow and particularly through the night), then it seems as though beneath it there is someone immense, connected with it in some way (not holding it, not carrying it, but how—I can't express it). Generally it's the most difficult thing to express, you can only find it, but I can't say it, perhaps I said it worst of all in "The Twelve" (but I still don't repudiate the essence of it, in spite of all the critics).

In F. D. Reeve's *Alexander Blok, Between Image and Idea*, p. 248, there is an English translation of Blok's elaboration of this letter in conversation with S. M. Aliansky, and N. Pavlovich ("Воспоминания об Ал. Блоке", *Думы и Воспоминания*, Moscow, 1962, p. 32) remembers how, in the winter of 1920, she walked with Blok through the falling snow and he told her how he saw Christ:

Фонарь за снегом впереди.
За нами темнота.
Он руку сжал мою: Гляди!
Я так видал Христа:

Идут двенадцать человек,
Он впереди идет,
Я не поверил: это снег
Свивается, метет.

Я не поверил, — снег кружил...
Но вижу венчик роз,
Но, к сожалению, это был
Действительно Христос.

И я, я должен был сказать...
Тот грохот шел три дня.
С тех пор уж больше не слыхать
Ни ночи мне, ни дня.

Perhaps the best single description of "The Twelve" written at the time by a contemporary whose feelings for events were evidently very close to those of Blok himself is the account given by E. Lundberg in his *Записки Писателя, 1917–1920* (Leningrad, 1930, p. 131).

*March, Petersburg, Moscow*

> A. A. Blok's poem "The Twelve" has appeared in *Знамя Труда*. Ivanov-Razumnik told me in passing that the poem is remarkable both in the unexpectedness of its form and in its intensity. But it is not in the least what I expected. There hasn't been anything like it in Russian literature before. The basis of the poem is the street quatrain [частушка]. It is as though Blok has bound together a sheaf in his poem—a sheaf among the single ears of which are: (1) the Cosmic (Wind, wind over all God's earth); (2) something of the people (the revolution); (3) the personal (Van'ka and Kat'ka); (4) something consciously religious ("Christ, in the white crown of roses")

and (5) most complicated of all—the mutual interweaving of all these underground, earthly and supra-spatial currents.

When I got hold of the newspaper I read the poem and took the page to E.P. Half an hour later I came back to her—she was still reading, very serious.

—Well?—I asked, and realized at once that I should not have asked.

—It's good.

And that was all. Only with acquaintances have I talked, as everyone is talking, about "The Twelve" ... they mostly discuss odd details ... but what will Blok write, what will he *do* after "The Twelve"...?

I have tried here not to "interpret" "The Twelve", but to supply the reader with some "raw material" and "background information" not otherwise readily available in English which may help him to a deeper appreciation of Blok's poem. "The Twelve" is the culmination of a lifetime of work, thought and experience and this "background information" is incomplete if the reader does not follow up the cross-references to the notes on earlier poems.

For recent Soviet literature about "The Twelve" see Vl. Orlov's *Поэма Александра Блока "Двенадцать"*, Moscow, 1962, which contains a lot of bibliographical data in the notes.

Studies in English include D.S. Mirsky, who once declared that if he had to choose between "The Twelve" and all the rest of Russian literature put together, he would hesitate ("Russian literature since 1917", *The Contemporary Review*, August 1922, pp.205–11, in his *Modern Russian Literature*, pp.210–24); Maurice Bowra's interpretation of the poem in his article on Alexander Blok in his book *The Heritage of Symbolism*, London, 1943; V. Zavalishin's "Alexander Blok" in his book *Early Soviet Writers*, New York, 1958, pp.5–22; F.D. Reeve, "The Twelve" in his book *Alexander Blok, Between Image and Idea*, Columbia University Press, 1962, pp.202–18.

Since this note was originally written Scandinavian scholarship has contributed an interesting comparison between the finale of "The Twelve" and the end of Ibsen's "Brand" (Martin Nag, *Edda*, No. 4, Oslo, 1964, pp.324–8 and an introduction by N.O. Nilsson to a new Swedish translation in *Ord och bild*, No.1966. Commentaries in French and Italian have appeared with separate translations (see Addenda to Bibliography).

For variants see *C.C.*, Vol.III, pp.626–8.

Вся власть Учредительному Собранию!: the Constituent Assembly, a representative body elected on a system of universal suffrage which met in Petrograd on 18th January 1918 to decide what form the government of Russia should take in the future and which was dissolved by the Bolsheviki after its first meeting. On 5th January, Blok asked himself in his diary why the people referred to the Constituent Assembly by the contemptuous diminutive "учредилка". "Because", he answers for them, "how ought I to vote? Like everyone else? We are choosing in the dark. We don't understand. And how can anyone represent me? I am all on my own, for myself. The humbug attached to elections (not to speak of bribes at election which are an *open scandal* with all their Americans and Frenchmen)..." (*Дневники 1917–1921*, 5/I/1918).

разут: shoeless (lit. unshoed).

предатели: the Bolshevik determination to end the war was thought of by many as pro-German treason—an attitude particularly repugnant to Blok (see Note 104).

долгополый: long-skirted.

И у нас было собрание: the reference is to the famous Meeting of Prostitutes at which the street-walkers of Petrograd attempted to establish Trade Union rules.

бубновый туз: the ace of clubs—in Tsarist Russia the mark on the back of a convict's uniform.

Как пошли наши ребята: lines suggestive of a Revolutionary Lament in the style of the folk-song (see Note 53).

керенки: paper money issued by the Kerensky Government.

Шоколад Миньон жрала: an expensive brand of chocolate. This line was substituted by Lyubov' Dmitrievna for Blok's "юбкой улицу мела".

с юнкерьем, с солдатьем: с юнкерами, со солдатами. The form is a kind of derogatory collective.

ружьеца: form of plural for ружье (rifle) [vulg.].

родинка пунцовая: "the scarlet birth-mark"—the words are taken from a "жестокий романс".

Выпью кровушку за зазнобушку чернобровушку: again, Blok writes in the style of the жестокий романс.

Упокой, Господи, душу рабы твоея: from the prayers for the dead.

Не слышно шуму городского: suggested by one of Glinka's romances and a poem by Fet.

Невская башня: the tower of the old City Hall on the Nevsky Prospekt.

Вперёд, вперёд, вперёд, Рабочий народ: variations on an old revolutionary song—the "Varshavianka".

Бессознательный: revolutionary slang—"ignorant", "politically and morally not up to the mark".

эка: такая (such a...) [vulg].

В белом венчике из роз: this line still puzzles commentators (cf. Vl. Orlov, "Двенадцать", М, 1967, p. 108; François Flaman, *Revue des Etudes Slaves*, Vol. 45, Paris, 1966, pp. 91–92; S. Nebol'sin, "Александр Блок в современном западном литературоведении," *Вопросы Литературы*, Moscow, No. 9, 1968, p. 194). A possible explanation not advanced in these works is that Blok had in mind the wreaths of paper flowers which often adorn the head of the crucified Christ in churches or the metal frames (оклад) of peasants' icons. White roses seem to be a favourite embellishment of our Saviour and this visual image corresponds to Blok's idea of Christ and the Russian people—in all their simplicity—as related concepts.


104 (III. 360–2) Скифы

First pub.: *Знамя Труда*, 20th (7th) February 1918.

Trans.: Anon. In the article "New tendencies in Russian Thought", *Times Literary Supplement*, No. 992, London, 20th January 1921, pp. 33–34. B. Deutsch and A. Yarmolinsky, "The Scythians", *Russian Poetry, an Anthology*, New York and London, 1927, p. 187. R. Kemball, "The Scythians", *Russian Review*, April 1955, p. 117. J. Lindsay, "The Scythians", *Russian Poetry* (*1917–55*), London, 1956, p. 27. C. Kisch, "The Scythians", *Alexander Blok, Prophet of Revolution*, London, 1960, p. 152. A. Miller, "The Scythians" (as broadcast in the B.B.C. Third Programme, in 1962).

"The Scythians" was written in the same breath as "The Twelve"—in those first weeks of the year 1918 when Blok, to use his own words, was "living in contemporaneity" (cf. G. Blok, "Блок, герой Возмездия," *Русский Современник*, 1924, No. 3, p. 184). He had written virtually nothing since July 1916—everything had been too disturbed, he had had "no voice, only eyes' (*Дневник, 1917–1921*, 23/VII/1917), but his eyes had been fixed unwaveringly on the course of war and revolution:

> "Are you writing or not?—He's writing.—He's not writing. He can't write".
> Leave me alone. What do you mean by "writing"? To dirty paper with ink?... How do you know whether or not I am writing? I don't always know myself (*Записные Книжки*, 22/VI/1917).

The immediate impulse for "The Scythians" was the failure of the Bolshevik Government's attempt to reopen negotiations for peace with Germany at Brest-Litovsk which was announced in the Russian press on 11th January 1918—but Blok was then already possessed by the idea of "The Twelve" and only came to turn his thoughts on Europe and Asia into poetry after he had completed this, his greatest poem about Russia. The urgency of his inspiration is evident from the fact that he finished writing "The Twelve" on 29th January, began "The Scythians" on the same day and finished it the next. His notebook for the 29th reads:

> Asia and Europe.
>
> I have understood Faust's: "Knurre nicht, Pudel."
> A terrible roaring sound growing ever louder in me and around me...
> Today I am a genius.

"The Scythians" has often been compared to Pushkin's "Клеветникам России" and, paradoxically, was welcomed by strongly nationalist elements of the Russian *émigré* press as evidence of a revival of patriotism in Soviet Russia. (Cf. P. Struve, "Двенадцать Александра Блока", *Русская Мысль*, кн. I и II, Sofia, 1921, pp. 232–3; Petronik, "Идея родины в советской поэзии", *Русская Мысль*, кн. I–II, Sofia, 1921, pp. 214–25; N. A. Tsurikov, "Заветы Пушкина", *Правда и Свобода*, Первая Серия: *Вопросы истории и культуры*, №2, Belgrade, 1937, pp. 3–42: see also, for Blok's reaction to the first two articles, his diary for 20th April 1921).

National pride was indeed something which Blok carried "in his blood", but he appears to have regarded it as a form of original sin and "The Scythians" is an impassioned plea for internationalism, *not* a chauvinistic challenge. It was also the product of a lifetime of thought and "mystic" (in Blok's sense of the word) concentration. To understand this poem it is essential to review Blok's thought on the problems of Europe, Asia and Russia from the time of the first Russian Revolution and the Japanese war when they were first thrust on his attention. This does not appear to have been done before, and since not all the material is readily available, and "The Scythians" is one of Blok's most important poems—and still a political hot potato—this must serve as sufficient excuse for the disproportionate length of this note. Since writing this note the author has herself published a fuller and more coherent study of "The Scythians" in the magazine *Stand*, 8, No. 3, 1966/7, pp. 23–33. A useful study of Russian thought on Asia which also comments on the Scythians is G. Nivat, "Du 'Panmongolisme' au mouvement Eurasien", *Cahiers du Monde Russe et Soviétique*, VII, 3, 1966, pp. 460–78.

First, it must be remembered that for Blok, as for many Russians of his time, "Europe", "Asia" and "Russia" were not so much geographical or political or ethnic concepts as cultural and spiritual "Bearers", each of its own "idea" or "theme". These "ideas" and "themes", being of the spirit, were conceived as interchangeable. Thus, for Blok, there existed not only "Asia", "Russia" and "Europe"—but "Asia-within-Russia" and "Europe-within-Russia" and, even, "Asia-within-Europe". There was also the problem of Russia, Europe and Asia within Alexander Blok. As the peasant poet Kluyev wrote to him:

> You've got one foot in Paris and the other "on the wild bank of the Irtysh". I re-peat, all my talk with you was one long struggle against the foreigner in you. I called you to Nazareth. You were thinking about Paris. I spoke of the Russian shirt and cap and you ran off to your tailor's to try on a dinner jacket, blowing kisses to the Russian shirt as you went. (Letter No. 21, undated, Ф №. 55, опись, №. 3, ед. хр. №. 35, ЦЕАЛИ.)

Blok commented meekly on this letter: "*I know what should be done:* give away my money, repent, give away my dinner-jacket, even my books. But I can't, I don't want to" (*Дневник*, 6/XII/1911).

For Blok, Europe represented the daemonic qualities of "Will" and "Culture" (cf. Note 92) which he associated with Rome and with the Renais-sance, but first-hand acquaintance with modern Europe convinced him, as it had convinced so many nineteenth-century Russian writers, that the live spirit of Europe was dying, decomposing even (cf. Blok's Notebooks on Italy, France and the other European countries which he visited; also his letters to his mother from abroad and, in this book, the cycles "Итальянские Стихи" and "Родина" and notes). Yet there were times when the aura of past romance and the lovely outward forms of Europe seduced Blok almost to the point of making him forget his allegiance to Russia, whose sprawling formlessness exasperated him. Always, however, he was brought up short by the decadence of Europe and driven to seek renewal in the thought of Russia's untapped energies, perceiving in her, "perhaps", the triumph of "the inward man", a constant reproach to "the outward man" (*Записные Книжки*, 25/VI/1909). Blok's Italian journey convinced him that it was too late for Russia to apprentice herself to Europe: "... either she will never be, or she will take quite a different road than Europe's—we cannot wait for culture..." (*ibid.* 15/VII/1909). And, on the following day: "Culture must be loved so much that its ruin should not seem frightening (that is, it is among those things most worthy of love)..." (*ibid.* 16/VII/1909).

In 1911, Blok opened a new diary with the cautious words:

> To keep a diary, or at least from time to time to jot down notes about the most important events, is the duty of each one of us. It is very probable that our time is—great, and that it is we ourselves who stand at the centre of life, that is in that place where all the spiritual threads run together and from which all the sounds are audible... (*Дневник,* 17/X/1911).

So gradually, by observation and groping thought, Blok had reached the conclusion that, if anything new were going to happen in the world, it would happen in Russia. (In this he was just six years in advance of Winston Churchill, who is reported to have remarked to a friend in 1917: "Russia, Russia—that's where the weather's coming from.") But Blok's Russia, too, was infected with European decay, to which she added her own particular brand of destructive "Asiatic" nihilism—"tatarshchina", as Blok called it. Before the First World War the Yellow Peril was considered a very formidable bogey. To Blok, it sometimes seemed as though not only Europe, but his own country, too, was ripe for invasion by barbarian hordes. His contemporaries, D. S. Merezhkovsky and Andrey Bely, whose thought certainly coloured if it did not actually influence his, and his teacher Vladimir Soloviev, saw in the "idea" of Asia the negation of the individual soul, a huge indifference to Man and a destructive nostalgia for non-being. Soloviev even went so far as to connect the Yellow Peril with the coming of Anti-Christ. In the "terrible years" before the Revolution, Blok saw this "idea"—or rather this negation of all ideas—perilously dominant in his own civilisation:

> ... from all sides a frightful bestial face materialises and seems to be trying to say "Aaa—so that's the kind of man you are, is it? ... Why are you so tense, why do you think, act, construct—why? ..."
> And so we too yawn over the yellow peril, but China is already within us.
> Irresistably and with gathering momentum the purple blood of the Aryans is becoming yellow blood. The frightful bestial faces in the tram-cars bear witness to this and to this only... There remains a brief last act: the physical occupation of Europe. It will happen quietly and sweetly, to judge by outward appearances. The clever puppet, the Japanese, will lay a firm, friendly hand on the shoulder of the Aryan, will look "with lively, black, curious" little eyes into the leaden eyes of the ex-Aryan...

> That will be the moment when we shall have to unseal all the secret renaissances of the New World (Poe) and of the Slavonic World (Pushkin, Russian History, Polish "Messianism", Mickiewicz's island in Paris\*, the secret of Ravenna, to awake Galla†).
>
> We shall have to discover in our Aryan culture a gaze which will be able to look calmly (solemnly) and without emotion into the "curious, black, fixed and naked" gaze of (1) the old man in the tram, (2) the author of that letter to a female agent-provocateur which Sologub read out in the ex-Café-de-France, (3) Men'shikov who sold us to the Japanese, (4) Rozanov, advocating that we should lie with our sisters and with animals, (5) Suvorin after his thrashing, (6) the ladies of the Nevsky Prospekt, (7) the Russo-German Sodomite... There's no naming them all. The sense of tragedy is in the *hopelessness* of the conflict; but there is no despair, no flabbiness, no folding of the hands. A high dedication is essential (*Дневник, 1911–1913*, 14/XI/1911).

A few days later Blok returns to the theme:

> A splendid lecture. The blood is not yellowing, there is both conflict and passion... From Theodosius of the Caves to Tolstoy and Dostoyevsky the great theme of Russian culture has been religious. In our day society has taken to "aesthetic idealism" (that is, by definition, their blood is turning yellow) (*ibid*. 21/XI/1911).

The idea continued to haunt him, even in his own home. He feared to see something "yellow, satiated, in the family, in the blood from which I tore away Lyuba" (*ibid*. 18/XII/1911). Arguing with friends, Blok explained that, in his view, West and East are branches of the road which lies before Russia, but not "*the* road": "From the West—the bitter scent of almonds, from the East—the blessed reek of smoke and burning", (*ibid*. 22/XII/1911).

This thought of a third "hidden" road is taken up again in an article written two and a half years *after* the poem "The Scythians", in which Blok compares the present crisis of our civilization to the crisis resulting from Christ's entry into history (for the same comparison cf. the article "Катилина", *С.С.*, Vol. V, pp. 60–91; [Что сейчас делать?—Ответ на анкету] *С.С.*, Vol. V, pp. 58–59; and the letter to Z. Hippius quoted in Note 97):

> If the comparison is allowable, the ever-watchful civilizers, armed with all their ancient cunning, the Romans—were sleeping a deep sleep; no less deep asleep were the barbarians, brushing the civilizers from their body with wild sweeps of their clenched fists even as they slept and snored and, in doing so, breaking every past and future law of human societies, as only the people are capable of breaking them; also deep asleep, for that matter, was that genius Tacitus, who chronicled all these goings-on a century after the death of Christ—without apparently suspecting that the wind was blowing not from Rome, not from Germany, not from Britain, not from Spain, not from Asia Minor, but from some other continent. This continent was at one time remembered by Plato and the Eleatics; but Aristotle made civilized people forget about it: and, for the uncivilized, there was nothing to remember. ("Владимир Соловьев и наши дни", *С.С.*, Vol. VI, p. 158.)

In "The Scythians", Blok is not taking sides with either West or East. He is fulfilling his function as an artist—which he described variously as that

---

\* A Polish Library on the Île de la Cité which had caught Blok's imagination when he was exploring Paris in 1911 (cf. letter of 20/VIII/1911 to his mother, *Письма к Родным*, II, p. 168).

† Galla Placidia—see note to "Ravenna", No. 70.

of "a witness", "an uncoverer of truth", a "releaser of harmonies" and—a "catacomb": he is stating a situation, and spreading and preserving the knowledge of a Third Road.

The picture which Blok draws of the confrontation of West and East (in all the complexity of meaning which these terms had for him) is as black and terrifying as our present reality. But the hope is also "real". Although Blok claimed that Russia "could not wait for culture", he did not think his country unfit, in the long run, to preserve what was best in Western civilization: "... for the measure of our refinement is full, that is refinement is already a part of our flesh and blood, a part of ourselves, we no longer tremble for it (of course, I say this only in the certainty that there will be new people and at the moment there are undeniably but few of them)..." (letter of K. S. Stanislavsky, 9/XII/1908).

So, when the Revolution finally came, he believed that culture would survive if the "Europeans" (here both the Russian intelligentsia like himself and the inhabitants of Europe) would only renounce the "patriotic" fratricidal lunacy of war. War, *not* revolution, was the enemy.

By the middle of June 1917 it appeared as though the Russian Revolution were indeed about to spread like wildfire across the borders. For some time, Russian soldiers had been fraternizing with their German counterparts at the front and it seemed as though the German officers would never again be able to force their men to fight. This was the moment of Blok's maximum optimism: "There's nothing new to tell you about myself and, if there were, it would be impossible to work up any excitement over it because the whole content of life has become the World Revolution, at the head of which stands Russia. We are so young that in a few months we could recover completely from a 300-year-old sickness...."

At the same time, he feared Kerensky's policy of not letting down the allies and the intelligentsia's indifference to the need for Peace, their obvious fear of the threat of mob rule:

> If the "brain of the country" is going to go on nourishing itself on the same ironies, the slavish fears, the slavish experience of weary nations, then it will stop being the brain and will be ripped out—quickly and cruelly and authoritatively, as everything is done which really does get done nowadays. What right have we to fear our great, clever and good people? And our experience, bought with the blood of children, could be shared with these children... (letter of 21/VI/1917 to L. D. Blok; see also Blok's diary for 19/VI/1917).

However, with the reopening of the offensive at the front on 18th June and the suppression of the workers' demonstrations on 3rd July, the hope of peaceful co-operation between the people and the intelligentsia, as between Russia and Europe, began to fade. Blok retailed distressfully the circumstances of the recommencement of the killing at the front (*Дневник, 1917–1921,*

14/VII/1917), noting bitterly: "Without this offensive and with fraterniza
tion the war would have been over." Nevertheless, he became more rathe
than less convinced that the forces of revolution needed the co-operation o
the old culture:

> There's one more thing I have come to understand: that is the workaday side o
> bolshevism behind the flying, behind the winged. That's where we must help them. The
> people have wings, but in skills and knowledge they need our help... But surely it can-
> not be that many who could help them will not go over to them... (*ibid.* 18/I/1918).

On the eve of the October rising, Blok noted: "This morning Mama was
talking very sensibly about the necessity of putting an end to the war: the
crassness of the word 'dishonour'. We have the wealth: the West the ability,"
(*ibid.* 19/X/1917). After the takeover: "To hate internationalism is not to
know and not to feel the strength of the nation," (*ibid.* 5/I/1918). Then, on
hearing the news of the failure at Brest-Litovsk, came the outburst which
was to become "The Scythians". Addressing foes and allies alike, Blok
writes:

> If you do not wash away the shame of your wartime patriotism with at the least a
> "democratic peace", if you destroy our revolution, then you are no longer Aryans.
> And we shall open wide the Eastward Gates.
>   We looked at you with Aryan eyes, so long as you still had a face. But your animal
> muzzle we will run over with our squint-eyed, cunning, glancing look; we will turn
> ourselves into Asiatics, and the East will flood over you.
>   Your skins will go for Chinese tambourines. He who has brought down such shame
> on his own head, who is so sunk in lies—is no longer Aryan.
>   We're barbarians? All right then. We'll show you what barbarians really are. And
> our cruel reply, our terrible reply, will be the only answer worthy of man.
>   But as to evolutions, progresses, constituent assemblies—all that is an old joke. We
> have understood your poison better than you yourselves (Renan).
>   Life is illiterate. Life is truth (Pravda). Riddled with falsehood... [word missing in
> the original], but—Truth—and it leaps to the eye, like the newspaper "Pravda" on
> every street corner.
>   You can't tone down life. What Europe tones down she tones down delicately,
> tenderly (Renan; the scientific spirit; the spirit of enlightenment; esprit gaulois; Eng-
> lish comedy). We (Russian professors, writers, public figures) can only tone things
> down to a dirty grey, water them down. Using the hands of our intelligentsia (and for
> so long as it so lacks the sense of music it is cannon-fodder, the honourable weapon of
> barbarity)—we are fulfilling our historical mission (and in the accomplishment of this
> task the intelligentsia are manual labourers carrying out a manual job)—which is to
> uncover Truth. The last Aryans are We.
>
>                    Truth is only revealed to fools.
>                    . . . . . . . . . . . . . . .
>                    Europe (her theme) is art and death. Russia is life.

Also for 11th January Blok's notebooks contain the still more cryptic entry:

>                    Музыка иная. Если — жолтая?
>
> (The music has changed. If it should be—yellow?)
> (For spelling of "желтый" see note to "Фабрика", No. 22.)

"The Scythians" is the culmination of hope, anger, fear and fierce, loving concern expressed in these scattered statements. A week or two after it was written, hope for a short-term solution had faded still further, although faith in the inevitable eventual outcome remained:

> Perhaps all the world (the European world) will grow angry, take fright and sink back still deeper into its illusion. But *that will not be for long*. It is hard to fight the "Russian infection", because *Russia has already infected humanity with health*. All dogmas are toppling, they have not long to go.
> Movement is infectious. (*Дневник 1917–1921*, 20(7)/II/1918).

A year after writing "The Scythians", Blok was still insisting on internationalism:

> ... it is the same two spirits which are now locked in combat in ancient Europe as in youthful Russia, and there is no important difference between them, in spite of all the immense apparent difference, because the world already stands under the sign of spiritual internationalism; beyond the din of artificially blown up national conflicts and quarrels it is already possible to foresee an era when the youngest races will walk arm in arm with the most ancient under the sound of that joyful music which, for the civilization* which divides them, will sound like a funeral march. (*Ibid.* 31/III/1919.)

Only later that year did Blok begin to qualify his belief in the beneficence of the overthrow of the old world: "What destroyed the revolution (the spirit of music)?—the War" (*Записные Книжки*, 4/IV/1919).

Soberly, he records and examines news from abroad: the bolshevik revolution in Europe is over; the Scandinavians are too well fed, the Germans too busy recovering from the war; the English are perhaps in the process of evolving towards socialism—at least the Trade Unions had prevented Lloyd George declaring war on Russia but this, Blok had been informed, was not because they were against war with *Russia* but simply because they were fed up with war (*Дневник*, 22/X/1920). He is cheered, however, by the thought of Wells' convinced and methodically constructive internationalism (*ibid.* 9/XI/1920).

It is an accepted cliché to say that Blok died profoundly disappointed with the Russian Revolution. It would be truer to say that he died exhausted by the pilgrimage through the world which, as a young man, he had undertaken—like the Red Guards of the Twelve—"without one Holy Name", and bitterly disappointed by the failure of the forces of enlightenment to hear "the music of history", a failure in generosity, love and coinherence which left that which was best in his people no alternative but to retire from the struggle, "to open wide the Eastward Gates"—which left the world and the individual unenlightened and untransformed:

> In the weather, and in the street, and in E. F. Knipovich, and in Mme Marie, and in Europe—all is the same. Life has changed (it is changed, but not new, not *nuova*), the

---

* Earlier in the same entry in his diary Blok defines "civilization" as anti-musical, a Tower of Babylon, and welcomes its collapse in the name of true "culture".

louse has conquered the whole world, it is already accomplished, and everything now is changing only in the other direction, not in that by which we lived and which we loved (*Дневник,* 18/IV/1921).

Yet still Blok elected to remain with his people. His aunt M. Beketova, his friend Zorgenfrei and many other witnesses of the poet's last years insist on this continued and loving fidelity. "My soul", he had written to Bely in 1907, defending himself from his "brother's" accusations of betrayal, "is a sentry unrelieved. When it is night though, even a sentry is not exempt from doubts and fears" (*Переписка,* letter of 15–17/VIII/1907, p. 206).

холопы: bondsmen, serfs.

провал и Лиссабона, и Мессины: "The fall of Lisbon and Messina"—both towns were overwhelmed by earthquake (cf. Note 100).

Крылами бьет беда: as in "На поле Куликовом" Blok uses images from the past to create a sense of historic continuity. Here, the image of Doom beating her wings is taken from the Lay of the Host of Igor.

от ваших Пестумов: Pestum—a centre of ancient Greek civilization in Southern Italy destroyed by the Arabs in the ninth century.

Эдип: Oedipus.

пред Сфинксом с древнею загадкой: according to the legend, the Sphynx is held to have asked Oedipus one riddle. Had the hero failed to guess the answer his life would have been forfeit.

галльский: Gallic (i.e. French). It is worth noting how much the use of the modern "французкий" or, in the next line, "немецкий" would have detracted from the solemnity of these verses.

гунн: Hun.

# CHRONOLOGY

### 1879

JAN. 7th*    Marriage of Blok's mother A. A. Beketova to his father A. L. Blok.

### 1880

Nov. 16th    Alexander Blok born in Petersburg at the home of his grandfather, the Rector of Petersburg University, A. N. Beketov. A. A. Beketova leaves her husband.

### 1881

DEC. 26th    Lyubov' Dmitriyevna Mendeleyeva, Blok's future wife, born.

\* Dates are given Old Style.

*1883*

A. N. Beketov resigns his rectorship.

*1883* to *1884*

Blok spends the winter in Trieste with his mother, aunt and grandmother.

*1885*

Blok's first attempts at verse date to the summer of this year.

*1887*

AUG. 24th        Blok's mother, Alexandra Andreyevna, officially divorces
SEPT. 17th       his father and marries Lieutenant F. Kublitsky-Piottukh of
                 the Grenadier Guards.

*1891*

AUG. 27th        Blok enters the Vvedensky school for boys in Petersburg.

*1894*

JAN. 16th        Blok's first visit to the theatre to see L. Tolstoy's *Fruits
                 of Enlightenment* (*Плоды Просвещения*). The beginning
                 of a life long passion for the stage.

*1895*

SUMMER           Blok meets Lyubov' Dmitriyevna at Boblovo (seven versts
                 from his grandfather's holiday home at Shakhmatovo,
                 Klinsk District, Moscow Province) for the first time since
                 their early childhood.

*1896*

SUMMER           First amateur dramatic production organized by Blok at
                 Shakhmatovo.

### 1897

MAY–JULY      At Bad-Nauheim in Germany with his mother and aunt.
              First romance with a married Ukrainian—K. M. Sadov-
              skaya.

OCT. 31st     "Ночь на землю сошла"—the first poem Blok thought
              worthy to include in the manuscript of his collected works.

WINTER        In Petersburg Blok goes in for amateur theatricals and
              studies the art of declamation.

### 1898

JAN.          "Пусть светит месяц — ночь темна", the first poem in
              Blok's published Collected Works and in this volume.

MAY           Blok leaves school.

JUNE–AUG.     At Shakhmatovo—amateur theatricals (scenes from *Ham-
              let*, *The Maid of Orleans*, *Woe from Wit* and *Boris Godu-
              nov*). At Shakhmatovo, Boblovo and Dedovo (the estate of
              Blok's great-aunt A. G. Kovalenskaya) Blok begins to fall
              in love with Lyubov' Dmitriyevna. Visit to Mikhail and
              Olga Solov'ev. Beginning of friendship with their son
              Sergey.

AUG. 31st     Blok enters the Faculty of Law at Petersburg University.

### 1899

SUMMER        At Shakhmatovo. Amateur theatricals at Boblovo con-
              tinue. Blok begins to take an interest in new "decadent"
              literature. Reads Z. N. Hippius' *The Mirror* (*Зеркало*).

AUTUMN        The theme of the Most Beautiful Lady begins to sound in
              his poetry in verses with such titles as "To the Unknown
              God" (Неведомому Богу) (September), "Servus-Regi-
              nae" (October) and "Dolor Ante Lucem" (December).

NOV.          Takes part in the "Petersburg dramatic society" under the
              name of "Borsky".

### 1900

SUMMER        Reads Plato and other philosophers during the vacation
              at Shakhmatovo. Studies the history of philosophy.

SEPT. 7th     Returns to Petersburg.

Oct.          First unsuccessful attempt to publish his poetry in the
              periodical *God's World* (*Мир Божий*) (see Note 7).
Nov.          Crescendo of Beautiful Lady theme—"I seek Salvation"
              (Ищу Спасения).

## *1901*

Jan.–Apr.     The theme of "The Most Beautiful Lady" continues to
              dominate Blok's poetry.
Apr.          Blok's mother gives him Vladimir Solov'ev's poetry as
              an Easter present. For Blok, this is a revelation, and a
              powerful confirmation of his own thought.
May           First reads Bryusov's poetry in the almanac *Northern
              Flowers* (*Северные Цветы*). End of May Blok leaves for
              Shakhmatovo.

### The mystic Summer

Aug.          Blok begins to study the philosophical works of Vladimir
              Solov'ev.
Sept. 10th    Returns to Petersburg and changes to the philological
              faculty. Sends a selection of verses to Bryusov at the
              Scorpion Press but they go astray.

## *1902*

Jan.–May      Continues to write of the Most Beautiful Lady.
Mar.          Makes the acquaintance of Zinaida Hippius and D.S.
              Merezhkovsky.
June 5th      Departure for Shakhmatovo.
July 1st      Death of Blok's grandfather A. N. Beketov.
Sept. 7th     Returns to Petersburg.
Oct. 1st      Death of Blok's grandmother E. G. Beketova.
Oct.          Begins to take an active part in the literary life of Peters-
              burg. Attends the Religious-Philosophical Meetings and
              the gatherings of contributors to the periodical the *World
              of Art* (*Мир Искусства*). Offers his verses to Z. Hippius
              for publication in *The New Way* (*Новый Путь*) and to
              V. Bryusov for publication in one of the Moscow alma-
              nacs.

| | |
|---|---|
| Nov. 7th | Lyubov' Dmitriyevna agrees to become Blok's wife. |
| Dec. | Bryusov accepts Blok's verse for publication in *Northern Flowers*. |

### 1903

| | |
|---|---|
| Jan. 2nd | Becomes officially engaged to Lyubov' Dmitriyevna. |
| 3rd & 4th | Blok's and Bely's first letters to one another cross in the post. |
| 16th | death of Mikhail and Olga Solov'ev. |
| Mar. | Ten verses about the Most Beautiful Lady published by *The New Way*. (Later that spring he also publishes three poems in a student's "Литературно—художественный сборник" and ten in the Almanac *Northern Flowers*. By the time of this, his début in print, Blok had already written over 600 poems.) |
| May 26th | Leaves for Bad Nauheim with his mother. |
| July 6th | Returns from Germany to Shakhmatovo. |
| Aug. 17th | Marriage to L. D. Mendeleyeva. |
| Sept. | Blok's first prose publication—a review for *The New Way*. |
| Nov.–Dec. | Greater frequency of "Town" themes in his poetry. "The Factory" (Фабрика), "From the Newspapers" (Из Газет) (Nos. 22 and 23). The publishing house Гриф asks him to prepare a collection. |

### 1904

| | |
|---|---|
| Jan. 10th–24th | Blok and his wife in Moscow where they make the acquaintance of the Moscow symbolists—Bryusov, Balmont, Bely, Ellis and others. |
| Apr. 21st | Leaves Petersburg for Shakhmatovo where he spends the summer editing the first collection of his verse and entertaining Sergey Solov'ev and Andrey Bely. |
| June 18th | The poem with which Blok later chose to conclude the First Volume, "Вот он — ряд гробовых ступеней" (see No. 25). |
| Aug. 25th | Return to Petersburg, which is in a state of revolutionary ferment. During the autumn, Blok writes his first "revolutionary" poems (see Nos. 27 et seq.). |
| Oct. | Blok completes his university thesis on "Bolotov and Novikov". |
| | Стихи о Прекрасной Даме, published by the publishing house Гриф in Moscow. |

### 1905

| | |
|---|---|
| JAN. 9th | "Bloody Sunday"—the suppression of a peaceful worker's demonstration by troops (see No. 29 and Note). |
| APR. 27th | Blok leaves Petersburg for Shakhmatovo. |
| SUMMER | Uneasy relations with Bely and Solov'ev, who again spend some part of the summer at Shakhmatovo. |
| AUG. 27th | Returns to St. Petersburg. |
| OCT. 17th | The Tsar grants a Constitution and the first Russian Parliament (the Duma) is convened. Blok carries a Red Flag at the head of a revolutionary demonstration (see Note 31). |
| 18th | First notes for the long poem "The Night Violet" (Ночная Фиалка). |
| NOV. | Writes a survey of the literature on Griboyedov and translates Byron. |

### 1906

| | |
|---|---|
| JAN. | Blok completes the rough draft of the play *The Puppet Show* (*Балаганчик*). First meeting with Maxim Gor'ky. |
| MAR. | Blok's second book of verse—*Нечаянная Радость*—is ready for print at the end of this month. |
| APR. | *The Puppet Show* printed in almanac *Torches* (*Факелы*) to which the chief contributors were M. Gor'ky and L. Andreyev. This fact—and the satyric content of the play—make Blok seem a traitor to Andrey Bely, who is also horrified by what seems to him to be the degradation of Blok's Solov'evian muse in the poem "The Stranger", written in this month. |
| MAY 5th | Blok graduates from Petersburg University with a First Class degree. |
| 11th | Leaves for Shakhmatovo. |
| SUMMER | Writes another play *The King in the Square* (*Король на площади*) and the dialogue "On love, poetry and the Civil Service" (О любви, поэзии и государственной службе). |
| AUG. | Relations with Bely, which have been very uneasy since the spring, come to a head when Bely challenges Blok to a duel. Blok travels to Moscow to meet Bely and achieves a reconciliation. |
| 24th | Return to Petersburg. Bely leaves for Munich and Paris. |

| | |
|---|---|
| AUTUMN | Blok's poetry is full of the sad, muted themes of a life of poverty in the big city. Blok and his wife living away from Blok's mother and stepfather for the first time. "The Stranger" continues to haunt him and, on 11th October, he finishes a play of that title. He is also writing lyrical prose: the articles "Поэзия заговоров и заклинаний" and "Девушка розовой калитки и муравьиный Царь". |
| DEC. | Blok meets the actress Nataliya Volokhova. |
| | *Нечаянная Радость* published by Скорпион. |
| 29th | First poem of the cycle "The Snow Mask". |
| 30th | First performance of *The Puppet Theatre* directed by Vsevolod Meyerhold and acted by Vera Kommissarzhevskaya's troupe. |

### 1907

| | |
|---|---|
| JAN. | "The Snow Mask" is completed by the 13th. Edits Pushkin's early verse. |
| APR. | *The Snow Mask* is published by Оры. |
| 16–20th | Visit to Moscow. Begins work on "The Song of Fate" (Песня Судьбы). Accepts regular work as literary critic to the periodical *The Golden Fleece* (*Золотое Руно*). |
| MAY | First poem to be included in the Third Volume and in the cycle "The Motherland" (Ты отошла, и я в пустыне). |
| | Work on an article on The Realists, "О Реалистах". |
| JUNE | Work on "Free Thoughts" (Вольные Мысли) and on the articles "О Реалистах" and "О лирике". Throughout this summer Blok is working on verses eventually included in both the Second and the Third Volumes. |
| JULY | "Free Thoughts" and articles completed. Blok leaves for Shakhmatovo. |
| AUG. 8th | Blok calls Bely out for insulting him in the course of literary polemics but again the two are reconciled. |
| 29th | Returns to Petersburg. Begins work on the article "О Драме". |
| AUTUMN | The cycles "Autumn Love" (Осенняя Любовь) and "Invocation by Fire and Darkness" (Заклятие огнем и мраком) (Nos. 51, 53) and other poems to Volokhova, who is also back in Petersburg. |
| OCT. 2nd–7th | In Kiev with Andrey Bely. |

| | |
|---|---|
| Oct. 31st | Completes translation of Rutteboef's mystic play *Théophile* (*Действо о Теофиле*). |
| Nov. 15th–17th | Visits his mother in Revel' (Tallin). |
| Dec. 7th | First staging of *Théophile* at the Старинный Театр. |

## 1908

| | |
|---|---|
| Feb. 14th–23rd | In Revel'. |
| | Blok's lyrical plays are published in the collection *Лирические Драмы* by Шиповник. |
| | Writes the article "Три вопроса", translates Maeterlinck's verses and Little Tragedies. |
| Mar. 2nd | Blok lectures on the theatre at the theatrical club—article "О Театре" published in *The Golden Fleece*. |
| Apr. 28th | Completes translation of Grillparzer's *Die Ahnfrau*. |
| 29th | Finishes the first variant of the play *The Song of Fate*. |
| May | Blok's uneasy relations with Bely boil up in a third quarrel. They break off correspondence and personal relations until the summer of 1910. |
| June 3rd | Leaves for Shakhmatovo. |
| | "On the Field of Kulikovo" (На поле Куликовои). Reworks the third Act of *The Song of Fate*. |
| July | Returns to Petersburg. Publication of Blok's third collection of verse "Земля в снегу" by *Золотое Руно*. |
| | Writes the article "Об одной старинной пьесе". |
| Aug. 20th | Returns to Shakhmatovo. |
| | Writes the article "Солнце над Россией" on Lev Tolstoy and re-reads the works of Tolstoy, Turgenev, Belinsky, Dobrolyubov and Saltykov-Shchedrin. |
| Sept. | Continues re-reading the Russian classics. |
| Autumn | This autumn Blok takes up his great theme of "Russia and the Intelligentsia". |
| Oct. 4th | Returns to Petersburg. Writes articles "Вечера 'Искусств'" and "Генрих Ибсен". |
| Nov. 2nd and 21st | Lectures on Ibsen at Kommissarzhevskaya's theatre. |
| 13th | Reads the article "Россия и Интеллигенция" as a lecture in the Religious–Philosophical Society. |
| 25th | Second session of the R.-P. Society devoted to discussing Blok's lectures. |
| | Wrote articles "Вопросы, вопросы и вопросы" and "Ирония". *Die Ahnfrau* published by *Пантеон*. |

| | |
|---|---|
| DEC. 12th | Second reading of "Россия и Интеллигенцяи" in the Literary Society. |
| 30th | Reads "Стихия и культура" in the Religious–Philosophical Society. |

## *1909*

| | |
|---|---|
| JAN. 29th | Première of Blok's translation of *Die Ahnfrau* in Kommissarzhevskaya's theatre. |
| FEBR. 2nd | Lyubov' Dmitriyevna is delivered of a son. |
| 10th | Death of Lyubov' Dmitriyevna's son (cf. the poem "На смерть младенца" written in March this year). |
| | Blok writes the article "Душа писателя". |
| MAR. 19th | Blok reads the article "Дитя Гоголя" to commemorate the 100th anniversary of Gogol's birth at an evening organized by the "League of Education". |
| 25th–29th | Visits his mother in Revel'. |
| APR. 14th | Left with Lyubov' Dmitriyevna for Italy (Venice). |
| MAY | From Venice the Bloks go on to Ravenna, Florence, Perugia, Assisi, Foligno, Montefalio, Spoleto, and Orvieto. Blok begins work on the Italian verses. |
| JUNE | They go on to Siena, Pisa, Marina de Pisa, Milan. On the 11th—at Marino de Pisa—Blok is attacked by strong feeling of the futility of the literary grind. Resolves to live more quietly on his return to Russia and to study more. |
| 21st | Return to Petersburg, having travelled via Bad Nauheim, Frankfurt-on-Main and Berlin. |
| 29th | They go down to Shakhmatovo. |
| JULY–SEPT. | Work on the Italian cycle and the cycle "Через Двенадцать Лет" dedicated to K. M. Sadovskaya. |
| SEPT. 30 | Return to Petersburg. |
| OCT. | Begins work on a book of Italian impressions which resulted only in the fragments "Молнии Искусства". |
| NOV. 30th | Blok leaves for Warsaw having heard his father is mortally ill. |
| DEC. 1st | Blok's father dies. Blok remains in Warsaw until 19th seeing to the funeral and other arrangements and making friends with his half-sister Angelina. On the 19th he returns to Petersburg which he leaves again on the 29th to spend the New Year with his mother in Revel'. |

## 1910

| | |
|---|---|
| JAN. 9th | Blok returns to Petersburg. |
| | Begins work on the article "Противоречия". |
| FEB. 10th | Death of Vera Kommissarzhevskaya in Tashkent. Blok reacts with the poem "На смерть Коммиссаржевской". |
| MAR. 7th | Speech about Vera Kommissarzhevskaya at an evening held to honour her memory. |
| APR. 3rd | Speech at the funeral of the artist M. A. Vrubel, whose paintings on the theme of Lermontov's "Demon" had exercised a profound influence on Blok's poetry. |
| 8th | Reads "О современном состоянии русского символизма" in the "Society of the lovers of Belles Lettres" (Общество Ревнителей Художественного Слова). |
| 30th | Leaves for Shakhmatovo where he remains until November. |
| JUNE 7th | First notes for the long poem "Retribution". |
| OCT. | Prepares for publication the collection "Ночные Часы". |
| NOV. 1st–4th | In Moscow. Negotiates publication of "Collected Verse" with "Мусагет". |
| 5th | Returns to Petersburg. |
| | Work on the First Volume of his "Collected Verse." |
| DEC. 14th | Reads "Рыцарь-Монах" at a memorial evening in honour of Vladimir Solov'ev. |
| 24th–30th | In Revel'. |

## 1911

| | |
|---|---|
| JAN. | Continues work on "Retribution". |
| 19th | Repeats speech on Solov'ev at the Religious–Philosophical Society. |
| FEB.–APR. | Continues work on "Retribution". |
| MAY | Мусагет publishes First Volume of "Collected Verse". |
| 17th | Blok leaves for Shakhmatovo—Lyubov' Dmitriyevna for Berlin. |
| | Blok first discovers works of August Strindberg. |
| JUNE | Reads Strindberg. |
| 30th | Returns to Petersburg. |
| JULY 5th | Leaves to join his wife in Aberwrach, Brittany. Arrives 22nd July (European style), having travelled via Berlin, Hanover, Cologne, Liège, Namur, Paris and Brest. |
| AUG. 15th (E. s.) | Leaves Aberwrach for Quimper. |
| 26th E. s. | Leaves Quimper for Paris. |

| | |
|---|---|
| SEPT. | Travels home via Antwerp, Ghent, Bruges, Flushing, Dordrecht, Rotterdam, The Hague, Amsterdam and Berlin. Arrives 7th September (Russian style). Resumes work on "Retribution". |
| OCT. | Мусагет publishes *Ночные Часы*. Blok begins to keep a regular diary which he keeps up until 1913. On the opening page he suggests that Russia may be the point at which, at this moment of history, "all the sounds converge". |
| DEC. | As all through this autumn he continues work on "Retribution". Мусагет brings out the Second Volume of his "Collected Verse". |

### 1912

| | |
|---|---|
| JAN. 20th | Article "Дневник женщины, которую никто не любил". |
| MAR. | Begins work on "The Rose and the Cross" (Роза и Крест), using much material gathered in France the previous summer. The play was first conceived, on the suggestion of M. I. Tereshchenko, as the scenario for a ballet from the lives of Provençal troubadours of the fourteenth to fifteenth centuries. |
| APR. | Мусагет publishes the Third Volume of Blok's verse. Work on "The Rose and the Cross" continued. Blok thinks of it now as "an opera". The article "От Ибсена к Стриндбергу". |
| MAY 9th | Finishes article "Памяти Августа Стриндберга". Works on "The Rose and the Cross". |
| JUNE 6th | Finishes first rough draft of the first Act of "The Rose and the Cross". |
| JULY 4–18th | At Shakhmatovo. |
| | Moves into new flat at 57 Ofitserskaya Street (now the Street of the Decembrists) where he remained till his death. |
| AUG. 8th–17th | At Shakhmatovo. |
| AUTUMN | Two collections of verse for children, *Круглый Год* and *Сказки*, published by Сытин. Continues to work hard on "The Rose and the Cross". |
| NOV.-DEC. | November and December see the completion of three articles. "Памяти К. В. Бравича", "Непонимание или нежелание понять" and "Искусство и Газета". During this autumn Blok is writing some of his most powerful and pessimistic lyric verse. |

## 1913

| | |
|---|---|
| JAN. 19th | Finishes "The Rose and the Cross". |
| FEB. | The play *The Stranger* staged in Moscow. |
| 17th | First rough draft of the uncompleted drama about "a man of power"—connected with thoughts of industrialization. |
| JUNE 7th | Revised "The Rose and the Cross" for the last time. |
| 12th | Leaves for Paris. |
| 14th–25th | In Paris. |
| 25th | Leaves Paris for the Pyrenees travelling via Bordeaux, Saint Jean-de-Luz, Guètary and San Sebastian. |
| JULY 19th–26th | At Biarritz. |
| 26th–31st | In Paris. |
| AUG. 3rd. | Returns to Petersburg. |
| 8th | Returns to Shakhmatovo. *The Rose and the Cross* published by Сирин. End of the summer returns to Petersburg. |
| OCT. | Writes the article "Пламень". |
| DEC. | Thoughts on industrial expansion in Russia which have been occupying Blok throughout this year culminate in the poem "The New America". (Cf. No. 94.) |
| | On the second sees and is favourably impressed by Mayakovsky's drama "Vladimir Mayakovsky". |

## 1914

| | |
|---|---|
| JAN. | Begins work on the poem "The Nightingale Garden"—inspired by his Pyrenean holiday the previous summer. |
| MAR. | Makes the acquaintance of the singer L. A. Delmas, whose performance in the opera *Carmen* has fascinated him throughout this month. Writes, for her, the cycle "Carmen" (4th–31st). |
| APR. 7th–11th | *The Stranger* and *The Puppet Show* staged daily in Petersburg. |
| JUNE 8th | Leaves Petersburg for Shakhmatovo. |
| JULY 19th | (August 1st new style) Germany declared war on Russia. |
| 20th | Blok returned from Shakhmatovo to Petersburg. |
| AUG. | Work on "Retribution". |
| SEPT. | Lyubov' Dmitriyevna having volunteered as a Red Cross nurse, Blok sees her off to the front (cf. the poem "Petrograd skies were darkened by rain" (Петроградское небо мутилось дождем). Blok begins editing the Collected Works of Apollon Grigoriev. |

| | |
|---|---|
| Autumn | Continues work on the poem "Retribution". The passage on the Twentieth Century beginning "Двадцатый век еще бездомней" (No. 100) written in December of this year. Franz Feliksovich (Blok's stepfather) called to the front in October. |

### 1915

| | |
|---|---|
| Jan. 14th | Finishes the article "Судьба Аполлона Григорьева". |
| Mar.–May | Work on editing a new three-volume edition of his verse and one volume of plays. |
| May | Publication of *Verses about Russia* (*Стихи о России*). Work on an article about the play *The Rose and the Cross*. Lyubov' Dmitriyevna returns to Petersburg (10th–14th August) and Moscow (6th–7th September) and resumes her career as an actress. |
| June 30th | Leaves Petersburg for Shakhmatovo where he remains except for short trips to Petersburg until… |
| Sept. 29th | On his return to Petersburg undertakes a commission from M. Gorky to translate works by Armenian, Latvian and Finnish poets for an anthology of works by the various peoples of the Russian Empire. The poem "Years followed Years" (Пролетели за годами годы) is Blok's first for this year. |
| Oct. 14th | Finishes work on "The Nightingale Garden". |
| 23rd | Ponders plan for a drama on "The Industrial Renaissance of Russia". |
| 24th | Шиповник publishes the first volume of Flaubert's letters edited by Blok and translated by his mother. |
| Nov. | Blok's edition of Appollon Grigoriev's verses published with his introduction. |
| Dec. 25th | "The Nightingale Garden" published in *Русское Слово*. Since September Blok has written only ten verses: none for earlier this year. |

### 1916

| | |
|---|---|
| Feb. | Writes one poem—"She" (Она). |
| Mar. 29th | Blok goes to Moscow for rehearsals of *The Rose and the Cross* in the Moscow Arts Theatre. Two poems—"The Wind" (Ветер) and "The Vulture" (Коршун). |

| | |
|---|---|
| APR. 6th | Returned to Petersburg. First Volume of his Verses and the "Plays" published. |
| MAY | Works on "Retribution". |
| JUNE | Writing more freely again: "The Daemon" and the Prologue and first chapter of "Retribution". Second Volume of Verses published. |
| JULY 7th | Receives his call-up papers to active service as Accountant to the "13-ая инженерно-строительная дружина Всероссийского Союза Земств и Городов". |
| 18th–22nd | At Shakhmatovo. |
| 26th | Blok leaves for his posting behind the lines in the Pinsk marshes. Third Volume of his Verses published. |
| SEPT.–NOV. | On leave in Petersburg. |
| NOV. 2nd | To end of year—on active service. |

## 1917

| | |
|---|---|
| JAN. | Prologue and Chapter I of "Retribution" published in *Russian Thought* (*Русская Мысль*). |
| FEB. | Revolution in Petersburg. Establishment of the "dual power" of the Provisional Government and the Soviets of Workers' and Soldiers' Deputies. |
| MAR. 10th | Blok elected in his absence to the Presidium of the Temporary Committee of Servants of the Arts (Временный Комитет деятелей искусств). |
| 19th | Returned to Petersburg. |
| APR. 9th | Leaves for Kryukovo near Moscow. |
| 13–17th | In Moscow for rehearsals of *The Rose and the Cross* at the Moscow Arts Theatre. |
| 25th | Elected member of the Literary Commission to the Alexandrinsky Theatre. |
| MAY 8th | Blok appointed as one of the editors of the stenographic reports of the Special Commission of Enquiry to examine the records of dignatories of the Imperial Court who had been involved in the Rasputin scandal—a work which required his presence at the cross-examinations. |
| JUNE 16th | For the first time, Blok attends a meeting of the Soviets of Workers' and Soldiers' Delegates. |
| 18th | Hostilities resumed at the front after a period of fraternization. |

| | |
|---|---|
| JULY 3rd | Workers' demonstrations against the resumption of hostilities put down by the Provisional Government. |
| AUG. | Bolshevik party recalled from a brief spell "underground" to help repel the advance of General Kornilov. Blok begins editing the findings of the Special Commission for his published account "The Last Days of the Old Régime". |
| SEPT. 7th | Blok elected a member of the Literary-Theatrical Commission of State Theatres. |
| OCT. | Work for the Theatrical Commission. |
| 25th | (November 7th new style) Seizure of power by the Petrograd Soviet's Military Revolutionary Committee and the establishment of a "Provisional Workers' and Peasants' Government" (Council of People's Commissars) with Lenin at the head. |
| | Blok's aunt writes that Blok welcomed this turn of events "joyfully, with new faith in the purifying force of Revolution. It seemed to him as though the old World were indeed collapsing and as though something new and beautiful must arise in its place. He went about looking young, merry, energetic, shining-eyed..." |
| NOV. | Blok takes part in the meeting of the literary and artistic intelligentsia called at the Smol'ny Institute on the initiative of the Central Committee of the Communist Party. |
| DEC. | Begins to contribute to the Left S.R. journal *The Banner of Labour* (Знамя Труда). |
| | Begins work on a plan for the publication of his "Collected Works" in ten volumes. |
| 30th | Begins the article "Интеллигенция и Революция". |

## 1918

| | |
|---|---|
| JAN. 7th | Plans for a play on the Life of Christ based on Renan. |
| 8th | First notes for "The Twelve". |
| 9th | Finishes the article "The Intelligentsia and the Revolution". |
| 11th | Breakdown of negotiations for Peace at Brest-Litovsk—entry in diary on theme of "The Scythians". |
| 27th–29th | "The Twelve". |
| 29th–30th | "The Scythians". |
| | Also in January, Blok undertakes to work on a commission for publishing the classics in popular editions. |

*(Dates Given In New Style From Now Onwards)*

| | |
|---|---|
| Feb. 1st | "The Intelligentsia and the Revolution" published in *The Banner of Labour*. |
| | First sketches for an uncompleted poem "Russian Delirium" (Русский Бред). |
| Mar. 3rd | "The Twelve" published in *The Banner of Labour*. |
| 12th | Finished the article "Искусство и Революция". Begins work in the repertory section of the Petrograd Theatrical Department of Narkompros. |
| Apr. 3rd | Finished work on "The Last Days of the Old Régime". |
| 19th | Finished the article "Дневник женщины, которую никто не любил". |
| 21st | Working on the article "Исповедь Язычника". |
| May | Wrote two feuilletons "Fellow-Citizens" (Сограждане) and "Russian Dandies" (Русские Дэнди). |
| 13th | Lyubov' Dmitriyevna gives first public reading of "The Twelve". (Blok never read this poem in public—not because he came to dislike it, as has been suggested, but because he could not do it well. His wife read it roughly and dramatically, and Blok approved her reading. His own technique of recitation was to speak quietly, almost metallically, quite without pathos, allowing the rhythm of the words to "carry" him.) |
| | Work on "Catalina" which he read in the School of Journalism on the 19th. |
| June | First separate publication of "The Twelve" and "The Scythians". |
| July | "The Nightingale Garden" in a separate edition. |
| Aug. | New edition of Blok's "Plays" published. |
| Sept. | The First Volume of a third edition of Blok's Collected Poems published. |
| 22nd | Blok invited to become a member of the editorial board of "World Literature" (founded by A. M. Gor'ky). |
| Oct. | Work on the collection of articles "Russia and the Intelligentsia" published by house "Алконост". |
| Nov. | Deeply impressed by the first anniversary of the October Revolution and by Mayakovsky's play *Мистерия Буфф*. |
| 27th | "Алконост" publishes "The Twelve" with illustrations by Annenkov. |

*1919*

| | |
|---|---|
| JAN. | Works on revision of the play *The Song of Fate* and prepares for publication the collection "Iambs"—poems written between 1907 and 1914 many of which had remained unpublished because of their overtly revolutionary content (see Nos. 66–69 and notes). In the spring of this year Alyansky begins to publish the journal *Dreamer's Notes* (*Записки Мечтателей*) to which Blok becomes a regular contributor. Helps to found the Free Philosophical Academy (Вольная философская Академия). |
| FEB. | "Catilina" published as a separate brochure. |
| MAR. 8th | Blok confirmed in his appointment as a member of the editorial board of "World Literature" and editor of the section "German Literature". |
| 15th | Blok arrested on suspicion of complicity with Left S.R.s but released within two days. |
| 25th | Speech at the publishing house "World Literature" on translating Heine. |
| 30th | Speech at the publishing house "World Literature" on the anniversary of A.M. Gor'ky. |
| APR. 9th | Reads "The Collapse of Humanism" at "World Literature". |
| 24th | Is appointed Chairman of the board of Directors of the Great Dramatic Theatre (Большой Драматический Театр). |
| MAY | Throughout the spring Blok works for the Union of Writers of Fine Literature (Союз деятелей Художественной Литературы) and on plans for a series of one-act historical plays or "tableaux". |
| JUNE | *The Song of Fate* published in a separate edition by "Алконост". Second edition of "Russia and the Intelligentsia". |
| JULY | Work on introduction to the poem "Retribution". All the summer Blok swam daily in the Gulf of Finland. With his grey eyes, weathered face and white pullover he looked—said his contemporaries—like nothing so much as a Scandinavian skipper. |
| AUG. | "Iambs" published by "Алконост". |
| SEPT. | Work on the article "О Романтизме" and, throughout this autumn, on "Исторические рошесмие Картины". |

| | |
|---|---|
| Oct. | Work for the Great Dramatic Theatre. |
| 12th | "Тайный смысл трагедии Отелло". |
| 29th | "Памяти Леонида Андреева". |
| Nov. 12th | "The Collapse of Humanism" read at the first session of the "Free Philosophical Association". Plans for the historical plays and other committee work continued into a dark, cold and hungry New Year. |
| Dec. 11th | Appointed member of the collegium of the Literary Department of Narkompros (Moscow). |
| 19th | Elected a member of the Soviet of the House of Arts founded by Gor'ky. |

## 1920

| | |
|---|---|
| Jan. 23rd | Death of F. F. Kublitsky-Piottukh. Blok's mother first comes to live with him and his wife: then, for convenience, and to avoid requisitions, they move into her flat in the same building. |
| Feb. 13th | Speech on the anniversary of the foundation of the Great Dramatic Theatre. |
| Mar. | Work on editing Lermontov for "World Literature". The first variant of Blok's introductory article refused. Work on the historical play "Rameses". |
| Apr. | Work on "Rameses". The collection "The Grey Morning" (Седое Утро) prepared for publication. |
| May 8th–18th | In Moscow. Great personal triumph. |
| 9th, 12th and 16th | Blok reads his poems in the Polytechnical Museum. On the 14th in the Palace of Art. |
| 11th | Discusses possibility of staging *The Rose and the Cross* with Stanislavsky. |
| June 27th | Blok elected Chairman of the Petrograd Branch of the All-Russian Union of Poets. |
| July 4th | Speech at the first Open Evening of the Poets' Union. |
| 31st | Speaks on *King Lear* at the Great Dramatic Theatre. |
| Aug. 15 | Speaks on Vladimir Solov'ev at the Free Philosophical Association ("Владимир Соловьев и наши дни"). |
| Summer | The collection "За гранью прошлых дней" published by Grzhebin. |
| Oct. | Blok elected to Governing Board of the Petrograd Branch of the All-Russian Union of Writers. "Алконост" publishes "The Grey Morning". |

| | |
|---|---|
| Autumn | Work on various committees. Material care for his family—including his aunt and biographer Mariya—and for many needy friends. Home life strained and unhappy. Lyubov' Dmitriyevna working at the theatre. No servants. Blok's mother in poor health, his wife on occasion unable to curb a perhaps natural irritation at the older woman's presence in the house and out almost all the time: working, shopping, queueing—and enjoying the more cheerful company of the theatre. Without her constant presence, Blok grows desperately depressed. His health begins to show signs of deteriorating. "World Literature" publishes the Fifth Volume of Heine's Collected Works edited by Blok and Grzhebin brings out his *Selected Works of Lermontov*. |

### 1921

| | |
|---|---|
| Jan. | Work on "Retribution". A poem written on the occasion of the foundation of the Pushkin House—"Пушкинскому Дому". <br> "The Last Days of the Imperial Power" published in *Былое*, No. 15. |
| Feb. 11th and 13th | "On the Calling of the Poet" read at the Pushkin House. |
| 16th | Repeated on 16th at the University. |
| Mar. | Work on "Retribution". |
| 15th | Blok's last attempt at poetry: "Как всегда были смешаны чувства". <br> He reworks a story begun in 1907–9, "Ни сны, ни явь". |
| Apr. 25th | Work on "Retribution". Towards the middle of the month Blok is suffering the first symptoms of fatal illness, but on the 25th he gives a recitation of his poetry in the Great Dramatic Theatre and he completes a polemical article against the Acmeists, "Без божества, без вдохновенья". |
| May 2nd–10th | In Moscow. |
| 3rd–9th | Gives recitals in the Polytechnical Museum (3rd, 5th and |
| 7th | 9th), in The House of the Press (Дом печати) (7th), and he reads also in the Writers' Union (9th) and in the Studio Italiano (7th). |
| 17th | Retired to bed though he continued to work on "Retribution". Lyubov' Dmitriyevna, deeply distressed but hopeful to the end, nurses him devotedly throughout his last illness, performing wonders in obtaining unobtainable |

foods and seeing that her husband is surrounded by every possible material comfort.

JUNE    "Rameses" published in a separate edition. Blok slightly better in first half of this month.

18th    Destroys part of his archive, having put the rest in perfect order.

JULY 3rd    Last entry in Blok's diaries. He destroys some of his notebooks.

July    Blok's mind begins to wander but in lucid intervals he still works on "Retribution".

AUG. 7th    10.30 a.m. Blok died. It was a Sunday and people came with flowers from all over Petersburg—people who had known the poet and complete strangers—sobbing openly.

10th    Blok was buried at the Smolensk graveyard (his remains were removed and re-interred in the Literary Volkovo Cemetery in 1944). Andrey Bely, Blok's lifelong friend, enemy and "brother", was one of the bearers. It was the feast-day of Our Lady of Smolensk.

WINTER 1921–2    The integrity of Blok's life, the timeliness of his death, lent his whole story a strangely sacrificial quality very evident in the stunned articles and poems which shortly began to appear "In Memoriam".

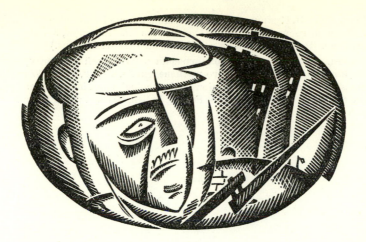

# BIBLIOGRAPHY

## Bibliographies

1. Приложение к книге К.Чуковского *Книга об Александре Блоке,* Эпоха, Петербург, 1922, составленое Е. Ф. Книпович (музыка на слова Блока, Книги, Александра Блока, Хронология стихотворений А. Блока).

2. Николай Ашукин. *Александр Блок, синхронистические таблицы жизни и творчества 1880–1921. Библиография 1903–1921,* Новая Москва,1923.(Отдельные издания, Заграничные Издания, Анонимное издание, Переводы, Редакторские Труды, Предисловия), Коллективные Труды, Журналы, Газеты, Альманахи (статьи, рецензии, пьесы, переводы) и отдел "Об Александре Блоке", отмечающий отдельные и журнальные и газетные статьи за годы 1904–1923).

3. Эмиль Блюм и Виктор Гольцев. «Литература о Блоке за годы революции (библиография)» в сборнике *О Блоке* под редакцией Е. Ф. Никитиной, Кооперативное Издательство Писателей, –Никитинские Субботники–, Москва, 1929 (Работы о Блоке за годы 1918–1928).

4. Е. Колпакова, П. Куприяновский и Д. Максимов. «Библиография А. Блока», Вильнюсский государственный Педагогический Институт, *Ученые Записки,* Т. VI, 1959. (Работы А. Блока и о Блоке за 1928–1957 годы.)

5. А. Пайман. «Материалы к Библиографии зарубежной литературе об А. А. Блоке и основных переводов его произведений», Тарту, 1964. (Works on Blok and translations in separate publications and anthologies (not in periodicals) published outside the Soviet Union in English, French, Italian, German and a few major works in other European languages.)

# Major Works on A. Blok

## 1921

1. *Об Александре Блоке* (Статьи Н. Анциферова, Ю Верховского. В Жирмунского, Вл. Пяста, А. Слонимского, Ю. Тынянова, Б. Эйхенбаума, Б. Энгельгардта), Картонный Домик, Петербург.

## 1922

1. *Памяти Блока,* Полярная Звезда, Петербург.
2. Вольная философская Ассоциация. *Памяти Александра Блока,* LXXXIII открытое Заседание Вол. фил. Ассоц., Петербург.
3. Бекетова, М.А. *Ал. Блок. Биографический Очерк, Алконост, Петербург.*
4. Белый, А. «Воспоминания об А.А. Блоке», в журнале *Эпопея,* №. 1, 2, 3, Берлин also in №. 4, 1923.
5. Княжнин, В. Н. *А.А. Блок,* Колос, Петербург.
6. Перцов, П. *Ранний Блок,* Костры, Петербург.
7. Чуковский, К. *Книга об Александре Блоке,* Эпоха, Петербург.

## 1923

1. Ашукин, Н. *Александр Блок. Библиография 1903–1923/Синхронистические таблицы жизни и творчества.* Новая Москва, Москва.
2. Бабенчиков, М. *Ал. Блок и Россия,* Гос. Издательство, Москва-Петроград.
3. Белый, А. См. 1922, №. 4.
4. Гиппиус, З. «Мой лунный друг», *Окно,* кн. I, Изд. Я Поволоцкого, Париж (Позднее в её-же Сборнике *Живые Лица, Прага,* 1925).
5. Иванов-Разумник, Р.В. *Вершины. А.Блок. А.Белый,* Колос, Петербург.
6. Пяст, Вл. *Воспоминания о Блоке,* Атеней, Петербург.

## 1924

1. Ашукин, Н. *А.А.Блок в воспоминаниях современников,* Изд. Т-ва «В.В.Думов», Москва.
2. Чуковский, К. *Александр Блок.* (See 1922, No.7—a revised and enlarged second edition. Chukovsky's fullest work on Blok.)

## 1925

1. Бекетова, М.А. *Александр Блок и его мать,* Изд. Петроград, Ленинград-Москва.
2. Гиппиус, З. См. 1923, №. 4.
3. Mel'nikova-Papauskova, *A.A. Blok,* Plamya, Praha.
4. *Письма Александра Блока,* Колос, Ленинград. (Со вступительными статьями С.М. Соловьева, Г.И. Чулкова, А.Д. Скалдина и В.Н. Княжнина.)

## 1926

1. Цинговатов, А. *А.А.Блок. Жизнь и Творчество,* Критико-Биографич. Серия, Москва–Ленинград.

## 1928

1. Медведев, П. *Драмы и поэмы Ал. Блока. Из истории их создания.* Изд-во Писателей в Ленинграде.

## 1929

1. Никитина, Е.Ф. *О Блоке.* Сборник литературно-исследовательской ассоциации Ц.Д.Р.П., Кооперативное Изд-во Писателей «Никитинские Субботники», Москва (Со статьями М.А. Бекетовой, Ив. Розанова, В.Д. Измаильской, С.В. Шувалова, Д.Д. Благого, Е.Ф. Книпович, Л. Лозовского, М.Н. Розанова, В. Гольцева, Б.Я. Брайниной, А. Ильиной и с библиографиею Э. Блюма и В. Гольцева).

## 1930

1. Бекетова, М.А. См. 1922, №.3. A second revised edition.
2. Немеровская, О. и Вольпе, Ц. *Судьба Блока.* По документам, воспоминаниям, письмам, заметкам, дневникам, статьям и другим матерьалам. Изд-во Писателей в Ленинграде.

## 1932–1936

Собрание Сочинений в XII томах, Изд-во Писателей в Ленинграде. Ряд важных статьей и примечаний.

## 1936

1. Goodmann, Th. *Alexander Block. Eine Studie zur neueren russischen Literaturgeschichte,* Königsberg/Pr., Königsberg.

## 1937

1. *Литературное Наследство,* 27–28, Журнально-газетное Объединение, Москва (Публикации Вл. Орлова и его-же статья о литературном наследстве Александра Блока).

## 1940

1. *Александр Блок и Андрей Белый. Переписка.* – публикация Вл. Орлова, *Летописи Государственного Литературного Музея,* Москва.

## 1943

1. Bowra, M. "Alexander Blok", *The Heritage of Symbolism,* Macmillan & Co., Ltd., London, 1943.

## 1946

1. Bonneau, S. *L'Univers Poétique d'Alexandre Blok,* Bibliothèque russe de l'Institut d'Etudes Slaves, Vol.20, Paris.
2. Тимофеев, Л. *Александр Блок,* Сов. Писатель, Москва.

## 1947

1. BERBEROVA, N. *Alexandre Blok et son Temps*, suivi d'un choix de poèmes, Edit. du Chêne, Paris.

## 1948

1. GÜNTHER, JOHANNES VON. *Alexander Blok. Der Versuch einer Darstellung*, Willi Weismann Verlag, München.
2. Мочульский, К. *Александр Блок*, YMCA, Paris.

## 1956

1. Орлов, Вл. *Александр Блок. Очерк Творчества*, Гослитиздат, Москва.

## 1957

1. Тимофеев, Л. См. 1946, №. 2.

## 1959

1. LAFITTE, S. (S. Bonneau). *Alexandre Blok*, Poètes d'Aujourd'hui, 61. Editions Pierre Seghers, Paris.
2. Ременик, Г. *Поэмы Александра Блока*, Советский Писатель, Москва.

## 1960

1. KISCH, SIR CECIL. *Alexander Blok*, *Prophet of Revolution*, Weidenfeld & Nicolson, London.
2. RIPELLINO, ANGELO M. *Poesia di Aleksandr Blok*, Lerici Editori, Torino.

## 1961

1. Громов, П. *Герой и Время. Статьи о литературе и о Театре* (IV: театр Блока). Советский писатель, Ленинград.

## 1962

1. LATHOUWERS, M. A. *Kosmos en Sophia. Alexander Blok: Zijn wereldbeschouwing en het Russisch denken*, Groningen.
2. Орлов, Вл. *Поэма Александра Блока «Двенадцать»*, ГИХЛит, Москва.
3. REEVE, F. D. *Aleksandr Blok. Between Image and Idea*, Columbia University Press, New York and London.

## 1963

1. Венгров, Н. *Путь Александра Блока*, Изд-во Академия Наук СССР, Москва.
2. MUCHNIC, HELEN, in the book *From Gorky to Pasternak*, Random House, New York and London (originally New York, 1961).
3. Орлов, Вл. В книге *Пути и Судьбы*, «Три очерка об Александре Блоке», Советский Писатель, Москва–Ленинград.
4. Тимофеев, Л. См. 1946, №. 2, 1957, №. 1. New and revised edition.

## 1964

1. *Блоковский Сборкик*. Труды наугной конференции, посвященной изугению жизни и творгества А. А. Блока, май 1962 года. Тартуский государственный университет, Тарту.
2. Долгополов, Л. К. *Поэмы Блока и русская поэма конца XIX – нагала XX веков*. Изд-во Наука, Москва–Ленинград.
3. KEMBALL, R. *Alexander Blok – A study in rhythm and metre*, Mouton et Cie, The Hague.
4. Жирмунский, В. *Драма Александра Блока «Роза и Крест», Литературные источники*. Изд-во Ленинградского Университета, Ленинград.


## 1965

1. Минц, З. Р. *Лирика Александра Блока (1898–1906)*. Специальный курс. Лекции для студентов заочного отделения. Выпуск I, Тартуский государственный университет, Тарту.
2. Соловьев, Борис. *Поэт и его подвиг. Творческий путь Александра Блока*, Советский Писатель, Москва.


## 1966

1. Громов, П. *А. Блок. Его предшественники и современники*. Советский Писатель. Москва–Ленинград.

# Blok in English

(Reprinted by kind permission of Tartu University from their collection "Блоковский сборник"

## Encyclopaediae

1. *Cassell's Encyclopaedia of Literature*, ed. S. H. Steinberg, Vol. II, Part III, Cassell & Co. Ltd., London, 1953, p. 1711.
2. *Chamber's Encyclopaedia*, Vol. 2, London, 1959, p. 362.
3. *Collier's Encyclopaedia*, Vol. 3, New York–Toronto, 1959, p. 510.
4. *Columbia Dictionary of Modern European Literature*, ed. H. Smith, New York, 1947, pp. 94–96.
5. *Encyclopaedia Americana*, Vol. 4, New York–Chicago–Washington, 1957, p. 103.
6. *Encyclopaedia Britannica*, Vol. 3, Chicago–London–Toronto, 1961, p. 738.
7. *Everyman's Encyclopaedia*, Vol. 2, New 1958 edition, London, pp. 320–1.
8. *Everyman's Concise Encyclopaedia of Russia*, S. V. Utechin, London, 1961, pp. 65–66.
9. HARKINS, W. E. *Dictionary of Russian Literature*, George Allen & Unwin, London, 1957, pp. 22–26.
10. KUNITZ, S. J. and HAYCRAFT, H. *Twentieth Century Authors*, New York, 1942, p. 153.
11. SNOW, V. *Russian Writers*, New York, 1946, pp. 20–22.

## Bibliographies*

12. ETTLINGER, A. and GLADSTONE, J. M. *Russian Literature, Theatre and Art*. A bibliography of works in English, published 1900–1945, Anglo-Soviet Public Relations Association, Hutchinson, London, *circa* 1946, pp. 21–24.
13. *Granger's Index to Poetry*, Columbia University Press, New York, 1950, Fourth Edition, p. 1428 (Supplement to the Fourth Edition, 1957, p. 345).
14. GRIERSON, P. *Books on Soviet Russia, 1917–1942*, Methuen & Co. Ltd., London, 1943, p. 247.

* See also G. Donchin, No. 82, Отдел *Англия и США*; M. A. LATHOUWERS, No. 2, Отдел *Другие европейские страны*; R. POGGIOLI, No. 62, Отдел *Англия и США*; F. D. REEVE, No. 63, там же; и статьи A. PYMAN: "Александр Блок в Англии", *Русская Литература*, No. 1, 1961, pp. 214–20; "Заметки об английских переводах стихотворений Александра Блока", *Международные связи русской литературы*, Moscow–Leningrad, 1963, pp. 417–33 the annual publication *The Year's Work in Modern Languages*, Cambridge University Press.

## Translations (Separate Publications)

15. BECHOFER, C.E. *The Twelve*, with illustrations by M.Larionov, Chatto & Windus, London, ix + 26 pp. (With translator's preface.)
16. DEUTSCH, B. and YARMOLINSKY, A. *The Twelve*. B.W.Huebsch, New York, 1920, IV, 7–23 pp. (With translator's preface.)
17. FREIMAN, I. *The Spirit of Music* (Selected Essays from the collections "Russia and the Intelligentsia", "Art and Religion" and "The Collapse of Humanism", translated by I.Freiman with an introduction by Elisabeth Hill), Lindsay Drummond, London, 1946, 70 pp.
18. O'DEMPSEY, FITZPATRICK. *Love, Poetry and Civil Service. A Comedy in One Act.* F.O'Dempsey, London, 1954, 20 pp. (First published in the American periodical *Poet Lore* (Spring No., 1953).)

## Translations (in Anthologies)

19. BARING, M. *The Oxford Book of Russian Verse* (see section on Blok in Russian (Outside the U.S.S.R.), No.1).
20. BOWRA, C.M. *A Book of Russian Verse*, Macmillan & Co. Ltd., London, 1943 pp. xix–xx and 97–110.
21. BOWRA, C.M. *A Second Book of Russian Verse*, Macmillan & Co. Ltd., London, 1947, pp.xv, xvi, 66–87.
22. CORNFORD, F. and SALAMAN, E. *Poems from the Russian*, Faber & Faber, London, 1943, pp.53–59, 72.
23. COXWELL, W.A. *Poems from the Russian*, the C.W.Daniel Co., London, 1929, pp.224–246, 300–2.
24. CUNNINGHAM, G.F. *Lyrics from the Russian*, Edinburgh, 1961, pp.59–66 (with a preface and notes by M.Greene).
25. ELTON, O. *Poems in Verse from Pushkin and Others*, Edward Arnold & Co., London, 1935, pp.175–85.
26. GANGULEE, N. *The Russian Horizon. An Anthology*, George Allen & Unwin Ltd., London, 1943, pp.22, 264–5, 266. (With a foreword by H.G.Wells.)
27. GUERNEY, B.G. *A Treasury of Russian Literature*, The Vanguard Press Inc., New York, 1943, pp.146–9 and index.
28. HORNSTEIN, YA. *Poems by Alexander Blok, Nicolai Gumilev, Ilya Ehrenburg and Nina Berberova*, copyright by Yakov Hornstein, 88 South Street, Dorking, undated, pp.6–9.
29. KAUN, A.S. *Soviet Poets and Poetry*, University of California Press, Berkely and Los Angeles, 1943, pp.33–34 and index.
30. KUNITZ, J. *Russian Literature Since the Revolution*, Boni & Gaer, New York, 1948, pp.22–32, 911.
31. LINDSAY, J. *Russian Poetry, 1917–1955*, The Bodley Head, London, 1951, pp. xiii–xvi, 27–29, 153.
32. OBOLENSKY, D. *The Penguin Book of Russian Verse* (cf. section on Blok in Russian (Outside the U.S.S.R.), No.5).
33. REAVEY, G. and SLONIM, M. *Soviet Literature, an Anthology*, Wishart & Co., London, 1933, pp.336–9.
34. SELVER, P. *Modern Russian Poetry*, Kegan Paul & Co., London, 1917, pp.17–19.
35. SHELLEY, G. *Modern Poems from the Russian*, George Allen & Unwin Ltd., London, 1942, pp.69–82.
36. YARMOLINSKY, A. and DEUTSCH, B. *Russian Poetry*. Martin Lawrence Ltd., New York, 1929, pp. (Part I) 141–7; (Part II) 173–89; (Notes) 223–34, first pub. John Lane, Bodley Head, London, 1923.

37. YARMOLINSKY, A. and DEUTSCH, B. *Russian Poetry*, John Lane, The Bodley Head Ltd., London, 1923, pp.126–37.

38. YARMOLINSKY, A. and DEUTSCH, B. *A Treasury of Russian Verse*. Macmillan & Co., New York, 1949, pp.1011–24.

## Books, Articles, Reviews

39. ANON. "New tendencies in Russian thought", *Times Literary Supplement*, No.992, London, 20th January 1921, pp.33–34.

40. ANON. "Romantic poet of Russia", *Times Literary Supplement*, No.2841, London, 10th August 1956, p.474. Review of Vladimir Orlov's *Александр Блок. Сочинения в двух томах*, М., 1955.

40a. ABERNATHY, R. "A vowel fugue in Blok", *International Journal of Slavic Linguistics and Poetics*, VII, 1963, Mouton et Cie, The Hague, pp.88–107.

41. ASEYEV, N. "The generation of Alexander Blok", *Soviet Literature*, No.8, Moscow, 1946, pp.43–45.

42. BECHOFER, C.E. "Russian literature today", *Times Literary Supplement*, No.1030, London, 13th October 1921, p.661.

43. BOWRA, M. "Alexander Blok", *The Heritage of Symbolism*, Macmillan & Co. Ltd., London, 1943, pp.144–79. (Cf. No.44—a revised version of this article. Bowra's book has become a classic of literary criticism and has been through five editions. In 1948 it was published in German under the title "Das Erbe des Symbolismus".)

44. BOWRA, M. "The position of Alexander Blok", *The Criterion*, No.XLIV, London, April 1932, pp.422–38. (The article which established Blok's place in European poetry, cf. No.43.)

45. BURGI, R.T. *The Plays of Alexander Blok*, Master's Thesis, typescript, Columbia University, U.S.A., 1947, 82 + 5 pp.

46. CIZEVSKY, D. and KARPOVICH, M. *Russian Literary Archives*, Harvard University, New York, 1956, pp.170–2. (E.Stenbok Fermor publishes a letter of Blok's of 20th September 1913 to the editor of *Новое Слово*. The addressee, as was shown by Gleb Struve in his review of this publication (see below), was M.M.Gakkebush (Gorelov), the editor of the morning edition of the newspaper *Биржевые Ведомости*.)
    Rev.: Глеб Струве, *Новый Журнал*, Нью Йорк, XLVIII, стр. 255–64;
          RICHARD HARE, *The Slavonic and East European Review*, Vol. XXXVI, No.86, p.263.

47. GUERSHOON, COLIN A. "The Russian Genius: Alexander Blok", *Russian Review*, No.4, Penguin Books, London and New York, 1948, pp.110–33.

48. HORVAT, J.A. *The Poetry of Alexander Blok, a Critical Analysis*, Thesis for the degree of Ph.D., typescript, Cambridge, 1953, xx, 441, xvii pp.

49. JACKSON, S. in "Correspondance", *Stand*, No.9, London, 1954–5, pp.16–18. (A letter regarding A.Miller's translation of "The Twelve" in the preceding number of *Stand*. For Miller's answer see No.59.)

50. KEMBALL, R. *Alexander Blok—a Study in Rhythm and Metre*, Thesis for the degree of Ph.D., typescript; Basel University, 1958, 547 pp., 46 tables and diagrams.

51. KISCH, SIR CECIL. *Alexander Blok, Prophet of Revolution, a Study of his Life and Work, Illustrated by Translations from his Poems and other Writings*, Weidenfeld & Nicolson, London, 1960, 202 pp.
    Rev.: M.FUTRELL, *Survey*, April–June 1961, pp.119–20;
          A.PYMAN, *Slavonic and East European Review*, Vol.XXXIX, No.93, 1961, pp.525–7;
          *Idem, The Cambridge Review*, No.2006, 1961, pp.555–7.

52. KISCH, C. "Alexander Blok on Russia", *Manchester Guardian Weekly*, Manchester, 22nd March 1951, p.13.

53. LAVRIN, J. "Alexander Blok", *Life and Letters*, Vol. V, London, July–December 1930 pp. 167–78.
54. LAVRIN, J. "Alexander Blok", *Aspects of Modernism from Wilde to Pirandello*, Stanley Nott, London, 1935, pp. 115–38.
55. LEDNICKI, W. "Blok's Polish Poem", *Russia, Poland and the West*, Hutchinson & Co., London, 1954, pp. 349–99. (In Russian in the monthly *Новый Журнал*, см. №. 71. Cf. the section Blok in Russian (Outside the U.S.S.R.), No. 83.)
    Rev.: L. R. LEWITTER, *Slavonic and East European Review*, Vol. XXXIII, No. 80, 1954, pp. 270–3;
      VIKTOR WEINTRAUB, *American Slavonic and East European Review*, Vol. XIV, No. 2, 1955, pp. 289–92.
56. LEVIN, B. "Alexander Blok", *Soviet Literature*, No. 8, Moscow, 1946, pp. 39–43.
57. LEWITTER, L. R. "The inspiration and meaning of Alexander Blok's 'The Rose and the Cross'", *The Slavonic and East European Review*, Vol. XXXV, No. 85, 1957, pp. 428–42.
58. MANNING, C. A. "The creed of Alexander Blok", *The Slavonic Review*, Vol. V, No. 14, London, 1926, pp. 332–9.
59. MILLER, A. In "Correspondance", *Stand*, No. 9, London, 1954–5, pp. 18–22. (Cf. No. 49.)
60. MUCHNIC, H. "Alexander Blok", *Russian Review*, Vol. XII, No. 1, New Haven, Connecticut, 1953, pp. 16–24.
60a. MUCHNIC, H. *From Gorky to Pasternak*, Random House, New York, 1961 (Глава о Блоке).
61. NILSSON, N. A. "Strindberg, Gorky and Blok", *Scandoslavica*, Vol. IV, 1958, pp. 23–42. (Cf. section Blok in Other European Countries, No. 5.)
62. POGGIOLI, R. "Aleksandr Blok", *The Poets of Russia, 1890–1930*, Harvard University Press, Cambridge, Mass., 1960, pp. 179–211. (For other works by this author, see the section Blok in Italian, Nos. 13, 14, 20 and 39.)
63. REEVE, F. D. *Aleksander Blok. Between Image and Idea*, Columbia University Press, New York and London, 1962, x, 268 pp.
64. REEVE, F. D. "Structure and symbol in Blok's 'The Twelve'", *American Slavonic and East European Review*, Vol. XIX, No. 2, 1960, pp. 259–75. (Identical with the chapter on "The Twelve" in No. 63.)
65. WILLIAMS, H. "Obituary", *The Slavonic Review*, Vol. I, No. 1, London, 1922, pp. 218–20.

## Histories of Russian Literature

66. HARE, R. *Russian Literature from Pushkin to the Present Day*, Methuen & Co., London, 1947, pp. 192, 193–5.
67. LAVRIN, J. *From Pushkin to Mayakovsky*, Sylvan Press, London, 1948, pp. 235–61.
68. LAVRIN, J. *Russian Writers*, D. van Nostrand Co., Inc., New York, 1954, pp. 267–89 and index.
69. MIRSKY, D. S. *Contemporary Russian Literature (1881–1925)*, G. Routledge & Sons, New York and London, 1926, pp. 210–24.
70. MIRSKY, D. S. *A History of Russian Literature*, edited and abridged by Francis J. Whitfield, Routledge & Kegan Paul Ltd., London, 1949, pp. 453–63 and index.
71. MIRSKY, D. S. *Modern Russian Literature*, Oxford University Press, London, 1925, pp. 107–8.
72. OLGIN, M. J. *A Guide to Russian Literature (1820–1917)*, Harcourt, Brace & Howe, New York, 1920, pp. 195–6.
73. REAVEY, G. *Soviet Literature Today*, Lindsay Drummond, London, 1946. See foreword and index.

74. SIMMONS, E. J. *An Outline of Modern Russian Literature (1880–1940)*, Cornell University Press, Ithaca, New York, 1944, pp. 33–35 and index.

75. SLONIM, M. *Modern Russian Literature—from Chekhov to the Present*, New York–Oxford University Press, 1953, pp. 196–210 and index.

76. STRUVE, G. *Twenty-five Years of Soviet Russian Literature (1918–1943)*, Second new and enlarged edition, George Routledge & Sons, London, 1944, pp. 1–3 and index. (First edition, 1935. Second extended English edition of the new post-war work came out in 1946 and in the U.S.A. in the University of Oklahoma Press in 1951. The book has been translated into French (Paris, 1946) and into German in a revised and extended edition (Insarverlag, München, 1957).)

77. TROTSKY, L. "Alexander Blok", *Literature and Revolution*, International Publishers, New York, 1925, pp. 116–25 (republished University of Michigan Press, 1960).

78. WILLIAMS, H. *Russia of the Russians*, Sir Isaac Pitman & Sons, London, 1914, 430 pp. (Cf. Chapter "Literature", pp. 178–227, and for Blok—pp. 212–13.)

79. ZAVALASHIN, V. *Early Soviet Writers*, Praeger publications in Russian History and World Communism, LXVI; research programme on the U.S.S.R., Study XX, New York, 1958, pp. 5–22 and index.

## Books, Articles and Memoirs Containing
## Substantial References to Blok

80. CALDERON, G. "The Russian stage", *The Quarterly Review*, No. 432, London, 1912, pp. 21–42. (For Blok cf. 37–39.)

81. DONCHIN, F. "French influences on Russian Symbolist versification", *The Slavonic and East European Review*, Vol. XXXIII, No. 80, London, 1954, pp. 161–87. (A chapter from the book *The Influence of French Symbolism on Russian Poetry*, cf. No. 82.)

82. DONCHIN, G. *The Influence of French Symbolism on Russian Poetry*, Mouton et Cie, Gravenhage, 1958, 239 pp. (For Blok see Index.)
   Rev.: A. SETSCHKAREFF. *Zeitschrift für Slavische Philologie*, Band XXVIII, Heidelberg, 1960, pp. 432–5.

83. ERLICH, V. *Russian Formalism*, Mouton et Cie, Gravenhage, 1955, XI, 276 pp. (For Blok see Index.)

84. ERLICH, V. "Russian poets in search of a poetics", *Comparative Literature*, No. IV, University of Oregon, 1952, pp. 54–74. (Chapter from the book *Russian Formalism*, pp. 16–32. Cf. No. 83.)

85. GORLIN, M. G. "The interrelation of painting and literature in Russia", *Etudes Littéraires et Historiques*, Bibliothèque russe de L'Institut des Études Slaves, Vol. 30, Paris, 1957, pp. 147–88. (Cf. pp. 187–8 for Blok and Vrubel. First published *The Slavonic and East European Review*, XXV, London, 1946, pp. 562–74. Cf. the section Blok in French, No. 40.)

86. JAKOBSON, R. "The kernel of comparative slavic literature", *Harvard Slavic Studies*, I, Cambridge, Massachusetts, Department of Slavonic Language and Literature, 1953, 396 pp. (See pp. 52 and 22.)

87. MASLENIKOV, O. *The Frenzied Poets: Andrey Biely and the Russian Symbolists*, California University Press, Berkely and Los Angeles, 1952, x + 234 pp.
   Rev.: G. IVASK, *American Slavonic and East European Review*, Vol. XII, No. 4, 1953, pp. 331–2;
   G. DONCHIN, *Slavonic and East European Review*, Vol. XXXI, No. 76, 1952, pp. 307–10.

88. MIRSKY, D. S. "A Russian letter, the Symbolists—II", *The London Mercury*, Vol. 3, April 1921, pp. 657–9. (Almost all about Blok—one of a series of articles on Soviet literature published in December 1920, February 1921, April 1921 and January 1922.)

89. MIRSKY, D.S. "Russian literature since 1917", *The Contemporary Review*, August 1922, pp. 205–11. (For Blok see pp. 208–9.)

90. MOHRENSCHILD, D.S. VON. "The Russian Symbolist Movement", *Publications of the Modern Languages Association of America*, No. 4, 1938, pp. 1193–1209.

91. PATRICK, G.Z. *Popular Poetry in Soviet Russia*, University of California Press, Berkeley, California, 1929, pp. 41, 53, 54, 143.

91 a. PRIESTLY, J.B. *Literature and Western Man*, London, W. Heinemann Ltd., 1960, pp. 220, 397–400, 402.

92. PERTSOV, V. "Realism and modernistic trends in Russian literature at the beginning of the twentieth century", *Soviet Literature*, No. 12, Moscow, 1957, pp. 122–8.

93. STRAKHOVSKY, L.I. "The silver age of Russian poetry: symbolism and acmeism", *Canadian Slavonic Papers*, No. IV, University of Toronto Press, 1959, pp. 61–87.

94. UNBEGAUN, B.O. *Russian Versification*, Clarendon Press, Oxford, 1956, xiii + 164 pp. (For Blok see Index of Poets. Also see Blok in French, No. 45.)
    Rev.: G. DUDEK. *Zeitschrift für Slawistik*, Band II, Berlin, pp. 460–7;
         A. SETSCHKAREFF. *Zeitschrift für Slawische Philologie*, Band XXVIII, Heidelberg, 1960, pp. 435–7.

## Translations of Individual Poems

(Reprinted from the collection *Международные связи русской литературы,* Moscow–Leningrad, 1963, pp. 429–33, by kind permission of the Сектор Взаимосвязи, АН СССР (П. Д.).)

*Abbreviations*

| | |
|---|---|
| *Anthology* | B.G. GUERNEY, *An Anthology of Russian Literature in the Soviet Period from Gorky to Pasternak*, New York, 1960. |
| *Blok* | SIR CECIL KISCH, *Alexander Blok, Prophet of Revolution*, London, 1960. |
| *Book I* | C.M. BOWRA, *A Book of Russian Verse*, London, 1943. |
| *Book II* | C.M. BOWRA, *A Second Book of Russian Verse*, London, 1947. |
| *Drunk Man* | H. MACDIARMID, *A Drunk Man Looks at the Thistle*, Edinburgh, 1926. |
| *Lyrics* | GILBERT F. CUNNINGHAM, *Lyrics from the Russian*, Edinburgh, 1961. |
| *Modern Poetry* | P. SELVER, *Modern Russian Poetry*, Kegan Paul & Co., London, 1917. |
| *Modern Poems* | G. SHELLEY, *Modern Poems from Russian*, George Allen & Unwin Ltd., London, 1942. |
| *Poems* | FRANCIS CORNFORD and E. SALAMAN, *Poems from the Russian*, London, 1943. |
| *PR* | *Poetry Review*, London. |
| *R. Poetry* (1927) | B. DEUTSCH and A. YARMOLINSKY, *Russian Poetry, an Anthology*, London, 1927. |
| *R. Poetry* (1957) | JACK LINDSAY, *Russian Poetry (1917–1955)*, London, 1957. |
| *RR* | *Russian Review*, Hanover, N.H. |
| *SEER* | *The Slavonic and East European Review*, London. |
| *St.* | *Stand*, Newcastle. |
| *Sov. Literature* | G. REAVEY and M. SLONIM, *Soviet Literature*, London, 1933. |
| *Verse* | O. ELTON, *Verse from Pushkin and Others*, London, 1935. |

Авиатор. 1910–1912.
"The Aviator", trans. Payson Loomis, *One Hundred Modern Poems*, p. 35.

Барка жизни встала. 1904.
    Life our bark has stranded, trans. O. Elton—*Verse*, p.177.
    The ship of life rose, trans. C. Kisch—*Blok*, p.71.

Бегут неверные дневные тени. 1902.
    The fickle shadows of the day are fleeting, trans. C. Kisch—*Blok*, p.25.

Болотистым, пустынным лугом. 1912.
    We fly o'er wastes of fens and marshes, trans. C. Kisch—*Blok*, p.104.

В лапах косматых и страшных. 1905.
    The sorcerer sang the spring-child to sleep, trans. Y. Hornstein—*Poems* (Dorking), p.6.

В октябре (Открыл окно. Какая хмурая). 1906.
    I opened the window, how sullen, trans. C. Kisch—*Blok*, p.78.

Возмездие. 1910–1921.
    Extracts from "Retribution", trans. C. Kisch—*Blok*, p.164 et seq.

Всё ли спокойно в народе? 1903.
    Is all quiet with the people?, trans. C. Kisch—*Blok*, p. 45.

Всё отлетают сны земные. 1901.
    All earthly dreams are flying past me, trans. C. Kisch—*Blok*, p. 20.

Всё это было, было, было. 1909.
    All that is finished, trans. C. M. Bowra—*Book I*, p.103.
    All this is over – over – over! trans. C. Kisch—*Blok*, p.97.

Вспомнил я старую сказку. 1913.
    There's an old tale I remember, trans. R. Kemball—*RR*, 1962, Vol. XXI, No. 2, p.151.

Второе крещенье. 1907.
    Second Christening, trans. C. Kisch—*Blok*, p.79.

Вхожу я в темные храмы. 1902.
    In sombre churches, dutiful, trans. R. Kemball—*RR*, January 1958, p.58.

Гамаюн, птица вещая. 1899.
    Hamayun the Prophet Bird, trans. A. L. Basham—*SEER*, Vol. XVI, 1938, p.288.

Голос из хора. 1910–1914.
    Voice from the Chorus, trans. C. M. Bowra—*Book I*, p.106.
    A Voice from the Chorus, trans. C. Kisch—*Blok*, p.82.

Грешить бесстыдно, непробудно. 1914.
    Russia, trans. B. Deutsch and A. Yarmolinsky—*R. Poetry* (1927), p.146.

Грустя и плача и смеясь. 1908.
    With tears and merriment and pain, trans. O. Elton—*Verse*, p. 179.

Двенадцать. 1918.
    The Twelve, trans. C. Bechofer (Chatto and Windus, London, 1920).
    The Twelve, trans. B. Deutsch and A. Yarmolinsky—*R. Poetry* (1927), p.173; *SEER*, Vol. VIII, 1930, p. 183.
    The Twelve (extracts), trans. G. Reavey and M. Slonim—*Sov. Literature*, p.338.
    The Twelve, trans. G. Shelley, *Modern Poems*, p.70.
    The Twelve, trans. C. M. Bowra—*Book II*, p.76.
    The Twelve, trans. A. Miller—*St.*, Winter 1955–6, p.11.
    The Twelve, trans. C. Kisch–*Blok*, p.257.
    The Twelve, trans. Anselm Hollo—*Evergreen Review* (New York), Vol. V, No.19, 1961, July–August, pp.31–43.

Девушка пела в церковном хоре. 1905.
    A maiden's song in the choir, trans. Anon., *Book I*, p.97.
    In the cathedral choir, trans. F. Cornford and E. Salaman—*Poems*, p.33.
    A young girl stood in a church choir singing, trans. R. Kemball—*PR*, vol. XLVI, No.I, 1955, p.30.
    From the choir her girlish treble blesses, trans. G. F. Cunningham—*Lyrics*, p.65.

Демон (Иди, иди за мной – покорной). 1916.
    Demon, trans. C. M. Bowra—*Book I*, p. 104.
День был нежно-серый, серый, как тоска. 1903.
    trans. P. Selmer—*Modern Russian Poetry*, London, 1917, p. 17.
Дикий ветер. 1916.
    Wild wind batters, trans. C. M. Bowra—*Book I*, p. 110.
Дома растут, как желанья. 1902.
    Like wishes, houses are ever growing, trans. C. Kisch—*Blok*, p. 27.
Друзьям. 1908.
    To my friends, trans. C. Kisch—*Blok*, p. 88.
Есть времена, есть дни когда. 1913.
    A season comes, a day comes, trans. C. M. Bowra—*Book II*, p. 69.
Жизнь медленная шла, как старая гадалка. 1902.
    Life dragged along, whispering in furtive fashion, trans. G. F. Cunningham—*Lyrics*,
       p. 63.
Здесь в сумерки в конце зимы. 1909.
    Here in the dusk as winter fled, trans. O. Elton—*Verse*, p. 180.
И я любил. И я изведал. 1908.
    Yes, I have loved, trans. C. M. Bowra—*Book I*, p. 101.
Идут часы, и дни, и годы. 1910.
    The hours and days and years are fleeting, trans. C. M. Bowra—*Book II*, p. 71.
Ищу спасения. 1900.
    I seek salvation, trans. V. de S. Pinto—*Book I*, p. 66.
К Музе. 1912.
    To the Muse, trans. R. Kemball—*RR*, October 1959, p. 307.
Как прощались, страстно клялись. 1909.
    Loved so kindly, swore so blindly, trans. R. Kemball—*RR*, 1962, Vol. XXI, No. 2,
       p. 156.
Когда вы стоите на моем пути. 1908.
    Whenever you stand before me, trans. A. Miller—*St.*, Winter 1956–7, p. 2.
Кольцо существованья тесно. 1909.
    How cramped the ring of our existence, trans. C. Kisch—*Blok*, p. 96.
Коршун. 1916.
    The Vulture, trans. C. M. Bowra—*Book I*, p. 109.
    The Kite, trans. F. Cornford and E. Salaman—*Poems*, p. 58.
    The Kite, trans. C. Kisch—*Blok*, p. 130.
Май жестокий с белыми ночами! 1908.
    May's white nocturne is with fury tainted, trans. C. Kisch—*Blok*, p. 96.
Мальчики да девочки. 1906.
    trans. P. Selver, *Modern Russian Poetry*, London, 1917, p. 19.
Мне страшно с Тобой встречаться. 1902.
    So fearful for me to meet Thee, trans. R. Kemball—*RR*, January 1958, p. 58.
Мой милый, будь смелым. 1909.
    My darling, be brave, trans. V. de S. Pinto—*Book II*, p. 68.
Мы встречались с тобой на закате. 1902.
    In the bay we met, with sunset gleaming, trans. G. F. Cunningham—*Lyrics*, p. 64.
На небе зарево. Глухая ночь мертва. 1900.
    A red glow in the heavens. Now murky night is dead, trans. A. L. Basham—*SEER*,
       Vol. XVI, 1938, p. 288.
На поле Куликовом. 1908.
    On the Field of Kulikovo, trans. R. Kemball—*RR*, January 1954, p. 33.
    On the Field of Kulikovo, trans. C. Kisch—*Blok*, p. 124.
На смерть деда. 1902.
    On the Death of his Grandfather, trans. C. Kisch—*Blok*, p. 28.

Не легли еще тени вечерние. 1899.
> Evening mist on the land was lying, trans. V. de S. Pinto—*Book II*, p. 66.

Незнакомка, 1906.
> As darknin' hings abune the howff, trans. H. Macdiarmid—*Drunk Man*, p. 7.
> The Lady Unknown, trans. B. Deutsch and A. Yarmolinsky—*R. Poetry* (1927), p. 143.
> The Stranger, trans. F. Cornford and E. Salaman—*Poems*, p. 54.
> The Unknown Lady, trans. C. Kisch—*Blok*, p. 43.

Новая Америка. 1913.
> New America, trans. G. Reavey and M. Slonim—*Sov. Literature*, p. 336.
> The New America, trans. V. de S. Pinto—*Book II*, p. 74.

Ночь, улица, фонарь, аптека. 1912.
> Night: the street, trans. V. de S. Pinto—*Book II*, p. 63.
> A street, a lamp, a chemist's shop, trans. G. F. Cunningham—*Lyrics*, p. 62.

О доблестях, о подвигах, о славе. 1908.
> Glory and gallant deeds and fame forgetting, trans. C. M. Bowra—*Book II*, p. 67.
> Valour, prowess and glory, trans. C. Kisch—*Blok*, p. 94.
> I care not for brave deeds of fame or fable, trans. G. F. Cunningham—*Lyrics*, p. 66.

Она пришла с мороза. 1908.
> She came in out of the frost, trans. A. Miller—*St.*, Winter 1956–7, p. 1.

Осенняя любовь. 1907.
> Autumn love, trans. C. M. Bowra—*Book I*, p. 99.

Осенняя любовь, 1. "Когда в листве сырой и ржавой". 1907.
> When mountain-ash, trans. B. Deutsch and A. Yarmolinsky—*R. Poetry* (1927), p. 147.

Отдых напрасен. Дорога крута. 1903.
> Rest unavailing. The road steep and straight, trans. R. Kemball—*RR*, January 1958, p. 56.

Песнь Ада. 1909.
> The Song of Hell, trans. C. Kisch—*Blok*, p. 84.

Песня Офелии (Он вчера нашептал мне много). 1902.
> Ophelia's Song, trans. C. Kisch—*Blok*, p. 32.

Пляски смерти. 1912–1914.
> Dance of Death, trans. C. M. Bowra—*Book II*, p. 72.

По городу бегал черный человек. 1903.
> A Little Black Man, trans. B. Deutsch and A. Yarmolinsky—*R. Poetry* (1927), p. 145.

Поет, поет. 1913.
> It sings, it sings, trans. R. Kemball—*RR*, 1962, Vol. XXI, No. 2, p. 150.

Поздней осенью из гавани. 1909.
> The Sailor, trans. F. Cornford and E. Salaman—*Poems*, p. 53.
> The winter day is cold and snowy, trans. Y. Hornstein—*Poems* (Dorking), p. 9.

Последнее напутствие. 1914 (three last verses).
> And again from an alien land, trans. C. Kisch—*Blok*, p. 129.

Предчувствую Тебя. Года проходят мимо. 1901.
> I ha'e forekennt Ye, trans. H. Macdiarmid—*Drunk Man*, p. 10.
> The Unknown Woman (I have foreknown Thee), trans. B. Deutsch and A. Yarmolinsky—*R. Poetry* (1927), p. 142.
> I have forebodings of Thee, trans. C. M. Bowra—*Book I*, p. 97.
> Presentiment of Thee, trans. R. Kemball—*RR*, January 1958, p. 57.

Приближается звук. И покорна щемящему звуку. 1912.
> Ever nearer the call, trans. R. Kemball—*RR*, October 1959, p. 308.

Равенна. 1909.
> Ravenna, trans. O. Elton—*SEER*, Vol. III, 1925, p. 750; *Book II*, p. 70; *Verse*, p. 182.

Разгораются тайные знаки. 1902.
> Into flame magic symbols have broken, trans. C. Kisch—*Blok*, p. 30.

Рожденные в года глухие. 1914.
>   Those who were born in years of quiet, trans. C.M.Bowra—*Book I*, p.109.
>   Born in the years of sloth and dull decay, trans. F.Cornford and E.Salaman—*Poems*, p.58.
>   Born in years of dreariness, trans. C.Kisch—*Blok*, p.129.
Роза и Крест. Песня Гаэтана. 1912.
>   The Song of Gaetan, trans. C.Kisch—*Blok*, p.133.
Россия (Опять, как в годы золотые). 1908.
>   Again as in the Golden Days, trans. C.Kisch—*Blok*, p.126.
Русь моя, жизнь моя, вместе ль нам маяться? 1910.
>   Russia, my life! trans. C.M. Bowra—*Book I*, p.108.
Свирель запела на мосту. 1908.
>   Pipes on the bridge struck up to play, trans. O.Elton—*SEER*, Vol.VII, 1929, p.393; *Book II*, p.68.
>   Over the rapids on the bridge, trans. Y.Hornstein, *Poems*, p.8.
Скифы. 1918.
>   The Scythians, trans. B.Deutsch and A.Yarmolinsky—*R.Poetry* (1927), p.187.
>   The Scythians, trans. R.Kemball—*RR*, April 1955, p.117.
>   The Scythians, trans. J.Lindsay—*R.Poetry* (1957), p.27.
>   The Scythians, trans. B.G.Guerney—*Anthology*, p.27.
>   The Scythians, trans. C.Kisch—*Blok*, p.152.
>   The Scythians, trans. A.Miller, St. 8, No.3, 1966/7, pp.20–22.
Сны. 1912.
>   Dreams, trans. R.Kemball—*RR*, October 1959, p.309.
Старик. 1902
>   My spirit is old, trans. O.Elton—*Verse*, p.175.
Старинные розы. 1908.
>   Dead roses and dying, trans. C.M.Bowra—*Book I*, p.99.
Сусальный ангел. 1909.
>   The Sugar Angel, trans. F.Cornford and E.Salaman—*Poems*, p.57.
Сын и мать. 1906.
>   Son and mother, trans. F.Cornford and E.Salaman—*Poems*, p.56.
Сытые. 1905.
>   The Glutted Ones, trans. C.Kisch—*Blok*, p.47.
Там, в полусумраке собора. 1902.
>   There, in the dusk of the cathedral, trans. R.Kemball—*PR*, Vol.XLVI, No.1, 1955, p.30.
Тебя я встречу где-то в мире. 1902.
>   I somewhere in the world shall meet you, trans. C.Kisch—*Blok*, p.20.
Тени на стене. 1907.
>   Shadows on the Wall, trans. C.M.Bowra—*Book I*, p.98.
Теряет берег очертанья. 1900.
>   Dim grow the edges of the river, trans. O.Elton—*Verse*, p. 176.
Ты в комнате один сидишь. 1909.
>   You are alone and not asleep, trans. Y.Hornstein—*Poems* (Dorking), p.7.
Ты в поля отошла без возврата. 1905.
>   Thou art far, in the fields—and for ever, trans. R.Kemball—*RR*, January1958, p.59.
Ты говоришь, что я дремлю. 1913.
>   You say that I'm asleep, trans. C.M.Bowra—*Book I*, p.100.
Ты, как отзвук забытого гимна. 1914.
>   You have entered my fate dark with passion, trans. C.Kisch—*Blok*, p.107.
Ты отошла, и я в пустыне. 1907.
>   Thou art afar, and I have laid me, trans. R.Kemball—*RR*, 1962, Vol. XXI, No. 2, p. 149.

Ты отходишь в сумрак алый. 1901.
    Into Crimson Dark, trans. B. Deutsch and A. Yarmolinsky—*R. Poetry* (1927), p. 41.
Ты твердишь, что я холоден, замкнут и сух. 1916.
    You say I am frozen, trans. C. M. Bowra—*Book I*, p. 107.
Увижу я, как будет погибать. 1900.
    I know that I shall see at last destroyed, trans. A. L. Basham—*SEER*, Vol. XVI, 1936,
    p. 289.
Унижение. 1911.
    Humiliation, trans. C. Kisch—*Blok*, p. 90.
Уходит день. В пыли дорожной. 1902.
    The day goes by. The last rays dwindle, trans. R. Kemball—*RR*, January 1958, p. 57.
Ушла. Но гиацинты ждали. 1907.
    She's gone—a hyacinth scent bequeathing, trans. C. Kisch—*Blok*, p. 76.
Фабрика. 1903.
    The Factory, trans. C. Kisch—*Blok*, p. 34.
Художник. 1913.
    Artist, trans. C. M. Bowra—*Book I*, p. 105.
    The Artist, trans. C. Kisch—*Blok*, p. 105.
Шаги командора. 1910–1912.
    The Steps of the Commander, trans. C. M. Bowra—*Book I*, p. 101.
    The Steps of the Commander, trans. C. Kisch—*Blok*, p. 100.
Я был смущенный и веселый. 1906.
    I saw your sombre silks and wondered, trans. C. Kisch—*Blok*, p. 75.
Я вижу блеск, забытый мной. 1913.
    What long forgotten gleam is this?, trans. O. Elton—*Verse*, p. 181; *Book II*, p. 19.
Я восходил на все вершины. 1904.
    I rose to every height, trans. C. Kisch—*Blok*, p. 40.
Я жду призыва, ищу ответа. 1901.
    I wait and watch with long insistence, trans. G. F. Cunningham—*Lyrics*, p. 61.
Я знаю день моих проклятий. 1902.
    I know the time when curses sway me, trans. C. Kisch—*Blok*, p. 22.
Я насадил мой светлый рай. 1907.
    I planted my bright paradise, trans. C. M. Bowra—*Book II*, p. 66.
Я не предал белое знамя. 1914.
    The white flag I never surrendered, trans. C. M. Bowra—*Book II*, p. 76.
Я пригвожден к трактирной стойке. 1908.
    "I'm nailed to the bench of a tavern", trans. G. Shelley, *Modern Poems*, p. 82.
Я шел во тьме дождливой ночи. 1900.
    A rainy night I trod in murk, trans. A. L. Basham—*SEER*, Vol. XVI, 1938, p. 288.
Явился он на стройном бале. 1902.
    He came to join the ballroom's glory, trans. C. Kisch—*Blok*, p. 22.

# Blok in French

(Reprinted by kind permission of Tartu University from their collection "Блоковский сборник"

## Encyclopaediae

1. *Encyclopédie de la Pléiade*. Histoire des Littératures. II. Littératures Occidentales, Volume publié sous la direction de Raymond Queneau, Gallimard, Paris, 1956, pp. 1528–30 (C. Wilczkowski, "Littérature Russe").
2. *Larousse du XXᵉ Siècle*, Vols. 1–2, Paris, 1928, p. 736.

## Bibliographies*

3. BOUTCHIK, VL. *Bibliographie des Œuvres Littéraires Russes Traduites en Français de 1737 à 1934*, Librairie G. Orobitz & Cie, Paris, 1935, pp. 6, 40. (Suppléments: 1936, p. 6; juin 1941 au 31 décembre 1942, No. 13.)
4. BOUTCHIK, VL. *La Littérature Russe en France*. Essai de Classification des Ouvrages en langue française rélatifs à la littérature russe parus jusqu'au 1ᵉʳ janvier 1947, Librairie Ancienne Honoré Champion, Paris, 1947, pp. 56–57.
5. VERHAEGEN, COSYNS E. *Traductions Françaises de Littérature Russe et Soviétique (1946/1960)*, Bibliographia Belgia, 50, Vol. 1, Commission Belge de Bibliographie, Bruxelles, 1960, pp. 19–22.

## Translations (Separate Publications)

6. DOKMAN, L. et BAUDOUIN, L. C. *Alexandre Blok. Elégies; Choix de Poèmes*. Traduits du russe. Ed. Les Cahiers du Journal des Poètes, Bruxelles, 1938, 43 pp.
7. GAUVAIN, J. et BICKERT, E. *Alexandre Blok, Poète de la Tragédie Russe (1880–1921)*. (Cf. No. 20.)
8. ISWOLKSY, HÉLÈNE. *Les Derniers Jours du Régime Impérial*, Paris, 1931, 223 pp. (The translation is from the "Алконост" edition, Petersburg, 1921, with an introduction by the translator.)
9. ROMOV, S. *Les Douze*. Avec illustrations de M. Larionov, La Cibe, Paris, 1920, éd. non paginée.
10. SIDERSKY, I. *Les Douze*. Avec illustrations de Yu. Annenkov, Au Sans Pareil, Paris, 1923, 45 pp.

* Cf. also S. Laffitte, No. 23; R. Poggioli, No. 62 in the section on Blok in English; F. D. Reeve, No. 63, Blok in English; G. Donchin, No. 82, Blok in English; M. A. Lathouwers, No. 2 in the section Blok in Other European Countries.

An important periodical bibliographical source is Professor A. Mazon's "Chronique" in the journal *La Revue des Etudes Slaves*, Paris.

## Translations (in Anthologies)

11. CHUZEVILLE, J. *Anthologie des Poètes Russes*, Paris, G.Crès et Cie, 1914, pp. 175–94.

11a. DAVID, G. *Anthologie de la Poésie Russe*, Stock, Paris, Vol.1 (1740–1900), précédée d'une introduction à la poésie russe, 1946, ix + 310 pp. (For Blok—cf. "Table d'ensemble. Tome premier. 1. Plan de l'introduction à la poésie russe".) Vol.2 (1900 à nos jours) 1948, ix + 418 pp. (For Blok—cf. pp. 12, 46–63, 140–55. Verses in Russian and in French.)

12. GORIELY, B. et BAERT, R. *La Poésie Nouvelle en U.R.S.S. Anthologie.* Ed. le Canard Sauvage, Bruxelles, 1928, p.14.

13. GRANOFF, K. *Anthologie de la Poésie Russe du XVIIIᵉ Siècle à Nos Jours*, Gallimard, Paris, 1961, pp.344–80. (Note on Blok's life and works pp.344–6. Brice Parain mentions Blok in the foreword—p.2.)

14. PIVOT, A. *Poèmes Russes, Poèmes Etrangers Unis en Poésie Française de Pouchkine à Nos Jours*, traduites avec la collaboration de Princesse E.Troubetskaia et S.Strogov, Paris, 1956, pp.102–9. (With a portrait of Blok on the cover.)

15. RAIS, E. et ROBERT, JAQUES. *Anthologie de la Poésie Russe du XVIIIᵉ Siècle à Nos Jours*, préface de Stanislas Fumet, introduction—Les auteurs, Bordas, Paris, 1947, pp.14–15, 217–36.

16. REAVEY, G. et SLONIM, M. *Anthologie de la Littérature Soviétique (1918–1934)*, Gallimard, Paris, 1935, pp. 268–73. (Extracts from the poem "Двенадцать" as translated by Brice Parain, cf. Nos.7, 20.)

17. ROBIN, A. *Quatres Poètes Russes; V. Maiakovsky, B. Pasternak, A. Blok, S. Essenine*, Edition du Seuil, Paris, 1949, pp. 12–14—about "Двенадцать", 15—briefly about Blok, 16–53—translation of "Двенадцать" and parallel Russian text.

## Books, Articles, Reviews

18. BERBEROVA, N.N. *Alexandre Blok et son Temps*, suivi d'un choix de poèmes. Edit. du Chêne, Paris, 1947, 247 pp. (A biography based in part on personal reminiscences by the widow of the poet V. Khodasevich.)

19. BONNEAU, S. Cf. LAFFITTE, S. (Nos. 24, 26).

20. GAUVAIN, J. et BICKERT, E. *Alexandre Blok, Poète de la Tragédie Russe (1880–1921)*, Nova et Vetera, No.3, Fribourg, 1943, pp.33. (Compilers' introduction pp. 1–6. "Двенадцать" translated by Brice Parain. Translations of twenty poems by Blok and of his foreword to "Retribution". Cf. No.7.)

21. HIPPIUS, Z.N. "Mon ami lunaire Alexandre Blok", *Mercure de France*, No.596, Vol. CLXI, Paris, 1923, pp. 289–326. (A short introduction for the French reader is followed by a straightforward translation of the article "Мой лунный друг", first published in the collection "Окно", Book No.1, pub. Polozkj, Paris, 1923, then in the book *Живые Лица*. Cf. No. 44 of the section Blok in Russian Outside the U.S.S.R.).

22. LABRY, R. "Alexandre Blok et Nietzsche", *La Revue des Etudes Slaves*, No. XXVII, Paris, 1951, pp. 201–8.

23. LAFFITTE, S. *Alexandre Blok, Poètes d'Aujourd'hui*, No.61, Seghers, Paris, 1958, 221pp. (Illustrations, portraits, chronological table, selected bibliography, excerpts from Blok's prose and poetry translated by author and G.Arout.)

24. LAFFITTE, S. (Sophie Bonneau). "Alexandre Blok", *Les Ecrivains Célèbres*, No.III, Edit. Lucien Mazenod, Paris, 1953, pp. 202–3.

25. LAFFITTE, S. " Le symbolisme occidental et Alexandre Blok", *Revue des Etudes Slaves*, Vol. XXXIV, Paris, 1957, pp. 88–94.

26. LAFFITTE, S. (Sophie Bonneau). *L'Univers poétique d'Alexandre Blok, Bibliothèque russe de l'Institut d'Etudes Slaves*, Vol. 20, Paris, 1946, 519 pp. (A very detailed work originally written as a doctor's thesis for the Sorbonne. The first part is an attempt to define the nature of Blok's inspiration. The second, a study of his dramatic works.) Rev.: WEIDLE, WL. "Sophie Bonneau: L'Univers poétique d'Alexandre Blok", Critique: *Revue générale des publications françaises et étrangères*, Vol. IV, No. 20, Paris, 1948, pp. 80–82. (Cf. No. 31.)

27. MONOD (PASTEUR WILFRED). *Les Douzes*, Sermon prêché à l'Oratoire du Louvre, le 14 octobre 1923, Fischbacher, Paris, 16 pp.

28. MOCHUL'SKY, K. V. "Un maître de la poésie russe contemporaine: Alexandre Blok" (signé C. Motchoulski), *Foi et Vie*, Cahier A, Paris, 16 décembre 1922, pp. 1168–75.

29. TRIOMPHE, R. "Étude de Structure", *Cahiers du Monde Russe et Soviétique*, Vol. 1, No. 3, Paris, 1960, pp. 387–417.

30. TRIOMPHE, R. "Sous le signe du printemps", *Revue des Etudes Slaves*, Vol. 38 (Mélanges Pascal), Paris, 1961, pp. 197–206.

31. WEIDLE, WL. "Sophie Bonneau: L'Univers poétique d'Alexandre Blok", Critique: *Revue générale des publications françaises et étrangères*, Vol. IV, No. 20, Paris, 1948, pp. 80–82. (Cf. No. 26.)

## Histories of Russian Literature

32. CORBET, C. *La Littérature Russe*, Collection Armand Colin, Paris, 1951, pp. 175–7 and index.

33. HOFFMANN, M. *Histoire de la Littérature Russe*, Edit. du Chêne, Paris, 1946, 255 pp. (For Blok, cf. the chapter "Temps Nouveaux", pp. 234–55.)

34. LEGRAS, J. *La Littérature en Russie*, Librairie Armand Colin, Paris, 1929, pp. 203–7.

35. PERUS, J. *Introduction à la Littérature Soviétique*, Editions Sociales, Paris, 1948, pp. 20–21.

36. POZNER, V. *Panorame de la Littérature Russe Contemporaine*, Edit. Kra, Paris, 1929, pp. 159–72 and index.

36a. STRUVE, G. (Cf. No. 76 in the section Blok in English.)

37. THORGEVSKY, I. "La révolution et le poète Blok", *De Gorki à Nos Jours, La Nouvelle Littérature Russe*. La Renaissance, Paris, 1945, pp. 33–47 and index. (See also No. 161 in the section Blok in Russian (Outside the Soviet Union).)

38. WILCZKOWSKI, C. *Ecrivains Soviétiques*, Editions de la Revue des Jeunes, Paris, 1949, pp. 129–45 and index. (For Wilczkowski cf. also No. 1.)

## Books, Articles and Memoirs Containing Significant References to Blok

39. GORIELY, B. *Les Poètes dans la Révolution Russe*, Gallimard, Paris, 1934, pp. 22–27 and index.

40. GORLIN, M. G. "The interrelation of painting and literature in Russia", *Etudes Littéraires et Historiques*, Bibliothèque russe de l'Institut des Etudes Slaves, Vol. 30, Paris, 1957, pp. 174–88. (First published in *The Slavonic and East European Review*, cf. No. 85 in the section Blok in English. For Blok and Vrubel see pp. 187–8.)

41. GORLIN, M. G. "Hoffmann en Russie", *Etudes Littéraires et Historiques*, Bibliothèque russe de l'Institut des Etudes Slaves, Vol. 30, Paris, 1957, pp. 189–206. (First published, *Revue de Littérature Comparée*, Vol. 15, Paris, 1935, pp. 60–76. Cf. pp. 203–4 for Blok and E. T. A. Hoffmann.)

42. MIRKINE GUETZEVITCH, B.S. *Les Scythes. Quelques Théories Russes sur la Crise Euro-péenne*. Préface de A. Aulard, Polozkj et Cie, Paris, 1925, viii + 48 pp. (For Blok cf. pp. 8 and 10.)
Rev. M.: Алданов, *На чужой стороне,* Том IX, Prague, 1925, pp. 313–15.

43. PASCAL, P. "Trois poètes russes à Venise" in the collection *Venezia nelle letterature moderna, Civilita Veneziana*, Studi 8, Istituto per la Collaborazione Culturale, Venezia–Roma, 1961, 375 pp. (For Blok cf. pp. 222–7. Cf. also No. 40 in the section Blok in Italian.)

44. STREMOOUKHOFF, D. "Echos du symbolisme français dans le symbolisme russe", *Revue des Sciences Humaines*, No. 78, Paris, 1955, pp. 297–319. (For Blok see pp. 301, 309, 313, 314, 315–18.)

45. UNBEGAUN, B.O. *La Versification Russe*, Librairie des Cinq Continents, Paris, 1958, 203 pp. (The same as No. 94 in the section Blok in English.)

46. N. Z. "La poésie russe moderne", *Le Monde Slave*, No. 16, Paris, 1929, pp. 1–30. (For Blok cf. pp. 7, 12, 13.)

# Blok in German

(Reprinted by kind permission of Tartu University from their collection "Блоковский сборник"

## Encyclopaediae

1. EPPELSHEIMER, HANS W. *Handbuch der Weltliteratur von den Anfängen bis zur Gegenwart*, Klostermann, Frankfurt/Main, 1960, p. 658.
2. FRAUENWALLNER, E., GIEBISCHE, H. und HEINZEL, E. *Die Welt-Literatur*, Vol. I, Wien, 1951, pp. 186–7.
3. *Der große Brockhaus*, Wiesbaden, 1953, 2. Band, p. 173.
4. LAATHS, ERWIN. *Geschichte der Weltliteratur*, Droemersche Verlagsanstalt, München, 1953, pp. 743–4.
5. *Lexikon der Weltliteratur*, Herder, Freiburg, Berlin, Wien, 1960, pp. 197–9. (F. Stepun's contribution on Blok.)

## Bibliography*

6. DOX, GEORGE. *Die russische Sowjetliteratur*. Namen, Daten, Werke, Walter de Gruyter & Co., Berlin, 1961, pp. 27–28 and index.

## Translations (Separate Publication)

7. CELAN, P. *Die Zwölf*, S. Fischer Verlag, Frankfurt/Main, 1958, 23 pp.
8. GRÖGER, WALTHER VON. *Die Zwölf*, illustriert und eingeleitet von dem Übersetzer, Newa-Verlag, Berlin, 1921, 34 pp.
   Rev.: A(лданов), M. "Alexander Block—Die Zwölf, Перевод В. Грегера", *Современные Записки*, Кн. XII, Париж, 1922, стр. 361.
9. GRÖGER, WALTHER VON. *Rose und Kreuz*, Berlin, 1923, pp. xxi, 92.
10. GÜNTHER, JOHANNES VON. *Alexander Block. Gesammelte Dichtungen*, Willi Weismann Verlag, München, 1947, 512 pp. (pp. 409–99, an article on Blok, later published as a separate book—see No. 26.)
11. GÜNTHER, J. VON. *Alexander Block. Die Stille blüht*. Willi Weismann Verlag, München, 1947, pp. 96.
    Rev.: DR. B. *Neue Welt*, 1. Jg., Heft 16, Berlin, 1947, p. 124.
12. LIEBKNECHT, S. *Der Untergang der Humanität*, mit Vorwort von Arthur Holitscher, Kleine Revolutionäre Bibliothek, Band 7, Der Malik-Verlag, Berlin, 1922, 48 pp. (Contents: Die Intellektuellen und die Revolution, Das Volk und die Intellektuellen, Die Erde und die Kultur, Die religiösen Probleme und das Volk, Das Kind von Gogol.)
13. ROHDE-LIEBENAU, A. *Die Unbekannte*, Aufbau-Bühnen-Vertrieb, Berlin, 1946 (Rototype edition, published in the periodical *Athena*, 2. Jg., Heft 4, Berlin, 1947/8, pp. 93–104.)

* See also J. Holthusen, No. 44; R. Poggioli, No. 62, section Blok in English; F. D. Reeve, section Blok in English No. 63; M. A. Lathouwers. No. 2. section Blok in Other European Countries.

14. WALTER, R. VON. *Alexander Block, Gedichte*, Verlag Skythen, Berlin, 1921, 48 pp. (With translator's introduction, pp. 3–5.)

15. WALTER, R. VON. *Skythen. Die Zwölf*, Verlag Skythen, Berlin, 1921, 47 pp. (Translator's commentary to "The Scythians", pp. 9–24, and to "The Twelve", pp. 26–28.)


## Translations (in Anthologies)

16. BETHGE, H. *Lyrik des Rußlands in neuerer Zeit*, Max Hesses Verlag, Leipzig, 1907, pp. 317–19. (Blok's verses translated by J. von Günther.)

17. DROHLA, G. *Russische Lyrik des 20. Jahrhunderts*, Insel-Verlag, No. 698, Wiesbaden, 1959, pp. 12–18, 62. (Blok's verses translated by D. Hiller von Gärtringen.)

18. GÜNTHER, JOHANNES VON. *Neue russische Lyrik*, Fischer Bücherei, Frankfurt/M and Hamburg, 1960, pp. 9, 80–90, 186–7. (With an introduction by Ju. Semyenov.)

19. GÜNTHER, JOHANNES VON. *Neuer russischer Parnaß*, eine lyrische Anthologie, ausgewählt, eingeleitet und übersetzt von Johannes von Günther, Musarion Verlag, München, 1921, pp. 105–10. (Cf. particularly the Introduction, pp. 13–43, especially pp. 37–38.)

20. HILLER VON GÄRTRINGEN, D. *Russische Dichter*, Kommissionsverlag Otto Harrassowitz, Leipzig, 1934, pp. 96–105.

20a. MATTHEY, W. VON. *Russische Lyrik von Puschkin bis Block*, 2te Auflage, B. Schwabe & Co. Verlag, Basel, 1956, pp. 25–26, 101–5 (First ed. 1943).

21. RÖLLINGHOFF, K. *Rossiya. Rußlands Lyrik in Übertragungen und Nachdichtungen*. Verlag ed. Stracke. Wien, Prag, Leipzig, 1920, pp. 34–35, 225–58.

22. TARTAKOWER, S. *Das russische Revolutionsgedicht*, Renaissance, Wien, Berlin, Leipzig, New York, 1923 (*circa*), pp. 7, 11, 14–19, 35, 39–50 ("The Twelve"), 107–24 ("The Intelligentsia and the Revolution").


## Books, Articles, Reviews

23. FASOLT, N. *Die literarische Kritik an der Lyrik Aleksander Bloks*, Dissertation, Maschinenschrift, Bonn, 1950, 136 pp.

24. GOLDBERG, H. "Majakovsky contra Block", *Heute und Morgen*, Heft 4, München, 1950, pp. 254–5.

25. GOODMANN, TH. *Alexander Block, eine Studie zur neueren russischen Literaturgeschichte*, Königsberg/Pr., Königsberg, 1936, IV, 104 pp.
  Rev.: CHISZEWSKI, D. *Zeitschrift für Slawische Philologie*, Band XV, Doppelheft 3/4, Leipzig, 1938, pp. 470–1.
    LUTHER, A. Aus der russischen Literatur (Rezension zur Diss. von Th. Goodmann, *Osteuropa*, 12. Jg., Heft 6, Berlin/Königsberg (Pr.), 1936/7, pp. 430–2.

26. GÜNTHER, J. VON. *Alexander Blok. Der Versuch einer Darstellung*, Willi Weismann Verlag, München, 1948, 95 pp. (Based on personal reminiscences of the author's acquaintanceship with Blok between the years 1906 and 1914. Dedicated to the memory of the poet's wife, L. D. Blok. Cf. No. 10.)

27. GURIAN, W. "Aleksandr Blok", *Hochland*, XIX. Jahrgang, Heft I, München, 1921, pp. 118–19. (Necrologue.)

28. MAYR, E. *Die lyrischen Dramen Aleksandr Bloks*, Dissertation, Maschinenschrift, Wien, 1950, 132 pp.

29. NESSELSTRAUS, A. "Aleksandr Blok", *Der Lesezirkel*, 10. Jahrgang, No. 2, Zürich, 1922, pp. 23–25.

30. RÜHLE, J. "Gestirn am Oktoberhimmel. Alexander Blok, S. Jesenin, W. Majakovskij", *Der Monat*, 12. Jahrgang, No. 140, Berlin, 1960, pp. 69–79. (For Blok see pp. 69–71.)

31. STEPUN, F. "A. Block's Weg von Solovjev zu Lenin", *Eckart*, 20/21. Jahrgang, Dez. 51/ Jan. 52, Witten–Berlin, 1951–2, pp. 111–22. (For Stepun's recollections of Blok cf. No. 5 and No. 187 in the section Blok in Russian (Outside the U.S.S.R.).)
32. TARTAKOWER, S. "Aleksandr Blok", *Die Wage*, 2. (XXIV), No. 33, Berlin, 1922, pp. 393–4.

## Histories of Russian Literature

33. ARSENIEW, N. VON. *Die russische Literatur der Neuzeit und Gegenwart*, Dioskuren Verlag, Mainz, 1929, pp. 269–79 and index.
34. BRÜCKNER, A. *Russische Literaturgeschichte*, Vol. II (1867–1914), Walter de Gruyter & Co., Berlin and Leipzig, 1919, p. 105.
35. ELIASBERG, A. *Russische Literaturgeschichte in Einzelporträts*, Zweite Auflage mit 16 Bildnissen, München, 1925, pp. 178–84.
36. LETTENBAUER·W. *Russische Literaturgeschichte*, Humboldt-Verlag, Frankfurt/M–Wien, 1955, pp. 231–6 and index.
    Rev.: GIROD, M. *Zeitschrift für Slawistik*, Band II, Berlin, 1957, pp. 630–5.
        PRIBIČ, N. *Die Welt der Slawen*, Jahrgang II, Heft 2, Wiesbaden, 1957, pp. 121–213.
37. LUTHER, A. *Geschichte der russischen Literatur*, Bibl. Institut, Leipzig, 1924, pp. 432–5 and index.
38. MATTHEY, WERNER VON. *Russische Lyrik von Puschkin bis Blok*, 2. Auflage, Benno Schwabe & Co. Verlag, Basel, 1956, pp. 25–26, 101–5.
39. SAKULIN, P. N. *Die russische Literatur*, A. V. Athenaion, Wildpark-Potsdam, 1927, pp. 209–10 and index.
40. STENDER-PETERSEN, A. *Geschichte der russischen Literatur*, Bd. II, C. H. Beck'sche Verlagsbuchhandlung, München, 1957, pp. 527–31 and index.
41. STRUVE, G. *Geschichte der Sowjetliteratur*. (Cf. No. 76 in the section Blok in English.)
42. ZENKOVSKIJ, V. V. *Aus der Geschichte der ästhetischen Ideen in Rußland im 19. und 20. Jahrhundert*, Mussagetes, No. 7, Mouton et Cie, Gravenhage, 1958, pp. 49–51.

## Books, Articles and Memoirs Containing Substantial
## References to Blok

43. HARTMANN, W. "Lux ab Oriente. Zur jüngsten russischen Literatur", *Münchene Blätter für Dichtung und Graphik*, Erster Jahrgang, Achtes Heft, Georg Müller Verlag München, 1919, pp. 127–8.
44. HOLTHUSEN, J. *Studien zur Ästhetik und Poetik des russischen Symbolismus*, Vandenhoeck & Ruprecht, Göttingen, 1957, 159 pp. (For Blok see index.)
45. JOLLOS, W. "Die heutige russische Literatur", *Wissen und Leben*, Jahrgang 16, Heft 16, Zürich, 1923, pp. 796–800.
46. LUNATSCHARSKIJ, A. "Eine Skizze der russischen Literatur während der Revolution", *Das heutige Rußland*, Berlin, 1923.
47. LUNDBERG, E. "Die jüngste russische Literatur", *Die Neue Rundschau*, 33. Jahrgang, Band 2, Berlin und Leipzig, 1922, pp. 921–32. (For Blok see pp. 923–5.)
48. MATTHIAS, LEO. *Genie und Wahnsinn in Rußland*, Ernst Rowohlt Verlag, Berlin, 1921, p. 40.
49. SELIGMAN, R. "Zur Charakteristik der neuen russischen Literatur", *Nord und Süd*, 37. Jahrgang, Band 145, Heft 463, Berlin, April 1913, pp. 92–99. (For Blok cf. pp. 97–98.)

# Blok in Italian

(Reprinted by kind permission of Tartu University from their collection "Блоковский сборник")

## Encyclopaediae

1. *Dizionario Letterario Bompiani*, Vols. 2, 5, 6, Milano, 1947, 1948. See index: Vol. 9 1950, p.164.
2. *Dizionario Universale della Letteratura Contemporanea*, Arnoldo Mondadori Editore, I Edizione, Verona, 1959, pp.456–8.
3. *Encyclopaedia Italiana*, Vol.7, Milano, 1930, pp.202–3.

## Bibliography*

4. ANON. "La letteratura sovietica in Italia" (elenco delle traduzioni), *Rassegna Sovietica*, V, nuova seri'e, 7 juglio 1954.
5. MESSINA, L. ' Le traduzioni dal russo nel 1920–1943", *Belfagor*, IV, 1949, VI.

## Translations (Separate Publications)

6. ANON. *Blok, A. L'Amore, la Poesia e lo Stato. Dialogo.* Prefazione di Paolo Flores, Ed. di "Fede", Roma (1925), 23 pp.
7. ANON. *Blok, A. Canti Bolscevichi (Dvienadzat).* Prima traduz. Italiano dal russo, Soc. R.Quintieri, Milano, 1920, 59 pp.
8. BOWISTEIN, G. e INTERLANDI, T. *A. Blok. Poesia e Arte Bolscivica. Gli Sciti, Dodici.* Casa Ed. "Rassegna Internazionale", Pistoia, 1920, 100 pp.
9. OLKIENIZKAIA, NOLDI R. *La Rosa e la Croce.* La collezione del teatro, 4, Ed. Alpes, Milano, 1925, 136 pp.
10. POGGIOLI, R. *A. Blok. Poemetti e Liriche.* 3 ediz., U.Guanda, Modena, 1947, 182 pp. (First Edition Modena, 1942).
11. RIPELLINO, ANGELO M. *Poesia di Aleksandr Blok.* (Cf. No. 21.)

## Translations (in Anthologies)

12. OLKIENIZKAJA, NOLDI R. *Anthologia dei Poeti Russi del XX Secolo*, Treves, Milano, 1924, pp.121–32.
13. POGGIOLI, R. *Il Fiore del Verse Russe, I milleni*, 7, Emulio Einaudi, Torrino, pp.191–298. (Cf. also the detailed preface.)
    Rev.: DI SARRA, D. D. *Fiera letteraria*, Roma, 1/I/1950, No.5, p. 4.

* See also Encyclopaediae, No. 2; E.Lo Gatto, Nos. 24 and 25; and R.Poggioli, No. 62, in the section Blok in English.

14. Poggioli, R. *La Violetta Notturna. Anthologia di Poeti Russi del Novecento*, Carabba, Lanciano, 1933, pp.31–62.
15. Reavey, G., Slonim, M., Spagnol, T. e Prampolini, G. *Scrittori Sovietici*, ed. Mondadori, Milano–Verona, 1935, pp.297–308.
16. Ripellino, Angelo M. *Poesia Russa del Novecento*, Nuova ed. riveduta e ridotta dall' autae, G.Feltrinelli, Milano, 1960, pp. 24–29, 170–85, 423, 436–7. (First published Parma, 1954.)

## Books, Articles, Reviews

17. Cukowskij, K. "Allessandro Blok" in the book *Critici Letterari Russi*, ed. E. Lo Gatto, Campitelli, Foligno, 1925, pp.287–8.
18. Cukowskij, K. "Il Bolscevismo in un poeta decadente: Aleksandr Blok", *Russia*, No.1, Napoli, 1920–1, pp.41–46. (Translated by E.Lo Gatto.)
19. Lo Gatto, E. "Versi d'Italia di A. Blok", *Russia*, No. III, Napoli, 1923, p. 40 et seq.
20. Poggioli, R. "Studi su Blok: I Versi della Bellissima Dama", *Rivista di Letterature Slave*, Vol. 5, No. 1, Roma, 1930, pp. 38–59.
21. Ripellino, Angelo M. *Poesia di Aleksandr Blok*, Lerici Editori, Torino, 1960, 487 pp. (A selection of Blok's poems printed in Russian and Italian with an introduction and notes by the translator. Portraits. Bibliography. Cf. No.11.)

## Histories of Russian Literature

22. Lo Gatto, E. *I Protagonisti della Letteratura Russa dal XVIII al XX Secolo*, V. Bompiani, Milano, 1958, pp.809–21.
23. Lo Gatto, E. *Storia della Letteratura Russa*, 3 edizione nuovamente riveduta e commentata, G.C.Sansoni Editore, Firenze, 1944, pp.488–92 and index. (Fourth ed. 1950.)
24. Lo Gatto, E. *Storia della Letterature Russa Contemporanea*, Nuova Accademia Editrice, Milano, 1958, pp.304–12 and index. ("L'histoire la mieux equilibrée et vraiment la meilleure de la littérature contemporaine" [A. Mazon, *La Revue des Etudes Slaves*, Vol. 35, p.163].)
25. Lo Gatto, E. *Storia della Letterature Russa Moderna*, Nuova Accademia Editrice, Milano, 1960, pp.163, 330, 405, 495.
26. Lo Gatto, E. *Storia della Russia*, G.C. Sansoni Editore, Firenze, 1946, 1003 + xv pp. (Cf. Index.)
27. Messina, G.L. *La Letteratura Bielorussa*, Valmartina, Firenze, 1952, pp.78, 107.
28. Messina, G.L. *La Letteratura Sovietica*, ed. Le Monnier, Firenze, 1950, pp.14–15.
29. Prampolini, G. "La Letteratura russa", *Storia Universale Della Letteratura*, ed. Utet, Torino, 1961, Vol.VII, pp.585–9.
30. Veselovskii, A. "(Storia della) letteratura russa", in the book Damiani, E., *Storia Letteraria dei Popoli Slavi*, ed. Valmartina, Firenze, 1952, p. 298.
31. Zweteremich, P. *La Letteratura Russa. Itinerario da Puschkin all'Ottobre*, Italia–U.R.S.S. Editrice, Roma, 1953, pp.468–76 and index.

## Books, Articles and Memoirs Containing Significant References to Blok

32. GOBETTI, P. "Problemi della letteratura russa e spunti d'interpretazione; 'Canti bolscevichi' di A. Blok", *Paradosso del Spirito Russo*, ed. Baretti, Torino, 1926, pp. 181–3.

33. LO GATTO, E. "L'Estetica e la poetica in Russia", *Scrittori d'Estetica*, No. II, G. C. Sansoni, Firenze, 1947, pp. 21, 37.

34. LO GATTO, E. "Gli ultimi cinquant anni della letteratura russa", *Pagine d'arte*, No. 7, 30/X/1951, pp. 3–4.

35. LO GATTO, E. "L'Italia nelle letterature Slave", *Studi di letterature Slave*, No. III, Roma, 1931, pp. 134–228. (For Blok cf. pp. 181–2.)

36. LO GATTO, E. *Il Mito di Pietroburgo, Storia, Leggenda, Poesia*, Feltrinelli, Milano, 1960, 289 pp. (For Blok cf. pp. 221–2, 229–34, 249–52.)

37. LO GATTO, E. *Poesia Russa della Rivoluzione*, A. Stock, Roma, 1923, 123 pp. (For Blok cf. pp. 23–41.)

38. LO GATTO, E. "Sulla poesia russa contemporanea", *Studi di letterature Slave*, No. I, Roma, 1925, pp. 151–86. (Re the anthology R. Noldi Olkienizkaja cf. No. 12.)

39. POGGIOLI, R. "Nota introduttiva a trad. da Blok, Gumilev e Esenin", *Il Convegno. Rivista di letteratura e arte*, No. XI, fasc. 3–4, Milano, 1930, pp. 81–83.

40. PASCAL, P. "Trois poètes russes à Venise", in the collection *Venezia nelle letterature moderna, Civilita Veneziana*, Studi 8, Istituto per la Collaborazione Culturale, Venezia-Roma, 1961, 375 pp. (For Blok cf. pp. 222–7. Cf. also No. 43, section Blok in French.)

# Blok in Other European Countries

1. FOOKHED-STOYANOVA, T. "О композиционных повторах у Блока", *Dutch Contributions to the Fourth International Congress of Slavists*, Moscow, September 1958, Mouton et Cie, Gravenhage, 1958, pp.175–203. (Holland: cf. Blok in Russian (Outside the U.S.S.R.), No.143.)

2. LATHOUWERS, M.A. *Kosmos en Sophia. Alexander Blok: Zijn wereldbeschouwing en het Russisch denken.* Druk V.R.B., Groningen, 1962, 257 pp. (In Dutch. Doctor's dissertation for University of Nijmegen. Bibliography. Résumé in French, pp.227–41.)

3. MEL'NIKOVA-PAPAUSKOVA, *A.A.Blok*, Plamya, Praha, 1925, 140 pp. (Czechoslavakia. First book on Blok in any language other than Russian. Chapters from this book were also published in Russian in the periodical *Воля России*; cf. No. 87 in the section Blok in Russian (Outside the U.S.S.R.).)

4. NILSSON, N.A. *Ibsen in Russland*, Stockholm, 1958 (in German).

5. NILSSON, N.A. "Strindberg, Gorky and Blok". (Sweden. Cf. No. 61 in the section Blok in English.)

# Blok in Russian
## (Outside the U.S.S.R.)

## Bibliographies

No bibliographies have been specifically devoted to collating the considerable body of emigré literature which, since 1917, has grown up around the work and memory of Alexander Blok. Two early Soviet sources do, however, provide much useful information on such publications. These are:

Н. Ашукин, *Александр Блок, Библиография*, Новая Москва, М., 1923; Эмиль Блюм и Виктор Гольцев, "Литература о Блоке за годы революции (библиография)", in the collection *О Блоке*, Кооперативное Изд-во писателей, "Никитинские Субботники", М., 1929.

Other sources are several works which have already been mentioned in other sections: S. Bonneau (Laffitte), No. 25, Blok in French; G. Donchin, No. 82, Blok in English; M. A. Lathouwers, No. 2, Blok in Other European Countries; E. Lo Gatto, No. 24, Blok in Italian; O. Maslenikov, No. 87, Blok in English; R. Poggioli, No. 62, *ibid.*; F. D. Reeve, No. 63, *ibid.*

## Blok's Verses in Anthologies

1. BARING, M. *The Oxford Book of Russian Verse*, Oxford University Press, London, 1925, pp. xli, 155–62, 297–8. (Frequently reissued. With an introductory article and notes in English.)
2. ELIASBERG, ALEKSANDR and DAVID, *Русский Парнас*, Insel Verlag, Leipzig, year not given, pp. 276–92.
3. HOLTHUSEN, J. und TSCHIZEWSKIJ, D. *Verdichtung der russischen Symbolisten, ein Lesebuch von Johannes Holthusen und Dmitrij Tschizewskij*, Heidelberger Slavische Texte, No. 5/6, Otto Harrassowitz, Wiesbaden, 1959, pp. 30–82.
3a. MILNER-GULLAND, R. *Soviet Russian Verse*, Pergamon, Oxford, 1964, pp. 1–15.
4. MIRSKY, D. S. *Русская Лирика*, Presse Franco-Russe, Paris, 1924, pp. 137–48, 196–9.
5. OBOLENSKY, D. *The Penguin Book of Russian Verse*, Penguin Books, London, 1962, pp. xliv–xlvii, 262–85. (The verses are printed in Russian with an English prose translation. Notes, an introductory article and notes on Russian versification by the compiler.)
6. PAMFILOVA, XENIA, *La Littérature Russe étudiée dans les Textes 1790–1944*, Librairie E. Droz, Paris, 1945, pp. 148–9.

## Books, Articles and Reviews

7. "А. Блок и «Двенадцать»", *Бюллетень Дома Искусств*, №.1–2, Берлин, 17/II/1922.

8. "А. Блок — Рамзес" (Rev.), *Воля России*, №.XII, Прага, 1922.

9. "А. Блок — Стихотворения Кн.11" (Rev.), *Руль*, №.378, Берлин, 12/II/1922.

10. "Блок о Пушкине", *Время*, №.198, Берлин, 7/IV/1922.

11. "Вечер памяти Блока и Гумилева", *Дни*, №.750, Берлин, 1925.

12. "Еще о Блоке (Беседа с А.Ремизовым)", *Свободное Слово*, №.118, Ревель, 1921.

13. "Из жизни А.Блока", *Голос России*, №.1025, Берлин, 6/VIII/1922.

14. "Памяти А.Блока", *Руль*, №.256, Берлин, 20/IX/1921. (Also in this number of *Руль*, cf. Тыркова, А., Офросимов Вл. и Сирин Вл. — Nos. 118, 137, 165.)

15. "Печать", *Последние Новости*, №.607, Париж, 7/IV/1922. (Re Andrey Bely's reminiscences of Blok cf. Nos.27 and 29.)

16. "Последние месяцы жизни А.Блока", газ. *Последние Новости*, №.413, Париж, 21/VIII/1921. (The source of the rumour about a mysterious foreigner who is supposed to have supported Blok financially during his last months.)

17. "Сговоритесь! (Обзор печати о причинах смерти А.Блока)", *Общее Дело*, №.402, Париж, 23/VIII/1921.

18. Адамович, Г. "Александр Блок", *Современные Записки*, №.XLVII, Париж, 1931, стр. 283–305. (Begins with the author's reminiscences of Blok on Pushkin's Anniversary in the winter of 1921. There follows an analysis of his poetry on the basis of which Adamovich claims Blok's right to be considered among Russia's greatest poets.)

19. Адамович, Г. "Наследство Блока", *Новый Журнал*, кн. XLIV, Нью Йорк, 1956, стр.73–87.

20. Адамович, Г. "Памяти Блока", *Последние Новости*, №.3522, Париж, 13/XI/1930.

21. Адамович, Г. "Смерть Блока", *Цех Поэтов*, №.111, Берлин, 1922, стр. 83–87.

22. Аль. "Поэтическая вера в Россию", *Жизнь*, №.8, Нью Йорк, 1925.

23. Анненков, Ю. "Об Александре Блоке", *Новый Журнал*, кн. XLVII, Нью Йорк, 1956, pp.108–32. (Personal reminiscences. Blok's letter to Annenkov of 12/1918. For Annenkov's lecture on the same subject cf. Н.Лидарцева, "Александр Блок", *Русская Мысль*, №.1653, Париж, 9/III/1961.)

24. Ашукин, Н. "Ал. Блок (Двенадцать)", *Сполохи*, Nos. 6 и 7, Берлин, 1922, pp.28–35, 21–27.

25. Бальмонт, К.Д. "Снежный Лик (Памяти Блока)", (verse) *Звено*, №.4, Париж, 1923.

26. Бальмонт, К.Д. "Три встречи с Блоком", газ. *Звено*, №.7, Париж, 19/III/1928. (On a meeting at Sokolov-Krechetov's in 1903, at the editor's "Сирин" in 1913 and in the home of Fyodor Sologub in 1915.)

27. Белый, А. "Блок в юности", газ. *Голос России*, №.892, Берлин, 26/II/1922.

28. Белый, А. "Воспоминания об А.Блоке", *Эпопея*, Nos. 1 и 2 (1922), Nos. 3 и 4 (1923), Изд. Геликон, Берлин, стр. 123–273, 105–299, 125–310, 61–305.

29. Белый, А. "Из воспоминаний об А.Блоке", газ. *Голос России*, №.934, Берлин, 2/VI/1922.(On Blok in 1905.)

30. Бердяев, Н.А. "В защиту А.Блока", *Путь*, №.26, февраль, Париж, 1931, pp. 109–13. (Defending Blok against the "Петроградский Священник", whose speech, originally pronounced in Petrograd in 1926, is printed here in the same number of *Путь*. Cf. Nos. 126 and 175.)

31. Бердяев, Н.А. "Мутные Лики — ("Эпопея" Андрея Белого")", *София*, Кн.1, Берлин, 1923, pp. 155–66. (On the cult of Sophia and the "narodnichestvo" of Blok and Bely.)

32. Бинокль. "Ал. Блок", *Рижсский Курьер*, Рига, 12/VIII/1921.

33. Блюм, В. "Поэт и революция", *Новый Путь*, №.279, Рига, 6/I/1922.

34. Богданов, Е. "На поле Куликовом", *Современные Записки*, Кн. XXXII, Париж, 1927, стр. 418–35. (The author advances the thesis that Blok is more attracted to the "Asiatic" than to the "Slavonic" elements in Russia.)

35. Бурлюк, Д. "С кем был Ал. Блок автор поэмы «Двенадцать», *Русский Голос*, №.4372, Нью Йорк, 6/XI/1927.

36. В.А. "Двуликий", *Накануне* (Литературное приложение), №.106, Берлин, 13/VIII/1922, pp. 5–7.

37. Валентинов, Н.В. "Чревовещатель невнятиц", газ. *Новое Русское Слово*, Нью Йорк, 4/VII/1961, 5/VII/1961, 6/VII/1961. (In 1907 the author of these reminiscences was a close friend of Andrey Bely's and his attitude to Blok was shaped by what Bely told him about his erstwhile friend at this time (cf. Chronology).)

38. Василевский, И. (Не Буква). "Безпартийный Блок", газ. *Накануне* (Лит. прилож.), №.106, Берлин, 13/VIII/1922, pp. 2–3.

39. Василевский, И. (Не Буква). "Куриная слепота (А. Блок — «Последние дни императорской власти»)", *Накануне*, №.76, Берлин, 29/VI/1922.

40. Василевский, И. (Не Буква). "Последние стихи", *Последние Новости*, №.406, Париж, 1921.

41. Вейдле, В. "Похороны Блока", *Новый Журнал*, кн. 65, Нью Йорк, 1961, стр. 270–6. (Personal reminiscences.)

42. Ветлугин, А. "Жизнь без начала и конца", газ. *Общее Дело*, №.392, Париж, 19/VIII/1921. (Based partly on personal recollections, the author recalls how, in 1916, Blok compared his own presentiment of early death with Lermontov's "unfailing presentiments".)

43. Ветлугин, А. "Третья годовщина", *Русский Голос*, №.3091, Нью Йорк, 9/VIII/1924.

44. Гиппиус, З. "Мой лунный друг", in the book *Живые Лица* – выпуск I, Пламя, Прага, 1925, стр. 7–70. (First published in the collection "Окно", кн. I, изд. Половоцкого, Париж, 1923. Translated into French—see No. 21 in the section Blok in French.)

45. Rev.: В. Ходасевич. *Современные Записки*, кн. XXV, Париж, 1925, стр. 535–41; С. Мельникова-Папаушкова. *Воля России*, кн. XI, Прага, 1925, стр. 216–18.

46. Голлербах, Э. "К воспоминаниям о поэте рыцаре", *Новый Мир*, №.230, Берлин, 1921.

47. Голлербах, Э. "Из Воспоминаний о Блоке", газ. *Новый Мир*, №.253, Берлин, 27/XI/1921.

48. Голлербах, Э. "Образ Блока", *Возрождение. Альманах*, №.1, 1923.

49. Голлербах, Э. "Памяти Ал. Блока", *Новый Мир*, №.31, Берлин, 1922.

50. Голлербах, Э. "Поминки Блока", *Накануне*, №.122, Берлин, 1/IX/1922. (On a meeting held on the first anniversary of Blok's death in the "Дом Литераторов" on 7th August 1922.)

51. Голлербах, Э. "Студенческие годы Блока", *Новости*, №.5, Берлин, 1922.

52. Горький, М. "А. А. Блок" in the book *Заметки из дневника. Воспоминания*. Изд. "Книга", Берлин, 1924, pp. 204–11.

53. Горный, С. "Урна. (Памяти Блока)", *Руль*, №.352, Берлин, 13/I/1922.

54. Горская, А. "О Блоке", *Возрождение*, кн. 83, Париж, 1958, pp. 123–7 "Двенадцать".

55. Гофман, М. Л. "А. Блок (Отрывок из воспоминаний)", *Руль*, №.1335, Берлин, 25/IV/1925.

56. Гофман, М.Л. "А. Блок (Поэма "Двенадцать и смерть Блока)", *Последние Новости*, №.1485, Париж, 26/II/1925.

57. Грибовская, М. "Воспоминания об А.Блоке", *Рижский Вестник*, №.208, Веч. Изд., Рига, 1921.

58. Даманская, А. "Воспоминания об А. Блоке", *Рижский Вестник*, №. 208, Рига, 1921.

59. Дроздов, А. "Блок", *Время*, №. 164, Берлин, 22/VIII/1921.

60. Дроздов, А. "А. Блок — Ямбы", *Русская Книга*, №. 3, Берлин, 1921, p. 34.

61. Елшанский, Н. "А. Блок о себе и других", *Дни*, №. 1383, 8/IV/1928.

62. Ершов, П. "Символическая лирика на сцене, «Балаганчик» А. Блока", *Новый Журнал*, №. 67, Нью Йорк, 1962, pp. 98–117.

63. З.—"Воспоминания о Блоке", *Путь*, №. 240, Гельсингфорс, 4/XII/1921.

64. Забежинский, Г. "Александр Блок. (80-летие со дня рождения)", *Новое Русское Слово*, Нью Йорк, 8/I/1961.

65. Завалашин, В. "А. Блок и русская революция", *Грани*, №. 36, Франкфурт/Майн, 1957, pp. 163–84. (Mostly about "Двенадцать". See also No. 79 in the section Blok in English.)

66. Зайцев, В. "Побежденный", *Современные Записки*, кн. XXV, Париж, 1925, pp. 250–61. (Reminiscences of Blok between the years 1907 and 1921. "The Twelve" and the idea of a "compilative Christ", in whom "everything of significance is of the people". For the polemical follow-up of this theme see Nos. 26 and 31 in the section Blok in French.)

67. Зайцев, К. "Дневник А. Блока", *Россия и Славянство*, №. 10, Париж, 2/II/1929.

68. Замятин, Е. "Воспоминания о Блоке" в книге *Лица*, Изд-во Имени Чехова, Нью Йорк, 1955, pp. 15–28. (First published in the journal *Русский Современник*, №. 3, Ленинград, 1924.)
    Rev.: Струве, Г. *Новый Журнал*, кн. XLIII, pp. 297–302.

69. Зноско-Боровский, Е. А. "А. Белый и А. Блок", *Последние Новости*, №. 672, Париж, 27/VII/1922. (A propos Bely's reminiscences of Blok.)

70. Зноско-Боровский, Е. А. "О Блоке", in the book *Записки Наблюдателя*, кн. I, Чешско-Русское Изд-во, Прага, 1924 г.

71. Иванов Г. "Блок", *Последние Новости*, №. 1968, 12/VIII/1926.

72. Иванов, Г. "Блок и Гумилев", *Возрождение*, кн. 6, Париж, 1949, стр. 113 до 126. (The same as pp. 200–19, *Петербургиские Зимы*, cf. No. 200.)

73. Иванов, Ф. "Эпопея. Литературный ежемесячник", *Новая Русская Книга*, №. 7, Берлин, 1922, стр. 14–15.

74. Иванов-Разумник, Р. *Испытание в Грозе и Буре*, Изд. "Скифы", Берлин, 1920, pp. 7–44.

75. Карцевский, С. "Пушкин—Достоевский", *Современные Записки*, кн. X, Париж, 1922, стр. 390–2. (Rev.)

76. Киселев, А. "А. Блок и его «Двенадцать»", *Путь*, №. 17, Гелсингфорс, 6/III/1921.

77. К-Г, Н. (Кноринг, Н.). "Дневник А. Блока", *Последние Новости*, №. 407, Париж, 1921.

78. Койранский, А. "Лицо ужаса", *Последние Новости*, №. 407, Париж, 1921.

79. Корин. "«В зеленой лампе». Судьба Александра Блока", *Дни*, №. 1418, Париж, 14/V/1928.

80. Лаврецкий, Вл. "Поэт революционных исканий", *Путь*, №. 150, Гельсингфорс, 24/VIII/1921.

81. Ланин, Б. "Из последних стихотворений А. Блока", *Руль*, №. 408, Берлин, 19/III/1922.

82. Левинсон, А. «Незрячий пророк. (Новые книги Блока)», *Жар-птица*, №. 1, Берлин, 1921, p. 44.

83. Ледницкий, В. А. "«Польская поэма» Блока", *Новый Журнал*, кн. II and III, Нью Йорк, 1942, pp. 309–24, 260–87. (Cf. No. 55 of the section Blok in English.)

84. Leo Ly. "Двенадцать (собственный комментарий А. А. Блока)" and "А. Блок — в последние дни", *Руль*, №. 237, 266, Берлин, 1921. (Two publi-

cations of letters addressed (if Leo Ly is to be believed) to the author by Blok on 19th June 1920 and towards the end of July 1921. The pseudonym Leo Ly has yet to be identified. Cf. Струве, Г. П., №. 147.)

85. Литовцев, С. (Поляков). "Александр Блок", *Голос России*, №. 736, Берлин, 14/VIII/1921.

86. Лоло. (Мундштейн, Л. Г.). "Памяти Блока" (verse), *Последние Новости*, №. 419, Париж, 1921.

87. Л—р. "Возмездие Блока", *Голос России*, №. 1019, Берлин, 30/VII/1922.

88. Лундберг, Е. "Памяти А. Блока", *Новый Мир*, №. 170, Берлин, 1921.

89. Лундберг, Е. "Памяти А. Блока", *Новый Мир*. №. 170, Берлин, 21/VIII/1921.

90. Лундберг, Е. "Россия А. Блока", *Новый Мир*, №. 172, Берлин, 24/VIII/1921. (Cf. also Lundberg's book *От вечного к преходящему*, Изд. Скифы, Берлин, 1923, pp. 1–102.)

91. Лутохин, Д. "А. Блок — Стихи (1898–1921)", *Воля России*, кн. VII–VIII, Прага, 1925, p. 267.

92. Львов, Л. "А. Блок", *Мир и Искусство*, №. 14, Париж, 1931, pp. 1–3.

93. Маковский, С. "Александр Блок 1880–1921", in the book *На Парнасе Серебрянного Века*, Изд. Цопэ, Мюнхен, 1962, pp. 143–76. (First published in the newspaper *Русская Мысль*. Cf. №. 93.)

94. Маковский, С. "Двенадцать Александра Блока" and "Как вспомнился Блок — Итальянские стихи" *Русская Мысль*, №. 927 and 980, Париж, 10/VII/1956 and 22/IX/1956. These articles represent an attempt to debunk Blok as a poet of the first magnitude, although the author admits the "charm" of his poetry and personality. For polemical reactions to these articles see Nos. 120 and 147 and for Makovsky's answer to his critics cf. No. 95. (The articles were later reprinted in the book *На Парнасе Серебрянного Века*. cf. No. 93.)

95. Маковский, С. "Еще о Блоке", *Русская Мысль*, №. 1812, Париж, 15/III/1962. (Reply to criticisms of No. 93.)

96. Масютин, В. Предисловие к книге А. Блока *Двенадцать*, Изд. "Нева", Берлин, 1921. (Foreword to Groeger's translation—cf. No. 8 in the section Blok in German.)

97. Мельникова-Папаушкова, Н. Ф. "А. Блок—Неизданныестихи (1897–1919)", (rev.), *Воля России*, кн. VI–VII, Прага, 1926, pp. 229–32.

98. Мельникова-Папаушкова, Н. Ф. "Дневник Ал. Блока (1917–1921)", *Воля России*, кн. VII, Прага, 1928, pp. 115–19.

99. Мельникова-Папаушкова, Н. Ф. (signed Н. М. П.). "Новый материал к изучению А. А. Блока. (Дневник Ал. Блока 1911–1913 гг.)", *Воля России*, кн. VII, Прага, 1928, pp. 128–32.

100. Мельникова-Папаушкова, Н. Ф. (signed Н. М. П.). "Письма Александра Блока к родным, Том I", *Воля России*, кн. XI–XII, Прага, 1927, pp. 296–7.

101. Мельникова-Папаушкова, Н. Ф. "Россия (из книги Блок)", *Воля России*, кн. VII–VIII, Прага, 1925, pp. 176–93. (A chapter from the book *A. A. Blok* published in Czech—cf. No. 3 in the section Blok in Other European Countries.)

102. Милюков, П. Н. "Кончина поэта Александра Блока", *Последние Новости*, Париж, 12/VIII/1921.

103. Минский, Н. М. "От Данте к Блоку", *Современные Записки*, кн. VII, Париж, 1921, pp. 188–208. (Later published in a separate edition, *Книга для всех*, №. 81, изд. Мысль, Берлин, 1922, pp. 54.)

104. М-к, В. "А. А. Блок в Москве", *Голос России*, №. 1025, Берлин, 6/VIII/1922.

105. Мон. Мария (Е. Ю. Скобцова, *née* Пиленко and, by her first husband, Кузмина-Караваева). "Встречи с Блоком — к пятнадцатилетию со дня смерти", *Современные Записки*, кн. LXII, Париж, 1936, pp. 211–28. (Elizaveta Yurevna Skobtsova was the addressee of Blok's "Когда вы стоите на моем

пути": apart from the story of this blank verse poem the author has much of interest to say of their later meetings and in particular of Blok's attitude to theosophy and to the First World War.)

106. Москвич. "А. Блок", *Новый Путь*, №.165, Рига, 1921.

107. Мочульский, К. В. *Александр Блок*, YMCA-Press, Париж, 1948, 441 стр.

108. Мочульский, К. В. "«Возмездие» А. Блока", *Последние Новости*, №.700, Париж, 30/VII/1922.

109. Мочульский, К. В. "Лирика Блока (А. Блок — Стихотворения, кн. III)", *Последние Новости*, №.585, Париж, 12/III/1922.

110. В. Н. "К кончине Ал. Блока", *Руль*, №. 225, Берлин, 14/VIII/1921.

111. Е. Н. "Al. Block—Les Douze" (rev.), *Своими Путями*, №.12.–13, Прага, 1926.

112. Наблюдатель. "В литературно-научном кружке Союза русской национальной молодежи", *Новое Время*, №.1454, Белград, 5/III/1926.

113. Надеждин, Л. "Блок и революция (Воспоминания К.И.Чуковского)", *Новый Путь*, №.324, Рига, 2/III/1922.

114. (Никольский) Н-ский Б. "Из недавнего прошлого русской литературы (Воспоминания об Ал. Блоке)", *Новая Русская Книга*, №.5–6, Берлин, 1923, pp.10–14.

115. Никольский, Ю. "Пророк", *Общее Дело*, №.429, Париж, 19/IX/1921.

116. Новицкий, Гр. "А. Блок, А. Рославлев, А. Гумилев", *Что делать*, №.1, Берлин, 23/X/1921.

117. Новицкий, Гр. "Памяти А.Блока. Загадка поэта", *Что делать*, №.1, Берлин, 23/X/1921.

118. Офросимов, Ю. "Блаженны алчущие", *Руль*, №.227, Берлин, 17/VIII/1921.

119. Офросимов, Ю. "Вечер союза журалистов (памяти Блока)", *Руль*, №.256, Берлин, 20/IX/1921.

120. Офросимов, Ю. "А. Блок. Собрание сочинений: Стихи. Том I–III, Берлин — Пб, 1921", *Новая Русская Книга*, №.1, Берлин, стр. 14–15.

121. Оцуп, Н.А. "Лицо Блока", *Русская Мысль*, №.989, 909, 991, Париж, 11/XII/ 1956–15/XII/1956. (Personal reminiscences combined with a series of literary meditations on: Blok and Heine; Blok and Tolstoy ("The Twelve" and Tolstoy's "Resurrection"); Blok and Lermontov; Blok and Baudelaire; Blok as a bridge to a contemporary interpretation of Pushkin, Lermontov, Nekrasov and Tyutchev. In part devoted to polemics with Makovsky (cf. Nos. 92–94) and others. Reprinted in Otsoupe's *Собрание сочинений*, том 4, см. №. 122.)

122. Оцуп, Н. А. "Лицо Блока", *Собрание сочинений в 4-х томах*, Том 4, Париж, 1961, стр. 55–77. (First published in the newspaper, *Русская Мысль*, см. №.121. Blok is also mentioned in passing in other articles of Vols. 3 and 4.)
Rev.: Н.Ульянов, *Новый Журнал*, кн. 66, Нью Иорк, 1961, pp.287–92.

123. Оцуп, Н. "О поэзии Александра Блока", *Цех Поэтов*, №.III, 1922, Берлин, pp.108–10.

124. Павлович, Вл. "Александр Блок", *Новое Русское Слово*, Нью Йорк, 23/XII/ 1961.

125. Пекелис, А.Г., Др мед. "Болезнь и кончина Блока (отчет врача)", *Голос России*, №.1025, Берлин, 6/VIII/1922.

126. Петроградский Священник, "О Блоке", *Путь*, №. 26, февраль, Париж, 1931, pp.86–108. ("Двенадцать" as a vision of demons; cf. Nos.30 and 175.)

127. Петроник. "Идея родины в советской поэзии", *Русская Мысль*, кн. I–II, София, 1921, pp.214–25. (Mainly devoted to "The Scythians": the author welcomes the "Pushkinian element" and the "patriotic enthusiasm" of Blok. For a similar view cf. *Цуриков*, №. 223.)

128. Пильский, П. "Двенадцать", *Сегодня*, №.260, Рига, 1921.

129. Потресов (Сергей Яблоновский). "Роза и Крест", *Руль*, №.231, Берлин, 21/VIII/1921.

130. Раич, Е. "О Блоке", *Голос России*, №.754, Берлин, 4/IX/1921.

131. Рахманов, Н. "Вечер памяти А. Блока", *Воля России*, №. 314, Прага, 24/IX/1921.

132. Рахманов, Н. "Кончина А. Блока", *Воля России*, №.281, Прага, 17/VIII/1921.

133. Ремизов, А. *Ахру. Повесть петербургская*, изд. Грежбина, Берлин, 1922, pp. 7–27. ("К звездам — памяти А.А. Блока" is the subtitle of this piece, which is written as a kind of conversation with the dead poet. Here rather fuller than in "Взвихренная Русь", См. №.209.)

134. Ремизов, А. М. "Из огненной России (памяти Блока)", *Последние Новости*, №.500, Париж, 3/XII/1921.

135. Росимов, Г. "О «Двенадцати»", *Жизнь*, №.7, Берлин, 1920, pp.23–27.

136. Росимов, Г. "Они и мы («Скифы» А. Блока)", *Жизнь*, №.II, Берлин, 1920, pp. 29–33.

137. Сирин, Вл. "На смерть А. Блока" (verse), *Руль*, №.225, Берлин, 14/VIII/1921.

138. Сирин, Вл. "На смерть Блока" (verse), *Руль*, №.256, Берлин, 20/IX/1921.

139. "Скиф". "Блок о Пушкине", *Возрождение*, кн. 3, Париж, 1949, pp. 106–9.

140. Слезкин, Ю. "Томительная ночи повесть (память А. Блока)", *Накануне*, лит. прилож., №.15, Берлин, 1922.

141. Словцов, Р. "Мать А. Блока", *Последние Новости*, №.1710, Париж, 19/XI/1925.

142. Слоним, М. "А.Блок («За гранью прошлых дней»)", *Воля России*, №.198, Прага, 8/V/1921.

143. Слоним, М. "Седое Утро" (rev.), *Воля России*, №.224, Прага, 9/VI/1921.

144. Слоним, М. "Творческий путь А. Блока", *Воля России*, №. 283, Прага, 19/VIII/1921.

145. Смоленский, Вл. "Мистика Александра Блока", *Возрождение*, кн. XXXVII и XXXVIII, Париж, 1955, стр.110–27 и 91–102.

146. Станюкевич, Н.В. "Блок и Гумилев", *Возрождение*, кн. ЛIУ, Париж, 1956, стр.114–27.

147. Столник. "Книги о Блоке", *Воля России*, кн. XI, Прага, 1925, стр. 210–11. Rev. М.А.Бекетова, *Ал. Блок и его мать* and the book *Письма Ал. Блока* published by "Kolos".

148. Струве, Г. "Дневник читателя — еще о 'Двенадцати' Блока", *Русская Мысль*, №.1793, Париж, 30/I/1962. (Survey of periodical literature on Blok over recent years. Also on "Leo, Ly" (cf. No. 84), Zamyatin (cf. No. 68) and Pyotr Struve (cf. No.150).)

149. Струве, Г. "Три судьбы (Блок, Гумилев, Сологуб)", *Новый Журнал*, кн. XVI и XVII, Нью Йорк, 1947, стр. 209–28 и 193–211.

150. Струве, П.Б. "Двенадцать Александра Блока", *Русская Мысль*, кн. I и II, София, 1921, стр.232–3. (The review of Suvchinsky's publication of "The Twelve" which Blok copied into his diary (cf. No.154).)

151. Струве, П.Б. "In memoriam — Блок — Гумилев", *Русская Мысль*, кн. X–XII, София, 1921, стр. 88–91. (Also in *Руль*, №.261, Берлин, 25/IX/1921.)

152. Струве, П.Б. "Памяти А. А.Блока", *Русская Мысль*, кн. VIII–IX, София, 1921, стр. 273–8.

153. Струве, П.Б. "Воспоминания о Блоке и Гумилеве", in the collection *Правда и Свобода (первая серия: Вопросы истории и культуры)*, №.2, Белград, 1937, стр. 43–49.

154. Сувчинский, П. Предисловие к поэме А. Блока *Двенадцать*, Российско-Болгарское Книгоиздательство, София, 1921, pp.36.

155. Сувчинский, П. "Типы творчества / памяти А. Блока", in the collection *На путях. Утверждение евразийцев*, кн. II, Геликон, Берлин, 1922, pp. 147–76.

156. Сумский, С. "Ал. Блок и революция", *Социалистический Вестник*, №.18, Берлин, 1921, p.59. (Partly based on personal reminiscences about the poem "The Twelve".)

157. Т[укалевский], Вл. "О Блоке", *Воля России*, №. 18–19, Прага, 1924, pp.252–3.

158. Тарасов, Г. "Последние дни старого режима", *Жизнь*, №.21–23, Ревель, 15–17/V/1922.

159. Терапиано, Ю. "Спор Блока и Гумилева", *Последние Новости*, №.3447, Париж, 30/VIII/1930.

160. Терапиано, Ю. "Тайна поэта" in the book *Встречи*, Изд-во имени Чехова, Нью Йорк, 1953, стр. 159–71. (Blok from the point of view of spiritism.)

161. Толстой, А. Н. "Падший Ангел", *Последние Новости*, №.413, Париж, 23/VIII/1921. (It is not without interest to compare this article with Tolstoy's satyric portrayal of Blok (Bessonov) in his book *Хождение по Мукам*.)

162. Толстой, А. Н. "Памяти Блока", *Накануне*, №.106, Берлин, 13/VIII/1922 (and in the literary supplement to the same paper, No.13, p.2).

163. Третьяков, В. "Утрата невознаградимая", *Сегодня*, №.183, Рига, 13/VIII/1921.

164. Трубецкой, Ю. "Памяти Александра Блока" (стихотворение), *Возрождение*, Кн. 6, Париж, 1949, стр. 127.

165. Тыркова, А. "Беглые встречи (из воспоминаний о Блоке)", *Руль*, №.256, Берлин, 1921, 20/IX/1921. (Interesting reminiscences, see also No.219 for later recollections.)

166. Угрюмов, А. (А.И.Плюшков) "А.А.Блок и семья Ивановых", *Русская Мысль*, Nos. 887, 888, 890, Париж, 17/IV/1956, 19/IV/1956, 24/IV/1956. (Personal reminiscences of the author, who is a distant relative of E.P. Ivanov.)

167. Флоровский, Т. "Дом Литераторов. — Пушкин, Достоевский", *Русская Мысль*, апрель, Прага, 1922, стр. 221–3. (Review of the first collection of articles to be published by the Pushkin House, a publication which included Blok's speech "On the Calling of the Poet".)

168. Фортунатов, Л. "Жизнь А. А. Блока", in the lit. supplement (No.13) to the newspaper *Накануне*, №.106, Берлин, 1922.

169. Фоохд-Стоянова, Т. "О композиционных повторах у Блока", Dutch Contributions to the Fourth International Congress of Scientists, Moscow, September 1958—s' Gravenhage, Mouton et Cie, 1958, pp.175–203.

170. Ходасевич, В. "Гумилев и Блок", *Некрополь ( Воспоминания)*, изд. Петрополис, Брюссель, 1939, pp. 118–40.
Rev.: Вейдле, *Современные Записки*, кн. LXIX, Париж, 1939, pp. 393–4.

171. Ходасевич, В. "М.А.Бекетова. Ал. Блок. Биографический очерк", *Новая Русская Книга*, №.9, Берлин, 1922, pp. 20–21.

172. Ходасевич, В. "О Блоке и Гумилеве (Воспоминания)", *Дни*, Nos. 1069, 1075, Париж, I и 8/VIII/1926. (In №. 1069 the poet's own reminiscences of Blok from November 1920.)

173. Цветаева, М. *Стихи к Блоку 1916–1921* г., Огоньки, Берлин, 1922, 47 pp.

174. Цетлин, М. "Заметки о Блоке", *Последние Новости*, Nos. 706, 707, Париж, 6, 7/VIII/1922.

175. Чуковский, К. *Книга об Александре Блоке*. приложение списка стихотворений А. Блока, составленного Е. Ф. Книпович, Изд. 2-ое, "Эпоха", Берлин, 1922, 169 pp.

176. Шаховской, Иоанн (Архиепископ Сан-Франциский). "О Блоке", *Новое Русское Слово*, Нью Йорк, 10/XII/1961. (A commentary on the article by a "Petrograd Priest", cf. Nos.30 and 126.)

177. Шолудко, Д. "Об источниках драмы «Роза и Крест»", *Slavia*, кн. IV, Прага, 1930–1, pp. 103–38.

178. Шрейдер, А. Предисловие к книге А. Блока *Россия и интеллигенция*, изд. Скифы, Берлин, 1920, pp.5–7. (On Blok's "narodnichestvo".)

179. Штейн С. В. фон, "Воспоминания об А. Блока", *Последние Известия*, Nos. 203, 205, Ревель, 21 and 25/VIII/1921.

180. Э. А. "Стихи Александра Блока на хорватском языке", *Воля России*, кн. IV. Прага, 1928, pp. 100–2. (Review of a book by Doctor Josip Badalic, *Iz sovremene rusk knjizevnosti pjesne Aleckandra Bloka*, Zagreb, 1927.)

181. Эренбург, И. "Письмо в редакцию", *Русская Книга*, №. 9, Берлин, 1921, pp. 5–6.

182. Эренбург, И. "А. А. Блок" in the book *Портреты Русских Поэтов*, изд. Аргонавты, Берлин, 1922, pp. 36–39.

183. Ющенко, А. *Личина и лик. О поэмах: А.Блока "Двенадцать" и Алексея Масианова "Лик Зверя"*, серия "Отклики жизни", Обзор Выдающихся Произведений Современности, Париж, 1925, 23 pp. (A chat between "a scholar", "a theologian" and "a poet" on the true meaning of "The Twelve".)

184. Яблоновский, А. "А. А. Блок (1880–1921)", *Общее Дело*, №. 392, Париж, 19/VIII/1921.

185. Яковлев, Н. Рец. на книгу: "Избранные Сочинения Лермонтова под редакцией Блока", *Русская Книга*, №. 3, Берлин, 1921, pp. 20–21.

## Истории Литературы на Русском Языке

186. Айхенвальд, Ю. И. *Силуэты русских писателей*, Том III, *Новейшая литература*, 4-ое издание, Изд. Слово, Берлин, 1923, стр. 250–64.

187. Иванов-Разумник, Р. В. *Русская литература от 70-х годов до наших дней*, изд. Скифы, Берлин, 1923 (see Chapter IX, "От декаденства к символизму", and index).

188. Тхоржевский, И. *Русская литература*, 2-ое издание исправленное и дополненное, Возрождение, Париж, 1949, pp. 475–82 and index.

## Книги, Статьи и Мемуарная Литература, Содержащие Существенные Упоминания о Блоке

189. Адамович, Г. "Литературные Беседы", *Звено*, Nos. 183, 226, Париж, I/VIII/ 1926, 29/V/1927. (In No.183—a review of Tsingovatov's book on Blok (cf. Major Works on A.Blok, 1926, No.1). In No.226—an attempt to evaluate Blok as a poet whose reputation rested largely on the popularity of the symbolist movement—an opinion which the critic was later to revise quite radically—cf. Nos.18 and 19.)

190. Аничков, Е. "Родное: Александр Блок и Андрей Белый", in the book *Новая русская поэзия*, Изд. Ладыжникова, Берлин, 1923, стр. 90–108.

191. Бицилли, П. "Этюды о русской Поэзии", *Пламя*, Прага, 1926, стр. 7–9, 47–58. (A study of Blok's use of metre and of his place in the development of Russian prosody.)

192. Булгаков, С. *На Пиру Богов* — pro и contra — *Современные Диалоги*. Российско-Болгарское изд-во, София, 1921, стр. 63–66. (On "Двенадцать" as a form of "spiritual provocation".)

193. Василевский, И. (Не Буква). "Роман имени Нэпмана V", *Накануне*, Лит. приложение, №.16, Берлин, 1922.

194. Венус, Г. "Русская Литература в немецком переводе", *Накануне*, Лит. приложение, №.44, Берлин, 17/II/1924.

195. Гиппиус, З. *Синяя Книга 1914–1918*, Белград, 1926, 234 стр. (For Blok see pp. 211–12: his attitude to the war, Germany, England and the Bolsheviki in 1917.)

196. Гиппиус, З. "Слова и люди, заметки о Петербурге 1904–1905", *Последние Новости*, Nos. 4083 и 4091, Париж, 1932.

197. Гиппиус, З. "Черная Книга", *Русская Мысль*, Nos. 1, 2, София, 1921, pp. 139–96, 49–99. (Published in the same year as a separate book by Drei-Masken Verlag, Munich. For Blok see No. 1, pp. 164, 169 and No. 2, pp. 60.)

198. Голлербах, Э. "Старое и новое — заметки о литературном Петербурге", *Русская Книга*, №. 7, Берлин, 1922, pp. 1–6.

199. Гофман, М. Л. "Петербургские воспоминания", *Новый Журнал*, кн. XLII, Нью Йорк, 1955, pp. 120–33. (Of the author's acquaintanceship with Blok in 1906—their mutual love of Pushkin.)

200. Данилов, Ю. "Последние римляне", *Воля России*, кн. XVIII–XIX, Прага, 1924, p. 110.

201. Иванов, Г. *Петербургские Зимы*, Родник, Париж, 1928, pp. 200–19, and scattered references throughout. (Based on personal reminiscences and, frequently, on literary gossip. The chapter on Blok appeared also in the periodical *Возрождение*, cf. No. 72.)
Rev.: *Воля России*, XII, 1928, pp. 120–2.

202. Иванов, Г. "Поэты (Воспоминания)", *Дни*, №. 854, Париж, 15/II/1925.

203. Иванов, Ф. *Красный Парнас*, Русское Универсальное Изд-во, Берлин, 1922, pp. 8, 23, 27–36, 127–38. (About Blok ,"The Rose and the Cross" and "The Scythians".)

204. Ключников, Ю. Б. "Смена вех", in the collection *Смена Вех*, Прага, 1921. (See also a second edition, Берлин, 1922.)

205. Констал. "Денонощь", *Годы*, №. 4 (26), pp. 31–33.

206. Ло Гатто, Е. "Воспоминания о Клюеве", *Новый Журнал*, кн. XXXV, Нью Йорк, 1954, pp. 123–9. (On p. 124 Lo Gatto quotes Kluyev on the "Scythian" element in Blok.)

207. Лундберг, Е. *Записки Писателя*, изд. Огоньки, Берлин, 1922, pp. 139–40 ("Скифы"), 147–50 ("Двенадцать") and scattered references throughout.

208. Мочульский, К. В. *Андрей Белый*, YMCA-Press, Париж, 1955, 293 pp. (Blok's relationships (literary and personal) with Andrey Bely.)
Rev.: Дм. Чижевский, *Новый Журнал*, кн. XLII, Нью Йорк, 1955, pp. 290–97; О. А. Масленников, *American Slavonic and East European Review*, Vol. 14, No. 4, pp. 572–4.

209. Н. Н. "Архив русской революции, т. IV", in the collection *Историк*, №. 1, Изд. Слово, Берлин, 1922.

210. Ремизов, А. М. *Взвихренная Русь*, "Таир", Париж, 1927, 524 pp. (Blok as intercessor for "Obezvolpol" before Lunacharsky and other scattered references throughout the text. Cf. Nos. 113, 114 for the chapter "К Звездам — памяти А. А. Блока", pp. 501–15.)

211. Ремизов, А. М. "Временник — 27/II–I/IV. 1917", *Эпопея*, №. 2, Берлин, 1922, pp. 61–104. (For Blok cf. p. 80.)

212. Ремизов, А. М. *Подстриженными глазами*. (For Blok see p. 14.)

213. С. "Отношение к революции русской интеллигенции в Советской России и за рубежом", *Русская Мысль*, кн. I–II, Прага, Берлин, 1923, pp. 177. (On "Двенадцать".)

214. Сазанов, Ю. "Андрей Белый", *Современные Записки*, №. LXVI, Париж, 1938, pp. 417–23. (About the picture which Bely gives of Blok in his memoirs.)

215. Слоним, М. "Литература наших дней", *Новости Литературы*, №. 1, Берлин, 1922.

216. Степун, Ф. А. *Бывшее и несбывшееся — воспоминания*. Изд. имени Чехова, Нью Йорк, 1956, Т. I. 396 pp. (For Blok cf. pp. 286–90. Stepun writes of his meetings with Blok in 1910–11, of the second staging of *The Puppet Show*, of Blok's love for Russia and of his death. Cf. also Nos. 5 and 31 in the section Blok in German.)

Rev.: М. Карпович, *Новый Журнал*, кн. XLVI, Нью Йорк, 1956, pp. 220–237.

217. Степун, Ф. "Памяти Андрея Белого", *Современные Записки*, №. LVI, Париж, 1934, pp. 247–83.

218. "Судьба и работы русских писателей, ученых и журналистов", *Русская Книга*, №. 1, Берлин, 1921, pp. 17–18.

219. Треплев, М. "Два литературных вечера", *Руль*, №. 293, Берлин, 3/XI/1921.

220. Тыркова-Вильямс, А. "Тени Минувшего", *Возрождение*, кн. XXXVII, Париж, 1955, pp. 77–94, кн. XLI, 1955, pp. 78–91, кн. XLII, 1955, pp. 83–96. (Blok is mentioned briefly in the first part of these reminiscences. In the second part— "Тени Минувшего вокруг башни", кн. XLI — the author tells of her acquaintanceship with Blok, of the poet's meeting with Maurice Baring, of his work for *Русская Молва*.)

221. Филиппов, Б. "Николай Клюев: материалы к биографии", in the first volume of *Полное собрание сочинений Клюева*, Изд-во Имени Чехова, Нью Йорк, 1954, pp. 11–110. (Blok and Kluyev.)

222. Цветаева, М. "Герой Труда (записки о В. Брюсове)", *Воля России*, кн. XI, Прага, 1925, pp. 42–43.

223. Цветаева, М. "Искусство при свете совести", *Современные Записки*, кн. L, Париж, 1932, pp. 305–26. (For Blok and "The Twelve" see pp. 315–16, 323.)

224. Цуриков, Н. А. "Заветы Пушкина", *Правда и Свобода (Первая Серия: Вопросы истории и культуры)*, №. 2, Белград, 1937, стр. 3–42. (For Blok cf. pp. 30–39. "Клеветникам России" compared with "Скифы"—Blok's attitude to the words "Родина" and "Отечество". On the same theme, see *Петроник*, №. 126.)

225. Ященко, А. "Русская Поэзия за последние три года", *Русская Книга*, №. 3, Берлин, 1921, pp. 11–12.

# ADDENDA TO BIBLIOGRAPHY

Owing to my absence from the U.K. while the manuscript of this book was being prepared for press a certain time elapsed between the acceptance of the manuscript and the first printing. So much of interest has since appeared about Blok outside Russia that, at the risk of delaying publication for a further year, I have brought the Bibliography up to date in so far as this has been possible working in Soviet libraries only. I am most grateful to the staffs of the Lenin Library and particularly of the Fundamental Library of Social Sciences for their help in this task.

It will be appreciated that I have not this time been able to check all the works listed, but I have marked with an asterisk those publications which I have not actually seen. This goes for the Addenda, a straightforward continuation of the Tartu Bibliography covering the years 1963–8†.

A different problem is that of works overlooked in the Tartu Bibliography which I have come across in preparing the 1963–1968 Addenda. In the German section, particularly, there are many important lacunae, especially in the division Translations in Anthologies, perhaps the most regrettable of which is JASPERT REINHARD's anthology *Lyrik der Welt. Ausland*, Safari-Verlag, München, 1947 (2nd edition 1948) which, I understand, includes translations not only of "The Twelve" and "The Scythians" but of three of Blok's lyric dramas. Since, however, I have not been able to check these and many other works which I should have liked to add to my bibliography of Blok in German before 1963, I cannot do

† The only parts which I have not been able to bring up to date are the sections on translations of individual verses into English and on Blok in Russian outside the Soviet Union. I therefore take the opportunity here of calling attention to two important republications:

1. A. Белый. *Воспоминания об Александре Блоке.* (1922). With a preface by Georgette Donchin, published by Bradda Books Ltd., Letchworth, 1964*. Also republished by Dmitrij Tschižewskij and others, Wilhelm Fink Verlag, München, 1969 in the Series *Slavische Propyläen*, Band 47. Tschižewskij's publication is, however, according to the text published in the journal Эпопея, whereas G. Donchin's corresponds to an earlier and briefer version orginally published in *Записки Мечтателей*.

2. A. Белый. *Начало Века Между двух революций;* published as numbers 60 and 61 of the Russian Study Series, Chicago, in 1965 and 1966 respectively.*

And to one fascinating and immensely detailed linguistic study: R. JACOBSON, "'Девушка пела в церковном хоре...' Наблюдения над языковым строем стансов А. Блока", *Orbis Scriptus. Dmitrij Tschizewskij zum 70. Geburtstag*. Wilhelm Fink Verlag, München, 1966, pp. 385–401.

Apart from these the only new Russian language articles to have come my way are V.N. IL'YIN's "Александр Блок и Россия", *Возрождение*, No. 2, 1966, pp. 70–89*, F. STEPUN's "Историософское и политическое мировоззрение Александра Блока", *Воздушные Пути*, No. 4, 1965, pp. 241–55* and MARIA WIDNÄS's "Владимир Соловьев и символисты", *Scandoslavica*, Vol. XIII, 1967, pp. 67–76 which sees Blok in a role which would have distressed him: as one who fell back from Soloviev's positive idealism into the decadence of Mallarmé and the Russian interpreter of French 'Symbolism' Valery Bryusov.

better than to send the reader to my own source, an exhaustive bibliography of Blok in German letters compiled by M. BAADE, "Aleksandr Blok: 60 Jahre deutsche Rezeptionsgeschichte. Ein Überblick (1905–1966)", *Zeitschrift für Slawistik*, Band XII, No. 3, Berlin, 1967, pp. 328–63. This is a work of most painstaking research in which every mention of Blok (from monographs entirely devoted to his life and work to passing references in articles or books not even specifically concerned with Russian literature) has been systematically catalogued, and shows how much scope my bibliographies of Blok in other European countries leave to the professional bibliographer and scholar on the spot. In spite of these reservations, I would still like to draw attention to two (unseen) pre-1963 publications in the German language, which promise glimpses of Blok or his work from unusual viewpoints and which, unlike the gentlemen inscribed for punishment on a more celebrated little list, would most certainly be missed. These are MARGARETA WOLOSCHIN's memoirs "Die Grüne Schlange", Stuttgart, 1954, 380 pp.* (reviewed by Joachim T. Baer, *The Russian Review*, Vol. 27, No. 3, July, 1968, p. 378 and containing, according to the reviewer, descriptions of "revealing short encounters" with various literary luminaries of the two decades before and the few years immediately after 1917, including Blok), and H.B. HARDER's article on the grotesque in Blok's and Leonid Andreyev's drama "Die tragische Farce", *Theater unserer Zeit*, Bd. 3 (Sinn oder Unsinn? Das Groteske im modernen Drama. 5 Essays), Basel–Stuttgart, 1962, pp. 147–70.

In cases where I have actually read works not in the Tartu bibliography and considered them of sufficient interest, I have simply included them in the 1963–1968 Addenda without further explanation than the date given — a tidier method than trying to insert them in the original Bibliography at proof stage.

While on the subject of omissions I should apologize to East European scholars for having made no attempts to include their works. Although aware of the contributions made by such Bulgarian specialists as E. DASKALOVA and N. CEKARLIEVA and of the appearance of a number of interesting articles in Poland, including one by TELESFOR POZNIAK on the promising and little-studied theme of Blok and Dostoyevsky (*Slavia Orientalis*, Vol. XIV, No. 4, Warsaw, 1965, pp. 419–34), I am not linguistically qualified to extend these addenda to cover the Slavonic countries, Hungary, Romania, Finland or Greece, in which last country "The Twelve" is apparently still considered politically dangerous, since a Greek journal was actually taken to court for publishing a translation as recently as 1958 (cf. E. BAZZARELLI's review of two books about Blok in the *Annali*, *Sezione Slava* of the Istituto universitario orientale, Naples, 1964, pp. 229–46). Neither do I know Spanish or Portuguese. In the journals which I have looked through, many of them multilingual, I have found no references to Spanish or South American works on Blok.

While aware of the imperfections both of the original Bibliography and of the Addenda, I am nevertheless confident that they may together prove of some help to scholars, translators and to those who simply want to read more in their own language about a great poet and a remarkable man of our times.

# Blok in English

## Encyclopaediae

1. *Penguin Companion to Literature*, 2nd European ed. Anthony Thorlby, Harmondsworth, 1969, pp.118–19.

## Bibliographies

None.

## Translations (Separate Publications)

None.

## Translations (in Anthologies)

2. MARKOV, VL. (ed.), MERRIL SPARKS (tr.), *Modern Russian Poetry: An Anthology*, London, 1966 and Indianapolis, 1967, LXXX, 842 pp.*
   Rev.: H. MUCHNIC, *The Russian Review*, Vol. 27, No. 2, Hanover, April, 1968.
3. YARMOLINSKY, A. (ed.), *An Anthology of Russian Verse 1812–1960*, paperback, USA, 1962.*

## Books, Articles, Reviews

4. ANNENKOV, GEORGE, "The poets and the Revolution – Blok, Mayakovsky, Esenin", *The Russian Review*, Vol. 26, No. 2, Hanover, April, 1967, pp. 129–43 (for Blok see pp. 129–36). (Reminiscences.)
5. ERLICH, VICTOR, "Images of the poet and of poetry in Slavic Romanticism and Neo-Romanticism", *American Contributions to the 5th International Congress of Slavists*, *Sofia, 1963* (Preprint), Mouton et Cie, The Hague, 1963, pp. 73–113.
   (A part of No. 6. Blok's "image" is that of "the seer" whose vision is acquired at the cost of self-immolation.)
6. ERLICH, VICTOR, "The Maker and the Seer". *The Double Image. Concepts of the Poet in Slavic Literatures*, Johns Hopkins, Baltimore, Maryland, 1964.* (The chapter "The Maker and the Seer" is devoted to Bryusov and Blok.)
   Rev.: E. J. BROWN, *The Slavic Review*, Vol. XXIV, No. 2, Illinois, 1965, pp. 343–4.
   *The Russian Review*, Vol. 23, No. 4, Hanover, October, 1964, pp. 404–6;
   HUGH McCEAN, *Comparative Literature*, Vol. XVII, No. 3, Oregon, Summer 1965, pp. 280–2.
7. GIFFORD, H., "Pasternak and the 'realism' of Blok", *Oxford Slavonic Papers*, Vol. 13, Oxford, 1967, pp. 96–106. (Pasternak seen as the successor to Blok's "realism"; their "sacrificial" attempt to let the contemporary world speak through their verse, "a cross and a predestination" which "costs not less than everything".)

347

8. KEMBALL, R., *Alexander Blok. A study in rhythm and metre*, Mouton et Cie, The Hague, 1964, 539 pp.
   Rev.: J. BAILEY, *Slavic and East European Journal*, Vol. II, No. 1, Madison, 1967, pp. 92–95;
   R. F. GUSTAFSON, *Russian Review*, Vol. 25, No. 4, Hanover, October, 1966, pp. 421–3;
   R. D. B. THOMSON, *Slavonic and East European Review*, Vol. 46, No. 106, London, January, 1968, pp. 229–31.

9. KISCH, SIR CECIL, No. 51 in the section Blok in English of the Tartu Bibliography (reviews):
   I. ARIAN, *Modern Language Review*, Vol. 58, No. 2, London, April, 1963, pp. 306–7;
   E. MORGAN, "Blok and Tyutchev", *Anglo-Soviet Journal*, vol. 22, No. 1, London, 1961, pp. 37–38.
   G. PHELPS, *Daily Telegraph and Morning Post*, Friday, 2 December, 1960.

10. KOSTKA, E. K., "Blok, Schiller and the Bolshevic Revolution", *Revue de Littérature Comparée XXXIX Année*, No. 2, Paris, April/June, 1965, pp. 255–67. (An expanded version of the same author's remarks on Blok and Schiller in his book *Schiller in Russian Literature*, Philadelphia, Pennsylvania U.P., 1965, 314 pp. Both book and article deal with Blok's speeches on Schiller's plays during his post-revolutionary period of work with the Great Dramatic Theatre and his treatment of Schiller as "the last great European humanist" in the article "The Collapse of Humanism").

11. LEDNICKI, W., "Mickiewicz, Dostoevski and Blok", *Slavic Studies*, Ithaca, New York, 1943*.

12. MAKOVSKY, S., Reviews of No. 93 in the section Blok in Russian in the Tartu Bibliography:
   N. GORODETZKY, *The Slavonic and East European Review*, Vol. XLI, No. 97, London, June, 1963, pp. 548–9;
   ARTHUR P. MENDEL, *Slavic Review*, Vol. XXII, No. 1, Illinois, 1963, pp. 146–8;
   G. STRUVE, *Russian Review*, Vol. 22, No. 1, pp. 104–5.

13. MUCHNIC, H. Reviews of No. 60a of the section Blok in English of the Tartu Bibliography:
   N. GORODETZKY, *The Slavonic and East European Review*, Vol. XLIII, No. 161, London, July 1965, pp. 433–5;
   R. MATHEWSON, *The Russian Review*, Vol. 22, No. 1, Hanover, January 1963, pp. 86–87.

14. POGGIOLO, RENATO, Review of No. 62 of the section Blok in English of the Tartu Bibliography:
   R. E. STEUSSY in *Comparative Literature*, Vol. XV, No. 1, Oregon, Winter 1963, pp. 80–81.

15. PUTNAM, G. "Aleksandr Blok and the Russian Intelligentsia". *Slavic and East European Journal*, Vol. 9, No. 1, Madison, 1965, pp. 29–46. (About Blok's ventures into the realm of sociology between 1906 and 1908 and their reception among the intelligentsia in the wider sense of the word.)

16. PYMAN, A., "The Scythians, a Critical Note", *Stand*, 8, No. 3, Newcastle-on-Tyne, 1966/7, pp. 23–33. ("The Scythians" as the culminating expression of Blok's thought on Europe, Asia and Russia.)

17. REEVE, F. D., Reviews of No. 63 in the Section Blok in English in the Tartu Bibliography:
   R. KEMBALL, *Russian Review*, Vol. 22, No. 2, Hanover, April 1963, pp. 203–5;
   H. MUCHNIC, *Slavic Review*, Vol. XXII, No. 3, Illinois, 1963, pp. 602–3;
   G. STRUVE, *Slavic and East European Journal*, Vol. VII, No. 2, Madison, Summer 1963, pp. 179–82.

18. THOMSON, R. D. B., "Blok and the October revolution", *Coexistence*, Vol. 4, No. 2, Oxford, July 1967, pp. 221–8. (In a popular article the author makes good use of little-known factual material.)

19. THOMSON, R.D.B., "The non-literary sources of 'Roza i Krest' ", *Slavonic and East European Review*, Vol.45, No.105, London, July 1967, pp.292–306. (A supremely tactful handling of the biographical drama behind the textual development of "Roza i Krest". Enlightening also on such extra-literary sources as Wagner's operas and on the lyrical intensity of the imagery of the play, much of which is traced back to earlier poetry).

20. VOGEL, L., "Blok in the land of Dante", *Russian Review*, Vol.26, No.3, Hanover, July 1967, pp.251–63. (Blok's attitude to Italy compared with Byron's. Particularly illuminating on the omnipresence of Dante's influence in the Italian verses, especially in the malediction of Florence).

21. WOODWARD, JAMES B. (ed.), *Selected Poems of Aleksandr Blok*, O.U.P., Oxford, 1968. 186 pp.* (The poems in Russian with stress marked for students. Introduction and notes in English.)
    Rev.: *Times Literary Supplement*, No.3491, London, 23 Jan. 1969, p.76.

## Histories of Russian Literature

22. ALEKSANDROVA, VERA, *A History of Soviet Literature*, Doubleday and Co., New York, xiv + 369 pp. For Blok see pp.8–12 and index.

23. BROWN, E.J. *Russian Literature since the Revolution*, Collier-Macmillan, London, 1963, 320 pp. For Blok see index.

## Books, Articles and Memoirs
## Containing Substantial References to Blok

24. ANNENKOV, JU.P., *People and Portraits – Дневник моих встреч. Цикл трагедии I–II*, Inter-Language Literary Associates, New York, 1966, 350 + 350 pp.* (With portraits.)

25. BOWRA, C.M., *The Heritage of Symbolism*, Schocken Books, New York, 1961*. (A paperback reissue of No.43 of the section Blok in English of the Tartu Bibliography.)

26. BOWRA, C.M., *Poetry and Politics 1900–1960*, C.U.P., Cambridge, 1966, 157 pp. For Blok see index. (Blok "the greatest poet and most inspired visionary" of his generation as one of Europe's chief "prophet poets to restore the grand manner and grand themes".)

27. IVANOV, VYACHESLAV, "Symbolism" (tr. by Thomas E.Bird from the *Enciclopedia Italiana*, Vol.31, 1936, pp.793–5), *The Russian Review*, Vol.25, No.1, Hanover, January 1966, pp.24–34. (For Blok see p.33.)

28. KOSTKA, E.K., *Schiller in Russian Literature*, Pennsylvania U.P., Philadelphia, 1965, 314 pp. (Cf. this section, No.10.)
    Rev.: VYTUS DUKAS, *Comparative Literature*, Vol.XIX, No.1, Oregon, Winter 1967, pp.91–94;
    C.CORBET, *Revue de Littérature Comparée*, Vol.41, No.3, Paris, juillet–septembre 1967, p.478.

29. TARANOVSKI, KIRIL, "The sound texture of Russian Verse in the light of phonemic distinctive features", *International Journal of Slavic Linguistics and Poetics*, The Hague, 1965, pp.114–24. (Interesting to compare this wider study—the author ranges from Lomonosov to Blok and Bely—with R.Abernathy's "A vowel fugue in Blok" and R.Jacobson's *Девушка пела в церковном хоре*).

30. TODD, A., "The Spiritual in recent Soviet Literature", *Survey*, No.66, London, Jan., 1968, pp.92–107. (Blok, with others, as the perpetrator of the poet-prophet image.)

# Blok in French

## Encyclopaediae

None.

## Bibliographies

None.

## Translations (Separate Publications)

31. ANON., *Les Douze*. Publications Internationales, Bruxelles, 1931.*
32. BICKERT, ELIANE, *Les Douze*, Librairie des Cinq Continents, Paris, 1967, 122 pp. (A most satisfactory publication with Annenkov's original illustrations and two later works and parallel French and Russian texts, the Russian reproducing the print and spelling of the original Alkonost edition, followed by a felicitous *choix de textes*.)

## Translations (in Anthologies)

None.

## Books, Articles, Reviews

33. BERNSTEIN, L., "A. Blok", *La Grande Revue*, Paris, juin, 1925.*
34. BLOT, J., "Alexandre Blok et 'Les Douze'", *Preuves*, Année 17, No. 196, Paris, 1967, pp. 76–77. (A propos of the Bickert "Twelve" but not, strictly speaking, a review.)
35. DUTEIL, D., "Blok et la jeunesse", *France–URSS*, No. 3, Paris, avril, 1968, p. 43. (The journalist chats about Blok to some Moscow young people: not calculated to give a high impression of the latter's critical acumen.)
36. FLAMAND, FRANÇOISE. "A propos d'un vers encore obscur des 'Douze' de A. Blok". *Revue des Etudes Slaves*, Vol. 45, Paris, 1966, pp. 91–92. (The line "В белом венчике из роз" is traced back to a comment in Blok's diary of 26 March, 1902 on Andrey Bely's concept of a "white", apocalyptic Christianity.)
37. HYART, CH., "Les conceptions théatrales d'Alexandre Blok", *Revue belge de philologie et d'histoire*, T. 43, No. 1, Bruxelles, 1965, pp. 365–6. (Critical comment on Ю. К. Герасимов, "Театр и драма в критике А. Блока в период русской революции", *Вестник Ленинградского Университета*, Серия История, Язык, Литература, № 20, 1962, с. 73–85.)
38. JUIN, H., "Alexandre Blok, poète voyant", *Critique*, vol. 15, No. 142, Paris, 1959, pp. 214–27. (A general article which suffers from inaccuracies both of fact and translation and is therefore shakier in interpretation than the author's critical prestige should warrant.)

39. NIVAT, G., "A. Blok et A. Belyj: étude de la correspondance des deux poètes", *Revue des Etudes Slaves*, vol. 45, Paris, 1966, pp. 145–64. (An excellent study, closely documented, perceptive and tender, of the relationships of two men each of whom carried in himself his own tragedy. Their points of contact: the apocalyptic and the absolute.)

40. WEISBEIN, N., "Alexandre Blok et 'Les Douze'", *France–URSS*, No. 3, Paris, avril, 1968, pp. 38–42. (Thoughtful article unfortunately preceding No. 35 and adorned by wrongly captioned illustrations from Annenkov.)

## Histories of Russian Literature

41. EHRHARD, M., *La littérature russe*, Que sais-je, PUF, Paris, 1962, 128 pp.*

42. LO GATTO, *Histoire de la littérature russe des origines à nos jours*. Trans. M. et A. M. Cabrini, Bibliothèque Européenne, section historique, Desclée de Brouwer, Paris, 1965, 923 pp*.
    REV.: F. DE LABRIOLLE, *Revue de la Littérature Comparée*, T. 42, No. 1, Paris, janvier–mars 1968, p. 134.

## Books, Articles and Memoirs
## Containing Significant References to Blok

43. NIVAT, G., "Du 'Panmongolisme' au mouvement Eurasien", *Cahiers du Monde Russe et Soviétique*, Vol. VII, No. 3, The Hague, juillet–septembre, 1966, pp. 460–78. (Russian thought on "Asia" from Gogol to Pilnyak. Cf. No. 16 of Addenda.)

44. TRIOMPHE, R., "Le thème du printemps: contribution à l'étude des rapports entre le folklore et la littérature savante en Russie," *Contribution au V<sup>e</sup> Congrès international des Slavistes* (cf. Blok in French, Tartu Bibliography, No. 30. The observations on Blok's treatment of the theme of spring gain when considered in the wider setting of this study.)

# Blok in German

## Encyclopaedia

45. WILPERT, G.v., *Lexikon der Weltliteratur*. Biographisch-bibliographisches Handwörterbuch nach Autoren und anonymen Werken. Alfred Kröner Verlag, Stuttgart, 1963.*

## Bibliography

46. BAADE, M., "Aleksandr Blok: 60 Jahre deutsche Rezeptionsgeschichte. Ein Überblick (1905–1966)." *Zeitschrift für Slawistik*, Band XII, No. 3, Berlin 1967, pp. 328–63. (The most exhaustive bibliography of Blok in any country outside the Soviet Union to appear to date, preceded by a survey in which Blok, regrettably, figures as just one more apple of discord coveted by both East and West Germany.)
47. HANISCH, E., "Zur Bibliographie der vornehmlich in Deutschland erschienenen slawischen Belletristik und Literaturgeschichte", *Jahresberichte für Kultur und Geschichte der Slawen*, Breslau, 1924. For Blok see pp. 157–9. (A detailed bibliographical survey of early translations of and literature on Blok.)

## Translations (Separate Publications)

48. KAEMPFE, A., *A. Blok. Ausgewählte Aufsätze*. Erstveröffentlichung. Ausgewählt und alus dem Russischen übertragen von Alexander Kaempfe, 11 Essays, Suhrkamp Verag, Frankfurt/Main, 1964, 135 pp.

## Translations (in Anthologies)

49. BAUMANN, HANS, *Russische Lyrik 1185–1963*. Sigbert Mohn Verlag, Gütersloh, 1963 255 pp., 6 poems.*
50. CELAN, PAUL, *Drei russische Dichter: Blok, Jessenin, Mandelstamm*. Fischer Bücherei, Frankfurt/Main, pp. 72–76, 137–8. ("The Twelve" and a bio-bibliographical note.)
51. HARDER, JOHANNES, *Proteste. Stimmen russischer Revolutionäre aus zwei Jahrhunderten*, Jugenddienst-Verlag, Wuppertal-Barmen, 1963.* ("The Twelve", two poems, one essay.)
    Rev.: O.E.H. BECKER, "Stimmen russischer Revolutionäre", *Die Bücher-Kommentare*, 12. Jg., H. 2, Stuttgart/Berlin, 1963, p. 20.*
52. KALMER, J., *Weltanthologie des 20. Jahrhunderts. Europäische Lyrik der Gegenwart 1900–1925*. Verlagsanstalt Dr. Zahn und Dr. Diamant. Wien/Leipzig, 1927, pp. 100–1, 117–33.

53. MIROWA-FLORIN, E., *Sternenflug und Apfelblüte. Russische Lyrik von 1917 bis 1962*, herausgegeben von Edel Mirowa-Florin und Fritz Mierau mit einem Geleitwort von E. Mirowa-Florin und Paul Wiens. Verlag Kultur und Fortschritt, Berlin, 1963–4, 3 poems. (A presentation edition.)

54. OPITZ, R., *Solang es dich, mein Russland gibt. Russische Lyrik von Puschkin bis Jewtuschenko.* Leipzig, 1961, 275 pp. For Blok see pp. 81–89.

55. SCHICK, MAXIMILIAN, *Nachdichtungen*, Verlag Kultur und Fortschritt, Berlin, 1961. For Blok see pp. 7–8, 12–13, 14–15.

56. STEINBRINKER, GUENTHER, mit HARTUNG, RUDOLF, *Panorama moderner Lyrik. Gedichte des 20. Jahrhunderts in Übersetzungen.* Sigbert Mohn Verlag, Gütersloh, 1960, 535 pp., 2 poems.*

## Books, Articles, Reviews

57. BAADE, M., "Aleksandr Blok: 60 Jahre deutsche Rezeptionsgeschichte. Ein Überblick (1905–1966). (See this section, No. 46.)

58. BAADE, M., "Bemerkungen zur Blok-Monographie von V. Orlov" (rev.), *Zeitschrift für Slawistik*, Band VII, Berlin, 1962, pp. 738–43.

59. BAADE, M., "Die deutsche Literaturkritik zu dem Poem 'Die Zwölf' von Alexander Blok", *Wissenschaftliche Zeitschrift der Humboldt-Universität Berlin*, Gesellschaftliche und Sprachwissenschaftliche Reihe/Mathematische-Naturwissenschaftliche Reihe, Jg. VII (1957–8), No. 1, Berlin, 1957, pp. 107–17.

60. BAADE, M., "Orlov, B.: Поэма Александра Блока "Двенадцать" (rev.), *Zeitschrift für Slawistik*, Bd. X, H. 2, Berlin, 1965, pp. 318–23.

61. BAADE, M., "Zur Aufnahme von Aleksandr Bloks Poem 'Die Zwölf' in Deutschland" (Teil 1: 1920–1933; Teil II: 1945–1963), *Zeitschrift für Slawistik*, Bd. IX, H. 2 und H. 4, Berlin 1964, pp. 175–95, 551–73.

62. BAADE, M., "Die deutschen Übersetzungen des Poems 'Die Zwölf' von Alexander Blok", Slawisches Institut der Humboldt Universität zu Berlin, Mai 1965, and "Die Aufnahme des Poems 'Die Zwölf' von Alexander Blok in Deutschland (1920–64)" Berlin, 1965 (Dissertation).

63. CELAN, PAUL, Reviews of No. 7 of the section Blok in German in the Tartu Bibliography:
ANON., *Die Zeitschrift für modernes Leben*, Heft 25, Schauberg/Köln, 1959, p. 73;
ANON., *Bücherschiff*, Jahrgang 11, Heft 1, 1961, p. 8;
ANON., "Lyrik—russisch oder deutsch", *Deutsche Rundschau*, Jahrgang 86, Heft 2, Baden-Baden, 1960, pp. 183–4;
MIERAU, F., "Zur Edition und Interpretation sowjetischer Lyrik in Westdeutschland", *Wissenschaft am Scheidewege, Kritische Beiträge über Slawistik, Literaturwissenschaft und Ostforschung in Westdeutschland*, Berlin, 1964, p. 188;
WEISS, E., *"Kritische Auseinandersetzungen" Ostforschung und Slawistik*, Berlin, 1960, pp. 65 et seq. (Here quarrelling not so much with Celan as with Professor Dr. Neumann's interpretation of "The Twelve").

64. ENDLER, E., "Zwei Dichter der Revolution: Alexander Blok und Wladimir Majakowski", *Die Kinder der Nibelungen. Gedichte*, Halle, 1964, pp. 178*. (A poem about Blok and Mayakovsky.)

65. HOLTHUSEN, J., "Nachwirkungen der Tradition in A. Bloks Bildsymbolik", *Slawistische Studien. Opera Slavica. Band IV, zum V. Internationalen Slawisten-Kongreß in Sofia, 1963.* Herausgegeben von Maximilian Braun und Erwin Koschmieder, Vandenhoeck und Ruprecht, Göttingen, pp. 437–44. (A fascinating discourse on such traditional symbols as snow and fire in Goethe and Petrarch, juxtaposed as oxymorons in Blok. Suggests the analysis of Blok's use of recurrent symbols in his earlier poetry might lead to a better understanding of "The Twelve".)

66. JUNGER, HARRI, Review of N. Vengrov's *Путь Александра Блока*, Moscow, 1963, pp. 413, in *Deutsche Literaturzeitung*, Jahrgang 87, Heft 5, pp. 426–8, Berlin, 1966.

67. KLAUS, V., "Alexander Blok als Essayist", "DSF", Jahrgang 4, No. 7, Berlin, 1965, p. 11*.

68. KLUGE, ROLF-DIETER, "Die Rolle Polens in Aleksander Bloks Versepos 'Vozmezdie'", *Die Welt der Slawen*, Vol. IX, No. 4, Munich, 1964, pp. 426–35. (The idea of retribution, both as revenge and as exculpation through suffering, perhaps suggested by the poetry of Mickiewicz, Slowaskis and Kasinski. Poland as a symbol of all oppressed nations, generations.)

69. MAKOVSKY, S., Review of No. 93 in the section on Blok in Russian in the Tartu Bibliography:
    HOLTHUSEN, J., *Zeitschrift für Slawistische Philologie*, Band XXXII, Heft 2, Heidelberg, 1965, pp. 434–8.

70. METZGER, H., *Ein Beitrag zur Poetik A. A. Bloks*, Inaugural Dissertation, Cologne, 1967, 192 pp. (An incisive study with chapters on Blok's place in Russian literature, literary criticism of Blok in Russia and the West, the concepts "Image", "Metaphor" and "Symbol" in Blok's poetry, the theme of the town and colour-symbolism. Conclusion: Blok's style is metaphoric and expresses his essential idealism.)

71. NAG, MARTIN, "Ibsen, Čechov und Blok", *Scandoslavica*, Vol. X, Copenhagen, 1964, pp. 30–48. (For Blok see pp. 43 et seq. Enlightening on Blok's attitude to "Brand" and the possible influence of the finale of this play on "The Twelve", its undisputed influence on Retribution. Cf. Blok in Other European Countries, No. 96).

72. NEUMANN, F. W., "Aleksandr Bloks 'Neznakomka'. Versuch einer Interpretation", *Die Welt der Slawen*, vol. VIII, Heft 1, München, 1963, pp. 5–17. (A curiosity of detailed textual analysis locating Ozerki, the setting of the poem, with the help of a contemporary map of St. Petersburg, identifying the "друг единственный" reflected in Blok's glass as Georgy Chulkov, placing Blok himself among the испытанные остряки and suggesting a complicated pun in the last line between вино and вина. Soundest on questions of rhythm.)

73. SILLAT, N., "Die Quellen der Tschastuschkaelemente", *Wissenschaftliche Zeitschrift der Karl-Marx-Universität – Kulturell-geistige Probleme beim voll entfalteten Sozialismus* – Jahrgang 13, Heft 5, Ges.- und Sprachwissenschaftliche Reihe, Leipzig, 1964, pp. 1001–4. (Based largely on Soviet studies (Pomerantseva, Orlov, Pertsov and Vykhodstsev), the author shows sound critical sense in his analysis of the origins of Blok's use of chastushka rhythms and turns of phrase in "The Twelve".)

74. STEPUN, F., "Aleksandr Blok", *Mystische Weltschau. Fünf Gestalten des russischen Symbolismus* (W. Solowjew, N. A. Berdjajew, W. Iwanow, A. Belyi, A. Blok), Hanser, München, 1964, pp. 356–427. (Stimulating not only because Stepun bases his observations not on books about Blok but upon a profound study of the actual texts and his own recollections, but also because, for Stepun, the Sophianic philosophy of Vladimir Solov'ev is as important a factor in his conception of things as it was in Blok's. One of the few books on Blok since Andrey Bely in which we feel a live relationship, a vigorously immortal dialectic between the writer and his subject. The description of Blok's death is a masterpiece of emotive writing. Only in the rare excursions into literary-critical polemics, particularly with Soviet criticism which is unfairly lumped together as a monolithic whole, is Stepun more than a trifle slapdash. Nevertheless, this work is the most important in these addenda.)
    Rev.: J. HOLTHUSEN, *Zeitschrift für Slawistische Philologie*, Band XXXII, Heft 2, Heidelberg, 1965, pp. 438–42.

75. STEPUN, F., "Das Wesen des Symbolismus", *Orbis Scriptus, Dmitrij Tschizewskij zum 70. Geburtstag*, Wilhelm Fink Verlag, München, 1966, pp. 805–10. (One of the chapters on Blok from *Mystische Weltschau*, cf. No. 74.)

## Histories of Russian Literature

76. ELIASBERG, A., *Russische Literaturgeschichte in Einzelporträts. Von Puschkin bis Majakowski*, München, 1964* (cf. No. 35 in Blok in German, Tartu Bibliography).
77. GUENTHER, J.v., *Die Literatur Russlands*, Union-Verlag, Stuttgart, 1964, 223 pp.*
    Rev.: W.B.EDGERTON, *The Slavic Review*, Vol. XXIV, No. 3, Illinois, 1965, pp. 549–58.
78. HOLTHUSEN, J., *Russische Gegenwartsliteratur 1890–1940; Die literarische Avantgarde*, Dalp Taschenbücher (Band 368B), Bern/München (for Blok see pp. 26–32 and index).
    Rev.: Z.FOLEJWESKI, *The Slavic and East European Journal*, vol. X, No. 1, Madison, Spring 1966, p. 107.
79. MIRSKY, D.S., *Geschichte der russischen Literatur* (Aus dem Englischen von G. Mayer), München, 1964*.

## Books, Articles and Memoirs
## Containing Substantial References to Blok

80. DEDECIUS, K., "Das Russland der Revolution im Spiegel seiner Literatur", *Neue deutsche Hefte*, Jahrgang 10, No. 98, Gütersloh, März/April 1964, pp. 55–80*.
81. DEMETZ, P., *Marx, Engels und die Dichter. Zur Grundlagenforschung des Marxismus* (Vorwort), Stuttgart, 1959, 342 pp. For Blok see p. 7.
82. KLUGE, ROLF-DIETER, "Johannes von Guenther als Übersetzer und Vermittler russischer Literatur", *Die Welt der Slawen*, Jahrgang XII, Heft 1, Wiesbaden, 1967, pp. 77–96. (Contains a bibliography of von Guenther's works and retells the story of his acquaintanceship with Blok.)
83. LESCHNITZER, F., *Wahlheimat Sowjetunion. Stadien und Studien eines deutschen Intellektuellen*. Halle (Saale), 1963. For Blok see p. 205 (Maximilian Schick's translations).
84. WALLMANN, J.P., "Poesie aus Russland", *Deutsche Zeitung und Wirtschaftszeitung*, 4. Januar, 1964, Stuttgart.*
85. WEINERT, E., *Dichter und Tribun 1890–1953*, Berlin/Weimar, 1965, p. 61.*

# Blok in Italian

## Encyclopaediae

86. *Enciclopedia Italiana*, Vol.31, Roma, 1936, pp.793–5.

## Bibliography

None.

## Translations (Separate Publications)

87. POGGIOLI, R., *A.Blok. I.Dodici*, with a preface by CLARA STRADA JANOVICH, Einaudi, Torino, 1965, pp.68. (Parallel text Russian/Italian plus translator's note and preface.)*
Rev.: P.ZVETEREMICH, *Rinascita*, anno 23, N 31, Roma, 30 juglio, 1966, p.17.
"Segnalazioni", *Richerche Slavistiche*, Vol. XIII, Firenze, 1965, p.260.

## Translations (in Anthologies)

None.

## Books, Articles, Reviews

88. BAZZARELLI, E., "Note sulla sintassi poetica di Alesandre Blok", *Rendiconti* (Istituto Lombardo, Accademia di scienze e lettere), Vol.96, fasc. 1, Classe di lettere e scienze morali e storiche, Milano, 1962, pp.259–91. (A study of the grammatical constructions of Blok's poetry leads to a comparison with other European symbolists.)
89. BAZZARELLI, E., Review of "Вл. Орлов. Пути и судьбы" and "Поэма Александра Блока" *Annali, Sezioni slava.* Istituto universitario orientale. 7. Napoli, 1964, pp.229–46.
90. IVANOF, A., "Realismo equivico nella prose di A.A.Block (Note al suo saggio su Catilina)", *Atti dell Istituto Veneto dei scienze, lettere ed arti*, T.CXVIII, Anno acad. 1959–1960, Classe dei scienze morali e lettere, Venezia, 1960, pp.75–92.
91. IVANOF, A., "Blok 1909: significato di una protesta", *Atti dell Istituto Veneto dei scienze, lettere ed arti*, T.CXIX, Anno acad. 1960–1961, Classe dei scienze morali e lettere, Venezia, 1961, pp.125–44 (Blok's Italian journey).*
92. MAURA, W., "La poesia di Blok", *Fiera letteraria*, anno 16, No.1, Roma, 1 genn., 1961, pp. 3–4. (A propos of Angelo Ripellino's translations, cf. section on Blok in Italian, Tartu Bibliography, No.21.)

93. POGGIOLI, R., Chapter on Blok in *I lirici russi 1890–1930*, Lerici, Milano, 1964, 435 pp. For Blok see pp. 211–44 and index. (Italian edition of *The Poets of Russia*: see the section Blok in English, Tartu Bibliography, No. 62).

## Histories of Russian Literature

94. LO GATTO, E., *Storia della letteratura russa*, V$^a$ edizione, Sansoni, Firenze, 1964, 892 pp. For Blok see pp. 623–8 and index. (The editors having placed no restrictions on the author's revisions, both text and bibliographies have been thoroughly reworked since the earlier editions, of which the third is noted as No. 23 in the section Blok in Italian in the Tartu Bibliography.)
Rev.: In *Ricerche Slavistiche*, Vol. XII, Firenze, 1964, p. 230.

## Books, Articles and Memoirs
## Containing Significant References to Blok

95. RIPELLINO, A. M., *Il trucco e l'anima*, Einaudi, Torino, 1965, 424 pp.*

# Blok in Other European Countries

96. NAG, M., "Ibsen, Čechov and Blok" (Norway. Cf. No. 71 in the section Blok in German).
97. NAG, M., "Ibsen og Blok og 'Deus Caritatis'", *Edda*, Argang 51, Hefte 4, Oslo, 1964, pp. 324–8. (The finale of "The Twelve" compared with the finale of Ibsen's "Brand".)
98. NILSSON, N. A., Foreword to a new translation of "The Twelve" by Ulf Bergstrem and Gunnar Harding published in *Ord och bild*, No. 2, Stockholm, 1966.
99. NILSSON, N. A., "Blok's 'vowel fugue'—a suggestion for a different interpretation", *International Journal of Slavic Linguistics and Poetics*, V. 11, The Hague, 1968.*
100. JOHANSSON, T. and K., "Blok A. Om August Strindberg", *Ord Och Bild*, No. 5 Stockholm, 1962, pp. 415–17. (Translations of the articles "От Ибсена до Стриндберга" and "Памяти Августа Стриндберга".)

# GENERAL INDEX

# INDEX OF FIRST LINES AND TITLES

(*Note.* Titles are given in *italics*)

P1